# Reading Matthew as the Climactic Fulfillment of the Hebrew Story

# Reading Matthew as the Climactic Fulfillment of the Hebrew Story

Martin C. Spadaro

WIPF & STOCK · Eugene, Oregon

READING MATTHEW AS THE CLIMACTIC FULFILLMENT
OF THE HEBREW STORY

Copyright © 2015 Martin C. Spadaro. All rights reserved. Except for brief quotations in critical publications or reviews, no part of this book may be reproduced in any manner without prior written permission from the publisher. Write: Permissions. Wipf and Stock Publishers, 199 W. 8th Ave., Suite 3, Eugene, OR 97401.

Wipf & Stock
An Imprint of Wipf and Stock Publishers
199 W. 8th Ave., Suite 3
Eugene, OR 97401

www.wipfandstock.com

ISBN 13: 978-1-4982-0068-4

Manufactured in the U.S.A. 09/09/2015

All Bible references in this thesis are taken from the NIV, unless otherwise stated.

THE HOLY BIBLE, NEW INTERNATIONAL VERSION®, NIV® Copyright © 1973, 1978, 1984, 2011 by Biblica, Inc.™ Used by permission. All rights reserved worldwide.

In memory of a beautiful man:
Tarcisio Spadaro (1910–2001)
*He blessed me with both hands*

With special thanks to:
Dr. Katherine Spadaro
Dr. Geoff Jenkins
Dr. Jeff Pugh

# Table of Contents

1 Introduction | 1
2 History and Prologue: Jesus' Authority to Judge | 39
3 The Sermon: Understanding the Legal Requirement | 61
4 John the Baptist: God's Ultimatum | 89
5 Miracles, Gentiles and Mission: The Rejection of Amnesty | 113
6 Parables as Principal Indictment Tool | 146
7 The Universal Priest and the Judge of Israel | 186
8 Subpoena, Trial, Execution and Vindication: The Termination of Aaron | 235
9 Conclusion | 280

*Bibliography* | 285

# 1

# Introduction

IT IS DAUNTING AND audacious to attempt to read a Gospel in such a way that it will produce interpretations that have not been part of historic biblical discussions. It is unlikely that a new approach to any New Testament work would be plausible after nearly 2,000 years of consideration and discussion. Nonetheless, new approaches do emerge, and they are judged by the academic community, by church leaders and ultimately, by time. For a student of the Bible and a believer in its declarations about the finished work of Jesus Christ, the task is not just to be novel, but also to actually bring new information to the table in order to advance a more biblical hermeneutic. This generation stands on the shoulders of those who have gone before, and it is necessary to honor former generations by advancing their work, and at times by proposing alternative paradigms. From the outset, no claims are being made about the contribution that this work can make—the only hope here is that it would receive some consideration, so as to determine whether this work is plausible and/or profitable.

This book is attempting to make a prima-facie case that the author/final redactor of Matthew[1] intended to advance the Hebrew narrative by demonstrating that Jesus was the fulfillment of Moses and the Prophets, and that he anticipated the arrival of YHWH at his temple for the express purpose of judging its priesthood and terminating the Mosaic administration.[2] It will be proposed that Matthew had a particular theological agenda

---

1. Matthew, in this work, is the name given to the author/final redactor. It is not intended to imply that Matthew the tax-collector was this person, nor does it preclude the possibility.

2. Various scholars have proposed that Jesus' death brought judgment upon Jerusalem and Judah (Bolt, *The Cross*; Hamilton, "His Blood"; Moffitt, "Righteous Bloodshed"; Watts, "The Lord's House"), so this work is not unusual at this point. This reading

to present Jesus as the judge of Israel, and as a new priest, who would displace the existing administration and appoint a new generation of leaders to administer the long-anticipated new covenant. Within this reading, it will be shown that Matthew's priority was not to highlight the salvific intention of God, but to square the ledger with Israel: that is, to conclude a covenant that had a predetermined end point when YHWH would either terminate his contractual obligations with the nation, or bring the blessings associated with covenant fulfillment. To make this case, Matthew will be read as though it were a prophetic indictment against the nation of Israel. The reading will not be comprehensive, but it will attempt to identify the peaks and troughs of Matthew's advancing narrative, the way that "Scripture" is used in Matthew, and the unique features of the Gospel, in order to make the case that Matthew is best understood as a book that presents "just cause" for the termination of God's exclusive covenant with national Israel and the decommissioning of her temple and priesthood.

A statement made by N. T. Wright in his epic work entitled *The New Testament and the People of God* in part triggered this project. One sentence within the work led me to consider the possibility that Matthew was written as the conclusion of the Torah. Wright commented: "Mark, like Matthew and Luke, has written a story which presupposes a larger story of which it will provide the strange but crucial final chapter."[3] This, on the one hand, appears self-evident and uncontroversial, yet the reality is that biblical scholarship has rarely allowed for the possibility that the Gospel writers were self-consciously completing "the story"—advancing the Hebrew narrative.[4] Matthew, in academic circles, is generally accepted as a work that attempted to influence the direction of the Christian project along Torah observant lines, but failed due to the widespread influence of the Apostle Paul.[5] There are scholars who take the rather extreme position that Matthew's inclusion in the canon can be seen as a complete accident. John Marshall in a review of Anthony Saldarini's book, "Matthew's Christian Jewish Community" reported:

> According to Saldarini, the position of the Matthean community is that of a deviant and relatively minor sub-group which fails to achieve the influence over Judaism that its gospel strives to exert. The irony which has distorted the interpretation of the

---

seeks to demonstrate that Matthew intended the entirety of the work to be read as an escalating indictment against Jerusalem and its stewards.

3. Wright, *People of God*, 396.

4. The Hebrew narrative, for this reading, refers to the story of Israel recorded in the Tanach.

5. This approach has been advanced most recently by Daniel Harrington, S.J. Harrington, "Matthew and Paul," 25.

gospel of Matthew is its spectacular and accidental success in a movement which it did not envision, namely Christianity.[6]

If we are to allow for the possibility that Matthew had intentionally attempted to complete the Hebrew story, and, therefore, was not simply a first-century "Chauncey Gardiner," certain and prevalent paradigms for understanding Matthew will need to be temporarily suspended.[7]

## The Purpose of Matthew

There has been no shortage of scholars who have observed the severity of the conflict between Jesus and the religious hierarchy in Jerusalem.[8] Some scholars have viewed the denunciation of the scribes and Pharisees as the cause of the ensuing destruction of Jerusalem in AD 70.[9] There is little disagreement with this proposition;[10] however, some suggest that Matthew's delegitimization of Israel's leaders was self-serving. Saldarini, for instance, asserts that the Matthean diatribe is a means of elevating the Matthean community's religious claims and standing.[11] Saldarini's approach implies that the author of Matthew did not consider the document would have universal import or significance; it was written to address the immediate pressing circumstances of the Matthean community.[12] The conflict between Jesus and the Pharisees cannot be denied. Few, however, have attempted to make the

---

6. Marshall, "Community," 85.

7. "The notion of the four gospel communities, with their particular circumstances and theology, has driven Gospel scholarship for several decades" (Sim, "Response to Richard Bauckham," 4). David Sim goes on to propose that the writing of "open texts" by the Evangelists would imply that they were not communicating a specific message; their writings could be interpreted as the reader saw fit (17). That being the case, it would be impossible for any message to be a public statement with universal relevance.

8. "The city of Jerusalem, its temple, its leadership and people constitute a conglomerate of opposition in Matthew" (France, "Matthew and Jerusalem," 126).

9. Moffitt, "Righteous Bloodshed," 306; Senior, *Matthew*, 23.

10. "The received gospel tradition appears to suggest that the catastrophe of 70 C.E. and its aftermath was brought about by Jewish leaders who plotted Jesus' death, the Jewish mob who had demanded it, and the stiff-necked Jews who refused to follow Jesus' way" (Garber, "Jewish Jesus," 141).

11. Saldarini, "Delegitimisation," 660.

12. Matthew's narrative should not be pressed beyond its own boundaries. It is not necessary for Matthew to have an ongoing skirmish with Pharisees to justify a historical retelling of the Jesus event. Kingsbury, "Reflections," 457.

case that this was anything more than a conflict of sects: Jesus' followers against the sect of the Pharisees.[13]

There has also been a tendency to downplay the Matthean rhetoric of denunciation in an attempt to avoid the implications that might arise from the termination of Israel's exclusive covenant with YHWH. A remarkable instance of this is found in a paper by John Paul Heil, in which the Gospel is read in the light of Ezekiel 34, which speaks of the raising up of new shepherds for the new community.[14] Heil, in his narrative analysis, manages to completely avoid Matthew 23, which so pivotally denounces the shepherds of Israel as being neglectful and self-serving guides: the very indictment of Ezekiel 34. On the other hand, Pheme Perkins acknowledges the interest of all the Gospels to "advance a striking supercessionist socio-religious agenda in imagery which alludes to the destruction of that sanctuary [temple]."[15]

Still others note the unique intensity of denigration found within Matthew's gospel towards Christ's institutional opponents. Craig S. Keener makes the case that Matthew's portrayal of Pharisees and Sadducees as a "brood of vipers" (Matt 3:7, 12:34, 23:33) implied that they were morally reprehensible in the ancient world; for, it was believed, viper young consumed their mothers at birth.[16]

Therefore, there is no particular shortage of interesting research that has observed, or denied, the obvious conflict with Jesus of Nazareth, which led to the final denunciation of Israel's religious establishment. Interestingly, then, Matthean scholars have generally not seen this polemical rhetoric as a unified feature and purpose of Matthew.[17] Invariably, Matthew has been seen as a historical biography that attempts to retell the "gospel" of Jesus, and interpret its meaning. Keener writes, "Matthew is more interested in interpreting tradition than in creating it."[18] For Keener, Matthew has an historical interest, and seeks to integrate the life of Jesus with pertinent and judicious quotation from the Tanach in order to establish a case for Christ as Mosaic

---

13. Morris, *Matthew*, 5.
14. Heil, "Ezekiel 34."
15. Perkins, "If Jerusalem Stood" 201.
16. Keener, "Brood of Vipers," 11.

17. Jack Kingsbury is an exception. He does see that conflict is central to the Matthean plotline. Kingsbury broke new ground in his treatment of Matthew as a unified narrative. This work builds on his approach, but is quite different. The focus on metanarrative, Matthew being written as Scripture, the priestly subtext, and the covenantal nature of Matthew's document are features that differentiate this work from Kingsbury's. Kingsbury, *Matthew as Story*.

18. Keener, *Matthew*, 22.

fulfillment.[19] William Hendrickson proposed another alternative: that the Gospel was written as an evangelistic tool to convince and win Jews.[20]

John Nolland presents several possibilities as to the purpose of Matthew's gospel. The first is that it conforms, in character, to ancient biographical writings.[21] The next possibility is that the Gospel is akin to the biographies of Israel's ancients, particularly those of Elijah and David, thus emphasizing conformity and continuity.[22] Nolland's third option is that it was written to facilitate Christian proclamation—that is, as a preaching manual to facilitate relationship with the abiding Christ. Another possibility is that the document serves as a catechetical aid, to ground the new communities in the teaching of Jesus, referred to in the commissioning of the disciples (28:18–20). In other words, the Great Commission is essentially the reason for the manuscript. Christ's teaching is documented so that the church would know what to teach as required by the commission. Nolland also considers the possibility that Matthew was written to be read liturgically, and as a Jewish Midrash. For Nolland, the polemic of Matthew 23 does not go unnoticed; its purpose, however, is to define the Christian community, that is, to demonstrate the disciples' acceptance by God via the foil of the Jewish establishment's rejection by God.[23] Michael Goulder has also made the case that Matthew can be divided in such a way as to suggest that it was written as a lectionary.[24] Jack Kingsbury, however, does consider that the conflict narrative is "central to the plot of Matthew's Gospel."[25]

Matthew's unique Jewish perspective of Jesus' life is a key feature of the document. Ulrich Luz finds agreement with H. Frankemölle who "designates the Gospel of Matthew as a *kerygmatic work of history* of an Old Testament style, as a new sketch of a sacred foundational history which has a literary orientation to Deuteronomy and the Chronicler's history."[26] There-

19. Ibid.

20. Hendriksen, *Matthew*, 97–98.

21. This view has the most support amongst commentators. Richard Bauckham has argued convincingly for this position having observed the generic character of ten Greco-Roman βίοι. Bauckham, *Gospel for All*, 121. However, the use of this *bios* genre may not satisfactorily explain the interest of Matthew's author in connecting his document to the existing Hebrew story with its specific emphasis on fulfillment.

22. The use of the Elijah story as a template in Luke/Acts has been noted. Evans, "Elijah/Elisha Narratives."

23. Nolland, Gospel of Matthew, 19–22. Donald Hagner had developed almost identical categories to Nolland's. Hagner, *Matthew 1–13*, lxii–lix.

24. Goulder, "Sections and Lections," 77–94.

25. Kingsbury, *Matthew as Story*, 3.

26. Luz, *Matthew 1–7*, 45–46.

fore, there is some interest in the proposition that Matthew is modeled on Israel's former documents. Luz, however, derived no inference as to why Matthew was written in this way.

At this stage no significant work has emerged that has developed a sustained argument that Matthew was seeking to advance the Hebrew narrative by comprehensively engaging the existing story.[27] Just as Frankemölle's thesis proposed a Deuteronomic[28] and Chronicles connection with Matthew, various others have argued that Matthew modeled his story of fulfillment on Isaiah,[29] Ezekiel,[30] Jeremiah,[31] Zechariah,[32] Moses,[33] and Hosea.[34] In addition to this we can also acknowledge the inspiration that Matthew gleaned from Esther in writing his theodicy—Mordecai was exalted while his vehement enemy Haman was slaughtered. Matthew's "bridegroom" motif must surely also have resonance with Song of Songs, while the proverbs found in the Sermon on the Mount and Matthew's interest in wisdom "being proved right" surely was intended to recall Solomon's writings. The allusions, typologies, and echoes of the Tanach in Matthew are too numerous to mention here, and no doubt many have escaped the notice of the modern reader. Yet it is practically impossible to find a paper that argues that Matthew is engaging and utilizing the whole Hebrew canon.

In a review of a paper that proposed Matthew had used Zechariah as his template, the reviewer, Jason Hood, could not disguise his frustration:

> Ham follows Donald Senior and Michael Knowles in initially studying citations, then moving to the study of allusions. One wonders if there is a still larger base from which to begin: namely, Matthew's representation of, reliance on, or interaction with Israel's story as a whole? Can one successfully isolate use of one book of the OT without reference to the use of the whole? Is there a "grand narrative" element, a sense that Matthew is in some way concluding Scripture's Story, which Ham with many

---

27. Vicki Balabanski believes that Matthew should be understood as a theodicy, as it addresses all the issues that are integral to the four apocalypses associated with the destruction of Jerusalem. Balabanski, *Eschatology*, 175–77.

28. Also Grassi, "Matthew as a Second Testament Deuteronomy."

29. Carter, "Evoking Isaiah."

30. Heil, "Ezekiel 34," 698–708.

31. Whitters, "Jesus in the Footsteps."

32. Ham, *Coming King*.

33. Westerholm, *Understanding Matthew*, 68–70.

34. Hill, "Meaning of Hosea 6:6."

others, including the majority of scholars reviewed in his first chapter has left untapped?[35]

Hood had seen the need for an assessment of Matthew against the background of the whole story (metanarrative), and not just individual parts of it. This book seeks to address this concern, and argue that Matthew was not retelling the Jesus event as the fulfillment of a book or potion of the Old Testament alone, but the whole of the Hebrew narrative.[36]

## An Alternative Proposal

This work is an attempt to explore the possibility that Matthew had intended to integrate his Jesus narrative as a well-anticipated concluding chapter to a complex, yet unified, metanarrative. To this end, an attempt will be made to demonstrate a deliberate and systematic treatment of the diverse Hebrew sacred texts on the part of Matthew in order to draw the story to its profound and confounding end. Further, rather than interpreting the widespread resistance to Christ in Matthew's gospel as necessary for the enactment of the passion narrative, it is being proposed here that the conflict motif was central to the prophetic expectation associated with YHWH's day of reckoning in the temple/Jerusalem.[37] Matthew, it is here proposed, drew from some of the most austere threats to Israel found in both the Major and the Minor Prophets. These texts and their contexts painted a dire picture for Israel, which was portrayed in Matthew as a hostile and unwilling participant in a peace treaty that YHWH sought to broker. This rebuttal was met by YHWH's wrath, expressed primarily at the apocalyptic crucifixion of the Christ, which was the means by which God concluded his exclusive covenant with national Israel.

---

35. Hood, "Coming King."

36. "Through the use of the Old Testament, especially the so-called formula quotations, Matthew indicates that the coming of Jesus means the time of prophecy has been brought to an end and the time of fulfilment inaugurated" (Kingsbury, "Form and Message," 16).

37. Jerusalem and the temple in the literature of second temple Judaism were interchangeable and almost synonymous. den Dulk, "Measuring the Temple," 442.

## Retelling History for the Purpose of Vindication and Indictment

A central feature of the Hebrew narrative is its dependence on covenant as the basis of YHWH's dealing with his people. Though covenant as a legally defined contractual agreement between a purported deity or monarch and his subjects was not unique to the Hebrew story, it is certainly the case that the Hebrew metanarrative is the one story that sustained and advanced this paradigm as foundational. This story consistently told of YHWH's condescension and willingness to enter covenant with individuals, as well as with nations. The first such covenant was made at the beginning with the "Adam" (Hos 6:7).[38] The second was with Noah, on behalf of all living beings (Gen 9:9), which guaranteed the preservation of the planet from future universal judgments until the end. These covenants were perhaps instructional for the Hebrew narrative and gave the basis for understanding the Abrahamic covenant (Gen 12:1–3), which was foundational to the redemptive history of God's dealings. This covenant was made with Abraham and his offspring,[39] and was reiterated to both Isaac and Jacob. Later, YHWH was also to make an exclusive covenant with David, which gave his descendants exclusive claim to the throne of Israel (2 Sam 23:5).

However, the central covenant to the nationhood of Israel, against which most of the chapters of the narrative are set, is the Mosaic covenant made at Sinai. This contractual arrangement established the parameters of the exclusive relationship made between YHWH and the Hebrew nation, which he had delivered from Egypt (Exod 19:4). Central to this covenant were the detailed stipulations and obligations placed upon the nation as its part in maintaining the sacred relationship. Although a point of theological controversy, the Mosaic covenant appears to be a conditional arrangement (Exod 19:5–6); Israel was in covenant with YHWH, and the basis of this covenant was its judicial code—the Law.

It is against this background, then, that Hebrew literature makes sense. The individual "chapters" of the story are most meaningful when they are understood as "covenant" documents—that is, documents that chart the

---

38. There is some disagreement as to whether there was a covenant with Adam as the meaning of the Hosea text is disputed; however, it is sufficient to note that within the Hebrew story the first man breached a condition that God had imposed. This resulted in the condemnation foreshadowed by God for breach of the regulation (Gen 2:17).

39. The identity of Abraham's offspring was a central feature of early Christian literature. Most of these documents testified that the "offspring" was the "elect" of both Israel and the Gentiles. No doubt this was heavily influenced by the Gentile influx into the church. Whatever may have given rise to the notion of a reconstituted multinational "seed," however, it was by no means a straightforward or simple controversy to resolve.

progress or failure of Israel's contractual obligations. Therefore, it is not surprising to find in this framework that YHWH's identity should be that of a judge (Ps 7:11). The subordinate players in this great theodicy are the priests, who seek mercy for the guilty, and the prophets, who function as YHWH's accusing attorneys. The prophets' function, by and large, is to remind Israel/Judah of her covenant obligations and to predict the penalty for failure to comply.

Israel's history was, therefore, not simply a retelling of random disconnected events; it was the story of the covenant, which would find its ultimate destiny in the Day of YHWH—Judgment Day. In this context, Israel's history should be understood as the basis of reward or punishment. What can be observed within Israel's narrative is the selective retelling of events in order to provide the reason for either condemnation or vindication. This motif is apparent in the retelling of Israel's history found in Deut 32, Josh 24:1–27, Judg 2:6–3:6, 2 Chr 36:15–20, Neh 9:6–37, Ps 7, and Ps 106. In each of these passages Israel's non-compliance with its covenant obligations is central to the historical recasting. This continued even into the "Christian" documents. At a trial before the Sanhedrin (Acts 6–7), for instance, Stephen retold Israel's history in order to accuse his hearers and their forebears of their own covenant neglect. In this way, Hebrew history is invariably used for either the vindication of YHWH's actions, and/or the indictment of Israel's conduct.

Matthew appears to have used the Jesus tradition to write a theodicy that was dependent on the history of Israel's covenant as its backdrop. The accumulation of witnesses who would testify to Israel's crimes against YHWH,[40] and the failure of Jerusalem to find witnesses in their countersuit of Jesus,[41] as well as the appointment of the twelve disciples to be witnesses or judges[42] to these events, all play their part in this Judgment Day drama. And, of course, Satan is present (4:1–11), the ancient accuser prosecuting the righteous people of God. All the ingredients are evident for the reader to recognize the judicial arrangement of Matthew's work in advancing his final courtroom drama, which resulted in the execution/termination of the exclusive and sacred relationship of YHWH with national Israel.[43] It was not merely the immediate generation confronted by Jesus that was "in the

---

40. Matt 12:41–42; 23:31.

41. Matt 26:60.

42. Matt 19:28. It should also not escape the reader's attention that Matthew alone has Judas declaring Jesus to be innocent (27:4). Thus the disciples, in Matthew, were unanimous in the belief that Jesus was innocent.

43. "It is clear to the reader that Jesus is destined for speedy divine vindication (16:21; 17:1–9, 22–23; 20:18–19) and that his tormentors are destined for divine wrath (8:11–12; 23:29–39; 26:64) . . ." (den Dulk, "Measuring the Temple," 442).

dock," but also all the generations before it. The cumulative guilt of covenant transgressions would rise like a crushing debt and collapse on this ultimate generation; they would carry the demise of Israel's totality, and be punished for all the righteous blood shed from "Abel to Zechariah" (23:35). This analysis proposes that Matthew was by this means advancing the existing covenantal narrative of the Law and the Prophets: a possibility, which, hitherto, has not been developed from a reading of the entire narrative.[44]

## Methodology

This reading or interpretation of Matthew is based on a series of observations and presuppositions. Of course, all readers of any form of literature approach their task with presuppositions, which shape the way that particular documents are read. This project is a reading of Matthew as though it were written as the concluding chapter of the Tanach, as N. T. Wright has proposed. This purpose, however, demands further qualification as the interpretation or reading of an "ending" can produce any number of outcomes. Therefore, the lens through which this reading will take place needs to be clearly identified. When dealing with any portion of Matthew this lens will be utilized, and it is assumed that the use of this distinctive lens will invariably produce distinctive outcomes.

## Previous Lenses through which Matthew Has Been Read

It is self-evident that the presupposition/s that one brings to a reading of Matthew will shape its reading and interpretation. Matthew has most frequently been read as a Christian document—it was written to tell the Christian story, and consequently inform Christians concerning the origins of their belief and how they should live as a consequence of this story. This approach, viewing Matthew as a catechetical aid, has probably been the most utilized lens for reading the Gospel. As a consequence of this lens, Matthew has been read as a straightforward account of Jesus and his teaching, and readers who made use of this lens did not recognize the possibility that Matthew may have had meaningful subtexts.[45]

---

44. ". . . narrative understanding is the comprehension of a complex of events by seeing the whole in which the parts have participated" (Polkinghorne, *Narrative Knowing*, 22). Therefore, the particular parts of this reading should fit comfortably within this paradigm of narrative advancement and completion.

45. What is considered a subtext for a twenty-first century readership may have been obvious to a first-century readership. For instance, in a world that was dominated

Another lens through which Matthew is often read is the dominant or consensus lens. The last four decades of Matthean scholarship have been dominated by the "communities" view of the Gospels. Matthew's community, it is believed, was under siege, and this lens has been utilized to identify this group, its location, its opponents, its theology and its struggles. Most of this community-focused research is a quest for subtext. Matthew is read to find clues as to where the community existed, and to identify its particular concerns and opponents. For instance, in a recent offering by David Sim, Matthew 16 is read as a contra-Pauline statement, a denunciation of Paul and his churches.[46] Sim's lens allows him to read Matthew as the product of a vulnerable and regional expression of a Torah-observant Christian/Jewish community that had access to Paul's writings. As this lens allows for the possibility that Paul's "law-free" gospel was an anathema to Matthew's Torah observant sect, Paul's claim, that he got his message directly from God is seen as an assertion that would be contested. Therefore, Matthew's community included a statement by Jesus in which he declared to Peter that flesh and blood had not revealed important information to him, but that it came from his father in heaven. This then, for Sim, is the subtext of Matthew 16—Paul is being put in his place, if not denounced. Peter's claim to divine instruction is much more substantial than Paul's unconfirmed claim. If one accepts this lens, then Sim's reading is plausible, although never proven. It is the results of the reading that vindicates the lens, or at least, establishes its plausibility.

## The Lens through which this Reading Will Be Undertaken

When doing a reading, any lens is permissible, but not all lenses are profitable. The task here is not simply to create a lens, but to try to replicate the lens that the author may have used. This requires some (although not too much) speculation. It is reasonable to assume that Matthew was a devout follower of Jesus, and a Jew who had a conservative view of the Scriptures. It can also be assumed that he was well versed in the Scriptures, and expected certain events to take place on the basis of them. Some aspects of the lens may be harder to justify, but in a reading they don't necessarily have to be justified. Although some aspects of the lens may be intuitive or speculative, they remain completely plausible. The lens for this reading includes:

- Matthew believed the Tanach to be the word of God.

---

by a priestly culture and issues of ritual cleansing etc., Jesus would obviously have been functioning as a priest, whereas this may not even occur to a modern generation.

46. Sim, "Matthew and the Pauline Corpus."

- Matthew believed the Tanach to convey the story of Israel (metanarrative) that was consistent, progressive, and unified. Therefore, Matthew would not have engaged in anything resembling modern critical methods to interpret the Scripture.
- The Scriptures of Matthew anticipated fulfillment, and Matthew attempted to document the Jesus event as the fulfillment of them.
- The trajectory of the message of the Minor Prophets (particularly Malachi) indicated that the Day of YHWH was imminent.
- This Day of YHWH was a day of judgment (Mal 4:1).
- The main object of God's scorn was the priests/Levites, who would be judged and displaced (Mal 2:1–8).[47]
- The coming of Elijah would precede the Day of the Lord (Mal 4:5).[48]
- The theology contained in the Epistle to the Hebrews is representative of Matthew's view of the law.[49]
- The writer of Hebrews interpreted the law primarily as cultic ordinance, rather than moral instruction.[50]

## The Major Presuppositions that Will Influence this Reading

This work is primarily a literary analysis of Matthew from a canonical perspective. As such, it should produce a biblical theological paradigm; that is, one that reads the document as part of an existing body of work, intended

---

47. "The attention that the Book of Malachi devotes to the priesthood stands without precedent in biblical literature. Nowhere else does the priesthood receive such extended or scathing beratings; the priests will, indeed, have dung spread upon their faces. Conversely, nowhere else is such exalted language used for the priesthood" (O'Brien, "Priest and Levite," 147).

48. "John is identified with the prophecy of Malachi 3 and subsequently directly with Elijah" (Goodacre, "Mark, Elijah," 79).

49. The theology represented in Hebrews was not the only perspective available in the first century; however, as the clearest presentation of the Gospel as it pertained to Jewish concerns, it will be utilized as representative of the Jewish Christian understanding of the priesthood and cult for the purposes of this reading. Obviously, many would strongly disagree that Matthew's theology was consistent with the theology of Hebrews; however, for the purposes of this reading it will be accepted that Matthew and Hebrews shared a worldview and theology.

50. This is a significant feature of this lens. Christians have not usually read the Law through the Levitical lens that is found in Hebrews. Therefore, Messiah has invariably been understood as referring to kingly function alone. For Hebrews, Jesus is the great High Priest, and Matthew, it is proposed, also presented Jesus as an effectual priest.

to complement the existing narrative and advance the story/history of Israel and its dealings with YHWH. This approach to reading Matthew has been built on certain assumptions, which require some explanation.

Some of the presuppositions that are used to justify this reading may appear to be unusual, but they are not arbitrary. Each is selected for very good reasons. It is hoped that by using this lens a number of Matthew's conundrums can be satisfactorily resolved, conundrums that seem to remain while the existing paradigms are used. By reading Matthew's narrative as part of a continuum, a chapter within an existing narrative, and allowing the plot to expose itself without the constraint of looking for meaning within a particular limited and local context, it is hoped that the narrative will fulfill a natural and justified role within the Hebrew metanarrative.

It can be demonstrated from the Epistle to the Hebrews that there was an acute necessity within the early church to explain how the Jesus event had seemingly brought the inviolable requirements of Torah to an end. Hebrews explores how it was possible for God to abandon his temple, to decommission his sacred priesthood, and to declare unclean foods and people clean. These abrogated concepts had been enshrined in the Torah of Israel's nationhood; without these key identity markers and her exclusive access to YHWH, Israel had become diminished, if not desolate. The Hebrews writer gave an explanation for why the temple and the Aaronic mediation had become obsolete as a consequence of Jesus' death and exaltation. As a consequence of this perspective, it appears possible that Matthew also tried to explain the judicial cause of the AD 70 cataclysm, not by means of a theological explanation as the Hebrews writer had done, but by retelling the Story, in order to achieve similar outcomes.

## Presupposition 1: Final Matthew Was the Intentional Product of a Redactor/Author for Theological Purposes and Not Simply a Biography of Jesus

Within this work no claims will be made concerning many of the background issues that may have been instrumental in shaping Matthew. Therefore, there will be no detailed analysis of authorship, dating, audience or community. Nor will any attempt be made to understand the particular struggles that the author or his community were involved in that may have given rise to the Gospel. Matthew will be read as though it were written for a universal audience and, secondly, intended to seamlessly integrate with the existing Hebrew narrative.

The primary document under investigation here is "final Matthew," which is the document that is accepted as the distilled and final form of the Gospel, textual variants notwithstanding. We are working on the assumption that the document had a redactor,[51] who shaped this final form into a cohesive unity for distinctly theological reasons. The text will be read as a deliberate undertaking to present the Jesus data, in terms of both the selection of the material and its sequence, in order to make specific points. Therefore, it is assumed that the narrative has a distinctive agenda that can be examined and relied upon to make certain conclusions about the document as a whole. It is against this plotline that each pericope will be considered and assessed. In the case that many of the "kernels" or significant pericopae are better understood against this plotline, it will be argued that a particular plot or storyline is legitimate, and a case can be made for Matthew's intention in writing his gospel.[52] While structure is critically important in Matthew, it does not necessarily expose the plotline, from which meaning is derived.[53]

## Author

The Gospel of Matthew does not name its author and has taken its name from the designation found upon it, *According to Matthew*, which is found in the earliest of manuscripts. Interestingly, there was no dispute from the earliest times concerning the document's author.[54] Patristic literature overwhelmingly identified the apostle as its source, with no exception. No claims, however, concerning the identity of the author will be made here. There is little doubt, certainly, that this author was keenly aware of the Jewish story and had intimate knowledge of many of its ancient documents, in both Hebrew and Greek. It is reasonable to suppose the author to have been Jewish.[55] It is also reasonable to believe that this author had enormous confidence in his ability and authority to transmit this account. In other words,

---

51. This does not negate the possibility that the document was written by Matthew the tax-collector.

52. The plot is the central theme which each particular within the work seeks to serve—it is what keeps the story moving forward. "Kernels indicate the story's logic by presenting the major turning points in the narrative" (Matera, "The Plot," 238).

53. Carter, "Kernels and Narrative Blocks." Warren Carter has advanced a plausible structure, but did not advance a convincing new hermeneutic as a consequence of it.

54. Turner, *Matthew*, 21.

55. There has been a case made that a Jew would never get the Shema wrong, but this has been adequately explained so that Matthew remains, according to the consensus, thoroughly Jewish. Foster, "Why Did Matthew?"

this was not a private work that accidentally became Scripture.[56] We can also conclude that the author was a Christian who sought to advance the fame of Jesus, and was prepared to suffer for the opportunity.[57] Throughout this work, the author/redactor will be referred to as Matthew.

## Date

There will be no attempt to establish a date for Matthew's document. The consensus dating of this work (AD 80) has been influenced by a limited set of presuppositions, which will be suspended for the purposes of this new reading. Matthew's dependence on Mark, its dependence upon Q or Primitive Matthew, references to the destruction of Jerusalem and the reference to ἐκκλησία have all had a significant influence on the dating of this document. Our interest is not so much in its date, but in the impression that the author/redactor sought to give.

Matthew does not intend his readers to assume that it was written after the destruction of Jerusalem.[58] The document anticipates the cataclysmic events, and gives no obvious indication that the events had already transpired. The Gospel is the fulfillment of many prophecies, but the largest single prophecy in Matthew (the destruction of the temple) is set in the near future, unfulfilled. As such, Matthew presents itself, in part, as a prophetic work.[59] A case can be made that signals may be embedded within the text to show that Jerusalem had fallen, and this possibility is not completely rejected. However, within a document that has a clear intention to demonstrate the fulfillment and advancement of the Hebrew narrative, it seems unlikely that its author would seek to veil such a momentous event, unless his work was intended to be understood as preceding the event. So the date of the document is not considered to be of very great significance to this particular project.

---

56. There is a case to be made within the narrative that the Gospel was commissioned by Matthew's Jesus.

57. There can be no doubt that this document was written in a milieu in which it was a dangerous activity to denigrate the high priest and the Pharisees, as well as to predict the destruction of the temple. Had the work been written after AD 70, it would have been no less hazardous to suggest that the destruction was the consequence of the appalling treatment of Jesus by the Jerusalem establishment.

58. See France and Nolland, "Reflections on the Writing," 280.

59. Vicky Balabanski identifies Matthew as an apocalyptic scribe, his work having quasi-prophetic authority. Balabanski, *Eschatology*, 179. Also see 248.

## Audience

It is perhaps at this point that the greatest latitude is asked of the reader. The overwhelming tide of Matthean studies has identified Matthew's audience as a particular Jewish sect on the fringes of Christian/Jewish relations and developments at the end of the first century. This work is not challenging that hypothesis, but only asking that it be suspended for this reading. There is little doubt that Matthew's interpretation has been dominated, in modern scholarship, by a desire to understand the immediate concerns of his particular community.[60] This reading, however, must be freed from this constraint if it is to have any hope of reading Matthew as a document designed to complement the existing metanarrative; there must be some latitude given to free the document from localized and particular minority concerns, in order to elevate it and allow for the possibility that it sought to conclude Israel's great story.[61]

## The Polemic within Matthew Was Not Incidental to the Story

All the Gospels advance a narrative of polemic with Jesus' opponents, but none highlight this aspect of the Jesus story to the same extent as Matthew. It will be shown in this reading that Matthew used almost every occasion to expose the entrenched animosity of Jesus' detractors, even extending this motif, as it were, beyond the grave.[62] Jesus' opponents were roundly condemned from the outset, and their vilification continued to the closing verses. Rather than observing these as an anomaly of Matthean excess in an otherwise "good news" story, it will be shown that Matthew's project was uniquely driven by this plotline.[63]

## Presupposition 2: The Existence of an Early Hebrew Matthew

While this work will be primarily an examination of Final Matthew, there is sufficient and compelling evidence to believe that a Hebrew version of this

---

60. Keener, *Matthew*, 11. Bauckham, *Jesus and the Eyewitnesses*, 290.

61. Richard Bauckham has advanced the hypothesis that an "apostolic collegiate" existed in Jerusalem that both collected and critiqued the cumulative stories of Jesus. Bauckham, *Jesus and the Eyewitnesses*, 290.

62. Kingsbury, "The Developing conflict," 72.

63. " . . . Matthew's eschatological perspective was not of secondary importance nor simply a disciplinary stick, but integral to the evangelist's theology" (Balabanski, *Eschatology*, 147).

document was in circulation at the beginning of the second century. This is still the subject of some controversy; however, in the context of this reading a case will be made for the limited use of what may remain of this document. The rationale for this will be based on some excellent preliminary work[64] in the evaluation of the Shem-Tob Hebrew Matthew, and a philosophical appeal to consider the Hebrew sensibilities and the probable need for a Hebrew Matthew. The hypothesis of this book is not dependent on the existence of an early Hebrew Matthew, which makes it a minor presupposition; nonetheless the occasional use of the Hebrew version will further advance and strengthen the plotline that is being advanced from Final Matthew.

## Philosophical Appeal

There is no doubt that Matthew was intended for an audience who was fully conversant with the Hebrew story. Perhaps this is why the document had long been considered to be the Gospel to the Hebrews. If it is the case that Matthew was written primarily for a Jewish readership, it would have been peculiar if it was exclusively circulated in Greek, the global language of the Gentile world.[65] In the event that Matthew was attempting to write a chapter of the existing narrative, it would have been imprudent to avoid using the historical communication and heart language of the Hebrew people. The former belief that Hebrew literature was not being produced in Judea during the first century has been corrected by the discovery of documents found at Qumran. These testify to the production and dissemination of Hebrew Scriptures and commentaries. So logically, there could be no reason to believe that the Gospel could not have existed in an early Hebrew version, and it would have been eminently appropriate if it did.

## Patristic Testimony

From the earliest of the Patristic writings there have been references to the primacy of Matthew and its existence in the Hebrew dialect.[66] Papias (60–130) observed early in the second century, "Matthew collected the oracles

---

64. Howard, "The Textual Nature"; Shedinger, "A Further Consideration."

65. Jews in the Diaspora and in Judea spoke Greek. This does not negate the point. In Jerusalem, Paul spoke to the crowd in Hebrew, which won their attention and gave Paul emotional access (Acts 21:40). This was the effect of using the sacred language.

66. Black, "The Use of Rhetorical." Black makes a strong case for Hebrew or Aramaic language, rather than style.

in the Hebrew language, and each interpreted them as best he could."[67] This testimony was not contradicted, but affirmed, by a succession of references from other "fathers" including Irenaeus, Origen, Eusebius and Jerome. The reliability of these accounts has been questioned, and so has the issue of whether they were referring to the Gospel of Matthew, or some compilation, such as Q or first Matthew.[68] However, Jerome gives a strong account of a Hebrew Matthew's existence in the fifth century:

> Matthew, also called Levi, apostle and aforetimes publican, composed a gospel of Christ at first published in Judea in Hebrew for the sake of those of the circumcision who believed, but this was afterwards translated into Greek though by what author is uncertain. The Hebrew itself has been preserved until the present day in the library at Caesarea which Pamphilus so diligently gathered. I have also had the opportunity of having the volume described to me by the Nazarenes of Beroea, a city of Syria, who use it.[69]

This testimony should not be treated lightly and quickly jettisoned in support of the prevailing Two-Source Hypothesis, which asserts Matthean dependence on Mark and Q.[70] There is little doubt that Final Matthew had some dependence on Mark's gospel; however, this does not necessarily negate the possibility of another Hebrew version, one that may have even informed Mark.

### The Preliminary Evidence from Shem-Tob

George Howard has examined the fourteenth-century polemical document called *Even Bohan* (Shem Tob), written by Shem-Tob ben-Isaac ben-Shaprut, which contained a Hebrew version of Matthew interspersed by detailed criticisms as part of a wider diatribe that sought to ridicule the Catholic Church in Spain.[71] Howard had extracted from *Even Bohan* the Hebrew text of Matthew, which was not complete, and sought to identify its origins. His conclusion regarding the text was that it was not a translation from Greek, but had a Hebrew substratum. Howard concluded that this substratum was

---

67. Eusibius *H. E.* 3.39.16.

68. Abel, "Who Wrote Matthew," 148. Abel placed First Matthew between AD 64–70.

69. Jerome and Gennadius, *Lives of Illustrious Men.*

70. See Farnell, "The Synoptic Gospels."

71. Howard, *Gospel of Matthew*, ix.

unlikely to be from a Greek translation, and therefore, it may have had some connection with a very early Hebrew Matthew.[72]

Apart from numerous linguistic considerations and Hebraisms that Howard traced back to a much earlier period in the development of the Hebrew language, he has observed the numerous instances where the Hebrew version was compelling as a consequence of its use of puns, word connections and alliterations, which are lost in a Greek translation.[73] Perhaps the most compelling reason to believe that this is not a translation from a Greek version, however, is the inclusion of the divine name (or a derivative of it) within Shem-Tob.[74] Howard describes how unlikely it is for the "name" to exist in any "heretical" document, as it was the practice of Jewish scribes to extract the name from its unholy context. How unlikely, then, would it be for a Hebrew translator to take the liberty of translating κύριος (Lord) into the divine name?

The dependability of Shem-Tob is questionable, as it was not in sympathetic hands. Howard acknowledges that, should Shem-Tob be a copy of an ancient Hebrew version, there would have been many scribal errors, and possibly even some deliberate alterations. For this reason alone, this version should not be heavily relied upon in tight exegetical considerations.[75] However, where a text is clearly more sensible in the Hebrew version, particularly when it adds to the credibility of the Christian version of the Christ event, the Hebrew possibility ought to be seriously considered.

So within this work the occasional appeal will be made to the possibility of a relevant Hebrew text, which could facilitate a richer explanation of a given pericope. However, as has already been mentioned, this reading will not be dependent on Shem-Tob; it will simply make occasional references to its translation.

## *The Synoptic Problem*

While dwelling on the likelihood of an original Hebrew Matthew, it is almost irresistible to propose an alternative solution to the Synoptic problem.[76]

---

72. Ibid., 225.

73. Ibid., 194.

74. Ibid., 201–3. The name is used nineteen times.

75. Ignatius had a version of Matthew that does not completely conform to Final Matthew. So alternative versions were in circulation. Trevett, "Approaching Matthew," 62.

76. It is generally accepted that Markan priority does not completely resolve the Synoptic problem, though Gordon Fee is committed to it. Fee, "A Text-Critical Look," 23. Malcolm Lowe considers that Fee's arguments are not supported by his evidence.

It is unlikely that Hebrew Matthew, presuming its early existence, could displace the necessity of Q for many scholars. However, there has been a growing interest in the viability of a primitive Matthew, even if it were simply a collection of Jesus data. Could this Hebrew Matthew be the distant offspring of primitive Hebrew Matthew?[77] Could Mark also have utilized this Hebrew Matthew, who's Greek Gospel was in turn used by the redactor of final Matthew, who believed it unnecessary to improve upon Mark's Greek translation? The possibilities are tantalizing, but perhaps a distraction in this introduction.[78]

## Presupposition 3: Matthew Was Written to Advance and Fulfill the Hebrew Narrative

This presupposition has been foreshadowed by the previous request for the indulgence of the reader—here the point is more explicitly made. Matthew may have written a document for the immediate context and particular needs of his community; however, the author manages to give the impression that he is writing a story that has universal relevance (See Matt 26:13). The freedom of Matthew to plunder the vault of Israel's sacred texts would appear sacrilegious if it were not for the highest possible objective—the retelling of YHWH's long awaited appointment with Israel at her temple. There exists in this document a certain audacity, perhaps only rivaled by John's Jesus epic, which gives every impression to the readers that they are witnessing a suitable and even superior chapter to the sacred story of God's dealing with Israel and the implications it has for the destiny of humanity.

N. T. Wright argued strongly that first-century Judea expected the advancement of the Hebrew narrative—a grassroots expectation in which New Testament writers would no doubt have been indoctrinated. There was a heightened eschatological expectation, as Wright noted:

> Few will doubt, in fact, that the great majority of Jews in Jesus' day were looking for a major action of their god within history to liberate his people. Even those who want to minimize this have to allow for a huge groundswell of this belief bursting out in the

---

So there is still some dispute to Markan priority, even apart from a Hebrew Matthew. Lowe, "The Demise of Arguments."

77. Proto-Matthew and Hebrew Matthew may be synonymous, and may have been written prior to AD 40. Lowe and Flusser, "Evidence Corroborating," 39–40.

78. There is increasing evidence that Luke had access to a Greek Matthew. Tuckett, "On the Relationship." Also, Argyle, "Evidence for the View." And, Goulder, "Two Significant Minor Agreements," 370.

mid-60s of the first century. The point here is that, in thinking about and longing for this event, they did not merely draw upon patterns and types, such as the Exodus, culled at random, allegorically or typologically, from a past conceived as a scattered bunch of unconnected events. Rather, they saw themselves *in sequence with*, and continuing, Israel's whole past story, waiting for that story to reach its promised goal. They were not living in an ahistorical mode, in which the only question of weight were timeless salvation or ethics, with such issues being "illustrated" by ideas taken in a fairly random fashion from her distant past. Rather, they read that past not least as a story; as a story which was continuing, and in which they themselves were characters; as a story with an ending, which can variously be characterized as "return from exile"; "return of YHWH to Zion"; "salvation"; "forgiveness of sins"; "new covenant"; "new exodus"; and perhaps even, for some at least, "new creation" and "resurrection."[79]

While this book may not make identical conclusions to Wright's, it is fair to say that his assessment of the first-century milieu has provided an eminently reasonable foundation for the pursuit of intentionality within the Christian documents. Matthew exhibits this cultural awareness and willingness that Wright speaks of to unpack the Jesus data as an integral extension and fulfillment of the Story—the arrival of the kingdom of heaven. As Wright wrote in another place concerning the writing of Matthew's Jesus biography: "he [Matthew] has told it as a continuation and climax of the story of Israel, with the implicit understanding that this story is the clue to the story of the whole world."[80]

## *The Advancement of the Hebrew Narrative*

The uniqueness of Israel's story is the way that it had advanced over millennia, each new episode building upon the previous narrative and moving it forward. There is no comparable ancient story. This advancement is not only evident within the historical books, it is apparent that the writings and Prophets also deliberately sought to extend the Hebrew narrative at certain times. This uniqueness is extraordinary in its own right, but it almost pales by comparison with the other distinctive that testifies to the deliberate extending of a single narrative: the prophecies that anticipate the following

---

79. Wright, "The Law in Romans 2," 131–50.
80. Wright, *People of God*, 390.

chapters and, as it were, write them in advance.[81] The Hebrew narrative advanced in this way:[82]

- Genesis anticipated Exodus (Gen 15:13–16), which in turn connected its story back to Genesis (Exod 1:5).
- Following the giving of Law and its second reading, Deuteronomy anticipated Joshua (Deut 31:1–8), which in turn connected back to Deuteronomy (Josh 1:1–9).
- Joshua retold the history of Israel from Abraham and anticipated the period of the judges (Joshua 24), which in turn reflected back on Joshua (Judg 1:1).
- Judges anticipated the rise of Samuel, the king-maker, by acknowledging that Israel's lawlessness was in part due to the absence of a king (Judg 17:6, 18:1,19:1, 21:25); 1 and 2 Samuel presented Samuel as the last of Israel's judges, who's task it was to appoint kings, and ultimately preside over the ascension of David's house.
- Samuel ended with the purchase of Araunah's threshing floor (2 Sam 24:21), which became the site of the temple; Kings resumed the story with David's death, Solomon's enthronement and the building of the temple.
- The Kings history was completed in the two volumes that ended with the destruction of the temple, the exile of Judah and the incarceration of King Jehoiachin in Babylon.
- The Chronicles testified to this succession also and included references to Israel's major pre-exilic prophets. It concluded with an acknowledgment of Jeremiah's prophecy concerning the destruction of Jerusalem.
- Following the Exile, Ezra acknowledged the same prophet in an almost identical manner to the Chronicler (2 Chr 36:22–23, Ezra 1:1–3).[83]
- After the Ezra/Nehemiah return, certain Minor Prophets anticipate what can be best described as the final episode, when Israel's temple would be permanently established and YHWH would maintain fidelity and exalt Israel and Judah. At the same time, this day would be a

---

81. No claim is being made here concerning the dating of prophetic books; the observation is that the Hebrew narrative gives the impression that prophetic utterance, which may include the books within which they were preserved, preceded the events that they anticipated.

82. This is partially advanced in Schnittjer, "The Narrative Multiverse," 242–43.

83. It is realized that this is probably not coincidence; however, my interest here is to show the way the stories were crafted in order to advance the narrative.

day of cataclysmic proportions for Israel. These Minor Prophets, it is proposed, heavily shaped Matthew's script, and he was careful to connect their significance to his Jesus account.

Thus we are able to observe that Israel's history is in the main accounted for, even though some periods are a little sketchy. We also observe that the former documents anticipated what followed and the latter gained currency by their ability to integrate with the existing literature. Like a train carriage, each chapter had a coupling to connect itself with the previous chapter and left a coupling for what would follow.

This awareness on the part of the various writers/redactors of the importance of progressing the narrative is integral to the whole story. This makes the Hebrew Scriptures a marvel, and possibly unique in the ancient world. Matthew was acutely aware of this narrative dynamic, which is demonstrated by his deliberate retelling of the Jesus event as not unexpected, but completely anticipated; hence his repetitive insistence that the events were the fulfillment of Moses and the Prophets (the Tenach). This, it is proposed, was the very purpose statement of the Gospel (5:17). However, clear and direct connections are also made within Matthew to the most recent prophets, particularly to Malachi, and this will be considered under Presupposition 4.[84]

## *The Importance of Documentation to the Hebrew Narrative*

Connected to the importance of Matthew's role in narrative advancement is the acute awareness for the Hebrew people that God's dealings must be documented. The birth of Israel and the birth of its Book are simultaneous according to Moses. It would be hard to find another culture/people more committed to and dependent upon its literary heritage. Israel, according to its narrative, received written law from its beginning. While Israel's history may have come about differently from the record we have been given in Moses (though no suggestion is being made here that that was the case), it is clear from the record that these events were documented from the earliest of times and were not the product of intergenerational folk reflection. So, for instance, Joshua had a book of the law upon which he was required to meditate (Josh 1:8). Similarly the prophets were instructed to write down YHWH's testimony (Isa 8:1; Jer 30:2). Even, in what is possibly the earliest Hebrew writing, Job would not accept an indictment from YHWH that was not clearly documented (Job 31:35).

---

84. Rikk Watts maintains that Mark had used the lens of Malachi in establishing his YHWH arrival narrative. Watts, *Isaiah's New Exodus*.

It is interesting, then, that many scholars have interpreted Israel's history using the same anthropological methods applied to pre-literate societies. Without wishing to make too strong a case, it would be amazing if the apostles had no awareness of the necessity to document the Jesus event, particularly in the light of their commissioning to be witnesses to the story. The New Testament period demonstrates the critical importance of documentation. It was born out of a culture that had the highest regard for the γραμματεύς (scribe/teacher of the law). Letters were circulated freely, and outcomes of events of significance, such as the Jerusalem Council, were recorded as edicts (Acts 15:20). Paul, though he had planned to declare "his Gospel" to the Romans (Rom. 1:5), ensured they had a clear presentation of it in written form. Some of these early documents were given the highest possible standing, even being referred to as Scripture (2 Peter 3:16). Even within the concluding apocalyptic of Revelation a command can be found to write it down (Rev 1:11), and it even emphasized the inviolability of the document itself (Rev 22:18–19). The author of Matthew certainly was enculturated with this same viewpoint; his document, should it have been written to extend the Hebrew metanarrative, was written to be Scripture. It would seem that the early church accepted the writer's assessment of his own work.

### Matthew Did Not Write a Book, but a Chapter

It is apparent within Matthew that he had a particular interest to show how Jesus was connected with the sacred Scriptures of Israel. The narrative draws specifically on many strands of the Hebrew story, and alludes to many others. Matthew did not write a stand-alone story, but one that relied on the readers' knowledge of the previous chapters. Without knowledge of the Hebrew story to that point, the Gospel of Matthew would make little sense.[85] This is incontrovertible, and assumed by every student of Matthew; nonetheless, it is imperative to make this point plain at the outset. Matthew's edifice was built on an existing foundation.

### The Importance of Context in the Hebrew Story

As the Hebrew books were concerned to tell their immediate situation, without negating their participation in the metanarrative, it is inconceivable

---

85. Matthew's gospel and Hebrews "are rooted theologically and literarily within the world and the texts of the Hebrew Scriptures and are unintelligible without them" (Hasitschka, "Matthew and Hebrews," 87).

that Matthew would use references to the previous narrative without expecting his readers to import the context of the passage quoted. In this way, meaning within Matthew's story cannot be found in an isolated reading, but against the totality of the Hebrew narrative. Therefore, it is reasonable to expect that any reference incorporated by Matthew be not simply intended to misappropriate Scripture for some expedient purpose, but to trigger in the memory of his audience the fullest historical significance of the text. Fundamentally, the story could not be both revered and misrepresent by an author for some personal localized skirmish. C. H. Dodd has noted that assuming the context of the verse quoted was the normal practice for New Testament writers in citing sections of the Old Testament, particularly major and minor prophets and the Psalms: "These sections were understood as wholes, and particular verses or sentences were quoted from them rather as pointers to the whole context than as constituting testimonies in and of themselves."[86] For this reason, this work will regularly seek to find meaning within the context of the imported texts.

Further to this, it is safe to assume that most of Matthew's readers had a common memory, which could be triggered by a reference or an allusion. Gary Schnittjer has recognized the "multiverse" character of the Hebrew narrative, in that an allusion will bring a former context, which in turn imports its own meaning from an earlier chapter of the story. Schnittjer observed:

> The fundamentally elusive character of biblical narrative, as well as other kinds of biblical writings, is rarely so confined. The reality is that often the context of origin for the biblical echo itself contains other echoes, which, in turn, also contain still other echoes. The essential allusive quality of biblical narrative is, therefore, by nature polyacoustic and often leads readers into networks of connections and interrelationships.[87]

## *Jesus As the Fullness of Israel's Story*

This will be covered at greater length in the course of the reading. Briefly, Matthew attempts to retell Israel's history through Jesus' life by using her significant events as the template for his early narrative, while not denying

---

86. Dodd, *According to the Scriptures*, 126. See also Borgen, "In Accordance with the Scriptures," 195.

87. Schnittjer, "The Narrative Multiverse," 236. Richard Hays argues a very similar line in Paul's writings. He believes that Paul made deliberate allusions to the greater narrative that his churches had been well versed in. Hays, *The Conversion of the Imagination*.

the historicity of the events.[88] Jesus as the endangered firstborn, his flight into Egypt, the baptism as metaphor for sea crossing, the temptation in the wilderness and the mount of Jesus' new Torah are all evocative images of Israel's central story. To this Matthew added slogans, which spoke of the Exodus and the Exile (2:15, 18). And, of course, many scholars have made note of Matthew's five discourses,[89] which they believe to be the new Torah symbolizing the five books of Moses.[90]

So what Matthew uniquely tried to provide was a panorama of Israel's history. This he did by using direct quotations of significant prophetic texts, and as mentioned, he used Israel's slogans, which called to memory the critical landscape of the existing narrative. In short, Matthew's masterful document was a collage of Israel's sacred history from Eden to Malachi. Where specific "chapters" were not directly quoted, they still warranted a mention or a clear allusion. Any document that sought to draw to a close an ancient covenant, with its writings and history, could not have done more to summarize and connect with the totality of what went before than Matthew. Matthew, above all New or Old Testament writings, presented a document that appears to be a summation and conclusion of Israel's history. As Donald Hagner notes: "For Matthew, all Israel's history finds its recapitulation in the life of Jesus."[91] Similarly, Daniel Kirk states, "The narrative perspective allows us to see that Jesus did not simply come to embody principles or even fulfill prophetic predictions, but to take the story of Israel to himself."[92] Matthew's Jesus was the eschaton of Israel; Israel's history, struggles, successes and destination were all to be recast and illuminated by the brief period in Judea, when Jesus came *to fulfill the Law and the Prophets.*

---

88. "Since Matthew characterizes many portions of his Gospel as strictly historical, and none in any other way, we must infer that he would have characterized his entire Gospel in this way" (Scott, "Matthew's Intention," 82).

89. Keegan, "Introductory Formulae." Keegan demonstrated the precise formulae used by Matthew to demarcate his teaching blocks. Also, Smith, "Literary Evidences," 550; Aune, *The New Testament*, 49. Kingsbury has argued for a threefold structure based on three significant superscriptions. Kingsbury, "Structure of Matthew's Gospel."

90. Keener, *Matthew*, 37. Keener also cites Bruce, Ellis and Sandmel.

91. Hagner, *Matthew 1–13*, 34.

92. Kirk, "Conceptualising Fulfilment," 91.

## Presupposition 4: The Existing Hebrew Story that Matthew Sought to Complement Anticipated the Conclusion of the Narrative with the Day of YHWH

Assuming, then, that Matthew was advancing the story of Israel by writing its ultimate chapter, we should be able to anticipate some key aspects of his story by examining the previous "chapters." Here we will explore the central prophetic declarations found within the Minor Prophets of Israel.

The Minor Prophets are a combination of pre-exilic, exilic and post-exilic literature. Several of these were prophecies against Gentile nations (Obadiah, Jonah and Nahum), and several anticipated the Exile of 586 BC (Hosea, Amos, Micah, Habakkuk and Zephaniah). Daniel, Haggai, Zachariah and Malachi were addressed to the exilic or post-exilic community.[93] So it may initially seem that many of these works had been fulfilled and were therefore not applicable to the latter chapters. However, this is not the way Hebrew literature works, and certainly Matthew did not consider any previously fulfilled prophecy to have been extinguished within its own context. An example of this is the Isaiahanic prophecy of the Exile found following the prophet's vision of YHWH (Isaiah 6). Though this prophecy clearly was fulfilled in 586 BC, it was readily incorporated into Matthew's metanarrative theodicy and became the rationale for Jesus' public ministry (13:10–17), for "In them is fulfilled the prophecy of Isaiah" (13:14).

### *The Day of YHWH*

The Day of the Lord was a primary focus of the Minor Prophets. This was anticipated as a Day of Judgment, darkness and terror.[94] The last of the Minor Prophets, Malachi, specifically focused on the imminence of YHWH's arrival. Matthew had informed his text with specific reference to Elijah (who in Matthew's estimation was John), the anticipated final prophet before the arrival of YHWH—"See, I will send you the prophet Elijah before that great and dreadful day of the LORD comes. He will turn the hearts of the fathers to their children, and the hearts of the children to their fathers; or else I will come and strike the land with a curse" (Mal 4:5–6). This portrayal of John as the last hope of Israel's redemption can be observed in Final Matthew, but more specifically in Shem-Tob. Howard had noticed that John played a greater salvific role in Shem-Tob, and that Jesus operated as a divine solicitor

---

93. Stuart, *Hosea–Jonah*, xliii.
94. Hos 5:9; Joel 1:15; Amos 3:14; Obad 1:12; Mic 7:4; Zeph 1:7; Zech 5:3–4; Mal 3:2.

and judge.⁹⁵ Regardless of this, it is obvious that Matthew's John portrayed Jesus as the coming eschatological judge (3:11–12).⁹⁶

## The Judgment of the Priestly Establishment

The pre-exilic and exilic prophets had attributed the demise of Jerusalem to the wretchedness of her priests (Mic 7:4; Lam 4:12–13). The whole of Malachi, it seems, was a prophetic indictment against the Levitical house and priesthood:⁹⁷

> "And now this admonition is for you, O priests. If you do not listen, and if you do not set your heart to honor my name," says the LORD Almighty, "I will send a curse upon you, and I will curse your blessings. Yes, I have already cursed them, because you have not set your heart to honor me . . ." (Mal 2:1–2).

The prophet continued, "'But who can endure the day of his coming? Who can stand when he appears? For he will be like a refiner's fire or a launderer's soap. He will sit as a refiner and purifier of silver; he will purify the Levites and refine them like gold and silver'" (Mal 3:2–3). Therefore, if Matthew were following the script written by Malachi, we should expect to see an indictment of the priesthood of Jerusalem.⁹⁸ This accounts for the sustained polemic against Jerusalem, which was already an object of YHWH's wrath according to Malachi.⁹⁹

---

95. Howard, *Gospel of Matthew*.

96. John Meier did not deny the salvific function of Jesus; however, he did observe Matthew's interest in portraying John as a co-evangel, calling people to repentance. Meier, "John the Baptist."

97. The majority of scholars consider the Levites and the priests to be synonymous in Malachi. O'Brien, "Priest and Levite," 24.

98. Indictments against Jerusalem's priests are found in Isaiah, Micah, Hosea, Jeremiah, Ezekiel, Lamentations, Zephaniah, Zechariah, Malachi, Jubilees, Testament of Levi, 1 Enoch, Psalms of Solomon and the Testament of Moses. Evans, "Jesus' Action in the Temple."

99. John the Baptist addressed the Jerusalem leadership as though it were not invited to the coming salvation, and were under the imminent judgment of YHWH— "Who warned you to flee from the coming wrath?" (3:7)

## Matthew Uniquely Portrayed Caiaphas as Jesus' Primary Opponent

Matthew, through his particular presentation, placed the responsibility for Jesus' death squarely upon the shoulders of Israel's high priest, Caiaphas. To this he added the consent and agreement/responsibility of the chief priests and elders,[100] and all the people themselves. In so doing, Matthew had connected the destruction of Jerusalem, its temple and the covenant standing of Israel to the conduct of the priestly class. This served Matthew's concept of narrative advancement by writing the script that Malachi had anticipated—the priests were under YHWH's imminent wrath.[101]

## The Priestly Subtext of Matthew

When viewed through a Levitical lens, Matthew's Jesus appears to be presented as an effectual priest who cleansed physical and internal impurity. This presentation of Jesus is spurred by the Hebrews presentation of Jesus, but also apparent in the thinly veiled subtext of Matthew. If Matthew were presenting Jesus as a greater priest, Jerusalem's priesthood would have recognized the threat that this posed to its tenure. A royal messiah would have posed little threat to priests, and would probably even be welcomed. A priestly messiah would explain the vehement opposition expressed by Caiaphas and his colleagues and supporters. Matthew's Jesus appears to be a Messiah priest/judge, not unlike the expected Melchizedekian priest anticipated by the Qumran community.[102] This is why Matthew makes his account an ultimate contest between two high priests; only one would survive Matthew's theodicy.

---

100. In Exod 18:22 leaders were appointed as judges within Israel and Deuteronomy confirmed their judicial status (Deut 16:18, 19:17, 21:2, 25:1). They were to be a wise and unbiased court, and function as the elders of the people. The "elders of the people" within Matthew's narrative should be interpreted, therefore, as appointed and representative judges of the people—the highest council.

101. The following questions have been asked, but not answered: "Did Matthew... see an enduring priesthood in Jesus, which he contrasted with the worldly high priesthood of Jesus' accuser, Caiaphas? Would Matthew's Jewish–Christian readers have seen an implicit [or subtext] contrast between Jesus, the eternal high priest, and Caiaphas, the earthly high priest?" (Bond, *Caiaphas Friend of Rome*, 127).

102. Kobelski, *Melchizedek and Melchireša*, 134, 181.

## The Two-House Motif

As a consequence of the adversarial nature of this priestly encounter, it is possible to read Matthew as the story of two houses that will face a common Judgment Day.[103] Jesus' apparently insubstantial "priestly" house would survive, while Caiaphas' indomitable priestly house would be made desolate. As an interpretative grid, therefore, it is proposed that reading the admonitions and directives within Matthew as directives for the corporate operation of Jesus' house, rather than simply as admonitions to individuals, has explanatory power in dealing with a good many of Matthew's conundrums.

One of the difficulties for advancing this observation is that the various leadership groups that are mentioned in the Gospel would need to be understood as a single "house" or enterprise. It is clear, for instance, that Matthew's Jesus berates scribes and Pharisees (Matt 23) but not the priesthood. If, however, the sects within Judaism are to be considered as a unified house, it is important to show that Matthew believed the scribes and Pharisees to be somehow connected to, and under the authority of, the High Priest. These clusters of sects that appear in Matthew are identified as a common identity in opposition to Jesus, while still maintaining their particular distinctive features at certain points within the Gospel. In order to make the case that Matthew saw the scribes, Pharisees, elders of the people, the Herodians and the chief priests as a single "house," it must be shown that Matthew did not bother to accentuate the differences between the variegated expressions of Judaism, which were unquestionably at odds with each other historically.

There does appear to have been considerable overlap of membership between these groups mentioned in Matthew, though this has also been disputed.[104] E. P. Sanders, however, has argued that most scribes and many Pharisees were priests. He believes that it is a "complex myth about late second temple Judaism" that "the priests withdrew from study, teaching, judging, and serving as legal experts."[105] Sanders claimed that from the time

---

103. This book is advancing the view that Matthew believed that the decisive moment of God's judgment took place on the cross; however, like the incident with the fig tree, the judgment would be evident to all some time later (AD 70).

104. Westerholm has argued that the authority of the scribes and Pharisees was "not dependent on any priestly statutes" (Westerholm, *Jesus and Scribal Authority*, 28–29, 39). Their authority, according to Westerholm, had been derived from their ability to interpret Torah. Therefore, the priests "enjoyed no monopoly on the knowledge of divine laws;" these sects operated alongside the priesthood, exercising influence as a result of their widely regarded understanding of Torah, and yet acting independently of priestly authority.

105. Sanders, *Judaism*, 173.

of Ezra (the priest/scribe), scribe and priest were all but synonymous.[106] He asserts that "Priests and Levites were often scribes, a title that covers a range of activities: copying texts, drawing up legal documents, and serving as experts of the law."[107] Regarding Pharisees, Sanders noted that when Josephus referred to "non-priestly Pharisees," he was noting an exceptional group, i.e., those who knew the law without being priests.[108] Therefore it is safe to assert that a number of the 6000 Pharisees at the time of Caiaphas were priests also. S. N. Mason also contends that the priesthood presided over the cult, the teaching of the law and additionally exercised authority over the judiciary.[109] Here, Mason quoted Josephus:

> Could there be a finer or more equitable polity than one which sets God at the head of the universe, which assigns the administration of its highest affairs to the whole body of priests, and entrusts to the supreme high-priest the direction of the other priests? . . . But this charge [to the priests] further embraced a strict superintendence of the law and the pursuits of everyday life (2.21 §185–87).[110]

Matthean scholars are generally agreed that Matthew intentionally blurred the distinctives of individual Judean sects, to portray them as a unified opposition to Jesus.[111] David Sim notes:

> Matthew refers to many groups which exercised leadership roles over the Jewish people in the time of Jesus—the Herodians, the Sadducees, the high priests, the elders, and the scribes and Pharisees. Studies of the theme of the Jewish leaders in the Gospel of

---

106. According to Mark Leuchter, many priests were regional scribes in the post exilic community. Leuchter, "'The Levite in your gates,'" 433.

107. Sanders, *Judaism*, 177.

108. Ibid., 172. It is also a mistake to assume that the majority of Pharisees were non-Levitical. Sanders also noted that the opportunity for advanced learning existed among the Levitical and priestly communities, who could be supported and had ample leisure time, unlike "the small number of Pharisees, most of whom probably worked from dawn till dusk six days a week" (ibid., 181). Sim also noted that the Pharisees were a coalition comprised of scribes, priests and nobility. Sim, *The Gospel of Matthew*, 113. Matthew manages to give the impression that the ultimate authority over this collective is the high priest, and perhaps this is the reason that the identities and functions of these groups are blurred within the narrative.

109. Mason, "Priesthood in Josephus," 658.

110. Ibid.

111. "All the sub-groups (Scribes, Pharisees, Sadducees, Herodians etc.) are portrayed as representatives of the Jewish establishment" (Anderson, *Matthew's Narrative Web*, 98). Stanton describes them as a monolithic group, opposed to Jesus. Stanton, *The Interpretation of Matthew*, 180; also, France, "Matthew and Jerusalem," 126.

> Matthew have emphasized that in his narrative the evangelist tends to blur the differences between the distinct groups which comprise the Jewish leadership. He does this by linking together quite disparate groups—the Pharisees and Sadducees (3:7; 16:1, 6, 11, 12), the high priests and Pharisees (21:45, 62), and the high priests and scribes (2:4; 20:18; 21:15) to select only three examples. It is often concluded from this that in presenting the Jewish leaders in this fashion, Matthew has no desire to differentiate between the groups in question; rather, he intends to present the different groups of leaders as one homogenous force that is totally united in its opposition to Jesus.[112]

Therefore, in this reading, the various leadership groups in Judea, Samaria, and Galilee,[113] who were opposed to Jesus, will be seen as a single entity that existed under the authority of Caiaphas, the only high priest that Matthew recorded.

## *The Separation of the Righteous*

Malachi anticipated that the Day of the Lord would be a day when YHWH would separate those who were his from those who were not. The prophet wrote:

> Then those who feared the LORD talked with each other, and the LORD listened and heard. A scroll of remembrance was written in his presence concerning those who feared the LORD and honored his name. "They will be mine," says the LORD Almighty, "in the day when I make up my treasured possession. I will spare them, just as in compassion a man spares his son who serves him. And you will again see the distinction between the righteous and the wicked, between those who serve God and those who do not (3:16–18).

An accusation that the priests had made was that the Lord did not differentiate between good and evil (Mal 2:17). YHWH's response was that he would separate the good from the bad when he came. In fact, he would make up his "treasured possession" (סגלה) on the day of his arrival. This Hebrew word was first found in Moses, and was presented as the eschatological hope for those who would obey Torah—"Now if you obey me fully and keep my covenant, then out of all nations you will be my "treasured

---

112. Sim, *The Gospel of Matthew*, 118.

113. Not only did the high priest exercise authority over the Jewish territories, but also over Jews in the Diaspora. Vanderkam, *From Joshua to Caiaphas*, 430.

possession" (Exod 19:5). The word סגלה had barely reappeared in the Hebrew canon until these very last lines of Malachi. This, no doubt, contributes to the argument that Malachi was anticipating the conclusion of the Mosaic covenant, and that this was now the time when YHWH would determine whether the conditions of Torah had been met in order to secure his "treasured possession." This set the stage for Matthew's Jesus story, which was focused on judgment, selection and separation, redemption and wrath. This paradigm was the backbone of Jesus' parables in Matthew—the kingdom was constantly portrayed as a harvest for separation before the day of wrath. The disciples were to be the harvesters.

## *Matthew Interprets the Death of Jesus As an Apocalyptic Event*

Lastly, under presupposition 4, it appears in Matthew that the routine slaughter of a capital offender in Judea was, in the case of Jesus, the eschatological judgment of God upon the theocracy that was Israel. Matthew interpreted the crucifixion as the defining moment when God concluded his exclusive relationship with Israel, while at the same time being the great event that expiated the sins of the new community, composed of Jew and Gentile.[114]

## The Commission and Mandate of Matthew

As has been previously noted, Matthew does not have an obvious purpose statement. There are commissions that carry significant force in Matthew. There is the obvious Great Commission, and the commission of Matthew 9–10, directed to proclaim the kingdom to Israel. The most serious of commissions, however, is perhaps the most neglected:

> A student is not above his teacher, nor a servant above his master. It is enough for the student to be like his teacher, and the servant like his master. If the head of the house has been called Beelzebub, how much more the members of his household! So do not be afraid of them. There is nothing concealed that will not be disclosed, or hidden that will not be made known. What I tell you in the dark, speak in the daylight; what is whispered in your ear, proclaim from the roofs. Do not be afraid of those who kill the body but cannot kill the soul. Rather, be afraid of the One who can destroy both soul and body in hell (Matt 10:22–28).

---

114. This motif is explicit in Luke and John also (Luke 19:42–44; 23:28; John 12:31).

This passage may contain the elusive purpose statement that has been overlooked, largely because of its Synoptic parallel in Luke. There is no parallel for this in Mark[115] and John, and its restatement in Luke is quite different to what is found in Matthew. Hagner has noted the differences:

> The crucial difference is that Luke says that what the disciples say in secret will become known. Thus, in Hebraic synonymous parallelism: "whatever you have said in the dark will be heard in the light, and what you have whispered in private rooms will be proclaimed upon the housetops." Matthew, on the other hand, refers to what Jesus says in secret and what the disciples hear as that which the disciples are to speak in the light and proclaim from the rooftops. Matthew, whose Greek is more awkward than Luke's, probably preserves the original meaning of the words (cf. Mark 4:22), while Luke has given them a secondary, moral application.[116]

So Matthew's version of the pericope is fundamentally different in intention to Luke's version. Hagner went on to note that the secret whispered was in fact the Gospel,[117] which was to be made public following the resurrection.[118]

Hagner's assessment is fair, but not complete. The central idea of proclaiming what had been made known in secret was sandwiched between warnings that the disciples would be identified with Jesus in his vilification; however, the disciples were not to fear "them," presumably, the ones who had identified Jesus as belonging to Beelzebub. Clearly, these same ones who would vilify the disciples also posed a real threat to their lives. The strong injunction, "not to fear them," was accompanied by a greater threat to their well-being—the disciples had better be more afraid of Jesus/God. So this commission must be given the highest gravitas, as it was accompanied with a distinctly punitive threat for non-compliance. That is why this may be the most important commission, as it seems to have dire consequences for the non-compliant.

It is not necessary to look far to identify those who would kill the body. The Pharisees, who were the regional foot soldiers of the priestly class in

---

115. Mark does not include a comparable pericope, but the commission to disclose hidden things does exist. Its context makes it difficult to ascertain what was to be brought out into the open—"He said to them, 'Do you bring in a lamp to put it under a bowl or a bed? Instead, don't you put it on its stand? For whatever is hidden is meant to be disclosed, and whatever is concealed is meant to be brought out into the open. If anyone has ears to hear, let him hear'" (Mark 4:21–23).

116. Hagner, *Matthew 1–13*, 284.

117. See also Carson, *When Jesus Confronts the World*, 147.

118. Hagner, *Matthew 1–13*, 284.

Matthew's account, are the same ones who accused Jesus of having the satanic heritage (9:34, 12:24). As we will read further into the narrative, however, it appears to be the priests who would have Jesus put to death. Hagner's assessment falls short then, for if the secret was the Gospel why would Jesus have restricted the admonition ("not to fear them") to the Jerusalem establishment? Shouldn't the disciples be fearful of everyone who hears the Gospel, for surely any offense in the "good news" would be universally applicable? So, exegetically, we would have to acknowledge that the Pharisees/priests were the community that Jesus had in mind with this admonition.[119]

If, then, it was not the Gospel that was being whispered in secret, what would the alternative be? This may be the mandate for Matthew. The disciples were being called upon to be whistle-blowers to the secrets of the corrupt system, which operated behind a façade of righteousness, but secretly conspired to commit the worst acts of evil.[120] It must be kept in mind that Matthew concludes by exposing the false account put around by Jerusalem's priests—would not this Gospel have some interest in setting the record straight?

This notion is further advanced by how the pericope was unpacked with the following warning. The disciples were called upon to testify/witness for Jesus (10:32); failure to take the dock and testify to the virtue of Jesus would result in Jesus' refusal to testify on their behalf. And so we have a second severe warning against cowardice; the disciples must declare what is spoken in secret and testify for Jesus, even if it should cost them their lives. This warning was further informed by a pithy but highly informative statement concerning the nature of the disciples' assignment, "Do not suppose that I have come to bring peace to the earth. I did not come to bring peace, but a sword" (10:34).[121] In view of this, the familiar perception of what was to be declared might need to be re-oriented, and a command

---

119. David Turner believes that the persecutor's crimes would be made known; however, this was to take place on the last day. Turner, *Matthew*, 278. Turner had not adequately accounted for the commission that the disciples were to declare the secrets from the rooftops. They were to follow Jesus' instruction without fearing the opponents. Why would they be fearful of these enemies at the last day?

120. Consider all the references to the underhanded and secretive machinations of Jesus' opponents: Matt 9:4, 12:25, 21:45–46, 22:15, 26:3, 26:59, 27:20, 27:41, 26:67.

121. Matthew had already used the Deuteronomic indictment with its implication that Jerusalem's destruction was going to be worse than the judgment on Sodom and Gomorrah; it is possible then that the sword that Jesus brought was intended to be the one referred to as the instrument for covenant termination. "When I sharpen my flashing sword and my hand grasps it in judgment, I will take vengeance on my adversaries and repay those who hate me" (Deut 32:41).

to condemn or expose the "opponents,"[122] while testifying to the honor of Jesus, may need to be considered.[123] There is more to this pericope, which may be further informed by a Hebrew translation.

Hebrew Matthew has a slight variation to this key text, which if correct, would go a long way to corroborating this interpretation. In the place of roofs or rooftops, the Hebrew has "gate."[124] The gate was, according to Deuteronomy, the judicial center of the community.[125] Further, this variation has particular resonance with the prophet Jeremiah, who was invariably instructed to go to the gate of the city to declare his indictments against the city.[126] The prophet was tortured and threatened with execution at the gate by the city's officials (priests and prophets) who accused him of testifying against Jerusalem.[127] This would cast a completely different light upon the meaning of the commandment; rather than just being a command to publicly declare whatever may be under consideration, the declaration would have a far more judicial character—an indictment or an appeal for justice. Did Matthew believe that the disciples were called to be whistle-blowers, and is this a significant aspect of his Gospel?

Interestingly, the first declarations of the apostolic community took place in the city public precinct, with the second such occasion being specifically at the temple gate. These declarations by Luke's Peter were not winsome evangelistic appeals, but declarations of culpability concerning the most heinous crime. According to Acts, the Apostle declared:

> Men of Israel, listen to this: Jesus of Nazareth was a man accredited by God to you by miracles, wonders and signs, which God did among you through him, as you yourselves know. This man was handed over to you by God's set purpose and

---

122. The apocalyptic character of chapter 10 resembles Matthew's larger apocalyptic in chapter 24. In both instances the disciples are told that they will be vilified and persecuted. In chapter 23 Jesus declared that he would send messengers to them (the scribes and Pharisees) that they, in turn, would put to death. Therefore, the message of Jesus' emissaries was not a gracious invitation to be saved, but rather condemnation similar to the one just meted out by Jesus to the scribes and Pharisees.

123. Bringing division is central to Matthew's gospel; as such the narrative cannot be reconciled without taking this into account. Combrink, "The Structure of the Gospel," 82.

124. Howard, *Gospel of Matthew*, 47. This phrase Howard translated "that which you hear in the ear tell it in the gate" was not in Shem-Tob, but drawn from a variant found in another Hebrew source.

125. Deut 17:5, 21:19, 22:15, 24, 25:7.

126. Jer 7:2–11, 19; 19:2.

127. Jer 20:2; 26:10–11.

> foreknowledge; and you, with the help of wicked men, put him to death by nailing him to the cross (Acts 2:22–23).
>
> Therefore let all Israel be assured of this: God has made this Jesus, whom you crucified, both Lord and Christ (Acts 2:36).
>
> The God of Abraham, Isaac and Jacob, the God of our fathers, has glorified his servant Jesus. You handed him over to be killed, and you disowned him before Pilate, though he had decided to let him go. You disowned the Holy and Righteous One and asked that a murderer be released to you. You killed the author of life, but God raised him from the dead. We are witnesses of this (Acts 3:13–15).

Surely these constitute public accusations concerning the guilt of the priestly establishment of Jerusalem, for this is how Jerusalem interpreted the declarations. It was the high priest, in the presence of the Sanhedrin, who declared: "We gave you strict orders not to teach in this name . . . Yet you have filled Jerusalem with your teaching and are determined to make us guilty of this man's blood" (Acts 5:28). Peter's response, on behalf of the Apostles with him, was not a clarification of their benign intentions, but to confirm the high priest's suspicion concerning the apostolic objective:

> We must obey God rather than men! The God of our fathers raised Jesus from the dead—whom you had killed by hanging him on a tree. God exalted him to his own right hand as Prince and Savior that he might give repentance and forgiveness of sins to Israel. We are witnesses of these things, and so is the Holy Spirit, whom God has given to those who obey him (Acts 5:29–32).

Therefore, Peter was obeying God when he condemned Jerusalem for its crimes against Jesus.

What Matthew is doing here is not groundbreaking in the Hebrew narrative. Israel's corporate crimes, as well as its private crimes against YHWH, were routinely placed on public record. The narrative is littered with this motif: two specific examples are David's sin of murder and adultery (2 Sam 12:1–23), and the sin of the priests who worshiped the sun with their backs to the temple (Ezek 8:14–18). Which other nation placed on public record the atrocities of both king and priest? This is unique in ancient literature, and integral to the Hebrew narrative. Gross atrocities were to be exposed, and these were usually the basis for the impending judgment. It seems perfectly plausible, then, that the disciples were also to make public the atrocities of Jerusalem, and this may well be the mandate that underlies Matthew's gospel. It was an attempt to place on public record the true story behind the death of

Jesus, in order to set the record straight, vindicate YHWH and his Son, and to incriminate the shadowy figures that conspired to "cut off" the author of life.

## Summation

What this book is attempting to do is to establish whether Matthew sought to advance the Hebrew narrative by using the existing story as the basis for the trajectory of his Gospel. The trajectory provided by the prophets, particularly the latter ones, anticipated the Day of YHWH as a day of judgment and possibly the conclusion of the Mosaic covenant. It should not be understood from this that YHWH was dissolving any former or latter covenants, such as the Abrahamic or Davidic covenants, which insured a place for both Israel and Judah in the new dispensation inaugurated by Jesus.

This reading of Matthew presupposes a certain belief that the Hebrews understood the necessity of advancing the narrative at its critical moments, for as a people of the book with a written covenantal agreement (law), it is certainly feasible that early Christians would have felt the necessity to document the Jesus story as part of that extraordinary narrative. Further, a written legally binding covenant would surely require a written conclusion, which would include just cause for the termination of the sacred agreement. Matthew may be doing this by citing specific crimes that would necessitate the termination of the Levitical system of mediation and the destruction of its temple. Rightly or wrongly, there is every possibility that a Jew who believed that Jesus had embodied the presence of YHWH, who had come to his temple as foretold by the prophets, would have felt a distinct obligation to record it with appropriate prophetic force.

It is also argued that Matthew 10:27 is possibly a commission to put on the public record the secret machinations of the religious community that conspired to dispose of Jesus. Such a document would be a necessary rebuttal to the "false" account that was put abroad concerning Jesus' resurrection by the chief priests. As suggested, Israel's history was never perceived as a series of random events; it was always understood against the background of the covenant stipulations. Failure to adhere to the covenant brought catastrophe, and faithfulness brought security and prosperity. The prophets played their part in this great theodicy as agents of information, to both warn and inform the Israelites as to why they had encountered such misery. Matthew, this book hopes to demonstrate, can be read as part of this prophetic tradition. Matthew had written his document as a justification of YHWH, who had gone far beyond his obligations within the covenant to secure Israel's affections, and also as an indictment of the priesthood and nation, which would soon experience the cataclysmic events of AD 70.

# 2

# History and Prologue: Jesus' Authority to Judge

> *Then the Lord will raise up a new priest*
> *To whom all the words of the Lord will be revealed;*
> *He will execute true judgment on the earth for a multitude of days*
> *His star will rise in heaven like that of a great king,*
> *Lighting up the light of knowledge like the midday sun . . .*
> *The heavens will be opened*
> *And from the temple of glory sanctification will come upon him*
> *With the Father's voice as from Abraham to Isaac.*
>
> (Testament of Levi 18:2–6)[1]

INTEGRAL TO MATTHEW'S DEPICTION of Jesus was his messianic authority, which was demonstrated by birthright, divine origin, meaningful identification with Israel's story and personal credibility. The first four chapters of Matthew present Jesus as the heir apparent, whose entitlement was established through divine and human connections and exemplary personal achievement. From the outset, the "christ" was presented as the antithesis of those who would oppose him; Jerusalem, as a conglomerate of leaders, had entitlement, but no authenticity. Jesus had far greater entitlement, and an authority that was derived from his superlative and unblemished character. As such,

---

1. Bruce, *Jesus and Christian Origins*, 77.

Jesus was the reality of everything that Messiah could and should be, whilst the anti-messiahs would be portrayed as a façade without substance.

In this chapter Matthew's early narrative will be considered as a construction designed to establish Jesus' authority. Matthew deemed it necessary to firmly establish Jesus' credibility, which would stand in stark contrast to that of the established leadership of Jerusalem. This mosaic of writings strategically informs Matthew's readers by using direct reference, clear allusion and eschatologically oriented appeals to the highest authority in the view of Matthew's audience: the Torah.[2] Within these early chapters, the adversarial character of the narrative emerges with some subtlety, but also in the most blatant form imaginable. Jesus' adversaries are almost concealed in these early chapters, but by the end of the narrative it becomes clear that they would complete the mission of Herod, and dispose of the one who fundamentally challenged their high authority.[3]

## The Genealogy

Matthew commences with a formulaic genealogy.[4] By beginning a document this way, Matthew had certainly flouted certain conventions: without an identification of author or audience and some suggestion concerning the purpose of the document, the narrative started as a divine decree reminiscent of the Torah. By avoiding commonplace preamble, Matthew's document is given a declaratory power. Matthew's intention was to establish Jesus' identity and history, and there is no attempt to establish the credibility or identity of the author. Matthew's work, like John's gospel, begins in a way that demands immediate respect of its readers, for its "sacred" formula immediately invokes the memory of Torah.

Matthew commences with βίβλος γενέσεως, a direct derivation from the LXX, which translated תּוֹלְדֹת. By adopting the Mosaic formula, which defined the divisions of Genesis, Matthew had connected his treatise to the

---

2. Matthew's first readers/audience, for the purposes of this reading, are primarily Jews as the covenant related to them, but also Gentiles, who would understand the basis of their inclusion through the New Covenant. Within the parameters of the lens, Matthew is considered to be a public document intended for a universal audience.

3. The reader was invited, at this early stage, to identify Jerusalem's priests and elders with Herod. Kingsbury, "The Plot of Matthew's Story," 348.

4. Biblical genealogies were used to establish legitimacy and continuity. They were also important to the "priestly narrative" (Levin, "Understanding Biblical Genealogies," 16).

beginning of the story, and intuitively, invoked the authority that the title of the first sacred book would imply to any Hebrew.[5]

The genealogy was constructed for distinctly theological purposes. Matthew's intention was to communicate a triple set of fourteen generations from Abraham to Jesus.[6] Luke's genealogy is considerably different to Matthew's. For some reason, Luke did not include Judah's kings after David. Matthew, on the other hand, was intent on demonstrating the Davidic dynastic progression. The three epochs presented in the genealogy (with their thirteen or fourteen generations: Abraham to David, David to Jeconiah and Exile, and from Jeconiah to Jesus) represent the beginning of the Hebrew story to its high point, through to its lowest point and then ultimately to Jesus, its highest point. The high point of David's reign was emphasized by the multiple repetition of his name (five times in these opening verses). Attention was also drawn to the Exile and its aftermath, during which Israel had no king. There is even the possibility that the use of fourteen (which is the numerical value of David in Hebrew) further emphasized the Davidic connection, which from the outset, is central to Matthew's story; Jesus was David's son, and as the narrative unfolds, David's Lord (22:43-45). Matthew's Messiah was clearly not Levitical, but from Judah. As Jesus was not the "natural" son of Joseph we have an interesting historical correlation: David was adopted as "son of God" (2 Sam 7:11-14) and the Son of God was adopted as the "Son of David."[7]

Matthew's inclusion of the women in this genealogy was irregular.[8] Women were not normally noted in genealogies, and if they were, they would certainly be the women of high reputation. Matthew chose to mention Tamar, who bore her father-in-law's child, Rahab, who was a Canaanite prostitute,

---

5. "'The book of the Genesis of Jesus Christ' is not a modest beginning" (Hauerwas, *Matthew*, 23). "In view of this language it seems likely that readers of Matthew's Gospel, who have read or heard the Scriptures read, could scarcely fail to hear the allusion(s) to Genesis" (Evans, "'The Book of Genesis,'" 68). "By opening his gospel with another book's title, Matthew almost certainly intended to set up the story as a counterpart to the story of Genesis" (Davies and Allison, *Gospel according to Saint Matthew*, 1:151). Jonathan Pennington sees an even greater connection with Genesis 1: "An important text in this regard is the climax of Matthew 28:16-20. In the grand conclusion to the First Gospel, which is understood by many as a summary of the whole work, the heaven and earth theme is again highlighted, and the passage likely serves for Matthew as an inclusio with Genesis 1:1, the matching bookend of God's revelation" (Pennington, *Heaven and Earth*, 345).

6. The fact that Jesus is not a natural son of Joseph according to the narrative does not pose a problem, for the naming of Jesus by Joseph constituted legal and full adoption. Jones, "Subverting the Textuality," 260.

7. Waetjen, "Genealogy," 228.

8. Jones, "Subverting the Textuality," 260.

Ruth the Moabite, and Bathsheba, named as Uriah's spouse to emphasize the scandalous adultery of David with the Gentile mother of Solomon. Of note is the absence of noble women such as Sarah, Rebekah and Leah.

The inclusion of these women invites some speculation, as no explanation is given. Undoubtedly, these women contribute significantly to the rich tapestry of Hebrew story. Stories of destitute foreigners, victims of war, kings' philandering and even intergenerational licentiousness are interesting, but not uncommon in the ancient world. Their inclusion, however, in this most noble genealogy in history (according to Matthew), must suggest that they are critical to this story.[9] Further, it is apparent with first-century hindsight that these women only became significant through their ultimate connection with Jesus. Therefore, the peculiar inclusions within the account only make sense when they are understood to be a piece of the mosaic that was Jesus' story.

This approach is plausible; however, it still fails to account for the absence of women with unblemished reputations. There is the possibility that Matthew simply wanted to flout convention by placing "sinners," even prostitutes, front and center. Within the wider narrative, outcasts and sinners appear to be welcome inclusions of the kingdom, so why not within the genealogy? This too is a possibility; however, there could be a few more layers to be uncovered concerning these intriguing inclusions.

Certainly these women were not simply bit players in the Hebrew story, but integral to it. At least in the cases of Tamar and Ruth, the sacred line would have terminated but for their peculiar intervention.[10] These women may also have lent some credibility to Mary, who appeared publicly to be a wayward woman. This being the case, these women were included to enable some to accept Matthew's story, despite the obstacle that Mary presented. A difficulty with Wilhelmus Weren's proposition, however, is that Mary was clearly portrayed as an innocent participant in the proceedings—she had not violated her vows to Joseph. In spite of this, Matthew was probably mindful of those who would seek to discredit the story based on the premarital pregnancy, so this genealogy may be anticipating and snuffing out those objections by reflecting on the "unsavory" mothers of David. Whatever the intention may be, Mary appears as a link in a peculiar genealogical chain of exceptional participants, and their inclusion may be significant for the development of Matthew's metanarrative.

---

9. Irene Nowell believes that they are bound by their personal struggles/alienation and their devious approaches to problem solving. Nowell, "Jesus' Great-Grandmothers."

10. Weren, "The Five Women in Matthew's Genealogy."

A reason why these women appear in this genealogy may be to indirectly connect this story to the wider human narrative, by hinting at the first woman. As mentioned previously, First Matthew may have been Hebrew. A Hebrew version would have rendered Jesus as *ben ʾādām* (Son of Man), which would be far more suggestive of the primal link of Jesus to Adam. Further, Matthew's portrayal of the Christ event, more than that of any other Gospel, emphasized the fundamental conflict between Satan and Jesus: Jesus' opponent was the enemy who would invariably try to destroy his work, the devil.[11] As the narrative progresses, it appears that Matthew strategically weaves the role of Satan and the Jerusalem hierarchy into a seamless identity. With the culminating event of the crucifixion, Matthew's metanarrative is played out—the vanquished "serpent's offspring" has bruised the heel of the "woman's offspring." The point being made here, concerning the unbecoming "mothers" of Jesus, is that they may remind the first readers of Eve; for they both represent an enormous problem and yet without them there is no ultimate solution. It was only through the offspring of the fallen woman that humans could be restored to God (Gen 3:15).

## First Fulfillment References

Matthew's story of Jesus did not commence in the first century: the Torah was the prelude of this dramatic story. The second pericope of Jesus' introduction unambiguously announced that the Holy Spirit conceived Jesus (1:18). Though no direct reference was made here to Zechariah, "the Zerubbabel" who would complete the temple of God (16:18) would, metaphorically, cast a mighty mountain into the sea (21:21). This was to be achieved "'Not by might nor by power, but by my Spirit,' says the LORD Almighty" (Zech 2:6).

Following the discovery of Mary's pregnancy, the Angel of the Lord addressed Joseph as "son of David," probably a first for Joseph and further emphasis of the Davidic connection. Joseph was instructed to name the child Joshua (Hebrew version),[12] for he would "save his people from their sins" (1:21). From the outset, the Messiah was identified as having a priestly function. Forgiveness was not a function of the king; according to the Law, priests were to dispose of sin through sacrifice (Lev 4–6).[13] Further, while Joshua as a

---

11. The devil confronts Jesus early in the narrative (chapter 4); he was also responsible for the sowing of the weeds (13:39). The temple of Jesus would endure and survive Hell's wrath (16:18).

12. Jesus, as a Greek transliteration, has no meaning apart from its Hebrew origin—YHWH saves.

13. In the Epistle to the Hebrews, Jesus' primary earthly task is assessed as the

name has lexical meaning, the significance does not end there. No descendent of David or Judah in Matthew's genealogy was called Joshua.[14] The heroic Joshua of the conquest was an Ephraimite, and therefore had no connection with Jesus. The first high priest after the Exile, however, was named Joshua, and he was forgiven his sin and given authority to rule (Zech 3:1–6). Joshua was advised that he and his associates (future high priests) were symbolic of what was to come, and before him (Joshua) was placed a rock with an inscription upon it (Zech 3:8). On a future day, God would "remove the sin of the land in a single day" (Zech 3:9), presumably by this rock. Joshua was inaugurated as a sign, and not as a fulfillment. By calling the child Joshua, Matthew may have indicated that the true High Priest had arrived—and it would be this child who would remove the sin of the people.[15]

Finally we can consider the direct reference (as opposed to indirect or even subliminal references) to fulfillment found in this pericope. For Matthew, the preceding events took place to fulfill the Scripture—the virgin will give birth, and the child will be called *Immanuel*, God with us. This reference to Isaiah is the first of a series of prophecies that had a former contextual fulfillment, but now a greater or primary fulfillment in the Jesus narrative.[16] In Isaiah, the child Immanuel is a sign of the coming of God's wrath against Judah.[17] This sign, in Isaiah, would lead to a judgment unlike any previously seen (Isa 7:16): the God-ordained Assyrian invasion. Matthew invoked this sign as a portent for impending judgment.[18]

---

forgiveness of sins. Hebrews notes, "after he had provided purification for sins . . ." (Heb 1:3).

14. Luke's genealogy runs a different course to Matthew's and consequently finds a plethora of different names, not the least Levi and Joshua. For some reason, Luke chose to trace Jesus through Nathan, the older half-brother of Solomon. This demands significant investigation, for Luke had specifically denied the Bathsheba connection and, more importantly, failed to connect Jesus to Solomon as the ultimate temple builder. Indeed, there is no king in Luke's genealogy, between David and Jesus. Further, Luke only minimally refers to Jesus as a builder. Matthew, on the other hand, avoids the Joshua connection, and has much to say about Jesus' reconstruction of the temple/house/church. So, clearly, Matthew utilized Zechariah as a significant prophetic template for the life of Jesus.

15. Another connection between Jesus and Joshua was the accusation made against both of them by Satan. This will receive greater consideration later in the chapter.

16. Consider 2:15; 2:17; 13:14.

17. The Isaiah pericope presented the sign of the virgin's offspring as a comfort that Israel and Aram would not devastate Judah as expected. God had planned something worse: an invasion of the new and aggressive rising Assyrian empire.

18. "As 'outsiders' Yahweh's manifest presence ('Immanuel') means only judgement" (Watts, *Isaiah's New Exodus*, 209).

## The Child and the Beast (Rev 12:4)

The extraordinary introduction of Jesus was juxtaposed with the almost complete indifference shown by Matthew to the peripheral characters in his story. The wise men, Herod and the Jerusalem conglomerate (all the chief priests and scribes) were not introduced, named (apart from Herod) or reflected upon, and there is no sense that these people are connected to the story of Israel in any significant way.[19] Matthew's unique inclusion of the magi incident can only be understood in the light of his over-arching theological agenda. Certainly they provide the first glimpse of Gentile elation concerning the Christ's arrival. They may well also have been included as another instance of implicit fulfillment (Isa 60:3). However, it appears that their inclusion serves as a convenient foil to identify Jerusalem's establishment as the villain in Matthew's story.

The Magi, in the first instance, are revealed as expectant and eager to pay homage to the foreign Messiah; this would be quite peculiar if there were no expectation on their part that the child had some authority greater than their own. The narrative reveals that the Magi were guided by heaven, and obedient to those promptings (2:10, 12). Further, by whatever means they had at their disposal to discern the Christ event, they managed to accurately predict its timing and understand its importance. Lastly, the Magi had sacrificed much to make the journey.

By contrast, Jerusalem has no interest in paying homage to the new arrival.[20] Unlike the Magi, the chief priests and their theologians received no heavenly messages, and as a consequence, were caught wrong-footed when the child arrived.[21] The Magi were warned to avoid Herod, while the priests were helpful advisors to the hostile king. Herod had to secretly consult the Magi, and deceive them as to his intentions. There is no suggestion that the Jerusalem priests had to be deceived, entreated or coerced; their cooperation and common concern was plain. The chief priests and the scribes were disturbed by the news, as was Herod (2:3).[22] They were of one mind—the

---

19. Narrative critics call these peripheral characters "flat," while more developed characters in the narrative are "round." Malbon, "Narrative Criticism," 81. The Jerusalem entourage are absolutely consistent and one-dimensional throughout Matthew.

20. Matthew's readers were probably aware that Bethlehem was only a short distance from Jerusalem.

21. As the child was almost two years old when the Magi arrived in Matthew's account, Matthew may have wished to imply that Jerusalem would have remained uninformed had it not been for the arrival of the foreign dignitaries.

22. "Fleeting though this initial appearance of the Jewish leaders in Matthew's story is, two things stand out. The one thing is that it is as allies of Herod that the leaders make their debut. Like Herod and as part of all Jerusalem, they react with fright and not

arrival of the Christ was disturbing to both king and priest.[23] There is no suggestion that Herod's brutal action was undertaken without the knowledge or consent of Israel's leaders.[24] Although this does not prove priestly involvement, there seems to be no attempt by the author to distance them from the actions of Herod.

The identity of these Magi has aroused considerable speculation. While kingship has been popularly ascribed to these men it is not clear in Matthew that they were royalty. It would be most peculiar for foreign kings to come to a land and not pay some homage to an existing sovereign as a guarantee of their safety and indication of their benign intentions. While there is the possibility that they were astrologers, it would be peculiar for Matthew to attribute virtue to idolaters. The most satisfactory way to understand this entourage is to recognize them as foreign priests (magoi being the Persian word for priest).[25] There is certainly a Melchizedekian echo about these individuals; they come from nowhere, and have no ancestry, and yet they offer gifts to the Most High. Their gifts are also particularly pertinent to priests: gold was prodigiously used for temple ornamentation, myrrh was the primary ingredient of the sacred anointing oil (Exod 30:22), and frankincense was used for consecration of gifts upon the golden altar (Lev

joy to the news of the Messiah's birth" (Jack Kingsbury in Stanton, *The Interpretation of Matthew*, 187).

23. David Bauer proposes that Matthew presents Herod and the Jerusalem establishment as partners in their enmity to Jesus. Bauer, "The Kingship of Jesus."

24. "The priestly leaders confirm that the Christ was to be born in Bethlehem . . . and do nothing to save the child from the king's plot" (Bond, *Caiaphas*, 121). It should also be noted that a succeeding Herod put John the Baptist to death without any apparent participation by the priests and scribes. And yet Matthew's Jesus declared that the priestly caste was responsible for John's death (17:12). Even if they did not participate in the commission to destroy the child, they certainly were portrayed here as giving tacit approval.

25. "No Father of the Church holds the Magi to have been kings. Tertullian ("Adv. Marcion." III, xiii) says that they were wellnigh kings (fere reges), and so agrees with what we have concluded from non–biblical evidence. The Church, indeed, in her liturgy, applies to the Magi the words: 'The kings of Tharsis and the islands shall offer presents; the kings of the Arabians and of Saba shall bring him gifts: and all the kings of the earth shall adore him' (Ps 71:10). But this use of the text in reference to them no more proves that they were kings than it traces their journey from Tharsis, Arabia, and Saba. As sometimes happens, a liturgical accommodation of a text has in time come to be looked upon by some as an authentic interpretation thereof. Neither were they magicians: the good meaning of magoi, though found nowhere else in the Bible, is demanded by the context of the second chapter of St. Matthew. These Magoi can have been none other than members of the priestly caste already referred to. The religion of the Magi was fundamentally that of Zoroaster and forbade sorcery; while their astrology and skill in interpreting dreams were occasions of their finding Christ" (Drum, "Magi.").

23:7). There is a distinct possibility, therefore, that these Magi may have been Persian priests (possibly Zoroastrian), who had come to submit to a much greater new priest. If this is the case, their submission to the universal priest is a contrast to the Jerusalem priesthood who would not recognize a priesthood other than its own.

Later in the narrative, Matthew calls to remembrance the Queen of Sheba, who "came from the ends of the earth" to visit and honor Solomon (12:42). Her action entitled her, according to Matthew, to be a witness against Israel generally, and the Pharisees and scribes specifically—for someone greater than Solomon was among them. The Magi do not overtly assign guilt to Jerusalem in this passage, but it is reasonable to assume that their primary role in the narrative was to indict Jerusalem for its failure to know the hour, to perceive its importance, and to act appropriately.

## Exile in Egypt

Following the angelic warning, Joseph fled with his family to Egypt (2:13–15). This occasioned the fulfillment of two significant scriptures for Matthew. The first of these was the slogan of the Exodus, and the second recalled the Exile. The reference to Hos 11:1, which in its context cast an eye back to Israel's deliverance from Pharaoh, was fulfilled by the evacuation of the "holy" family. Again, our interest here is not to question the validity of the assertion, but simply to recognize it. In Matthew's view, the Hosea oracle pointed particularly to this event. By making this connection, Matthew was presenting Jesus as the "new Israel" or at least, he was casting Jesus' early years as a recapitulation of Israel's significant events.

The same can be said of the Exile slogan of Rachel "weeping for her children." Rachel was buried in Bethlehem (Gen 48:7); however, a sepulcher was also mentioned in Ramah (1 Sam 10:2), north of Jerusalem. This would be on the road the exiles took when carried into Babylonian exile. In any case, Matthew made use of the prophecy and attributed its fulfillment to this Christ event. The issue then becomes whether Rachel (metaphorically speaking) is weeping for the slaughter of the children or for the exile of Jesus. Perhaps both are intended here: Matthew's interest was to reveal the scandal as it affected Jesus. Jesus was welcomed and honored by Babylonian/Persian priests, and sent into exile by Jerusalem. Jesus was safer in Egypt than in Judea. So Matthew presented his readers with an interesting new twist to both the Exodus and Exile episodes of Israel's history. Surely this irony would not have been lost on Matthew's readers.

## Jesus the Nazarene

Following the death of Herod, according to Matthew, Jesus journeyed from Egypt to Galilee, which was the safest place for the child due to its distance from Jerusalem (2:22). Jesus' settlement in Nazareth provided Matthew with the opportunity to be at his cryptic best, attributing the title of Nazarene to Jesus as fulfillment of what the Prophets declared. First we must note that there is no verse in the prophets that said, "He will be called a Nazarene." However, Matthew hints at the composite nature of his reference by claiming that it was a fulfillment of "the prophets," rather than "the prophet," his preferred source reference when he uses a direct quotation. What then is to be made of this reference?

The three preferred possibilities that have been put forward to explain this composite reference are the designation of Nazirite (Isa 4:3),[26] a designation of separation and holiness to the Lord; a wordplay on the Hebrew word נָצַר, $nāṣar$ (watchman or priestly overseer); and finally, $nēṣer$ (branch) as a messianic reference to Isa 4:2, 11:1, Jer 23:5 and Zech 3:8.[27] Any or all of these are a comfortable fit for Matthew's depiction of Jesus. Jesus' family had separated itself from Jerusalem, which had already been shown to be less than "righteous" by its complicitous connection to Herod,[28] so the Nazirite connection could have a dual meaning: separation from the unrighteous leaders, as well as Jesus' identification as the holy one of God. The play on "watchman" would also fit comfortably into Matthew's paradigm should Jesus have been cast in a priestly office. And the last reference, connecting Jesus to David as the "branch," has significant appeal; certainly it is easy to demonstrate that Matthew paid much attention to Isa 4–7, Jer 23:1–6 and Zech 3.

## John the Baptist

John the Baptist was integral to Matthew's paradigm of judgment; his role in Matthew was given greater prominence than in the other Gospels and requires a comprehensive treatment. For this reason, John and his role in Matthew will be considered in chapter 4. For now we will only consider those aspects of Matthew's third chapter that relate directly to this first section concerning the introduction of Jesus and others.

---

26. It has been suggested that Matthew may have sought to connect Jesus to Samson the Nazirite via a Greek version of Judg 13:5–7. Menken, "Sources of the Old Testament."

27. Keener, *Matthew*, 114.

28. By implication, the priestly class were safe in Jerusalem.

Matthew makes a seamless transition from Jesus' childhood narrative to the time of John's ministry. The focus of Matthew's drama shifted to another region and story—"in those days . . ." John was in the desert region baptizing. No indication is given as to how long John had been conducting his ministry, but it had commenced while Jesus was still resident in Nazareth.

John was introduced as a character well known to Matthew's readership; the author does not spend time describing John's personal background, but opts rather for the place of John in the metanarrative—as fulfillment of Scripture (3:3). Matthew's John, unlike the Jerusalem counterparts previously mentioned, received special attention and approbation. Only Christ exceeds his standing in Matthew, and even Jesus' parents receive less attention in Matthew. Matthew presented John as a kind of proto-Christ, in that his message, adversaries and destiny were predictive of the Christ story (17:12).[29] In this way, John was the distillation of the Law and the Prophets before him. He embodied the message of the Tanach and even the identity of its first condemnatory prophet, Elijah. John was, in effect, a heaven-sent testimony. John's authenticity was crucial to Jesus' introduction. For this reason, we can assume that John's reputation as an incorruptible and significant prophet was well established by the time that Jesus arrived.

John was the third aspect of Jesus' introduction. Jesus was confirmed by his birth narrative and genealogy, his identification with the significant events of the Hebrew story and now the distilled echo of the Mosaic and prophetic history found in John. This chapter also gives Matthew's story a clear connection with the end of the Tanach, for John is the last person anticipated at the end of Malachi.[30] So Matthew was able to use the account of John as a literary device that established his narrative as a continuation and complement of what it purported to fulfill, rather than a new and disconnected history.[31]

Matthew's John was definitely cast as a righteous emissary and prophet of Jesus. This was crucial to Matthew's depiction of the opponents, who were subject to the vitriolic condemnation of John, and, we can assume, those entities that John represented—the Law and the Prophets. Even in these early episodes of Matthew's story the lines were drawn as to who was with

29. ". . . Matthew combines a startling and thorough attempt to make the Baptist parallel to Jesus . . ." (Meier, "John the Baptist," 386).

30. The last book of the Hebrew Canon is 2 Chronicles, which records history from 970 BC to the decree of Cyrus. Nonetheless, Malachi wrote the prophecy that anticipated this next episode in the Hebrew story. Malachi presupposes the existence of the second temple and the functioning cultus.

31. It has been argued that Jesus' baptism also connected him typologically to Israel. Gibbs, "Israel Standing with Israel."

Jesus and who was against (12:30). This explicit "wedge" agenda has the effect of informing the reader that there is no possibility of neutrality in this story; each participant would either honor Jesus or oppose him (12:30). In a story that may be describing the last conflict and the culmination of a long struggle, there is no hint at this stage that a truce or new peace would be brokered. On the contrary, Matthew's language appears to escalate and intensify the conflict, until it evolves into a final death grip that only one of the antagonists can survive.[32] Matthew's "gospel" at this stage does not appear to be a message of peace, as much as a message of the sword (10:34).

## The First Conflict

John, who questioned how they had received the warning to flee the "coming wrath," did not receive the arrival of a delegation from Jerusalem kindly (3:7). This suggests two things: Jerusalem and those who spread its influence were not intentionally warned about the coming wrath, and John perceived that his ministry was the only possibility of escaping that wrath.[33] According to Matthew's John, the ruling and "righteous" class was beyond redemption. By implication, this Jerusalem community was the most culpable of all and possibly even the cause of the impending wrath. By presenting this sharp conflict between John and the Pharisees and Sadducees, Matthew was able to keep the readers' gaze of disdain fixed upon the anti-Christ community. At no stage in the narrative are they presented as good or benign; rather, the "villains" of this story are already obvious to the reader, and the unfolding narrative would remove any doubt that Matthew viewed this community as the object of God's scorn. Incrementally, the indictment builds. And even if the reader may be left to question whether the Jerusalem religious community was complicitous in the death of the innocents, by the end it becomes patently obvious, according to Matthew, that nothing would stop its determination to kill Jesus, not even Rome.[34]

---

32. "Literary critics have argued that Matthew's plot turns on progressively intensified conflict, especially between Jesus and the Jewish leaders, leading to Jesus' death (Kingsbury 1987; 1988:17–24, 115–27; Anderson 1994: 97–126; Powell: 171–77)" (Duling, "'Egalitarian Ideology," 124).

33. It should be noticed that, at this stage, the Jerusalem community has not done anything obvious to attract the condemnation of John. Therefore, it could be suggested that John started the public conflict.

34. Matthew portrayed the Roman officials as unwilling participants in Jesus' execution. However, Matthew did nothing to portray the chief priests as unwilling participants in the infant assassination attempt.

John's, and later Jesus' designation of the Pharisees and Sadducees as a "brood of vipers" (Matt 3:7, 12:34, 23:33) was no doubt intended to portray them in the worst possible way.[35] However, this interpretation may not be taking into account Matthew's keen interest in the metanarrative and its conclusion. It may well be that this is one of the few places where Matthew was avoiding subtlety and not concealing the import of these people to his story; these were the "offspring of the serpent"—a brood of vipers.

Following this initial encounter, John went on to describe the true threat to his Jerusalem opponents: the one who would follow him. The baptism of the Holy Spirit and fire are not presented in the pericope as a gracious endowment, but as the ultimate threat.[36] If the Jerusalem rulers had feared John's denunciation, they were soon to be horrified by what would come next. John's Jesus in Matthew was a judge, whose primary role was separation of the good from the bad. The Pharisees and Sadducees were deemed ineligible for John's baptism. They would, however, be subject to the terrifying baptism of the Christ/judge. Jesus' baptism was foreshadowed in Isaiah (Isa 4:2–4). The "Branch of the Lord" would be honored by the remnant of Zion; those separated by him would be holy. This was to take place after the Lord had cleansed, and presumably separated, Jerusalem with the "spirit of judgment" and the "spirit of burning."[37] This prophecy, then, pointed to the appearance of the *nēṣer* (branch, Isa 4:2) who would separate a holy remnant following his washing (baptism) with the "Spirit and fire." This judgment and conclusion motif in Isaiah bears a remarkable resemblance to John's depiction of Jesus' ministry.

## John's New Demeanor and Jesus' Heavenly Appointment

The pericope ends with the blustering and righteous Baptist assuming a subordinate posture to Jesus and confessing his need of him. When Jesus came, John no longer gave instructions and or made demands; rather he accepted instruction and performed Jesus' bidding. In this way Matthew was able to dramatize the importance of Jesus to his readers. John's meek

---

35. Keener, "Brood of Vipers," 11.

36. Peter Bolt makes the case that *baptizō* is far stronger than *baptō*, which as a simple verb conveyed washing or bathing. *Baptizō*, on the other hand, inferred being overwhelmed by floodwaters, immersed in troubles, and even on the brink of destruction. Bolt, *The Cross*, 67.

37. ". . . he will cleanse the bloodstains from Jerusalem by a spirit of judgment and a spirit of fire" (Isa 4:4).

posture before Jesus was in distinct contrast with those who would later seek the downfall of Jesus.

Matthew had already disclosed that the Holy Spirit had conceived Jesus; now, in this passage, the Spirit of God descended. This image of the Spirit falling on an individual was familiar to Matthew's readership; it also had clear prophetic relevance for "the Branch" (Isa 11:1–2, 42:1).[38] The descent of the Spirit, from the time of Moses, was the means by which God's appointed servant was demarcated from everybody else. Invariably, the Spirit was given for the purpose of leadership, and usually for judgment. The judges, for instance, seemed to routinely experience the Spirit's descent before devastating Israel's enemies. The message was resoundingly clear; the person who had the Spirit was the one God would use as his particular administrator on earth.

This is particularly pertinent when considering Israel's early dynastic history. Saul was given the Spirit, and subsequently, he became successful in battle (1 Sam 11:6). Similarly David, after Samuel had anointed him, was filled with the Spirit. At that same time the Spirit departed from Saul, replaced by an evil spirit (1 Sam 16:14). So the descent of the Spirit on David was both evidence of God's appointment of David, and evidence of God's rejection of Saul; it was a sure sign that the power had been transferred. This connection with David in Matthew's narrative is unmistakable. Matthew had amply portrayed Jesus as the Davidic heir. Further, this incident distinctly resembles the appointment of David: God spoke to Samuel confirming the new king (as he may have been doing to John), who was then anointed by Samuel and who then received the Spirit of the Lord with power (1 Sam 16:12–13).

If we assume that this influenced Matthew's narrative, Jesus' public appointment, in the presence of the Pharisees and Sadducees, was a testimony that Jesus had been exalted, while other "anointed" ones were now bypassed. This anointing was accompanied by a public declaration from heaven that acknowledged the sonship of Jesus, and his unprecedented acceptability. Mark and Luke recorded this declaration as a statement to Jesus—"You are my son . . ." Matthew, however, records it as a public declaration about him, rather than just a personal address: "This is my son . . ." So, in Matthew, the Father testified on behalf of the Son—the first, and most important, testimony concerning Jesus in this courtroom drama.[39] As this was a pub-

---

38. "The opening of the heavens is a familiar apocalyptic image" (Watts, *Isaiah's New Exodus*, 102).

39. The hearing of the divine voice was to pre-empt an apocalyptic judgment in Isaiah. "The LORD will cause men to hear his majestic voice and will make them see his arm coming down with raging anger and consuming fire, with cloudburst,

lic message, Matthew intended his readers to understand that those who witnessed the event included representatives of Jerusalem;[40] the heavenly endorsement, however, did not change their attitude to Jesus.[41] Matthew had left his readers in no doubt: Jesus was God's appointed, and this was placed on public record.[42]

The declaration from heaven, taken from the Synoptic tradition, has been integral to the development of the church's Christology. The composers of the Athanasian Creed were persuaded that divine sonship of Jesus constituted irrefutable proof of his equality with God. This was a reasonable deduction, particularly when informed by the Johannine documents. It is noteworthy, however, that the Hebrews writer considered the declaration of divine sonship was also an appointment to the high priestly office (Heb 5:5). Similarly, Psalm 2 noted the regal appointment as the inauguration of a divine relationship. The "anointed one" (King) was appointed, and his function was to ask for the nations and bring judgment through the administration of an unyielding scepter. Therefore, it may be that the weaving together of divine sonship, kingly prerogative, priestly function and eschatological judgment are all placed in the one "divine" appointment. As the Hebrews writer considered the appointment to sonship as being an inauguration of the high priestly office, this may have reflected a widespread Hebrew understanding.[43]

## The Testing of the New "Son"

Matthew continued the "credentials of Jesus" motif by inserting his account of Jesus' wilderness testing. There can be no doubt that Matthew intended the connection to be made with Israel's wilderness sojourning, which had proved to be a dismal failure. The response of Jesus to the temptations

---

thunderstorm and hail" (Isa 30:30).

40. "... the Pharisees and scribes have an obvious literary function as the agents of the Jerusalem authorities ..." (Bird, "Jesus as Law–Breaker," 10).

41. This declaration concerning Christ was a Matthean connection with YHWH's chosen servant in Isaiah: "Here is my servant, whom I uphold, my chosen one in whom I delight; I will put my Spirit on him and he will bring justice to the nations" (Isa 42:1). This connection was later made explicit (12:18).

42. This, however, should not be interpreted as a dismissal of the Jerusalem incumbents. As in the case of Saul, the Spirit could be removed, but not necessarily their covenantal offices; only God would remove the "anointed" at his discretion (1 Chr 16:22).

43. The declaration made of Jesus "You are my Son, today I have become your Father" was an appointment to divine authority according to New Testament writers. This is primarily to the kingly office, but does not negate the view presented in Hebrews that it also had distinctly priestly implications. Psalm 2 presented the Anointed One as king, priest and judge; all three are intertwined within his divine appointment.

was to quote exclusively from Deuteronomy 6 and 8. Deut 8:2 reminded Israel of its own testing—"Remember how the LORD your God led you all the way in the desert these forty years, to humble you and to test you in order to know what was in your heart, whether or not you would keep his commands." God had tested Israel; therefore, it was appropriate that Jesus be tested as a demonstration of his devotion to God and as a symbol of the "new Israel."

This temptation was at the Spirit's instigation, but the examiner was to be the devil. After forty days without food, the test began. A notable differentiation from Israel was that Jesus did not ask for food, and what is more important, he did not complain against God concerning its absence. The first two temptations were prefaced with the challenge by Satan that Jesus should demonstrate his divine sonship. Satan was not challenging Jesus' divine origin, but his divine prerogative to represent God on earth. In Psalm 2, the appointment of the earthly ruler and the designation of Son of God were synonymous. The baptism incident may be perceived as the divine call of Jesus to the highest office; this was what Satan wished to undermine. This notion that Israel's king/ruler was also the son of God was implied by the challenges to Jesus during the passion narrative (27:41–44). God's representative on earth could legitimately be called the Son of God. This notion will be considered at greater length in chapter 7.

The first temptation was addressed to Jesus' immediate need for sustenance. The temptation did not expose Jesus to any breach of Torah; the implication of the text was that to turn stones into bread was not according to God's will at that time. Jesus' response to the temptation, which is a direct quote from Deut 8:3, asserted that life was not sustained by bread alone, but primarily from doing everything that God required. Israel did not die in the wilderness for lack of food, but for disobeying God; as the Deuteronomy passage goes on to explain: "Like the nations the LORD destroyed before you, so you will be destroyed for not obeying the LORD your God" (Deut 8:20).

The second temptation called upon Jesus to fulfill Scripture. This inclusion is particularly interesting in Matthew, for his Jesus' credentials stemmed from being the fulfillment of the Law. Here Satan is tempting Jesus to fulfill the Law. Certainly, God would command his angels to lift up the righteous one and not cause his foot to stumble (Ps 91:11–12). However, Jesus believed a preemptive action on his part to invoke this protection was to test God's reliability. Jesus' time in the wilderness was not to test God, but to be tested by God. Israel, on the other hand, would not be tested by God; rather, the nation sought to test him (Exod 17:1–7).

Jesus' response to the temptation was derived from Deut 6:16: "Do not test the LORD your God as you did at Massah." This reference pinpointed the specific failure of Israel, which had some implications for the priesthood of the nation. Moses reflected on the incident which had some connection with the Levitical community—"You tested him at Massah; you contended with him at the waters of Meribah" (Deut 33:8). Matthew's Jesus did not test God, but was tested by God as Levi was. Jesus' use of the Deuteronomic text, however, may have been used to recall the Massah incident, where the inaugural priestly community was willing to contend with God.[44]

The last temptation was a desperate claim for Jesus' devotion. Jesus was presented with all the kingdoms of the world as the reward for subjugating himself to Satan.[45] This was not unlike the vassal treaties that promised reward for unfettered devotion. Satan's ability to deliver on his offer is not of interest to this reading; our interest is in the role that this played in Matthew's big story. How does this incident distinguish Jesus from Israel, and even from its primeval history?

The reason God called Israel (his son) out of Egypt was that Israel might worship him (Exod 4:23). However, the single biggest worship event in the Hebrew wilderness narrative was directed to the golden calf (Exod 32). The newly appointed high priest, Aaron, led this idolatrous worship. Jesus, by denying Satan's demand, refused to be a failed mediator. Aaron's commissioning, and the construction of the sanctuary in which he was to worship, was recorded in Exod 25–31:18. Aaron's immediate abandonment of his commission and holy standing before God provides a suitable lens for interpreting this temptation, for Jesus was commissioned prior to this event. However, there may be further metanarrative echoes to be found concerning these temptations, particularly the last.

Matthew's temptation sequence demonstrated Jesus' willingness to lay down his life. By denying himself food, Jesus was completely at God's disposal, and certainly at the point of death after forty days. The angels that attended Jesus at the end of the process were no doubt instrumental to his survival. This echoes another famous Hebrew story, the offering of Isaac. Isaac was all but dead but for the intervention of the angel (Gen 22:11–12). Abraham had endured the test of God successfully as evidenced by the need for heavenly intervention. This testing of Jesus may have recalled this significant Hebrew story, for Abraham's seed could now be seen as offering his own life.

---

44. Of interest concerning this temptation, Matthew did not fail to make the point that the angels were commissioned by God to attend to Jesus' needs (4:11), but not as a consequence of Jesus' pre-emptive action. So once again, the Scripture was fulfilled in Jesus.

45. Satan's offer of the kingdoms of the earth would be trumped by God, later in the narrative, who would give Jesus authority over heaven and earth.

While Matthew's references within this pericope relate to the wilderness testing, the striking echo of the primeval temptation must have resonated with Matthew's readers also. This would be most apparent as a consequence of the prominent role given to the devil and his dialogue with Jesus. The devil did not obviously feature in Israel's wilderness temptations, therefore, his appearance in Matthew's temptation narrative must have served some other theological purpose, and it is certainly complementary to a metanarrative conclusion. Unlike the first humans, Jesus was without the bounty of paradise and considerably weakened by the forty day fast. It is possible that Matthew's readers would have connected the devil with the ancient serpent,[46] in which case his appearance within this early stage of the narrative would strengthen the claim that this narrative had something to do with the final conflict foreshadowed by the first divine prophecy (Gen 3:15). It may be, therefore, that Matthew has attempted to weave together the human and Hebrew stories; the antagonists have been identified, and the reader would anticipate how Satan would reemerge and strike the heel of Jesus.[47] Not since Satan's conversation with Eve had a human been directly provoked by the ancient enemy.[48]

## The Light Dawns in the North

The commencement of Jesus' ministry was directly connected with the termination of John's ministry (4:12). This will be considered at greater length in chapter 4, but for now it is sufficient to note that this had strong implications for Jesus' role as the Messiah Judge. According to Malachi 4, John/Elijah was the last representative in YHWH's protracted negotiations and history with Israel; Jesus/YHWH would follow to settle accounts.

---

46. Rev 12:9 identified the devil as the ancient serpent. Kelly, "Exposition of Matthew 4:1–11," 62. Balmer Kelly considers this to be an accidental connection for Matthew.

47. Satan does not directly appear in Matthew's narrative again. The other Gospels have Satan entering Judas, but Matthew avoided this. In keeping with Matthew's subtle literary skills, the three tests of Jesus by the Pharisees, Sadducees and Herodians in chapter 22 revealed Satan's continuing entrapment agenda through the less obvious identity of the Jerusalem community. Satan (the accuser) was not presented as acting on his own behalf by the end of Matthew, and yet the condemnatory accusations against Jesus were numerous. Mark Powell disputes this, by saying that Satan and the leadership had separate and distinct agendas. Powell, "The Plot and Subplots." This, however, seems highly implausible.

48. The only possible exception to this is the satanic accusations of Joshua in the heavenly tribunal (Zech 3:2). Job was not directly tempted or accused.

In Matthew's assessment, Jesus went to live in Capernaum in order to fulfill the prophet's testimony concerning Zebulun and Naphtali being the first to see the dawning of light (4:15–16; Isa 9:1). This prophecy in Isaiah followed a declaration by God that he would be a sanctuary (temple) for those who fear him, a stumbling stone for both houses of Israel, and a snare for Jerusalem (Isa 8:13–15). In spite of this gloom, the people of Galilee would be honored by the first appearance of the "light."

Matthew was alone in quoting this text at the commencement of Jesus' ministry; however, this understanding of Jesus as "light" was not unique, and was of significant interest in later Christological development (John 1:1–5). Though Matthew does not exploit this notion excessively, clearly "light" and "sight" are synonymous, as were "darkness" and "blindness" within Matthew's hermeneutic.[49] This being the case, there is an allusion to the primeval darkness that was "formless and void"; the appearance of the "light" was God's means of separating the darkness from the light. The implications of this possibility are that Israel was in no better condition than its Gentile neighbors, for it also sat in the darkness; further, Jesus came to give light and, consequently, expose the darkness—an act of separation. Darkness is a metaphor for judgment in Matthew (8:12, 22:13, 25:30).

Jesus' ministry in Matthew commenced with the preaching of the kingdom's imminent arrival. The imperative to "repent," which was attached to the announcement, can perhaps be understood best by contrasting it with a benign alternative, such as, "rejoice, for the kingdom is near." Repentance was a well-known concept to a Hebrew readership, for it was the perennial call of the prophets for wayward Israel to enact righteous and YHWH-fearing beliefs and conduct. The imperative attached to the kingdom pronouncement made the message of the kingdom both ominous and yet accessible. Jesus had come to bring judgment, but there was still time to heed John's message—a final offer of amnesty. The character of this repentance would be demonstrated in Matthew by the conduct of the first disciples, who abandoned both livelihood and family (and, we can suppose, everything else) at Jesus' behest (4:18–22).

The calling of the fishermen, who were two sets of brothers,[50] was made striking by the immediacy attached to their response. This, no doubt, was the demonstration of repentance necessary to enter the kingdom, according to Matthew. The radical conversion of the disciples would later be set in contrast with others in the narrative that were not compelled to abandon their lives and interests immediately (8:21–22, 19:16–24). Such radical life

---

49. Matt 5:13–16; 6:22–23.

50. The stewards of the former covenant were also two brothers, Aaron and Moses.

change could only further emphasize the urgency of the call and, therefore, the severity of the impending kingdom to those who did not take such drastic action. The total abandonment by these followers has the same character as a person leaping from his burning dwelling empty-handed.

The calling of the disciples in Matthew was also noteworthy for the absence of any reflection upon their tribal associations. Their "pedigree" was not relevant; it was only their response to Jesus' message that was noteworthy. The fifth disciple named in the narrative, Matthew, similarly heard the command and immediately followed (9:9). Following Jesus, in Matthew's story, was the primary character of repentance.[51] This may have informed the reader's understanding of the two paths: one path led to life, the other to death. The individual that remained in the "darkness" and followed those who represented it, even after the light had dawned, pursued the path of death.

The disciples' defining role from this early pericope was that they would become "fishers of men" (4:19). This function has long been considered an evangelistic role of ingathering. This may be the case, but the narrative conveys more than this. For instance, Jesus taught that the kingdom of heaven[52] would be like a net with all kinds of fish in it, and the fisherman would then separate the "good" from the "bad" (13:47–50). This parable may have implicitly defined the role of the "fishermen" as judges, but it would later be made explicit. Jesus told the disciples in Matthew's narrative, "I tell you the truth, at the renewal of all things, when the Son of Man sits on his glorious throne, you who have followed me will also sit on twelve thrones, judging the twelve tribes of Israel" (19:28). Their role and authority to "bind and loose" indicated to the reader that the fishermen were the new judges, or separators of the good and the bad.[53] The disciples' testimony would be either believed or rejected; and separation would occur based on their firsthand witness. Matthew's narrative fits comfortably within the paradigm designated for these "apostolic" office-bearers, for it may be that this document was intended to function as a prophetic indictment tool—a book of judgment.

---

51. Kingsbury, "Verb *akolouthein*."

52. Matthew avoided using the term kingdom of God, preferring to use kingdom of heaven. Many scholars have considered this to be a "circumlocution for the divine name," however, it has also been argued that this was used to affirm the disciples as members of the heavenly kingdom. Foster, "Why on earth use 'kingdom of heaven'?" 497. Pennington rejects the circumlocution argument, and believes that Matthew's use of the phrase was to highlight the gulf between the kingdoms of men (earth) and God's kingdom. Pennington, *Heaven and Earth*, 7.

53. It has been commonly understood that this function to bind and loose involves the role of the church to make moral judgments on earth. Derrett, "Binding and Loosing."

## The Overwhelming Good News

The final pericope of Jesus' history and prologue was a summation of the things to come during the Galilee years (Matt 5–18). With a single sweep Matthew managed to summarize the events that preceded Jesus' fateful march to Jerusalem. The passage served several purposes for Matthew. It was an introduction to the particulars of Jesus' ministry, which commenced with the Sermon on the Mount—Jesus' new vision of kingdom righteousness.[54] It also emphasized the offer of God's grace that was attached to the ministry of Matthew's Jesus—he was exceedingly kind and compassionate, and all who came to him were healed. There was no limit to his ability to meet the spectrum of human need, even Gentile needs. Lastly this passage made clear that Jesus was not a fringe prophet—thousands of individuals throughout the land and even beyond the national borders came to him and were blessed by the encounter in Matthew's story. Even Jerusalem and Judea came to witness this marvel and be blessed—his ministry was "good news." So Jesus' gracious ministry and power were not a matter of contention in Matthew—the debates would revolve around the source of his power and the basis of his authority.

In spite of all this, the invitation to ask, seek, and knock (7:7), as well as the unconditional offer to carry the burdens of all (11:28), was not accepted by the vast majority of Israelites in Matthew. The gospel came, but its denial would function as one of two significant factors in the overwhelming indictment against Israel. Israel rejected the amnesty and offer of grace; its final offense was to conspire and "cut off" the bearer of the good news. These last two crimes against YHWH would serve as the cataclysmic end to a long history of unrequited love and faithfulness. The good news of Jesus was the necessary backdrop to the transition from the geographically and ethnically bound covenant of Moses to the universal and international covenant of Abraham (Gen 12:1).[55]

## Summation

This chapter has examined Matthew's early narrative as the means by which Jesus was introduced as the destiny of Israel, the true Israel and the successful Israel. Jesus was the Son of God, as Israel of old was called God's

---

54. Righteousness in ancient Israel was relational—"faithfulness to a covenantal relationship" (Talbert, *Reading the Sermon on the Mount*, 63).

55. The particular mission of chapter 10 is a contrast to the universal mission of the Great Commission. Clearly, a change of covenant was now being applied. Carlston, "Interpreting the Gospel of Matthew," 8.

son; yet unlike in the case of Israel, God was well pleased with Jesus. This introduction, therefore, established Jesus' credentials and authority as the human who would act as God's final emissary, the manager of God's business/household. Not only did the prophets testify to him in writing and in the person of John, but also his life testified for him—he overcame the most demanding of tests.

The priestly subtext is not a predominant feature of these early chapters; however, inferences can be made that the Jerusalem priests were disturbed by the possibility of a renewed Davidic descendent who could claim messianic and, possibly priestly, authority. Matthew's introduction left his readers with no doubt as to Jesus' identity and entitlement. It also introduced the central opponent, and the Jerusalem identities through which he would launch his last assault on YHWH, in this stylized account of how the Hebrew metanarrative would come to its end.

# 3

# The Sermon: Understanding the Legal Requirement

> *This is the shoot of David who is to arise with the Expounder of the Law . . . in Zion in the latter days.*
>
> (Q4 Florilegium; interpretation of 2 Sam 7:11–14)[1]

THE SERMON ON THE Mount is a significant feature of Matthew and any hypothesis concerning the purpose of this Gospel must account for it as part of the wider narrative. The Sermon appears to set the agenda for the ministry of Jesus and his followers, and it carries the reader along with the force of bold unexpected assertions. The Sermon is striking from the outset as it assaults any preconceived notions of how the kingdom of heaven would be accessed and what it would look like. Matthew's Jesus trumps whatever morality or law came before, by bringing clarity, amendment or complete overhaul, depending on which scholastic tradition is considered to have the right interpretation. Many scholars and church fathers have reflected in great detail on the Sermon, and it is not possible to fully acknowledge the many contributions. Many templates for interpreting the Sermon seem viable and persuasive, though numerous questions concerning it remain unanswered.[2] Consequently, this reading will not evaluate the interpretations of others; the intention here is to simply read the Sermon through the specified lens. The lens requires that the Sermon be read as an integral part

---

1. Bruce, *Jesus and Christian Origins*, 73.
2. Carter, "Some Contemporary Scholarship."

of the whole, not "detached from the narrative of Jesus as told by Matthew."[3] As this reading of the Sermon is premised on Matthew being an advancement of the Hebrew story, and consequently, a concluding prophetic judgment, this reading will take a unique form.

## The Sermon As the Word of God

The Sermon follows an introduction to Jesus, which established his genealogical, historical, prophetic and moral authority. The genealogy established Jesus' metanarrative credentials, the significant historical "slogans" connected Jesus to Israel's hard service of slavery and exile, "Elijah" and the heavenly voice introduced Jesus to demonstrate that he was not "self-appointed," and the temptation demonstrated his moral authority to preach to others.[4] With such a prelude it is unlikely that Matthew believed his work to be mundane, yet this is not the most striking feature that testifies to its author's belief in his divine task: that feature rests with the Sermon's content.

Jesus' sermon is at the very least a call to Torah revision. The call to consider what was formerly said and trump it with "but I say to you" places Matthew's Jesus in the league of lawgiver along with Moses, and, we should readily suppose, with greater authority.[5] This is an extremely audacious claim. Jesus was not critiquing contemporary applications of the Torah but the very law itself as given through Moses.[6] This is assumed by the introduction to the antitheses "you heard it was said to the people long ago."[7]

The Sermon, and its documentation, was placed in the public domain by Matthew. As the Sermon addressed Mosaic edicts authoritatively, it is likely that its author considered it to be a prophetic word on a par with Scripture. The Sermon is Jesus' "ninety-five theses;" a public challenge that addressed the failings of the incumbents and their system. It also defined Jesus' own ministry and life: Jesus would be judged by the precepts that he presented in the Sermon.[8]

---

3. Harrington, "Problems and Opportunities," 418.

4. Any sermon that advises its hearers to "remove the log" would surely be somewhat hypocritical without some demonstrable moral authority. Matthew's Jesus successfully came out of the wilderness, unlike his metanarrative forerunner, Moses.

5. There are fourteen triads within the Sermon, and the moral imperative fell on the last of these triads, according to Glen Stassen. Stassen, "The Fourteen Triads."

6. France, *Matthew*, 195.

7. Nolland, *Gospel of Matthew*, 229.

8. Once again it would be extraordinary hypocrisy to assert "For in the same way you judge others, you will be judged, and with the measure you use, it will be measured to you," without being prepared to be judged oneself by the espoused precepts.

## The Sermon's Introduction

Within the bounds of this reading, it is of interest to explore how the Beatitudes, and their amplification throughout the Sermon, testify to one overarching Matthean preoccupation: righteousness. The Beatitudes testify that the "righteous" will receive God's blessing. Each of the individual character traits of the "blessed" can be subsumed under the one virtue of righteousness, which in Hebrew (and Aramaic) carries a broad semantic range not dissimilar to those described within the Beatitudes. תָּם can refer to gentle and righteous.[9] עָנָו incorporates the idea of meek, humble, poor, oppressed and afflicted. צַדִּיק also translates righteous, but can reflect honest or innocent. Joseph, as an example of righteous conduct, did not seek to expose Mary, but rather quietly protect her. Moreover, Joseph responded obediently and promptly to the divine revelation; his righteousness was revealed by his willingness to please God. The Sermon is a revelation of the correct disposition of the ones who will be blessed. They are not without "righteousness," but abound in it. They meet the requirement of Torah, but also manage to seek mercy for those who fail to maintain Torah.

Throughout the Sermon, the practice of Jesus' "higher righteousness" was contrasted with the "lower righteousness" of the incumbents—the scribes and Pharisees. These lesser practitioners of righteousness are not capable of "entering the kingdom of heaven" (5:20), despite having some form of righteousness.[10] By implication, the disciples must attain the higher righteousness that Christ conveyed with the "new law" contained in this sermon. The disciples are required to meet Jesus' standards—by doing so they will have performed the "will of God," and have attained to the blessed state. The Sermon does not contrast righteousness with unrighteousness, but two standards of righteousness. The Jerusalem community represents an outward, harsh, self-serving righteousness, and it is the foil against which Jesus explains the righteousness that heaven requires.

As a result of the contrast between the two "schools" of righteousness, the Sermon may be best understood by considering the community opposed to Jesus' brand of righteousness. Matthew seems to have set the "blessings" of chapter 5 as a literary contrast to the "woes" of chapter 23, though commentators generally avoid making this kind of connection. By doing this Matthew has certainly invoked the memory of Deuteronomy's blessings and curses (Deut 28).[11] The final woes revealed the scribes and Pharisees

---

9. Jacob was תָּם. (Gen 25:27).

10. "[there needs to be something] more than [the righteousness of] the scribes and Pharisees" (Nolland, *Gospel of Matthew*, 223).

11. Tom Wright is one exception. Wright, *People of God*, 387.

to be practicing the inferior righteousness described in the Sermon. Rather than being poor in spirit, they were haughty and exalted (23:7); rather than showing mercy, they tithed and failed to practice justice and mercy—they placed burdens upon others that they were unwilling to lift (23:4, 23). They did not mourn, for they attended banquets and were filled with greed and self-indulgence (23:5–6). They were not pure inwardly, for they were satisfied with outward cleanliness (whitewashed sepulchers—23:7). They did not hunger and thirst for righteousness (23:30), for they were confident that they were more righteous than their fathers. They were not peacemakers, for they killed the prophets (23:37). They were not persecuted for righteousness' sake, for they were the persecutors of the righteous prophets (23:37).

These beatitudes are amplified throughout the Sermon and, either specifically or by implication, they feature the indictable practices of the adversaries of Jesus. This can be shown by a rapid sweep through the Sermon. Purity of heart would produce hearts without malicious anger or lust—the hypocrites were "full of uncleanness" (ἀκαθαρσίας 23:27). Rather than avoid the court and make peace, the hypocrites rushed to and presided over the courts (26:59–60). Jesus' prohibition on oaths was contrasted to the value that the hypocrites placed on the gold in the temple when they made their puerile oaths (23:16). In the narrative the Pharisees insisted on their Mosaic right to divorce (19:7), yet Jesus cited it as a cause for adultery. Jerusalem did not love its enemies; rather, it conspired to bring about their downfall (26:3–4). The hypocrites gave, prayed and fasted to be seen (6:5), and therefore received no reward in heaven.[12] It was impossible to serve mammon[13] and God—a choice needed to be made between earthly privilege, wealth and honor, and God.[14] The scribes and Pharisees had showy garments with long tassels and wide phylacteries, and they took the high places at banquets to ensure they enjoyed the best food; the disciples were not to be concerned with what they ate or wore, for that was a concern for the pagans (Gentiles),

---

12. In a judicial sense, no appeal for leniency (reward) can be granted on the basis of good works which were performed for self-exaltation—"they have received their reward in full" (6:16).

13. To limit mammon to money fails to appreciate the broader implication of wealth, both in reputation and material possessions.

14. "According to Matthew's Gospel, 'the scribes and Pharisees' conceive of themselves as guardians of religious behaviour. Ultimately, however, their authority is subverted by the fact that they place an illegitimate priority on their own reputation (honour precedence) rather than on mercy and love toward others in the sight of God (honour virtue). Those competitively displaying their social status and religious practice before others have already received their prize of worldly acclaim (6:2). For those who privately pursue altruistic moral goals, God offers the reward (6:6)" (Lawrence, "For truly, I tell you" 702).

who were, by implication, acting like the scribes and Pharisees. The disciples were to critique themselves first by taking the "log out of their own eye." Jerusalem was occupied by "blind guides" who strained gnats and swallow camels (23:24). A bad tree bore bad fruit, and the proselytes of the Pharisees were twice the heirs of *Gehenna* as the "priestly tree" (23:15). And finally, saying "Lord, Lord," would not suffice for those who produce this bad fruit, for their bountiful work was lawlessness (ἀνομία)—as was the work of the indicted hypocrites (23:28).

A preliminary reading bears out that there is a contrast between two righteous systems and two righteous communities. However, we are left with the thorny dilemma as to how the disciples were to attain to the higher righteousness, that the Pharisees had no hope of achieving. How would these fishermen attain blessedness? It is clear that without a radical reversal of character, the disciples were also destined to fail. It is proposed here that the solution to this problem is to be found in Matthew's wider narrative, and appropriately, also within the Sermon. Jesus' "law" revealed how it was possible to observe a higher righteousness that was not nuanced by personal perfection and self-vindication, but by corporate acceptance and love.

## The Sermon in the Wider Narrative

Before the Sermon's conclusion is found the parable of the two houses, in which Matthew's Jesus specified what was required to enter the kingdom of heaven. Admission to the kingdom was for those who "do the will of the Father." In the context of the Sermon, it may appear that the cryptic "will of the Father" was nothing less than perfect righteous conduct that surpassed even the requirements of Moses. The narrative, however, teaches that Jesus' disciples did attain this "blessedness," while still being rather ordinary characters.[15]

Matthew's Jesus announced the "blessed" state of the disciples on three occasions.[16] The first reference is important by virtue of its Synoptic distinction. Following the attempt by Jesus' family to call Jesus away, Mark recorded that Jesus gestured to those around him and said, "Here are my mother and my brothers! Whoever does God's will is my brother and sister

---

15. It should be noted that blessedness is the condition of those who would not perish in the imminent wrath. According to Matthew, the disciples were to be the only survivors in Israel. Menninger, *Israel and the Church*, 138.

16. The threefold report of their blessedness is consistent with the manner in which Matthew communicates a permanent or complete state—three fourteens, three temptations, three denials, three hours, three days etc.

and mother" (Mark 3:34–35). Matthew, on the other hand, recorded that Jesus pointed toward his disciples and said, "Here are my mother and my brothers. For whoever does the will of my Father in heaven is my brother and sister and mother" (12:49–50). Luke recorded something quite different: "My mother and brothers are those who hear God's word and put it into practice" (Luke 8:21). The Matthean distinction confirmed that it was the disciples who were doing God's will, by virtue of being his disciples/followers. Luke inverts this proposition; in the third Gospel, those who do God's will are Jesus' relatives.[17] So if we can assume that blessedness was attributed to those who did God's will according to the Sermon (7:21), Matthew had, for the first time, suggested that the disciples were entering or had entered the kingdom.

The second reference to the disciples' acceptability was noted in the parabolic set of chapter 13. In that instance, the disciples were described as "blessed" for they had seeing eyes and hearing ears—a disposition set in juxtaposition with the community on the "outside" who were denied the "hearing and seeing" necessary to be healed/forgiven.[18]

The third instance was the pivotal moment within the narrative.[19] Peter's declaration (16:16) resulted in an emphatic declaration of blessedness;[20] Peter had become the portrait of Jesus' ideal human—one who had attained the eschatological state of blessedness, and by implication, was now heir to all the benefits disclosed in the Beatitudes. Without having attained all the virtues prescribed by the Beatitudes, Peter had gained their eschatological rewards, simply as a consequence of knowing Jesus' true identity and glory. In short, Peter's faith in Jesus resulted in the acquisition of kingdom blessedness— perhaps what Paul would call justification.[21]

---

17. Barth in Przybylski, *Righteousness in Matthew*, 112. Luke can be reconciled with the other Synoptics, for it may be that being disciples was the basis of God's will for Luke also, but in this instance, it is not explicit.

18. Jack Kingsley has suggested that Matthew's primary purpose revolves around the notion of seeing and hearing. The readers were invited to see and hear what Israel and its leaders failed to comprehend. Kingsbury, "The Rhetoric of Comprehension."

19. Following Peter's revelation and disclosure, Jesus began to disclose to the disciples his destiny with Jerusalem, where he would be tried, executed and raised to life. As the explanation of these events was given to all the disciples, it is reasonable to assume that Peter had declared what they all had discussed and believed.

20. "Blessed are you . . ." (16:17).

21. If judgment was typified by denial of the "secrets," the blessedness of the disciples is fully affirmed by the greater intimacy/knowledge to which they were privy following Peter's confession.

## The Essence of Kingdom Morality

A neglected key that may prove useful to understanding the Sermon is its possible emphasis on community rather than the individual.[22] The lens that is typically used in reading the Sermon is that it is a set of moral precepts for individual Christians to follow. It is suggested here that this turns the Sermon into high and unattainable morality. In order to accommodate the traditional view, the Sermon has regularly been interpreted as a clarification of the Law's onerous requirements, in order that people understand their moral shortcomings and their desperate need of a Savior. This reading presented here, however, puts forward an alternative approach, one that exhorts the individual to subordinate all moral and legal entitlement for the benefit of the collective. In so doing, righteousness and blessedness are attained as a corporate gift, rather than an individual possession.

Before considering this approach through the introductory and concluding allegory/parables of the Sermon, this proposition will first be considered in the body of the Sermon. The first set of these is the moral imperatives of chapter 5.

## Concerning Wrath (5:21–26)

The prohibition of anger in Jesus' higher righteousness and its attendant exhortations are difficult to reconcile.[23] The command is plain enough: murder is subject to judgment, which according to the law involved the death

---

22. By reading the Sermon as a corporate directive, rather than as directives to individuals, there is no intention to downplay the significance of Jesus' words for the lives of his followers. If the Sermon is specific instruction for the "leadership team" this would not mean that it has no application for every Christian, any more than the instruction that elders should be the husband of one wife implies that it is permissible for all others to be polygamous. The whole Christian project is built upon a modelling principle, where Christians are directed to emulate their leaders. Letters addressed to leaders (e.g., 1 and 2 Timothy, Titus, Philemon and 3 John) have traditionally been accepted as having relevance for all Christians. Exegetically, it is plain that the Sermon is given to the disciples who came to him (5:1). Similarly the Great Commission was given to the same group. Nobody suggests that the Commission ended with the disciples, nor is there any suggestion here that the moral precepts within the Sermon only applied to these disciples.

23. The traditional interpretation of these "antitheses" is that Jesus is explaining the "spirit" of the command—what it really means. Hagner, *Matthew 1–13*, 118. The problem with this approach is that it indicts the Law for not being clear, and if it is not clear, how can it be good law? Secondly, and most importantly, Matthew's Jesus is contradicting what was "said to the people long ago"; therefore, the new directives are not the old law at all, but different law.

penalty. What followed, however, is complicated. Anger towards a brother would also be met with judgment, and yet the law makes no comment about such judgment. The judgment to which Jesus refers must be something other than the Mosaic legal system. This is then further complicated by the introduction of an incremental escalation of transgression and judicial consequences. The use of "raca" towards one's brother would result in being brought before the Sanhedrin, and referring to a brother as a moron would place a person in danger of the impending eschatological wrath of God.

Before any discussion of a solution to this, the next section of the Sermon, which encourages reconciliation, needs some consideration, as it appears to be connected with the wrath prohibition. This section is also puzzling. Knowing that the brother has an unresolved issue (presumably the reason for his anger), a person must leave her offering to God on the altar and go to be reconciled. The instruction continued with an exhortation to come to some agreement quickly to avoid facing a judge, who would exact full recompense for the misdeed. Basically, it is cheaper to settle out of court.

The complications that are attached to a formerly straightforward commandment and penalty are now bewildering. From the outset, it is plain that the Sermon is not going to surrender its pearls to fools. Nonetheless, Matthew's careful attention to literary form and detail would suggest that there is sense to be made of this small pericope. From the start it should be assumed that Jesus is directing these instructions primarily to disciples as part of a larger discussion subsumed under the category of "preaching the good news of the kingdom" (4:23). This would account for the differing legal requirements entailed within the anger pericope. Perhaps an embellished translation would look something like this:

> Torah told you that murder would be punished; therefore, if you do not commit murder you can remain a full participant of the Mosaic Covenant. However, I tell you, anger against your sister or brother will render you liable to judgment in the kingdom coming; therefore you will be in danger of covenant exclusion if you continue in anger. Moderate wrath will bring you before the elders, severe anger will subject you to the flames prepared for those outside the kingdom. On the other hand, you may consider that you are blameless before God, but you know that your brother is disturbed (possibly angry) with you. Therefore, subject yourself to that brother and bear his scrutiny. Make amends, for his anger may be justified. If you cannot resolve the matter between you, you will come before a third brother who will judge the matter. Without reconciliation, he will have no

option but to hand you over to the kingdom officials, who have the power to exclude you from the kingdom.

This embellished paraphrase can only be made possible by reconciling this teaching with instructions for kingdom inclusion and exclusion found later in the narrative (18:15–17). If there is some intertextual enlightenment to be had, we are able to observe that the ethics of the kingdom of heaven are set in contrast with the ethics of the kingdom of Israel—the Law. Subscribing to Moses, therefore, only enables one to exist safely in Israel; it does not entitle a person to participate in the permanent eschatological kingdom.[24] The kingdom of heaven requires its members to forgive and be reconciled; this is a fundamental tenet of the kingdom's existence, but not Israel's. On this score, membership in Israel only required that a member not kill his or her neighbor. And so there is the development of two differing legal systems, the higher righteousness being required of those who aspire to heaven's kingdom.

Another aspect to this "new" law is its emphasis on the unrestored brother. Contrary to the previous attempt at paraphrasing, it may also be the case that the individual at the altar was in fact individually righteous. Individual righteousness in heaven's kingdom, however, is not acceptable without seeking righteousness for one's brother and sister. This motif becomes more obvious further into these teachings, but even here a different perspective on what is moral emerges. If the brother offering the sacrifice is innocent under the Law, he is not innocent in the kingdom while he is unresolved with his brother. Such is the force of the new "law of love" that individual righteousness alone is of little worth in the face of a kingdom where all are called to bear the burdens of others. In short, the innocent righteous individual is deemed unworthy at the altar until all members of the kingdom are reconciled—each carries the burden of her sister before God, even the innocent party. There is more to this pericope, which will be considered later.

## Concerning Lust (5:27–30)

This prohibition does not entail the complications attached to the former; by comparison, it is rather straightforward. The Law does not specifically judge or condemn adulterous thoughts, but the kingdom's standards are

---

24. Hebrews develops this idea in terms of mediation. Aaron could not make one clean in heaven; to achieve acceptance in heaven, one needed a heavenly priest—one who serves in the heavenly tabernacle. Aaron's efficacy was limited to the externals and earthly domain (Heb 8:1–6; 9:11–14; 10:1–12).

qualitatively different. The judge can judge the heart and the kingdom stewards will not exceed their authority if they judge a polygamous heart. The kingdom requires inner purity and not simply the absence of fornication.

The drastic mutilation of body parts attached to this instruction has a counterpart later in the narrative (18:8–9). In that instance, the ruthless actions are attached to a warning not to cause the children of the kingdom to stumble. By implication, the kingdom stewards must deal harshly with those who do not welcome the children (who are the inferior members of society).[25] These directions for discipline may be helpful for interpreting the divorce imperatives; for once again, individual rights were to be diminished for the wider good.

## Concerning Divorce (5:31–32)

Once again, Jesus acknowledged that the Law permitted divorce; the kingdom, however, forbids divorce on trivial grounds. This prohibition differs from the Mosaic legislation and casts some light upon the rationale that shapes kingdom morality. Under Moses, a Hebrew was entitled to write a certificate of divorce if he was not pleased with his wife. However, he was not entitled to remarry the woman once she had been with another husband (Deut 24:1–4).

Jesus' teaching does not deny the entitlement found in Moses. It does, however, appeal to a higher righteousness, which ultimately does condemn the frivolous divorcé.[26] Moses said nothing about the standing of the woman who suffered the thoughtless divorce, or the state of her future partner. Jesus points out that the man was permitted to divorce; however, the spurned wife committed adultery when she remarried, as did her new spouse. So importantly, the entitled divorcé is responsible for their sin, for he "causes her to become an adulteress." Under Moses, this is not a consideration, but under Christ, kingdom participants are their "brother's keepers." Causing anyone within the kingdom to sin is a sin (13:41; 18:6). Perhaps it is in this light that the member of the body that causes the whole body to stumble (in the previous prohibition) must be removed.

There remained, however, the provision, for "just" divorce in covenant law; adultery could sever the bond, and according to Near Eastern custom,

---

25. Children, who were the quintessential disciples in Matthew, praised Jesus while the leaders did not. Grams, "Not 'Leaders.'"

26. Nolland interprets this as a warning against easy or trivial divorce. Nolland, *Gospel of Matthew*, 46–47.

dowries did not have to be repaid in such instances.[27] This being the case, YHWH too was entitled to divorce for serial unfaithfulness, without future obligation to the adulterer.

## Concerning Oaths

Once again the Law permitted oath-taking as proof that a person intended to fulfill his obligations. The oath served as a guarantee of the person's fidelity.[28] Ironically, the oath-taker had no control or ownership over the entities by which he swore. Taking the oath, however, ensured that the person was bound, and therefore potentially indictable for not undertaking his obligation. A thoughtless or unfulfilled oath was a sin before the Law, which required sacrificial intervention to enact restoration (Lev 5:4–13). In the kingdom, however, oaths are not required to bind individuals to perform an obligation—the members must simply be truthful and reliable, and need no coercion or penalty to honor their word.[29]

## Concerning Vengeance (5:38–42)

The Law entitles an individual to be repaid for losses inflicted upon her by a third party. Theft, for instance, entitles a person to be repaid as much as four times the value of the item removed (Exod 22:1). Similarly, the Law made provision for exact punishment—an eye for an eye (Exod 21:22–25). Conversely, if the subject was being sued and a demand was placed upon her, Jesus advised that, rather than contest the issue, even more should be given. In essence, Jesus' morality calls for the new community to deny its rights. So, in this way, the church exists without recourse to earthly justice in an age that will perish, as a testimony to its eternal vindication.[30] The import of the passage is found as the narrative unfolds and the wrath of Jesus' oppressors becomes plain. Jesus, as the kingdom's exemplar, accepted the full implications of his own teaching; he passively accepted his arrest,

---

27. Janzen, "The Meaning of Porneia."

28. Of interest is the Hebrews writer's view that when God takes an oath it is not to convince humans that he will do what he has said; rather it is to enact a permanent state of affairs. For instance, God's oath that Jesus will "be a priest forever" ensures that Jesus would be a priest forever by virtue of the oath (Heb 6:16; 7:20).

29. Hagner, *Matthew 1–13*, 128.

30. Strecker, Luz and Weaver believe that the command to not resist evil (5:39) is intended for the church, rather than for individuals. Carter, "Some Contemporary Scholarship," 200.

even though he had twelve legions of angels at his disposal, and not just the twelve disciples (26:53).

Israel existed as a nation that required vengeance for atrocities committed against her. The clearest example of this was the determination by God that Israel should wipe out the Amalekites, 500 years after their crime against the fledgling Israel (1 Sam 15:2–3). Israel was a nation that would be avenged in circumstances where they had been treated badly, but the kingdom of heaven would not seek vengeance in this way, and would actively pursue a different course of action. The call to submit to all authority was such a call to action; the church did not even reject the evil that it would suffer at the hands of its oppressors.[31]

## On Loving Enemies (5:43–48)

While it is not verifiable that the Law taught the hatred of enemies, clearly Israel was to be an exclusive community—the Mosaic covenant institutionalized the exclusion of marginalized people.[32] Illegitimate children, people with deformed genitals (eunuchs included) and former citizens from certain neighboring nations were excluded from participation in the "kingdom [assembly] of Israel" to the tenth generation (Deut 23:1–7). Israel was commanded, by contrast, not to abhor (hate) the Edomites and Egyptians, who could join the assembly after just three generations of exclusion. In this way Israel was able to be "pure" within the Mosaic covenant, and, by implication, "hate" certain clusters of people.

By contrast, the kingdom of heaven would be perfect, like its Father in heaven, by requesting the inclusion of its natural enemies and accepting them as full members immediately. The rationale here is that God is kind to all types of people, good and bad; therefore, the New Community must resemble its Father. A couple of obvious examples of this edict in the life of the New Community were the inclusion of its most driven enemy, Paul, and

---

31. This kingdom law found in the Sermon has regularly been cited as the basis of passive resistance and the transformation of society. Stassen, "Healing the Rift"; however, there is no concept of resistance found in the passage. It is, rather, a call to submission. Nolland, *Gospel of Matthew*, 259–60.

32. "The latter, though not taught in the OT, is an inference that was commonly drawn, for example, from such passages as Pss 139:21–22; 26:5; or Deut 7:2; 30:7" (Hagner, *Matthew 1–13*, 134). These verses are not all eligible, as two of them are not from the Law. The other two are references to corporate enemies and not personal enemies. There seems to be no command that implies the hatred of individuals by individuals. This would support the hypothesis that reading the corporate imperative into the Sermon may be profitable. In saying this, however, it should not be assumed that Jesus did not condemn hatred in all its forms.

the acceptance of a foreign (Ethiopian) eunuch.[33] In effect, the kingdom of Jesus would accept former enemies, social outcasts and those with physical disabilities without prejudice or probationary period.

## Concerning Alms, Prayer and Fasting (6:1–18)

Reserving the Lord's Prayer for separate consideration, these three issues can be assessed simultaneously.[34] Each of the categories is germane to the practice of righteousness. The lower righteousness is characterized by its pursuit of "people-pleasing," while the higher righteousness is characterized by its interest in securing the approbation of God. The lesser is, therefore, undertaken publicly so that it may be seen; the greater is conducted in secret for the eyes of God. It should not, however, be assumed that this implies that the kingdom righteousness is best practiced in private; for the disciples did not seem to interpret this admonition that way. From the outset of the new community the disciples prayed, fasted and gave alms collectively (Acts 2:42, 4:35, 13:3), though not in public for religious stature. These directives are not advocating private religion, but sincerely God-honoring motives.[35]

## The Lord's Prayer (6:9–14)

The Lord's Prayer has been extracted from its context within the Sermon and in the wider Matthean narrative to become a liturgical staple for many Christians. Is it possible, however, that the early church understood the prayer's covenantal limitations[36] and did not consider it to be an appropriate prayer for the new community? The incongruity of the prayer concerning forgiveness has surely caused some concern for Christians, as any authentic reading reveals that God's forgiveness is contingent on the forgiveness of the religious community or individual. It should not be assumed that reversing the order and suggesting that the prayer teaches that we ought to for-

33. While a case is being made for the corporate dimension of this, it is inconceivable that individuals within the new community would be permitted to hate former enemies.

34. Allison proposes that Matthew had in mind a re-defining of the three traditional pillars of Simeon with his instruction on almsgiving, prayer, and fasting. Allison, "The Structure of the Sermon."

35. The Ananias and Sapphira incident may be helpful here (Acts 5). They were not condemned for openly giving, but for seeking to gain glory by the gift; this led them to perpetrate the deception.

36. The covenantal limitation suggested here is that the prayer may have greater relevance to those who were under the Law.

give in the same manner we are forgiven can reconcile this—it is quite the opposite. Donald Hagner sees it this way: "These verses need not be taken to mean that the forgiveness we enjoy from God stands in a causal relation to our forgiveness of others, or that God's forgiveness of us is the result of our forgiveness of others."[37] This is theologically problematic for those who consider that forgiveness is without preconditions or works, for the prayer's stipulation for forgiveness cannot be that easily reconciled. In fact, the addendum to the prayer in Matthew drives the uncomfortable point home: "For if you forgive men when they sin against you, your heavenly Father will also forgive you. But if you do not forgive men their sins, your Father will not forgive your sins" (6:14–15). The problem posed by the prospect of conditional forgiveness will be considered shortly.[38]

The first petition of the prayer is for the kingdom of heaven to come.[39] There can be little doubt that this kingdom is the same kingdom that both John the Baptist and Jesus have foreshadowed and described as imminent. The petition's intention is clarified by the additional information that is incorporated into the request—"your will be done on earth as it is in heaven." We can safely assume that the kingdom has come when the Father's will is being done on earth in a comparable or identical manner to heaven. When would this event take place?

The general perception is that the kingdom's arrival would be characterized by the reign of peace on earth, when all God's enemies would be subdued and everyone would live at peace. It may be, however, that the kingdom's arrival occurred at Pentecost, and from that time on God's will was done on earth as in heaven. The key to understanding this may be found in Matthew 16, where the disciples (Peter particularly in that instance) were told that the things they would bind and loose on earth would also

---

37. Hagner, *Matthew 1–13*, 152.

38. "Jesus was not restricting the Father's power to forgive. He was simply repeating the Old Testament maxim that to the merciful he will show himself merciful" (O'Neill, "The Unforgivable Sin," 41).

39. The kingdom of heaven is not necessarily identical to the church. Although it will always be difficult to define exactly what is meant by the kingdom of heaven, it is presented here as God's domain, the place where he enacts his authority and where his will is done. The church, by extension, is something of an earthly "branch office" of the kingdom; it is the creation of the kingdom. George Ladd is probably correct that the church is the witness, custodian and instrument of the kingdom of heaven on earth. Ladd, *Theology of the New Testament*, 111–15. The kingdom's coming, as well as the setting up of the church as the instrumentality of God's salvation, also comes as an expression of the Day of the Lord, which carries with it the warrior/judgment motif. Beasley-Murray, *Jesus and the Kingdom*, 3–16.

be bound and loosed in heaven.[40] The Epistle to the Hebrews sheds light on this apostolic authority. The Hebrews writer proposes that the Aaronic Priesthood only had authority to atone for and forgive certain sins on earth (Heb 8:4, 9:1), but this forgiveness was not effective in heaven. For the Hebrews writer, heavenly transgressions required heavenly mediation (Heb 7:23–8:1). Jesus' priestly function was such that it was performed in heaven (the true sanctuary Heb 8:2), and his mediation was so efficacious that all who come to him can be cleansed (forgiven) permanently. Two priesthoods are therefore set in contrast: the limited and failed priesthood of Aaron, and the permanent and successful priesthood of Jesus. Sins that Aaron (and his successors) bound on earth were not bound in heaven. On the other hand, the church would accept people on earth who would also be acceptable in heaven. The church does not forgive sin, but it is capable of recognizing the penitent, and granting them admission through baptism. (Forgiveness, in this sense, is a public recognition and acceptance of a person who has put his faith in Christ.) Conversely, those that the church did not accept were not accepted in heaven. According to this wider context of God's will on earth, it would appear that the kingdom came when the church had commenced. Praying, therefore, for the kingdom's inauguration after the event may act as a denial of the reality that heaven has an effective branch office on earth—the church.

Returning, then to the problem of forgiveness being given to the merciful, it can be argued that the church can only be the church when it dispenses the forgiveness that is integral to the kingdom of heaven. If a "church" puts restrictions on forgiveness, or requires personal transformation before an individual can be received, or discriminates against certain individuals and groups, then it is failing to forgive those who come to Christ. Consequently, that "church" is no longer a forgiven entity, as it does not do heaven's bidding. Essentially, the church ceases to be acceptable in heaven when it does not freely forgive, or better, affirm the cleansing and forgiveness of Jesus to those who come to Jesus.[41]

This corporate dimension to the forgiveness requirement makes most sense of the prayer. The alternative is to consider that all Christians revert to an unforgiven state if they do not forgive from the heart; that is, that they would revoke their own forgiveness, if they fail to be as gracious as God (18:35).[42] True forgiveness of others, for many, will not be automatic, and it

40. These terms correspond to "putting in fetters" or "acquitting." Luz, *Matthew 8–20*, 365. This issue receives fuller treatment in chapter 6.

41. An example here is Matthew. Heaven had accepted him, but Jerusalem would not. Therefore, Jerusalem could not be the church or forgiven.

42. It should be noted that the imperative to forgive in the parable of the unforgiving

will usually require some emotional energy to fully forgive an offender from the heart. The church, however, did not have the luxury of half-hearted forgiveness or of withholding forgiveness to those who relied on Jesus as priest. The church is therefore recognized by its abundant willingness to fully forgive sinners in Jesus' name.[43] This kingdom requirement finds its natural contrast in the Jerusalem administration. Jerusalem withheld mercy and adopted an obstructionist agenda for those seeking admission into the kingdom (23:13, 23).

The principle of reciprocal mercy was developed again from a different angle in the Sermon. The standard of judgment meted out by the community would be the measure applied to it. If the community were not merciful, it would receive little mercy; if it judged harshly, it would be judged harshly (7:1). There can be no mistaking the inference from all this: the kingdom/church must demonstrate mercy as its *raison d'être*. In such a way, the kingdom of heaven exists on earth.

The third petition should naturally be interpreted in the light of the forgiveness paradigm set forth in the prayer, for it is sandwiched between the petition and its explanatory rationale. Deliverance from temptation, therefore, may have been a request to be delivered from becoming unwilling to show extravagant mercy to those coming to Jesus. It does not preclude other temptations, but certainly this would be the critical temptation, as it seems that without the merciful disposition that God requires, the church/kingdom does not exist.[44]

The other petition within the prayer is for daily provision, or for a foretaste of the future banquet.[45] If it is the latter, it would support the hypothesis

---

debtor was for the benefit of those who had asked for forgiveness and not for those who did not seek it.

43. On this reckoning, churches that placed strictures upon Christians that required them to carry the burden of their own sin, through penance, purgatory or good works, would not be authentic representatives of the kingdom of heaven.

44. Longenecker makes the point that the personification of evil in the Matthean narrative is the Pharisees. Longenecker, "Evil at Odds," 507–8. In this case, such a petition may have an immediate reference to the community who had rigorous standards, but no mercy. Deliverance from them, or deliverance from becoming like them, would both have a reasonable basis in the narrative. Interestingly, the early church was beset with the problem of full and unconditional acceptance in the kingdom on the basis of grace alone. Those who insisted upon a heavily fettered gospel were described as the Party of the Pharisees (Acts 15). Could this petition in the Lord's Prayer and the events around the Jerusalem Council be somehow connected? Could Matthew have had this Christian group in mind when the warning was issued to "Beware of the yeast of the Pharisees . . ."? (16:6).

45. The better translation of this petition is a request for "tomorrow's bread." This being the case, the petition is a request to participate in the eschatological bounty before

that the prayer is for the commencement of the eschatological community on earth—heaven's expression on earth, the church, would be a foretaste of the coming age. However, the more mundane reading is also pertinent.

In the absence of stored wealth, this prayer emphasized the kingdom's total dependence upon God for its survival. Unlike the system that stored wealth as a guarantee of its future viability, the kingdom, as a corporate identity, would exist as any other natural organism (lilies and birds of the air) on the planet—dependent on God's patronage, not its own perceived managerial ability.[46] This petition is further developed immediately after this section on "righteous acts"; the kingdom was directed to make heaven its storehouse (6:19). The incumbent system, by contrast, was beholden to Herod and its accumulated wealth. These would prove to be valueless when Jerusalem was under siege, and then totally destroyed.

## The Sermon's Method of Attaining the "Higher Righteousness" (7:7–14)

The analysis of the Sermon to this point has not simplified the question of how the kingdom of heaven is to be entered. God's demands are lofty, and the individual has no prospect of meeting these requirements. The lens applied to this reading allows for the Sermon to be interpreted as a corporate set of directives, which would make it possible for the community to attain the higher righteousness and take the immediate stress off the hapless individual. Placing these requirements on a community, however, may not place any member of the kingdom on safer ground, for the community is just as likely to fail as the individual. Nonetheless, there is a ray of hope that a righteous community was possible, not on the basis of individual righteousness, but on the basis of concern and love of neighbor. The Law can be fulfilled in this way (7:12).

Access to the kingdom was through mercy.[47] The kingdom/church was the place that disclosed this mercy and offered it to all who called upon Christ. The Sermon develops this proposition, and describes it as a "narrow door" and a "narrow path." Few find the narrow door, even though it does

---

its complete inauguration—a foretaste of eternity. "Give us today the eschatological bread that will be ours in the future" (Hagner, *Matthew 1–13*, 144).

46. Dillon, "Ravens."

47. "In the judgement of many, Matthew 5–7 is unremitting in its requirements and does nothing more than make demands . . . Such a view fails to understand aright four different portions of the discourse—4:23–5:2; 5:3–12; 6:25–34; and 7:7–11" (Allison, "The Structure of the Sermon," 441).

not press the legal demands of the Sermon or Moses upon those who enter. In the context, those who enter are those who seek, knock and ask. Good things are given upon request, and the kingdom is given to those who ask. Within the overarching Matthean narrative, few ask Jesus for anything, but those who ask do receive.[48]

So it appears that there are two soteriologies on offer in the Sermon, one through "advanced and higher" Torah-keeping, and the other through request. One is impossible, the other ridiculously easy. There is a catch, however, in taking the narrow door—it would lead to the narrow (or hard) path. The path is not made difficult by the inexhaustible righteous requirements attached to kingdom morality, but by persecution. Matthew proposed that following Christ was accessible to those who had formerly been ruled ineligible through Torah-keeping (9:13). By contrast, Jesus' yoke was easy (11:30), but following him would be made difficult, as opposition would attend it; this too becomes increasingly obvious as the narrative unfolds.

## The Validity of the Law

The Sermon established at the outset that the task of Jesus was not to undermine, change or dispose of the Law; the Law of Moses, according to Matthew's Jesus, was the binding requirement upon every Israelite (5:17–21).[49] This introductory stipulation, found before the particular directives of Jesus' kingdom requirements, has led many to the conclusion that the Matthean community was an advocate of Torah-observant Christianity.[50] There is no doubt that this introductory pericope demands the attention of Matthew's readers; indeed, in these verses Matthew presented to us the purpose statement of Jesus and, therefore, possibly the purpose statement of the entire document.

Matthew's Jesus came to fulfill Torah as an entirety, which included the directives of the prophets. By noting the "yod and tittle" as being indispensable within this commission, it may be assumed that Jesus was proposing to do what no individual had previously done—fulfilled the Law and the Prophets. Fulfillment, for any Hebrew, was certainly the goal of the Scriptures. The Scriptures did not exist as an eternal religious manual, but as

---

48. The exception to this is the request from the mother of James and John. Jesus' reply was pertinent—it "is not for me to grant" (20:23).

49. Matthew 5:17–20 has provoked many considerations. For a good treatment see Foster, *Community, Law and Mission*, chapter 5.

50. Brice Martin asserts that Matthew's Jesus wanted to fully interpret, enact and establish the existing Mosaic Law. Martin, "Matthew on Christ and the Law."

history that was directed toward a satisfactory and glorious eschatological completion. Jesus' statement cannot simply have meant that he was determined to be faithful to the Law, which was a requirement inherent to being a Hebrew; it had to mean much more. His accurate and comprehensive teaching of the Law and the Prophets, and his keeping of the same, would be the basis of Jesus' greatness (5:19). As the Sermon proceeded to enunciate the most rigorous interpretation of Torah possible, Jesus' statement must firstly be understood as his divine commission; his goal was to be the perfect law-keeper.[51] However, the inclusion of prophetic fulfillment demands that this statement of purpose be understood as something more than law-keeping, for the Prophets did not propose new laws—they spoke primarily of YHWH's next move in the grand story. Jesus was, in this way, the fulfillment of the Prophets.

Certainly it is clear that Matthew intended Jesus to be understood as Israel's eschatological moment. Having already gained a glimpse of how Jesus fulfilled the Prophets within the pre-Sermon narrative, we can have little doubt that Matthew's Jesus was not simply a participant in the story, but the subject and eschaton of the Hebrew metanarrative. As the story continues Jesus invoked the memory and fulfillment of both Major and Minor Prophets. His task of fulfillment can therefore be understood in no other way than as a significant development in the story, and probably as its culmination. Matthew considered that the Prophets pointed toward this event, and there is no evidence within Matthew that they were interpreted as pointing beyond it. It may be the case, then, that Matthew considered fulfillment (5:17) to be conclusion—the last chapter.

This, however, leaves the reader with an exegetical difficulty: what does Matthew mean by fulfillment, considering Jesus' mandate not to abolish the Law and the Prophets?[52] If it is the case that fulfillment implies completion or even termination, then the first aspect of Jesus' mandate, "not to abolish," would have to be somehow reconciled with the entire mission statement. The approach taken by many to reconcile this has been to accept the binding

---

51. As the narrative leads to a courtroom scene where witnesses are called and evidence sought to determine when and where Jesus had failed to keep Torah, it seems that Matthew considered that this was evidence of strict and complete observance. No legitimate claim could be made against Jesus in Matthew's courtroom drama. This was juxtaposed by the claims Jesus made against the Jerusalem leadership (Matt 23). Also, Jesus should not be interpreted as a transgressor of Torah because he opposed the *halakah* of the Pharisees. Bird, "Jesus as Law-Breaker," 25.

52. This verse has led many to believe that Matthew was dealing with an antinomian problem in his church. However, as ἀνομία was used for all kinds of lawlessness, including that of the Pharisees, this would have little textual support. Davison, "Anomia."

requirement of the Decalogue upon the new kingdom community.[53] This approach is difficult to sustain. Firstly, it reduces the intended comprehensive implications of *yod* and *tittle* to a specific and reduced block of requirements. Even if this understanding could be exegetically supported, it faces the difficulty of the *yod* and *tittle* which apply to the fourth commandment; the suggestion that the movement of Sabbath from seventh to first day does not constitute even a minuscule change of law is unsustainable. Further, supporters of this approach have great difficulty reconciling how the prophets play into this paradigm, for do their prophecies remain in force after they are fulfilled also?[54]

The proposal here is that Matthew viewed Jesus as the Messiah/Judge, with the task of bringing upon the nation YHWH's final edict. As such, the Law's demands and penalties would and could not be abrogated, but imposed. Jesus had not come to bring blessings in spite of the cumulative covenantal breaches and prophetic foreboding, but to settle accounts in line with the legal stipulations and prophetic warnings of Torah. Jesus came to foreclose on a debt that was never paid. Therefore, it is possible to consider that fulfillment without abrogation was the destiny of God's contractual arrangement with the nation that he called out of Egypt. As Deuteronomy 28 foretold the stipulated consequences of covenant keeping or denial, Matthew may be indicating that his account is the grand conclusion to the Hebrew story by strategically placing "blessings" and "woes" (curses) within his narrative.

Matthew's document is anything but obvious, and its message must sometimes be deduced, rather than simply observed. Key features of Matthew also demonstrate this conclusion motif, particularly the conditional requirements placed upon Israel, which would testify to its covenantal legitimacy. The preamble of the Mosaic legislature proposed that Israel's obedience would produce a universally distinct nation, in the following words:

> Now if you obey me fully and keep my covenant, then out of all nations you will be my treasured possession. Although the whole earth is mine, you will be for me a kingdom of priests and a holy nation. These are the words you are to speak to the Israelites (Exod 19:5–6).

The fulfillment of this conditional reward remained incomplete, as evidenced by the prophetic repetition of the offer (Mal 3:16–17). As Matthew clearly believed John was the Elijah anticipated by Malachi, it is reasonable

---

53. This is central to many Reformed traditions, as demonstrated by the confessions. See also, Hendriksen, *Matthew*, 292–3.

54. See, France, *Matthew*, 182–83.

to assume he identified Jesus as YHWH, coming to settle accounts on the covenant's last day. If Jesus had come to fulfill the covenant, the outstanding question to be addressed through the narrative would be whether Israel has fulfilled its covenantal obligations adequately enough to secure God's permanent blessing—the answer becomes plain, shortly after the Sermon.

The Israel of Jesus' day in Matthew's depiction was diametrically opposed to what was possible through covenantal fidelity; for it is inconceivable that a treasured possession could be destined for Gehenna,[55] or that the priesthood could be more devoid of "royal" priestly virtue than that depicted by Matthew, or that a nation could possibly be more impure (unholy) than the first-century Judea, which Matthew describes as being infested by unclean spirits. Matthew's depiction of Israel told the story of covenant failure; the impeachment and exile of Jesus (Israel's only righteous person) was the appalling last page of an atrocious, but consistent history.

If this was Matthew's intention, fulfillment without abrogation of the Law was not for the purpose of continued Torah, but for the purpose of wrathful termination—extracting everything that was contractually owed by the debtor (5:26, 18:34). The Law would continue to be fully binding upon Israel until the end of all things, or until its fulfillment. Jesus had come to fulfill it, and because he was doing this, the covenant could be terminated. Jesus' new Torah met the conditions of the old Torah; however, it demanded more. And this was the basis of Jesus' higher righteousness. Jesus required forgiveness of kingdom members, whereas forgiveness was not a requirement of Torah.[56] God was entitled, and indeed obligated, to demand full justice of those under Torah who refused the free offer of amnesty that Jesus made. As the narrative unfolds it becomes clear that God will not show mercy to those who will not come to Jesus for it.

## The Surreptitious References to Priesthood in the Sermon

There is no direct reference to priesthood within the Sermon; Matthew's propensity to finely nuance his material to recall Israel's history, however, suggests the possibility of a priesthood subtext at work here also. Clearly, within the Sermon, the Pharisees and teachers of the law constitute the

---

55. Gehenna was the rubbish tip of Jerusalem. "In the Synoptics Gehenna refers to the final irreversible, eschatological judgement . . ." (Scharen, "Gehenna," 470).

56. Torah required release of debts after seven years and after fifty years the release of lands and slaves. However, it also permitted the exact payment for property offenses. In this way Torah had a measure of ambiguity, but the "new righteousness" was not ambiguous.

failed and observable model. Their righteousness is not sufficient and their conduct is set in juxtaposition with the kingdom of heaven's values, for hypocrites have no reward in heaven. These scribes and Pharisees represent Jerusalem in Matthew; they are the kingdom antitypes. By using them as a foil, Matthew has indicted the whole priestly system. Apart from this, however, there are more implications for the priestly system community.

First, there are the oblique references that Matthew used to bracket the entire sermon. These commence with the references to salt and light (5:13) and conclude with the two houses (7:24). Salt is a symbol of preservation, which only has value while it remains salty—obvious enough. The disciples are being cast in this role, which clearly carries with it an admonition to remain functionally "salty" and thus take on the function of preservation. Failure to perform the function for which they were intended would result in their becoming cast out and useless.[57] Similarly, the disciples are the light of the world. A city on a hill that is illuminated cannot be hidden; neither can a light in a house fail to light the whole house. These statements are exegetically meaningful when it is understood that Jesus is speaking to the disciples as leaders and not just individuals. The corporate dimension is particularly important here.

Israel was a "people living in darkness" (4:16), which would suggest the current leadership had not provided light. If they had provided light, it could not have been hidden, and the land would not be in darkness. Absence of light within Israel testifies to a leadership without light. This analogy is drawn later in the Sermon with a slight variation: "The eye is the lamp of the body. If your eyes are good, your whole body will be full of light. But if your eyes are bad, your whole body will be full of darkness. If then the light within you is darkness, how great is that darkness!" (6:22). Again, dark eyes (eyes and lamp are synonymous in this analogy) make a dark body.[58] If the eyes are good, the whole body is good. This analogy highlights the importance of interpreting the Sermon as a community directive rather than as legislation for individuals.[59] Israel's problem is its leadership which

---

57. The salt of the Covenant may have some connection here (Lev 2:13). The kingship was promised to David in perpetuity by a covenant of salt (2 Chr 13:5), and the Levites were able to eat temple offerings into perpetuity by a covenant of salt (Num 18:19). This cryptic and barely understood covenant may be the focus of Jesus' teaching; it may also have connected the Davidic dynasty to some kind of priestly prerogative.

58. Jesus refers to the Pharisees as "blind guides." Those who follow them fall into a pit with them (15:14). So, once again, the followers' destiny is attached to the destiny of their leaders.

59. "The Sermon represents authoritative teaching entrusted to the authorized leaders, the four, against false authority and teaching and false prophecy, which are liable to judgment" (Draper, "The Genesis and Narrative," 34).

is comprised of blind guides (23:16). As it is blind, it does not welcome YHWH, but seeks to destroy him. Those under its guidance, or in its house, suffer the same fate as the leaders—the whole body is full of darkness. The converse of this is also true. If the disciples have "blessed eyes" (13:16), then the community they lead will have light. In the same way, leadership that does not preserve its people/house will be discarded and trampled upon like useless salt (Luke 21:24).[60]

The concluding analogy of the Sermon also exalts one system while denouncing another. The "two houses" are the two communities vying for God's approval. One "house" is built on sand, the other upon the rock. Without wishing to consider the full implications of the "rock" in Matthew, it is sufficient to note its importance in the commissioning of Peter and its historical significance as a place of decision and indictment in the "wilderness" years (Exod 17, Num 20).[61] By virtue of the wider context, there are two houses that will face judgment day. One house would be left desolate (23:38); the other would survive the worst testing imaginable, even Hell's gates (16:18). Jesus builds one house (the church) and the other is the work of Caiaphas/Herod.[62]

Within the analogy, the two houses must face impending calamity— an echo of the primeval flood: "the rain fell and the river rose."[63] From this devastation (AD 70), one house would survive—the house built upon the rock.[64] This will be considered at greater depth in another place; however, it is worth noting here that the emphasis of Zechariah was that Zerubbabel (not Herod) would build God's permanent house, both laying its foundation

---

60. Sinai Turan has sourced an ancient Hebrew story that connected the health of the eye with the health of the whole body. Turan, "A Neglected Rabbinic Parallel." There may be a connection here.

61. The prophet Zechariah noted the "Rock" set before Joshua the high priest. The Rock had seven eyes (a connection with divinity) and bore the "inscription"—presumably the inscription denied to Joshua that would normally be tied to his turban, which was "Holy to the LORD." This "Rock" would remove Israel's sin in a single day (Zech 3).

62. "The concluding parable of the wise and foolish people who build on the rock and sand respectively has usually been interpreted outside this context, in an individualistic way. But in the context of a struggle with false prophets/apostles, it takes on a somewhat different meaning, more akin to Paul's teaching in 1 Cor 3.9–17. The community is understood as the building laid upon sound or false foundations of teaching" (Draper, "The Genesis and Narrative," 44).

63. Matthew's Jesus would later refer to the flood to describe the coming judgment (24:37–41).

64. Concerning this parable, Wright observed: "Jesus, like some other Jewish sectarians, was inviting his hearers to join him in the establishment of the true Temple. The Jerusalem Temple was under judgment and would fall before too long" (Wright, *Victory of God*, 334).

and completing it (Zech 4:9). As Matthew relies so heavily upon Zechariah, it would be unlikely that Jesus' resolution in the narrative to "build my house"[65] would not be influenced by the ascension of Zerubbabel to take his rightful place in Joshua/Jesus, his descendant.

The overall structure of the Sermon can best be understood as an indictment of failed leadership, and instruction for what would constitute successful leadership, which necessarily has implications for the priesthood. These are not the only references. It has been noted that the great flood was set as a model for the coming judgment, and Matthew refers to coming wrath as being like the "days of Noah" (24:37). Further, Matthew's seventyfold seven as the new standard for forgiveness recalled the wrathful vengeance expressed by the first polygamist Lamech (Gen 4:24). So clearly Matthew has some antediluvian interests, which may relate to the Sermon.

One such instance has been noted concerning anger and the directive to leave the gift at the altar. As Israelites generally did not have an altar at which they may have left a gift,[66] it has been proposed that this is an indirect reference to the Cain and Abel incident.[67] If this was the intention of Matthew, the complex little pericope was intended to recall the actions of two priests, both offering sacrifices, one acceptable while the other was not. Clearly, Abel's blood was noted as a proto-Christ in the first century (Heb 12:24), and he was mentioned later in Matthew's narrative (23:35). Of particular interest to us, should Matthew be developing a priesthood displacement subtext, would be the wrath of the failed priest (Cain) against the righteous priest (Abel)—an echo of Matthew's own climactic ending.

Another possible instance of the priesthood subtext, which requires a little more speculative energy, is the lust/adultery imperative that followed. The final indictment against humanity prior to the flood was the action of the enigmatic "sons of god" toward the "daughters of men" (Gen 6:4). Although historically this episode has been interpreted as mythological,[68] some have challenged this to interpret the passage as a consistent part of the surrounding narrative.[69] These scholars have suggested that the "sons of god" were either the descendants of Seth, the holy line within which Enoch and Noah are found, or despotic kings who were the first of the divine monarchs that became a feature of ensuing royal dynasties. A feature of the "godly" line

---

65. While Greek translations have left us with ἐκκλησία, rather than "house," Shem Tov did not have "gathering" or "church," but "house of prayer."

66. Nolland acknowledges that the altar only exists in Jerusalem, but fails to remind his readers that only priests can serve at this altar. Nolland, *Gospel of Matthew*, 223.

67. Allison, *Studies in Matthew*, 65–78.

68. Westermann, *Genesis 1–11*, 74.

69. Fockner, "Reopening the Discussion"; Kline, "Divine Kingship."

was its ability to produce righteous individuals who could commune with YHWH.[70] Like Abel and Noah, they may have also offered sacrifices and thus functioned as priests.[71] The crime of these "sons of god" was first to "look upon" the daughters, that in turn led them to take any and probably every woman they chose. Their lust led to the sexual permissiveness.

In defense of this proposition, it would be something of a miscarriage of justice if humans were obliterated for the actions of non-human beings.[72] If the "sons of God" were not human, why would God have regrets about making human beings (Gen 6:3)? In this instance, there would be no human transgression, for the earthly participants in these elopements seem to be passive victims rather than active transgressors. Second, it appears that the most alarming aspect of this primitive atrocity was the indiscriminate nature of the selection. The "gods" took any women they chose, suggesting that they should have regulated and moderated their choices. If these "sons of god" are the descendants of Seth, and, therefore, the bearers of the promised deliverer that would come through the woman's offspring (Gen 3:15), they were polluting the sacred line with the daughters of Cain. Further, this community, had by their action, come to resemble the abominable Lamech (Gen 4:24), the first polygamist, known for his violence.

This ancient episode of the Torah would, no doubt, have acted as a cautionary illustration to the fledgling Hebrew community emerging out of Egypt, who was solemnly warned not to marry "outside the clan." Abraham, the highly significant Hebrew priest, was particularly attentive to have his offspring marry in-house (Gen 24:3). So this concept does have some broad cultural application in that ancient society.

The identity of the "sons of God" from the wider Hebrew narrative also needs some consideration. Job commences with a scene in heaven, where the "sons of God" are in some kind of court or council. The next glimpse we have of this council/court[73] was in Zechariah, where Joshua, the newly inaugurated high priest after the Exile, is the subject of a dispute (Zech 3). As in the depiction of the heavenly council in Job, Satan was present there also. Our interest, however, is the place of Joshua in this council. Joshua was told, "If you will walk in my ways and keep my requirements, then you

---

70. "... the Sethite had kept a tradition of its close and devoted relationship to God" (Coleran, "The Sons of God," 509). See also, Keil and Delitzsch, *The Pentateuch*, 129–33.

71. "In the Targum to Zechariah the verse [Zech 4:14 concerning the anointed sons] is apparently understood to refer to the beings mentioned in Genesis 6:2" (Evans, "'The two sons of oil,'" 567).

72. Fockner, "Reopening the Discussion," 438.

73. The courtroom character of the heavenly council has been observed by others. Vanderkam, "Joshua the High Priest," 554. Kee, "The Heavenly Council."

will govern my house and have charge of my courts, and I will give you a place among these standing here" (Zech 3:7). So the high priests of Israel were counted among the "sons of God" council, provided that they did not breach God's regulations.[74]

Considering the evidence overall, it appears plausible that a prediluvian priestly caste was instrumental and responsible for the prototypical divine apocalypse. In Matthew's narrative, it is also the sins of the priestly council, it would seem, which caused the demise of Jerusalem and the Mosaic covenant. No definitive claim can be made concerning the lust/adultery pericope; however, in the light of the wrath/murder pericope, this proposition may have some relevance.

## The Ultimate Indictment

Our last consideration of the Sermon will be the verse that seems not to fit—"Do not give dogs what is sacred; do not throw your pearls to pigs. If you do, they may trample them under their feet, and then turn and tear you to pieces" (7:6). Hagner considers that this verse "appears to be a detached independent logion apparently unrelated to the preceding (*pace* Guelich, *Sermon*; Davies-Allison) or following context, inserted here for no special reason but only as another saying of Jesus."[75] Within a narrative reading, however, this verse may take on significant meaning. It even has an immediate context, which is not so difficult to discern.

The three proverb-like wisdom sayings in this section build upon each other as a prelude to Matthew's significant solution to the human predicament. The first prohibition was on judgment, not for the intrinsic reason that it is wrong to judge, but because the judge writes his own judicial boundary (7:1-2). Later in the narrative, this was expressed in a different way—"For by your words you will be acquitted, and by your words you will be condemned" (12:37). The lesson from this was to judge in such a way as though you yourself were in the dock—mercifully.

The second proverb is similar. A person must acknowledge the serious impediment in his own eye, before seeking to remove splinters from the eyes of others (7:3). Once again this is a call to self-critique. Having learned the dire consequence of judging from an inferior personal standing and being prepared to assess soberly the significant personal shortcoming that

---

74. It is interesting to note that Zechariah was a theological treatise in visions for the restoration of the community, which had been previously condemned under the Deuteronomic provision. Petersen, "Zechariah's Visions."

75. Hagner, *Matthew 1-13*, 171.

renders one incapable of being a benefactor to others, a person is prepared to understand Jesus' "way of life." But there is still the third proverb, which places a caveat upon the one who distributes the gift/pearls.

The disciples would have the privilege of dispensing heaven's bounty, in the form of a gift. However, they should not cast the pearls before the ones who freely judge others while obviously being morally oblivious (with planks in their own eye). The disciples are told to ask, seek and knock, for God is generous and will give to you what you do not deserve and cannot earn. However, those who avail themselves of this invitation must understand their desperation and inability to attain what the Father is willing to give. The ones who receive must be humble. They must know that they have no credibility to judge and they must have their visual impairment removed; in effect, the gift was for sinners, not the righteous—the sick, not the well.

According to this scheme, the dogs and swine (terms which constituted a great insult in the ancient world)[76] are not Gentiles or outcasts, but those who consider that they are worthy or righteous. This notion reappeared later in the narrative in the words, "I tell you the truth, unless you change and become like little children, you will never enter the kingdom of heaven" (18:3). Therefore, do not offer to the proud/righteous the pearl of grace, for they will not value it.[77]

Like so much in this sermon, the mysterious saying is gradually clarified within the wider narrative. By the end of the story, it becomes clear that Jesus' proverb is fulfilled as part of the indictment/conflict narrative. As the significant treasure/pearl of the kingdom is Jesus (for this is what the prophets and the righteous longed to hear and see, 13:17), the disclosure of his identity must invariably be the essence of this prohibition to "not cast your pearls." While Jesus' identity became plain to the disciples midway through the narrative, Jesus' opponents in Jerusalem were left to make their own conclusions. This tension was finally resolved at the dramatic highpoint of Matthew's story, when Jesus condemned Caiaphas and Caiaphas condemned Jesus (26:63–65). It was at this point that Jesus was bound under oath to give the testimony that he had previously been reluctant to give: Jesus acknowledged himself to be the Christ of God. It was then that the force of the Sermon proverb found its full expression: having received the pearls of Jesus' self-disclosure, Caiaphas and his council, proceeded to turn and tear him to pieces (26:67).[78] The astute reader could observe the

---

76. McEleney, "The Unity and Theme of Matthew."

77. These, according to France, are those incapable of appreciating the gift. France, *Matthew*, 227.

78. This saying has some resonance with purity laws and what can be presented to the unclean (dogs). Holy food could only be consumed by priests; this may be

dramatic reality. It was not the abominable swine of Antiochus Epiphanes that made the temple desolate, but the unclean standing high priest—"let the reader understand" (24:15).

## Summation

This chapter has attempted to read the Sermon as an integral part of a prophetic indictment concerning the termination of the Aaronic priesthood and the national covenant of Israel, which is consistent with the proposed paradigm. The corporate character of the admonitions and instructions are consistent with the entire narrative that functions as a training manual for the leaders of the new community, and a condemnation of the existing Jerusalem establishment. It is apparent that the exacting demands of Torah are present, and even embellished to include inward attitudes. However, this should not lead the reader to infer that Jesus was advocating Torah observant Christianity as the means of admission to the kingdom; on the contrary, the narrow gate and road are accessed by request (grace), not works. Those who do the will of the Father and enter the kingdom of heaven are those who follow Jesus. The priestly subtext, though not overt, is arguably present. Therefore, the Sermon does seem to function as a declaration of what is acceptable to heaven, while implicitly and explicitly condemning Jerusalem's priestly aristocracy. Most importantly, the Sermon appears to be Jesus' mission statement, and the standard by which the reader is invited to judge the words and actions of Jesus. Will the house of Jesus stand on his words alone, or will the indomitable house of Caiaphas/Herod continue to stand by the force of incumbency, wealth and the patronage of Rome?

---

redefining, therefore, who are holy in Jesus' new economy. Sandt, "Do not give what is holy."

# 4

# John the Baptist: God's Ultimatum

> *All who hold fast to these rules, and go out and come in according to the law, and listen to the voice of the Teacher, and make confession before God, saying, "In truth we have acted wickedly, both we and our fathers, by walking contrary to the ordinances of the covenant; just and true are your judgments against us"; . . . God will make propitiation for them, and they will see his salvation, for they have trusted in his holy name.*
>
> (Zadokite Work, Qumran)[1]

NO INDIVIDUAL WAS MORE pertinent to the Gospel testimonies than John the Baptist.[2] In each Gospel, John was portrayed as the prophesied forerunner of Jesus, whose ministry was to prepare the "way of the Lord." John received various levels of treatment by the Gospels writers, and there is evidence from the first-century record that his ministry was not entirely understood, even by his own disciples (Acts 19:1–5). John's profile was such that popular opinion considered that Jesus might have been a continuation of John in some way (Matt 14:2, 16:14). No doubt, the high standing and forthright righteousness that John possessed equipped him to be a rival "Messiah"—a possibility that the Gospel writers were eager to dismiss (John 1:6–8). Jesus' own testimony concerning the prophet set him apart from all

---

1. Bruce, *Jesus and Christian Origins*, 68. The Zadokite Work was one of the Qumran documents known prior to the manuscript discoveries.

2. John "sets the context in which Jesus' work of both judgment and salvation will be carried out" (France, *Matthew*, 97).

other humans, for Matthew's Jesus declared that no one born of woman was greater than John (11:11).

For these reasons, few biblical characters have been assessed to the same extent as John. In Matthew, John is a doomsday prophet; his demeanor and declarations foreshadowed imminent judgment, which he expected the Messiah to bring. John's message was a clear warning—the coming of God's kingdom was synonymous with coming wrath (3:1–10). Jesus was the instrument of God's wrath for Israel. This was what John believed, and it was what his hearers heard. Consequently, the primary question that must be considered concerning the great prophet John is whether he had failed to understand the ministry of Jesus. Many have considered that he did not fully understand Jesus' mission. In doing so, however, they do not deal with the enormous implications of such a position; for if John himself was wrong concerning God's agenda, and he was the emissary of YHWH sent to introduce Jesus, how could any prophet be considered authoritative?[3]

This question is crucial. John believed that Jesus was bringing "bad news"; Jesus' primary message, however, was "good news" according to the general sweep of church history. Is it possible, then, to assert that Matthew's narrative was a message of "good news" for a few, while still maintaining that John did correctly understand the role of Jesus to involve condemnation for the many?

## John's Identity

Following Jesus' childhood narrative, Matthew introduced John as a character well known to his audience. He begins with the words "In those days John the Baptist came . . ." (3:1). John's introduction in Matthew, like the other Gospels, casts him as an exceptional and apocalyptic figure. His ministry was nationally known, and Jerusalem was aware of his influence. John bore the imprimatur of Isaiah, no less, and without explanation from Matthew, people confessed sins to him as a testimony to his divine mandate. The message of Jesus, "Repent for the kingdom of heaven is near," was first declared by John (3:2, 4:7); the effect of which was to demonstrate that John

---

3. In making a case that John was not a mistaken prophet, this reading has attempted to enter into Matthew's world. It is inconceivable that Matthew would have wished to present John as being a faulty prophet, as this would have fundamentally undermined his testimony about Jesus. The only significant human testimony regarding Jesus was John. He was in some way a distillation of the "Law and the Prophets." If John was deemed unreliable, and he was the greatest, then surely all other prophets would also be unreliable.

and Jesus were two witnesses of the same message.[4] John's appearance and dietary constraints[5] immediately recalled the prophet Elijah, who would be unambiguously connected to John later in the narrative. So clearly, Jesus' description of John as the greatest born of women was not faint praise, but an endorsement of the last in a great line.

John's role in Matthew was authenticated by his connection with former prophets. Luke, on the other hand, introduced John by his priestly heritage; he was the miraculous offspring of Aaron, through Zechariah and Elizabeth.[6] John had priority in Luke's account, and the recording of his birth narrative was critical to Luke's identification of him.[7] If Jesus was the eschatological destination of David in Luke, certainly, it can be argued, John was the eschatological fulfillment of Aaron in Luke.[8] By identifying the tribal and family connections of both John's parents, Luke strengthened the case of John's priestly entitlement;[9] Zechariah and Elizabeth were "righteous," and therefore causal to John's own standing before God.[10] The maturity of John's parents, the angel in the temple, the commands as to how John should be raised and the Spirit indwelling from the womb all echo some of Israel's significant characters.[11] Added to this was the connection to

---

4. There are a number of direct statements that are common to Jesus and John: "brood of vipers," the call to produce "good fruit," fruitless trees would be cut down, and grain gathered in the granary.

5. These should not be understood to be a brand of asceticism. Nolland, *Gospel of Matthew*, 139.

6. Elizabeth was also the name of Aaron's wife. Nolland, *Luke 1:1–9:20*, 26.

7. "John is not only born of priestly stock and dedicated to the service of Yahweh's house, but is associated by implication to patriarchal and prophetic figures of Israel's past" (Fitzmyer, *The Gospel according to Luke*, 317).

8. Caiaphas was appointed by Valerius Gratus, Pilate's predecessor. His father-in-law Annas was the first appointment by a Syrian governor. Vanderkam, *From Joshua to Caiaphas*, 420. As such, it is easy to understand how the legitimacy of Caiaphas and Annas could be questioned. John may have been presented in Luke as a priest who was acceptable to God.

9. Zechariah was introduced as a functioning priest. The incense offering that he was performing was a daily task of Aaron (Exod 30:1–10). This took place at the altar, a place where only one priest could serve; it was off-limits to all other Israelites. Whoever served at the altar was doing so in Aaron's place. David divided the "sons of Aaron" into twenty-four divisions that worked on a rotation of temple duties (1 Chr 24). When a division was on duty, they were required to do what God had stipulated through Aaron (1 Chr 24:29). In Luke's account, the lot fell to Zechariah, who was given the assignment of entering the Holy Place for his priestly division.

10. Luke clearly implies that John was receiving God's word in the wilderness while Annas and Caiaphas were being overlooked in Jerusalem (Luke 3:2). This too may have contributed to Luke's portrait of John as an unofficial, but worthy priest.

11. The age of Elizabeth recalls the birth of Isaac and Samuel. Zechariah's prayer

Isaiah and Malachi through their prophetic writings, and the reappearance of Elijah as the prophet who did not die; so John represented a formidable representation of spirit-filled Old Testament imagery.

John's priestly bloodline may have been well known to Matthew's Tanach-informed audience. Yet, clearly, Matthew did not record John's natural heritage in his account. Matthew's interest in John, which was considerable, did not portray John as a direct threat to Jerusalem's high priests. Matthew's John is the embodiment of the biblical testimony—almost a living Torah. John's purpose was to introduce the wrathful Messiah he was sent to proclaim, and to purify the nation for his arrival. The latter of these two functions has specific priestly overtones, for the cleansing of the people through the Day of Atonement was intended to remove uncleanness to ensure the continued presence of YHWH.[12] John's role in cleansing the nation achieved a similar outcome, and as such, was a declaration of the divine origin of Jesus.[13]

John's human relationship to Jesus was not important to Matthew's narrative. All the Synoptics observe the connection that John had with Elijah.[14] Matthew, along with Mark, however, sought to further develop John's prophetic forebear in several ways. John's garments were described, which were strikingly similar to Elijah's (2 Kgs 1:8). Matthew's John did not have a lengthy introduction; he simply appeared on the scene abruptly—as did Elijah in 1 Kings 17. Like Elijah, John also made his home at the Jordan in Matthew's account.[15] Elijah was also supernaturally fed by ravens at the Jordan (1 Kgs 17:4), while John only ate wild food.

John was unique among the prophets, for no other prophet was spoken of by former prophets. John was anticipated for 800 years (notwithstanding

---

recalls the prayer of Hannah (1 Sam 1:17). The commands concerning the child recall Samson (Judg 13:7). Lastly, the infilling of the Holy Spirit from the womb recalled the election to prophetic ministry of Jeremiah (Jer 1:5).

12. From Israel's beginnings as a "covenant" community, correct procedure was essential to be safe from YHWH. Yahweh's presence was assured, however, Israel had to be continually vigilant not to breach covenant protocol which would result in YHWH "breaking out" against them (Exod 19:22, 24). The Day of Atonement ensured Israel's safety from YHWH. Perhaps this is a function that John performs for Israel—making them safe for the arrival of Messiah.

13. In Josephus, baptism only purified the body, while atonement cleansed the soul. Klawans, *Impurity and Sin*, 140.

14. The Gospel of John downplayed this connection even to the point of denial (John 1:21).

15. Although there were no specifics in the Gospel accounts, John may have stayed on the east side of the Jordan as Elijah did. John's gospel does state that John baptized on the "other side" (John 1:28). The effect of this was to be away from the land that was under God's wrath.

various dates for sections of Isaiah); he was to precede the Messiah as darkness precedes the dawn. The prophet, identified as Elijah by Malachi, was intended to restore the nation, in order to avert a final curse by God. Malachi's final verses are a fitting ending to the Tanach:

> Remember the law of my servant Moses, the decrees and laws I gave him at Horeb for all Israel.
>
> See, I will send you the prophet Elijah before that great and dreadful day of the LORD comes. He will turn the hearts of the fathers to their children, and the hearts of the children to their fathers; or else I will come and strike the land with a curse (Mal 4:4–6).

This appendix[16] to Malachi fittingly concludes the Law and the Prophets by commending the observation of Moses as an abiding and binding requirement, whilst upholding the dignity and force of historical prophetic indictment.[17]

This ending of the Minor Prophets anticipated two future events: the coming of Elijah and the coming of YHWH in what would be a cataclysmic conclusion to Israel's history.[18] The great prophet would prepare the way for the Lord, and call for covenantal reform. Without significant reform the nation could expect the curse (חרם)—that is, be devoted to destruction.[19] The irony of the Matthean narrative then was that John, in spite of his wrathful presentation, was the restorer of the covenant; while Jesus, in spite of his pleasing manner and good works, was the apocalyptic judge. John was presented without ambiguity in Matthew as the anticipated Elijah. His task was to make clear the function of Messiah and to herald the dreadful day of the Lord.[20]

---

16. The substance of Malachi is a dispute between YHWH and Judah with special attention to the impure priesthood. This final entreaty has been widely accepted as an editorial conclusion.

17. Smith, *Micah–Malachi*, 341.

18. Morris Faierstein has contested the view that there was a widespread expectation that Elijah would come before Messiah in the first century. Faierstein, "Why Do the Scribes Say?" In Matthew's narrative, however, it is assumed that this was the expectation.

19. Smith, *Micah–Malachi*, 340.

20. Peter Bolt has proposed that the apocalyptic passage in Mark was fulfilled at the time of Jesus' death. Bolt, *The Cross*, 92. Similarly, Jesus' death, in this reading, is considered to be the singular apocalyptic event that enacted the termination of the Covenant and its associated terrors; however, its fallout would be experienced until the dismantling of the temple. What happened to Jesus "is a microcosm of what has happened or will happen to Jesus's disciples and Israel. The messianic woes come and judgment is poured out; in the aftermath, God's people emerge protected from and

The idea of John as "Elijah" returned may present a genealogical difficulty, but also some opportunity for meaningful comparison. The possibility that John could have been in some way the reincarnation of the former prophet is contextually set aside with Elijah's appearance with Moses (17:3). The record of Elijah's earthly departure also clarifies what an Israelite should make of Elijah's return. Elijah's spirit, like his mantle, was transferable (2 Kgs 2:9). Elijah's servant, Elisha, received a double portion of whatever capacity Elijah possessed.[21] On this reckoning, the third "Elijah" would have been greater than those who went before—the very testimony of Jesus. The biblical concept of Elijah must be more than an individual prophet, but a progression of identity that improves with each successive appearance. This is not dissimilar to the identity of Jesus, who may be the last Moses (Acts 7:37) and the last David (Luke 1:32).

There are some distinct parallels between John and Elijah, apart from the obvious ones that have been observed. Elijah's nemesis was Ahab and his Gentile wife Jezebel. John, unlike Elijah, stood fearlessly before Herod and bore the scorn of his wife (14:3–8).[22] Elijah's wrath fell substantially on the priest/prophet class of the northern kingdom (1 Kgs 18). John addressed his wrath to the priestly stewards of Jerusalem (3:7). Further, as Elijah/Elisha demonstrated comparable signs to Moses,[23] we can assume that John also had authority to enforce Moses—a key aspect to understanding the post-Elijah prophetic calling: prophets were not at odds with Moses, for they were the enforcers of the Sinai covenant. The appearance of Elijah and Moses together with Jesus could only reenforce the unity between Law and Prophets.[24]

## What Kind of Prophet was John?

From the earliest biblical record, prophets were instrumental in God's dealings with humans. Enoch and Noah were prophets who, according to

---

purified by the eschatological ordeal" (Bird, *Are You the One*, 135).

21. Similarly, Joshua was the second Moses, who completed the task of deliverance and received from Moses his identity before Israel (Deut 34:9).

22. As Elijah's standing was significantly diminished by his fear of Jezebel, John becomes even more significant as not only the "new Elijah," but also the greater Elijah.

23. Elijah and Elisha non-coincidentally reenacted many significant Mosaic signs. They parted the Jordan, multiplied food (for foreigners), purified polluted (bitter) water and witnessed YHWH's passing by. Elijah also found solace at Horeb, the mountain of God where Moses met YHWH. Perhaps this testifies to the strong and intractable connection between the Law and YHWH's prophetic prosecutors.

24. France, *Matthew*, 702.

post-exilic reflection, condemned the world through their righteousness.[25] Moses, too, was a prophet. He communicated God's intentions for both Egypt and Israel. Like Moses, Samuel was instrumental in taking Israel to its zenith—both by denouncing the godless Saul and by installing the heroic King David. From David's time, prophets were court advisors, and as such, seemed subordinate to kings. Elijah was a new order of prophet. He existed outside the system he was sent to denounce. Elijah existed for the glory of YHWH at a time of extreme and ubiquitous apostasy. From Elijah to John, prophets existed as a reminder of imminent wrath to all who showed contempt for Israel's covenant to honor YHWH.

The writing prophets, both major and minor, filled a unique role: they were prophets, like Elijah, but they also fulfilled the role of divine scribe. They catalogued Israel's covenantal breaches, disclosing just grounds for YHWH's enactment of the various contractual penalties—which concluded with the "fall" into Exile. These prophets fulfilled an important role for their audience and for future worshippers of YHWH. They made it abundantly clear that Israel's decline into humiliation and destruction was not the result of international aggression or poor economic decisions; the covenant partner's demise was the result of God's destructive hand against her—she had become YHWH's intransigent enemy. Yet these prophetic writings were also seasoned with mercy and hope; YHWH's long-suffering commitment was such that any reciprocation of his devotion would be lavishly rewarded.

These two prophetic strands may be represented in the Synoptic tradition. John the Baptist is the public voice of YHWH—his messenger. Matthew, like Isaiah and other scribal prophets, may have documented what he believed to be the unfolding of the prophecy concerning the demise of Israel. In Matthew's "prophetic denunciation," however, YHWH is barely mentioned—Israel's crimes against God were apparent through its opposition toward Jesus. This sets the Gospels apart from other prophetic writings. The former prophets' persecution and misery were not the reason for YHWH's indictment against Israel; Israel was judged for its covenantal unfaithfulness. Matthew, on the other hand, seems to have recorded the crimes against Jesus as the ultimate indictable offense.

Prophetic ministry, in Hebrew narrative, was integral to God's divine disclosure; the veracity of YHWH was confirmed by the reliability of the prophets. John appeared at the very end of the Mosaic covenant era. It is questionable, therefore, in view of Matthew's Hebraic sensibilities that he would attempt to portray John as a prophet possessed with self-doubt and an exaggerated or defective eschatological message. Any doubt he expressed

---

25. Jude 1:14–15; Heb 11:7; 2 Pet 2:5–6.

should not be interpreted as impinging on Matthew's central tenet, which is that John the Baptist spoke on YHWH's behalf, according to the Scriptures. Indeed, John's appeal to Jesus for clarity should rather be interpreted as an appeal to YHWH for clarity, in the finest prophetic tradition.[26]

John's prophetic ministry in Matthew was both traditional and unique. While John encapsulated the ministry of those who went before him, his unique function was to be the herald and sign that the Lord was coming. In this way, John was the last, and consequently the greatest. It may be the case that prophetic ministry continued after John; he remained, however, the last of the covenant prophets—Israel's last chance to be adequately prepared to give YHWH the reception to which he was entitled. John was an oddity and a nostalgic throwback, and yet he was widely accepted as legitimate. Jesus' words concerning him, in Matthew's presentation, leave no doubt that Matthew wanted his readers to believe that John truly was the prophet of YHWH.

One considerable anomaly of the Synoptics, found also in John's gospel, is John the Baptist's limited prophetic ministry when it came to anointing Jesus. Samuel and Elijah/Elisha anointed kings for the leadership task. John's baptism of Jesus, while spectacular for the heavenly appearance and testimony, was nothing more than a common baptism applied to many Jews. Therefore, it should not be construed as the action of anointing. Further, no oil was used. Jesus was anointed with oil at another time, however, and this presents a prophetic anomaly: was the unnamed woman who anointed Jesus a prophet?[27]

Obscure and unnamed prophets are not altogether unknown in Israel's history.[28] And certainly there are examples of female prophets throughout the writings (Exod 15:20; Judg 4:4). The woman who anointed Jesus performed a duty that would be a critical feature of the Jesus story (26:13).[29] To be sure, there are difficulties associated with reconciling the four different accounts.[30] John identified the woman in his Gospel as Mary, the

---

26. Gen 15:2; Exod 4:1; 1 Kgs 19:10.

27. It was only the high priest who had anointing oil lavishly poured upon him. Fleming, "The Biblical Tradition," 402. The image of Aaron being doused with oil in Psalm 133 is the only comparable image that is found in the Bible to this depiction in Matthew.

28. 1 Kgs 20:35–41.

29. There is good support for the view that the woman's action was to anoint Jesus as Messiah, though this is generally understood as Messiah King. Elliott, "The Anointing of Jesus," 105; Bird, *Are You the One*, 122.

30. It is not a concern to harmonize the story for this reading, as this is only a treatment of Matthew's story; however, while not all scholars would agree, there may be a common story that all Gospel writers have drawn upon. Holst, "The One Anointing of

sister of Lazarus, who wanted to express appreciation for the return of her brother. Luke used the incident to indict the host, Simon the Leper, who did not welcome Jesus—for he "did not love much." Mark's account indicated a general disquiet concerning the "waste," but generally matched the Matthean "low-level" narrative. Matthew chose to use the basic narrative to indict the "mean-spirited" disciples alone, and possibly for good reasons. The superficial lesson from the incident was that Jesus, who would remain temporarily, needed to be honored; there would be ample opportunity to remember the poor.

This woman, unidentified in Matthew, would be remembered universally, according to Matthew's Jesus. Remembering an undisclosed person is potentially difficult, and perhaps her anonymity was a further Matthean exhortation to "give in secret" (6:4). Another possibility is that a subjective genitive is at work, which would make her action an enduring memorial of her [to Jesus], rather than to herself.[31] My preference is this latter possibility, which both may identify the woman as a prophet, and her action as a divine declaration concerning Jesus.[32]

There may be a significant subtext to this narrative, which may not have eluded an early audience that was immersed in Torah and understood the role of oil for the installation of priests.[33] Perhaps this is the reason Matthew implicates the disciples alone in the surface reading of the incident. Certainly the outcome of the incident was to expose the disciples' belief that being lavish to Jesus was a waste of money; however, this is a particular consequence of the woman's action, not the reason for the action itself. A pious Jew may have seen greater significance in this event. The offense given by the occasion was such that it led Jesus' enemies to offer a bribe to secure an invalid testimony (26:14–16).[34] The great, and yet unuttered, offense may have been that this kind of ointment[35] was never to be applied to the

---

Jesus."

31. Hagner, *Matthew 14–28*, 759.

32. Susan Miller also proposed that Jesus was anointed for kingship in Mark's gospel. Miller, "The Woman Who Anoints Jesus."

33. Matthew did not record that this took place in the company of Pharisees, although this is mentioned in Luke. Simon the Leper, however, may have been well known as a Pharisee, even to Matthew's first audience.

34. If the Law placed a curse on the one who received a bribe, how much more the one who purchased the false testimony (Deut 16:19–20; 27:2).

35. μύρον—the same word used in the LXX (Ps 132) is used without qualification in Matthew and Mark. Both John and Luke refer to the oil as nard (νάρδος); Matthew and Mark leave the composition of the oil unidentified.

body—nor was it ever to be applied to any individual other than Aaron at his divine anointing (Exod 30:31–33).

Now it is impossible to conclude that this perfumed oil was identical to the fragrant oil commissioned for the sanctification of the temple furnishings and Aaron;[36] however, an allusion to the highly crafted and costly fragrant oil may be there.[37] The best artisans using the finest materials made the oil that was commissioned for God's use, and the ointment poured upon Jesus was clearly very impressive. The disciples were concerned that it should have been used for the poor; the priests, who may have been informed by Judas concerning this event, may have had different concerns—such oil should only be poured on the high priest, God's earthly representative.[38]

An implication of this action may be that this woman was acting as a prophet who foreshadowed Jesus' death and ensured that Jesus' body remained holy, even in death. Death and uncleanness were synonymous in the Law.[39] If Jesus were truly dead and truly under the Law, then it would be difficult to explain how he could avoid the uncleanness of death. The sacred oil was reserved for those things that belong to God—the oil, in some way, made these things holy. In Jesus' case, the ointment would not have sanctified him (made him holy), but was used to confirm his pure and irreproachable status, even by the Law's standards. It appears that the anointing oil could not be poured upon "men's bodies" (any person—Exod 30:32)[40] and the command concerning Aaron was that it be poured upon his head and garments only (Exod 29:7, 21).[41] It could not be poured upon non-priests/kings. The point that is being made here is that this anointing may have been integral to the woman's declaration, which would accompany the gospel wherever it was to

---

36. The Law even forbade the production of any imitation oil. Keil and Delitzsch, *The Pentateuch*, 215.

37. The Synoptics record that the oil was transported in an alabaster jar. Stone vessels were used to transport fluids that needed to be maintained from ritual contamination. Kazen, *Jesus and Purity Halakah*, 85.

38. "A woman, with motives unknown, impulsively performs an extravagant act which inevitably suggests Jesus' messianic status: he is the anointed one" (Davies and Allison, *Matthew: A Shorter*, 464).

39. "The human corpse is the most serious source of impurity" (Kazen, *Jesus and Purity Halakah*, 4).

40. Durham, *Exodus*, 406.

41. Most scholars believe the oil was only intended for priests, and not other men. Keil and Delitzsch, *Pentateuch*, 215. However, the prohibition is directed to its use on the flesh of men, and not simply mankind. As the Law specifies that the oil be used on the garments and head of the priest only, flesh could refer to the body of the priest himself.

be told. If John the Baptist, or even one of the disciples, had carried out this action, perhaps much more importance would have been attributed to the incident. As an unnamed woman carried it out, however, the meaning and purpose of her action will remain a matter of conjecture.[42]

## Matthew's Portrayal of John

The standing of John in Judea was such that many believed him to be the Christ (Luke 3:15). The Gospel writers all faced the difficult task of portraying John as greater than anyone who went before, and yet, not to be compared with the glory attached to Jesus. Although there is no record that John made a messianic claim for himself, the case can be made that he was a contender for the honor. The emphatic demarcation between Jesus and John in the introduction to John's gospel would be most peculiar if John the Baptist was universally accepted as simply Jesus' prophet.[43] Even within the Synoptic tradition, the first suggestion as to the identity of Jesus was that he was the continuation of John, in some way (14:2, 16:14). It is also clear from the Synoptic tradition that there was some disquiet between John's disciples and Jesus' disciples.[44] The quality of any teacher would be reflected in the piety of his disciples; Jesus' disciples did not practice the asceticism expected of a deeply religious sect. "Eating and drinking" would not have been appropriate behavior at a time of impending wrath. Therefore it is reasonable to assume that John's community may have been considered holier than any other—comparable to the Pharisees, who also fasted (9:14). Jesus' lack of asceticism and the tainted company he kept suggested something altogether different to his faultfinding generation (11:18).

Matthew's account admirably walked the fine line between John's lofty standing among humans and his paltry standing next to Christ. Matthew's John was not substantial enough to carry Jesus' sandals (3:11). John was also portrayed as being doubtful concerning Jesus, after earlier definitively identifying him as the Christ.[45] Jesus was never portrayed as double-minded. The most conclusive proof, however, that John was not the Christ was

---

42. One commentator did speculate concerning this incident: "The woman had in effect anointed Jesus' body for burial. This was certainly not her intent" (Hagner, *Matthew 14–28*, 758). How anybody can be certain as to the woman's personal intention is unknown.

43. Beasley-Murray, *John*, 12.

44. Matt 9:14; There is even the suggestion of some competitiveness concerning numbers (John 4:1).

45. The disciples are also portrayed this way, even after the resurrection (28:17).

the severing of his head (14:11).⁴⁶ The Messiah was God's righteous one; God will not allow the bones of a righteous man to be broken.⁴⁷ It is also noteworthy that John's disciples buried the body of John, thus confirming to them his decapitation. This grotesque ending to John's life also signaled the end of Elijah's ministry—confirming that there was no more to come. Elijah's first "appearance" did not leave the earth by normal means; he was transported in the heavenly chariot (2 Kgs 2:11). Elisha, though dead and buried, still managed to exercise a forceful ministry from the grave—even raising the dead (2 Kgs 13:20–21). John, it seems, was the conclusion of this enigmatic and prophetic dynasty.

The only direct encounter between John and Jesus is also instrumental to Matthew's messianic revelation. On this occasion there were three witnesses: John, Jesus and the heavenly voice. John was reluctant to baptize Jesus, who, under normal circumstances, would have baptized the lesser (3:14). Therefore, John presented himself to be baptized by Jesus. Apart from any previous prophetic identification of John's role as subordinate to Jesus, this of itself revealed Matthew's view of the lesser and greater. Even more relevant, however, was the role of confession in Matthew's paradigm.

People came to John for baptism, understanding the necessity of confessing their sins (3:6). When Jesus appeared, however, John confessed his own inadequacy "I am not worthy." John, rather than hear Jesus' confession, confessed Jesus' glory. Jesus was both extolled by John, and declared by heaven to be both the Son and eminently pleasing (3:17). From this point, in Matthew's narrative, confession of sin was not the means to attain a righteous or "blessed" standing before God; it was, rather, attained by agreeing with the heavenly testimony that Jesus was the Son of God.

Concerning the rite of baptism, as it applied to Jesus, Matthew's John submitted to the greater revelation of Jesus. Jesus revealed that it was in fact righteous for the baptism to proceed. Therefore, it was not a disputable point, but a divine imperative. God required that Jesus submit to John as God's emissary. While John had the imprimatur of God, it was his time to represent God.⁴⁸ For this reason, Matthew's John was incarcerated immediately before the commencement of Jesus' ministry. The seamless baton

---

46. Not coincidentally, perhaps, the death of Eli (another descendant of Aaron), by the breaking of his neck, was symbolic of the theocratic death of Israel—the glory had departed (1 Sam 4:21). The high priestly line had ended and the ark had been captured.

47. "A righteous man may have many troubles, but the LORD delivers him from them all; he protects all his bones, not one of them will be broken" (Ps 34:19–20).

48. Nolland believes that John interpreted the arrival of Jesus as the end of his ministry of baptising, as Jesus was to be a baptizer after him. Nolland, *Gospel of Matthew*, 153.

change from John to Jesus is reminiscent of Moses/Joshua, David/Solomon and Elijah/Elisha.

John's standing in Scripture is second to Christ alone. Jesus' confession concerning John, that the least in the kingdom is greater than he, should be understood within the totality of Matthew's paradigm for greatness. The greatest in the kingdom must become "the least" or the servant of all (20:26–27, 23:12); John is therefore not inferior to every Christian, but to Christ alone.[49]

## John's Message

John's message in Matthew is not heavily contested—he embodied the message that judgment was as imminent as a swinging axe at the root of a tree (3:10). Of interest to us is that John's message was subsumed under the same heading as Jesus' message—the kingdom of heaven (3:2). As mentioned earlier, both John's and Jesus' ministries were introduced with the call of repentance in view of the impending "kingdom." As the wrath of God was inextricably linked in John's message to the arrival of the kingdom of heaven, it may be necessary to understand the "kingdom" as less than benign or simply "good news." John appeared to be the heavenly gatekeeper; he did not ensure either admission to or safety from this "kingdom" to anyone, but he certainly denied the possibility of admission to some (3:7). Matthew's kingdom of heaven may have been intended to have parallels to a Babylonian or Assyrian invasion, for none could doubt its violent nature (11:12); certainly some could prosper from a radical changing of the guard, but most incumbents and citizens would have been wise to heed the message of impending disruption and destruction.

From a covenantal standpoint, John's most alarming revelation was that natural connection to the Patriarchs was worthless (3:9).[50] There was a widespread first-century view that Israel was a "faith community" who had Torah for guidance rather than as a binding regulation. The assurance that came as a result of one's direct connection to Abraham meant that many Jews believed that YHWH was inclined to dismiss the offenses of Israel. So Ed Sanders is correct in his observation that Jews believed themselves

---

49. Benedict Viviano argues that Dan 4:14 has bearing on John's position in relationship to Jesus. Therefore, God chooses to set over the kingdom of mortals the lowliest of humans. By implication, John is the greatest born of women, and will not be Lord. Nolland, *Gospel of Matthew*, 153.

50. This was also a challenge in John's gospel, made by Jesus (John 8:39). Israel would not be immune from judgment as a consequence of its Abrahamic connection. France, *Matthew*, 144.

to be a faith community that did not rely on the Law for its good standing with God.[51] However, Matthew's John was intent on dismissing the widely accepted soteriological perspective within second temple Judaism that Jews had entitlement because of their forebear Abraham or their possession of Torah. Judgment, in Matthew, was based on conduct alone; the Torah was not simply a set of guiding principles but binding law. In Matthew's unfolding narrative, the only exception to this "works" paradigm was for those who professed faith in Jesus.

The denial of the ritual cleansing of baptism to Pharisees and Sadducees meant that another frightening eschatological reality loomed on Judea's horizon. Even the temple stewards and Torah devotees were ruled ineligible by their conduct—a standard that was probably unsurpassed in Israel's history for its determination to fully subscribe to the *yod* and *tittle* of Moses. John's community was not the only religious sect that believed that the Jerusalem community was under indictment; however, reform movements (e.g., Zealots and Essenes) considered the established religious leadership in Jerusalem to be illegitimate—a contention denied in Matthew's indictment passage (23:2).[52] This being the case, Israel was effectively left rudderless in the face of its impending doom. Without covenantal favoritism or "acceptable" leadership, their only hope was to follow John's directive and honor the "one" who would follow him.

## John's Particular Role in Matthew's Narrative

Matthew plainly believed that John represented the terminus of the Law and the Prophets. This was established in his narrative through a series of statements by Jesus. Jesus confirmed that the teachers of the law were correct; the end could not come until Elijah had made an appearance (17:10–12). This, according to Jesus, had taken place, and the teachers had failed to comprehend (or believe) it. Matthew is determined not to let this point slip by unnoticed; the John/Elijah connection is made three times in Matthew.[53]

---

51. Sanders, *Paul and Palestinian Judaism*.

52. John, though bearing some similarities to them, should not be classified as a member of the Qumran community; "John the Baptist and the Essenes were strong competitors" (Stegemann, *The Library of Qumran*, 222).

53. The description of John's resemblance to Elijah is unique to Matthew and Mark (Matt 3:4, Mark 1:6). The post-transfiguration dialogue is also only found in Matthew and Mark (Matt 17:12; Mark 9:12). Luke's only specific connection between Elijah and John is in Gabriel's announcement to Zechariah—that he will come "in the spirit and power of Elijah" (Luke 1:17). Matthew makes the additional statement—"And if you are willing to accept it, he is the Elijah who was to come" (Matt 11:14). By stating that

This connection is further underwritten by Jesus' explicit assessment of John, "For all the Prophets and the Law prophesied until John" (11:13).[54] If nothing else, John represented, in Matthew's account, the conclusion to the existing Hebrew narrative.

As the terminus of Israel's narrative, all that remained was the settling of accounts—a significant theme of Jesus' teaching. John was the last teacher to show the way of righteousness (21:32); therefore, he was effectively the last chance on offer for restoration, and this was the ultimate function of Elijah before Judgment Day (17:11; Mal 4:6). John's lifeline, then, was to call people to recognize the Messiah/Lord, who had come to hold the nation to account. The complexity of Christ, according to this assessment, was that he had come to judge, and that in this role he would offer mercy to anyone who requested it. This is a key to Matthean soteriology found in the Sermon on the Mount, which is demonstrated throughout the narrative. Most Israelites asked for healing and signs; few asked for mercy. It is impossible, therefore, to have a one-dimensional view of Matthew's means of "justification." The Law bound every Israelite, and each one would be judged by the contents of their hearts (5:21–30); therefore, all were destined to Gehenna.[55] God too was bound; as the irreproachable covenant partner, his unrelenting commitment to show mercy was his prerogative, and this he delighted to do for all who asked (9:13, 12:7).

John's role was also as a covenant herald. Matthew's John fulfilled the moral obligation to warn of impending doom, a prime prerequisite to Hebrew indictment narrative. The prophet's role in Israel's story was to warn, for the purpose of repentance, and to condemn in the absence of it. There were various incidents when calamity was averted, and times when it was not. Although the Law made no demand upon God to warn transgressors of covenant failure, he did so, nonetheless, through his prophets. Thus, prophetic warning was the act of a judge who looked for a way to show mercy. Ezekiel, the prophet/priest, was specifically assigned to the "watchman task" (Ezek 3:17; 32:3–9). In this case, Ezekiel was held responsible for the blood of anyone he did not warn. On the other hand, those who had been warned had no excuse; they were responsible for their own blood. The prophetic herald was, therefore, an indictment instrument. Once warned, an Israelite was

---

"Elijah comes and restores all things," Matthew has made an unmistakable connection to Mal 4:6.

54. By reversing the natural order of Law and the Prophets Matthew was able to connect John to the pre-Mosaic history—a point that would have implications in the final indictment (23:35).

55. Matthew's understanding of punishment is that it takes place subsequent to the Day of Judgment and not before. Milikowsky, "Which Gehenna," 243.

completely culpable. The ownership of responsibility for the brutal "cutting off" of Christ by the single voice of the nation echoes Ezekiel's watchman responsibility (27:25). Matthew's account clearly portrayed John as an effective and successful herald, who testified in the wilderness and was known in the highest places. His profile and clear message left Israel without excuse; no one could claim that they were uninformed that Jesus was the Messiah.[56]

In the Synoptic traditions, John should not simply be cast as a prophet, even the final one. As mentioned earlier, John was an echo of Israel's covenantal narrative. Commencing in the wilderness (Sinai) and baptizing at the Jordan (a symbol for sea crossing—1 Cor 10:2), through to Elijah and then referred to by Isaiah and Malachi, John was surely the embodiment of all that went before. Rejection of John cannot be understood as the rejection of a single prophet, but as rejection of the whole of the Law and the Prophets. What Judea did to John was representative of the indictable behavior of all the generations that went before. Judea was the courtroom, and John was God's exhibit A. A nation that rejected God's word through John would certainly also reject the Lord that John represented.

Within this courtroom paradigm, John, along with Jesus, became instrumental in the escalating indictment against Israel. First, even though the narrative depicts John's decapitation as being the result of Herod's familial machinations (14:3–11), Jesus had no hesitation to lay John's death at the feet of Judea's Mosaic stewards in Matthew's account (17:12). How Matthew's Jesus came to this conclusion was not explained.[57] What is clear, however, is that John's death was a precursor to Jesus' death—the same injustice by the same people who got the gruesome result they wanted. Even though the other Synoptic Gospels do not implicate Jerusalem's leadership directly in John's death, it clearly served the purpose of Matthew to do so.[58] Matthew's Jesus laid John's blood to the account of the teachers of the law (17:12).

Matthew's reproach of the leadership did not leave the ordinary Judean guiltless. Again Jesus was the prosecutor of the indictment, and it directly related to the reception that Jesus and his prophet received. Jesus' parables often began with the comparison: "the kingdom of heaven is like . . ." It was

---

56. Though not specifically pertinent here, Christ also went to "all the towns and villages" preaching the kingdom (9:35). At this time the disciples were commissioned to do the same (10:5).

57. Making Jerusalem guilty of John's blood fits a pattern in Matthew. Later in the narrative Judas and Pilate would also seek to distance themselves from Jesus' execution. The net effect of all this is that Jerusalem alone would ultimately be held responsible for the crimes against Jesus in Matthew.

58. Interestingly, Acts 5:28 recorded the Sanhedrin distancing itself from the events that led to Jesus' death.

appropriate then for Jesus to also explain the "kingdom of Israel." The comparison was not flattering; "this generation" was like name-calling children that expected heaven's holy representatives to fit in with their meaningless religious parody (11:16–19). Rather than follow the lead of the spectacularly effective new "christs," they were disappointed by the unwillingness of Jesus and John to conform to their infantile expectations. This bungling Hebrew generation could not perceive the enormity of the occasion, or the implications that would flow from its own folly. Its response to the austere warning and impending calamity was to use derogatory caricatures to ridicule the ones who were their only hope. This generation's spiritual ineptitude did not lead to a willingness to be judged, but a renewed confidence in its ability to judge God's emissaries.[59] With the rejection of John and Jesus, all that was left to do was invoke the curses/woes (11:21, Mal 4:6). Matthew left his readers no doubt that Jesus' audience would not be judged like children, even if they chose to act like them. Sodom was less culpable than the northern towns (11:22), and Jesus and John would be vindicated by their wise conduct and speech (11:19b).

John's primary function within Matthew is the essence of his identity. As "the Baptist," John's preaching ministry, confessor function and water baptism all took place at the Jordan, and probably simultaneously. The strong priestly implications of John's ministry have already been alluded to; however, a clear understanding of John's baptism remains elusive. Any connection with post-resurrection baptism should be all but dismissed. John baptized many people who did not profess faith in Christ—some of the disciples for instance, according to John's gospel (John 1:35–37). Those who were baptized confessed sins, in Matthew's account, but there is no assurance that John was issuing pardons on the basis of the declarations. Certainly cleansing and consecration were necessary before any meeting with God (Exod 19:10), and perhaps this is how John's baptism is best understood. He was preparing the people to meet Messiah.

The role that John's baptism performed at the Jordan could possibly also be understood by the contrasting greater baptism that Jesus would administer. Jesus' baptism would use the media of the Holy Spirit and fire. Apart from the obvious contrast between water and fire, and the vast disparity between ubiquitous water and the Divine Spirit, John's baptism may be even harder to understand. Clearly, what John did was both ordinary and benign compared to the apocalyptic baptism that Jesus would bring. The meaning of Holy Spirit and fire can be readily discerned from the statement's context: Jesus would separate the good from bad, the wheat from the

---

59. See Cotter, "The Parable of the Children," 295–304.

chaff (3:12). One is made fit for God's barn (the kingdom of heaven) and the other is fit for unquenchable wrath—the Messiah's winnowing fork is in his hand (imminence) and he is ready to sort out the harvest (judgment).[60]

On this assessment, Jesus' baptism appointed individuals to their permanent destiny: either immersion into heaven's kingdom (God's eschatological reward of holiness from the Spirit) or the apocalyptic flames. Whatever John's baptism was, it certainly could not have had the permanent efficacy of Jesus' baptism—at least not in Matthew. Luke's identification of first-century Palestine emphasized that the people were "living in darkness and in the shadow of death" (Luke 1:79). This is also implied in Matthew (4:16). The default condition of the people was therefore one of hopelessness and morbid anticipation. John brought hope and his baptism should be interpreted as some kind of fresh start, representing a new beginning for those who received it. Without inward transformation provided by the Holy Spirit baptism, however, the Israelites were destined to be mindful of their need and yet remain untransformed. This is implicit in the Matthean text; John pointed to the greater "baptizer" who would bring a significantly greater baptism. John's baptism was not, therefore, anything more than the gateway to the permanent baptism. For these reasons, John's baptism cannot be understood as a new covenant rite, but as some kind of renewed commitment to covenant observance; the like of which had been undertaken at Moab (Deut 1:5), under Josiah (2 Chr 34:31) and under Ezra (Neh 8–10), with little long-term benefit. Luke's John baptized for the forgiveness of sins (Luke 1:77; 3:2); Matthew's John only heard sins confessed (3:6). There is no sense that John functioned as a priestly absolver of sin in Matthew.[61]

## John's Confusion

Jesus' endorsement and affirmation of John's ministry followed the prophet's prison question (11:7–15). John appeared to be confused over a matter of which he was formerly emphatically certain. It is this part of the narrative

---

60. The Greater Isaiah Qumran scroll had two Xs beside this Isa 41:8–16 reference, which Matthew attributes to John concerning Christ's ministry. "The large X in the left margin is connected to the page at the right and denotes to the editor an important passage which he wanted to highlight" (Miller, *Q—The Great Isaiah Scroll*, 16). If this is so, the apocalyptic message that Matthew attributed to John was certainly of interest to the Qumran community. They anticipated the Lord's appearance as a "thresher" and separator.

61. "For Matthew, forgiveness of sins only comes through the sacrificial death of Christ," Meier, "John the Baptist," 388. See also Pamment, "The Kingdom of Heaven," 212.

that has raised questions concerning John's "misunderstanding," and the apparent correction by Jesus. On the face of it, Jesus' response to John gave every indication that Jesus was bringing unparalleled blessing to Israel; the blind see, the deaf hear, the dead are raised, and the gospel is proclaimed. What is immediately apparent for modern readers is a conflict of understanding. John clearly enunciated that Jesus came to settle accounts and be the wrath-bearer of God. Jesus' assessment of his own ministry, it would seem by his response, was quite the opposite.[62]

Reconciling Jesus' ministry with John's anticipation is a tremendous challenge. If John had overstated Jesus' wrathful mission, then it would have implications for how Matthew's account should be interpreted. There is no doubt as to what John expected; therefore, Matthew 11 casts some doubt on John's reliability. Within the pericope, however, Jesus' affirmation of John would seem to be a contradiction. If no greater person than John existed, and he had got the message wrong, then surely every prophet's writings or declarations must be viewed with some cynicism. This, according to Mosaic legislation, would be problematic for Matthew's readers. Moses is emphatic at this point:

> If anyone does not listen to my words that the prophet speaks in my name, I myself will call him to account. But a prophet who presumes to speak in my name anything I have not commanded him to say, or a prophet who speaks in the name of other gods, must be put to death. You may say to yourselves, "How can we know when a message has not been spoken by the LORD?" If what a prophet proclaims in the name of the LORD does not take place or come true, that is a message the LORD has not spoken. That prophet has spoken presumptuously. Do not be afraid of him (Deut 18:19–22).

This legal requirement, which would certainly have been well known by the critics of Jesus and John, would essentially tell the Judean audience to ignore everything John had said. If we interpret Jesus' response to John as a corrective, then we must also conclude that Jesus was exposing John's prophetic inadequacy. This would be a direct contradiction of Jesus' affirmation of him. The legal safeguard placed upon a prophet to protect Israel was the "fulfillment" test. Such a provision enabled Israelites to make judgments concerning which prophets had divine endorsement. There is nothing in Jesus' statement

---

62. The following is representative: "There is in Jesus' concluding words, however, an indirect admission that not everything will work out in accord with John's expectations. If Jesus is the Messiah, he is not the kind of Messiah awaited by John and the populace at large" (Hagner, *Matthew 1–13*, 301).

about John that suggested that John had failed; therefore, another approach must be taken to understand John's "confusion" and Jesus' response.

The key to understanding Jesus' message to John is to be found in the context of the passages quoted by Jesus. John's question, if we may read between the lines, was: Where is the wrath? Jesus, in response, partially quoted Isa 35:5–6 and Isa 61:1. The slightly wider context of each of these passages casts light on the response. Isa 35:3–6 reads:

> Strengthen the feeble hands, steady the knees that give way; say to those with fearful hearts, "Be strong, do not fear; your God will come, he will come with vengeance; with divine retribution he will come to save you." Then will the eyes of the blind be opened and the ears of the deaf unstopped. Then will the lame leap like a deer, and the mute tongue shout for joy. Water will gush forth in the wilderness and streams in the desert. The burning sand will become a pool, the thirsty ground bubbling springs. In the haunts where jackals once lay, grass and reeds and papyrus will grow. And a highway will be there; it will be called the Way of Holiness. The unclean will not journey on it; it will be for those who walk in that Way; wicked fools will not go about on it.

This passage both answered John's question more fully and gave him some personal comfort at a particularly needy time. John appeared to be giving way, and these verses were both the particular response to John's question and a pastoral comfort. By applying this passage to John at this time, Jesus revealed himself to be John's teacher and shepherd. John was at his weakest point, and the Scripture was intended to strengthen his weak knees and fearful heart with fuller information.

The message of Isaiah's prophecy was that divine retribution, and the "opening of eyes and ears," were inseparable and simultaneous, and, therefore, not contradictory. God's wrath was premised on his acts of kindness. Israel's citizens widely benefited from Christ's heavenly bounty, which in the Matthean paradigm made the nation's rejection of Christ less justifiable and more contemptible (11:21–24). With the understanding that the wider context of Isaiah 35 brings, John would have taken solace that Jesus was still on his wrathful mission. Its obscurity was consistent with the "hidden from them" motif, which had also veiled John's eyes, albeit temporarily.

The second referent passage, Isaiah 61:1–3, bears the same message,

> The Spirit of the Sovereign LORD is on me, because the LORD has anointed me to preach good news to the poor. He has sent me to bind up the broken-hearted, to proclaim freedom for the

> captives and release from darkness for the prisoners, to proclaim the year of YHWH's favor and the day of vengeance of our God, to comfort all who mourn, and provide for those who grieve in Zion—to bestow on them a crown of beauty instead of ashes, the oil of gladness instead of mourning, and a garment of praise instead of a spirit of despair. They will be called oaks of righteousness, a planting of the LORD, for the display of his splendor.

Once again the passage assures John that his grief has been noted and will be reversed with the promised compensations. Most pertinent, however, is the fact that the day of the Lord's favor and the day of his vengeance are together the comfort of those who mourn. The activity of blessing and cursing are intuitively antithetical and inconsistent, yet they occur simultaneously in a peculiar symbiotic relationship. This perfectly fits Matthew's objectives. In the one document are both the blessed (Peter and his ilk), and the cursed (Jerusalem's establishment and those who follow their path to Gehenna). The prevailing consensus may be mistaken to believe that Jesus had two missions separated by millennia.[63] The wonders on display in Judea cannot be distanced from the wrath that fell upon that generation. John was correct according to this analysis; he had, however, failed to understand the strategic importance of the Messiah's kindness as a precursor to judgment.[64]

In order to substantiate this contention that John understood the import of the wider prophetic contexts, some objections must be anticipated. Could John in his prison cell have known the wider context of the Scriptures Jesus quoted and believed them to be relevant (according to Matthew's depiction)? If so, can a case be made that verses quoted in the New Testament were intended to be understood in their wider contextual significance?

Concerning what Matthew's readers could have expected of John's biblical literacy and his intimacy with prophetic writing, there is no doubt that Matthew's John was depicted as being fully immersed in the literature to which Matthew's Jesus referred. If we consider Luke's John there is ample reason to believe that the prophet had access to Scripture and the opportunity, if not the obligation, to have major prophetic thought imbedded in his memory. As the first son of Zechariah, according to Luke, John would have studied Torah as an integral part of his education. John was a plausible priest in Luke's account. The Synoptic Gospels do not reveal a priestly culture that is unaware of the minutiae of the Law and the Prophets or their importance;

---

63. See Nolland, *Gospel of Matthew*, 452; Hendriksen, *Matthew*, 484.

64. Hagner acknowledges the judgment motif found in the Isaiah references of Jesus; however, he considered that the judgment was not applicable, because Jesus did not mention it. Hagner, *Matthew 1–13*, 301. Hagner, therefore, would not believe that importing the context of these passages is integral to their meaning.

quite the contrary—if anything the community of priests appears to have over-studied Torah (23:23).⁶⁵ As a "righteous" priest, who understood the particular importance of his child to Israel's story, it is inconceivable that Zechariah would not have taught John to meditate on the Law day and night or bind it upon his heart (Deut 11:18–19). Further to this, John was not just an interested observer of the prophetic texts; they were texts that testified about him. Isaiah's testimony about John (Isa 40:3–4) has a natural connectedness to the passages that Jesus quoted in his response. They were speaking about the events of John's day, and he was aware of the eschatological moment in which he ministered (3:1–3).

A major theme of Matthew is that the Jesus story fulfilled what had been written in the Law and the Prophets (5:17). In view of this, it would be most peculiar for Matthew to use the Scriptures in a way that was unrelated to their original context. Isolated verses or portions of them, as in this case, could be used to prove almost anything. Matthew left little doubt that the metanarrative found in Israel's sacred texts had meaning, and, of necessity, had to be applied correctly. Formerly, modern biblical interpreters rarely considered the context of verses quoted in the New Testament. It seemed to be implicit within biblical scholarship that New Testament authors simply cobbled documents together and used Scriptures for the purpose of proof texting. Fortunately, this view is being replaced with a considerably more flattering view of the apostolic community. Scholars are now prepared to consider that the events surrounding the Jesus event explained and clarified the context of the earlier Scriptures.

As a first-century scribe, Matthew's most critical audience was likely to come from the γραμματεῖς—the teachers of the law. Consequently, Matthew would have been aware of the contemporary methods of exposition necessary to make a relevant point. An author that recorded the importance of every *yod* and *tittle* is unlikely to be contextually cavalier. Matthew expected his hearers to know and investigate the Scriptures he incorporated.⁶⁶ He does not rob Isaiah of its context, but assumes the readers' knowledge of it. As noted earlier, this was the normal practice for New Testament writers in citing sections of the Old Testament, particularly Major and Minor Prophets and the Psalms.⁶⁷

Another approach to John's misgiving concerning Jesus' conduct is to attribute the prophet's confusion to a failure to understand God's timetable.

---

65. E. P. Sanders believed that the majority of scribes were priests. Sanders, *Judaism*, 177.

66. It may be relevant that Luke implicitly encouraged his readers by the Berean example (Acts 17:11).

67. Dodd, *According to the Scriptures*, 126. Also, Shedinger, "Must the Greek," 459.

Nobody seriously challenges the notion that both John and Jesus portrayed the Christ's ministry as including violent eschatological judgment, distasteful though it may be to some.[68] Jesus' eternal redemptive program, however, is plainly uncontroversial. Most theologians with a high view of Scripture are loathe to state that John's message was mistaken, though, as mentioned earlier, there is little reluctance to observe his failure to understand the thousand-plus years between Christ's roles. However, if it is accepted that John got the timing of Jesus' wrath wrong, it must also be accepted that Jesus misunderstood the timing of his wrath. Jesus also taught that the apocalyptic judgment was imminent for his own generation (24:34). Therefore it is appropriate to conclude that Matthew's position on this is both plain and verifiable.

Matthew's document routinely referred to the coming judgment,[69] so much so that it has raised the specter, for some, that Matthew was obsessively vindictive.[70] With the many references to Judgment Day, which would both bless the righteous and damn the wicked, there is no suggestion that judgment would be delayed by, or separated from, the day of blessing and reward. And this is perhaps the crux of the issue concerning how Matthew has been interpreted; historically, few have been prepared to consider the possibility that Matthew believed his document to be the final chapter of God's exclusive covenant with the natural seed of Abraham and Jacob. Although it is plain to everyone that AD 70 was a cataclysmic event that terminated both the priestly line and the temple, many have been reluctant to accept that it was Israel's Judgment Day.[71] On a prima facie reading of Matthew, Matthew portrayed John's eschatological vision as identical to that of Jesus; judgment and reward were imminent for the covenant community.

## Summation

John the Baptist gets more exposure in Matthew's account than in any other Gospel. Understanding Matthew's John is imperative in any discussion of Matthew's objective in writing the document. The great standing of John is meaningful to Matthew for the purpose of clarifying Jesus' cosmological

---

68. Neville, "Toward a Teleology of Peace," 157.

69. Matthew's acute interest in the final judgment has resulted in it being classified as apocalyptic literature. See Sim, *Apocalyptic Eschatology*; Balabanski, *Eschatology*, 139.

70. Sim, *Apocalyptic Eschatology*, 246.

71. The Essenes had interpreted Daniel's prophecy to predict the end of the Roman Empire in AD 70. Stegemann, *The Library of Qumran*, 133. This, however, was their third attempt at pinpointing the Last Day. Conceding that they did get this date right, their message was still substantially wrong; for they anticipated the establishment of national Israel along with Gentile/Roman judgment.

significance. John was foretold by prophets as the great prophet (even the last "Elijah"). John resembled a living Torah. Like the Law and the Prophets before him, John's task was to prepare the nation for the Christ, to instruct Israel about his divine mandate and introduce the Lord to the nation. These functions were performed with the public approbation of his Lord. Though in appearance John was a caricature of ancient prophets, Matthew demands he be accepted as authentic and authoritative; therefore, his message was central to the totality of Matthew's eschatology.

John's message in Matthew is without dispute. He declared that the wrath of the "Anointed One" was imminent and palpable. The passion and urgency of John's message was underscored by his ruthless abandonment of privilege and comfort. The "repent or perish" declarations of John were not discredited or discarded by Jesus; indeed, Jesus' rhetoric was, if anything, more pointedly violent and urgent. John declared that Jesus would baptize with fire (a euphemism for destruction) and Jesus confirmed that the Son of Man would administer this judgment (13:40–41).

The only doubt cast over John's credibility has resulted from a one-dimensional interpretation of his question to Jesus and the answer he received. Truly Elijah did come, before the end, according to Matthew's Jesus. And it would require a considerable explanation to enlighten twenty-first century interested parties how the immediate end could be taking more than 2,000 years. Certainly the credibility of Jesus and his prophet were inextricably connected, as was their identical proclamation.[72] Their message was open to Mosaic censure if their eschatological vision was not fulfilled in the time that they predicted. Without clearly understanding the role of Jesus and John to Israel's national covenant, which was a specific Matthean interest, commentators and interested parties have had to resort to a complex array of justifications, which corporately amount to nothing more than a severe case of cognitive dissonance. If Jerusalem had not fallen in AD 70, it is conceivable that Christianity would have become as obscure to us as any other first century "messianic" community. The wrath of Rome confirmed the prophet's message. Jesus survived the wrath of God in Matthew's account; Israel's covenant status, however, did not endure the wrath of the resurrected Messiah.

---

72. "Repent, for the kingdom of heaven is near" (3:2; 4:17).

# 5

# Miracles, Gentiles and Mission: The Rejection of Amnesty

> . . .[Interpreted, this concerns] the Teacher of Righteousness who [expounded the law to] his [Council] and to all who freely pledged themselves to join the elect of [God to keep the law] in the Council of the Community; who shall be saved on the Day [of judgment]
>
> (1Q14 I,5; fragmentary commentary on Micah)[1]

THE PASSAGE OF EVENTS following the Sermon (Matt 8–12) is under consideration throughout this chapter. After the Sermon, Jesus was immediately confronted with one of Israel's most intractable problems—a leper. Jesus had spoken of mercy, and of upholding the Law. So how would Jesus do both? In this circumstance, how could mercy be shown to a man who was a permanent outcast and untouchable? This practical application of the Sermon would be proof of Jesus' mandate to instruct the disciples in a higher order of righteousness. The healing of this leper would prove that Jesus' teaching came with great substance; he could give deliverance and cleansing to the lowliest of Israel. He taught with authority, unlike the teachers of the law (7:29). Matthew may well have had this healing sequence in mind with this statement.

The record of this healing, and the chapters that followed, enabled Matthew's readers to witness David's astonishing son at work, undertaking his mission of compassion to the disparate communities of the Hebrew

---

1. Vermes, *The Dead Sea Scrolls*, 278.

people.² Matthew's readers would also witness the appalling response to Jesus by those who benefited most from his ministry. We cannot examine every pericope in this varied section; we will, however, reflect on those sections most pertinent to the narrative advancement, indictment and priesthood themes. Some sections within these chapters are also examined in chapter 7, and as a result, they will receive less attention here.

## The Leper and the Priest

This pericope is of particular importance to Matthew in that it was a confrontation with Jesus, and in turn a confrontation with the high priest. This will be considered more fully in chapter 7; however, there are some profitable observations that can be drawn concerning the section's immediate context. Matthew's awareness of Levitical cleansing law heavily influenced his presentation of this event. Its primacy set the stage for a confrontation between two priestly communities.³ Jesus was tested by the approaching unclean leper, and Caiaphas would be challenged by a cleansed leper.

The throngs that were enthralled by Jesus' mountaintop address and followed him down were nowhere to be seen for fear and disdain of the leper.⁴ The Law forbade "secret" leprosy, the stricken having to declare their condition in a loud voice whenever they were near other people (Lev 13:45). The man was a perpetual hermit, and his only prospect of companionship was with similarly dislocated individuals. It took great courage and faith for the man to come to Jesus, who, at the time, was with a large crowd. His request would test Jesus' claim: would he give to him who asked (7:7), and be found by the leper who sought him? Without hesitation, Jesus granted the man's request, and was probably the first Hebrew to touch him for many years.

The leper was the first Hebrew to worship Jesus (8:2).⁵ Many Bible versions avoid translating προσεκύνει with the word "worshipped" here, in the same way that they have deemed it inappropriate for the acts of the wise

---

2. The first three healings in Matthew were of people who, "from a Jewish point of view were disadvantaged" (France, *Matthew*, 304).

3. Matthew alone presented the leper incident as the first healing. Mark (1:23–28) and Luke (4:33–37) both led with the healing of the demoniac. Demons, however, are not even mentioned in the Law, while skin diseases get what seems to be disproportionate attention (Lev 13 and 14).

4. This assertion is based on the belief that a command to remain silent would seem somehow redundant if a large crowd had witnessed the event.

5. "With the leper we are beginning to be nudged in the direction of religious worship" (Nolland, *Gospel of Matthew*, 349).

men (2:8, 11),[6] a ruler (9:18),[7] and the Syro-Phoenician woman (15:25). This is hard to account for, as Matthew's story highlights the earnestness and drama attached to the approach of these unworthy or desperate characters. According to Matthew, these people are forcing their way into the kingdom (11:12). This leper had faith, and he acted upon it. The immediate contrast was with the crowd who heard the message, and made no appeals to be healed, or more importantly, to be cleansed. Jesus' first miracle in Matthew was priestly (an act of cleansing), and sending the believing ex-leper to the priest was a testimony to him.

Jesus muted the man's testimony in Matthew, but this should not be interpreted as being a feature of the "messianic secret" motif, which is more prevalent in Mark.[8] Matthew's understanding of the Law was such that he was aware that the priest alone could declare a person clean. This declaration was more than a clinical assessment, but a restoration of covenantal standing. A Hebrew could not declare himself covenantally clean, even if he were healed. In fact, the sin attached to leprosy was not removed without considerable sin sacrifices (Lev 13–14). This was the only time that Matthew's Jesus was to issue the instruction to see the priest, which could mean either that it was implicit on all other occasions, or that this testimony was not for the ex-leper's benefit, but for the priest's.[9]

Some have objected to the testimony being particularly for the individual high priest as the word indicates a plural—it was a testimony to them (αὐτοῖς). This does not present any real difficulty, as Matthew usually presented the officiating priesthood as "the chief priests." There was only one high priest in Israel, but at certain times the duty was shared between two people.[10] Nonetheless, within Matthew's narrative it would seem probable that he intended his audience to believe that Caiaphas would be confronted, in some way, by this cleansed man. While any Jerusalem priest could declare the man clean, ultimately, this procedure was under the authority of

---

6. "The leper approaches Jesus in the same way as the Magi did (2:2, 8, 11)" (Harrington, *Matthew*, 112).

7. Matthew avoided identification of this ruler, who was probably the synagogue ruler, Jairus, identified in Mark 5:22. Matthew may have attempted to obscure the identity of this man who was an Israelite who did worship Jesus.

8. Mark used this incident to explain why Jesus could not minister in the towns. This was not a priority for Matthew, who gave no suggestion of the leper's disobedience.

9. This testimony has traditionally been interpreted as a "sign of judgment," though Luz challenges this. He notes: "John Chrysostom says, 'not to improve them, nor to teach them, but . . . to accuse them, to convict them'; similarly, e.g., Euthymius Zigabenus (281) and Maldonat (1.173)" (Luz, *Matthew 8–20*, 6).

10. The priest (Aaron) or one of his sons could make the judgment concerning the leper (Lev 13:2).

Caiaphas, who alone was the priest of Israel. This being the case, it would have been a perplexing dilemma for the Jerusalem priests, who could not pronounce an individual clean without in some way acknowledging the source of his cleansing. It may also be that this was the first time that Caiaphas was confronted by the possibility that the Bethlehem child was not slaughtered by Herod (and possibly in collusion with Annas).[11] Matthew was setting the stage for a priestly conflict. Jesus' new community accepted lepers as a priority, but these were outcasts for Jerusalem;[12] therefore, two houses now existed, and their values and manner of operation were diametrically opposed to one another.[13]

## The Centurion's Indictment

Matthew's second recorded miracle (8:5–13) is noteworthy for its concluding invective against those who did not understand Jesus the way the centurion had. The healing of the centurion's son/servant[14] incident took place on the outskirts of Capernaum. Matthew's use of this event was to highlight the nobility and perceptiveness of a Roman representative as a foil to expose the wretched condition of the Israelites. This motif is easily demonstrable by comparing it to Luke's version.

Luke's account did not have the centurion approach Jesus directly; he sought to have influence via the synagogue elders (Luke 7:3). These elders entreated Jesus on the basis of the man's benevolence toward the covenant people expressed through contributions made for the synagogue. The substance of the story is the same: that is, the expression of faith, which the centurion delivered by another messenger. Luke ends by noting how exceptional the man's faith was in all of Israel. Matthew had Jesus express the same astonishment; for Matthew, however, the statement provided a springboard from which Jesus could launch a scathing indictment against Israel's leaders.

---

11. It is not necessary for Caiaphas to directly receive the leper for this to be a confrontation with him. The Law made it clear that the path to being fully restored involved a series of sacrifices that could only be performed at the temple (Lev 13). The ex-leper was a message that Jesus sent to Jerusalem. His readers would assume that Caiaphas got the message.

12. The Law set lepers and the high priest in juxtaposition. See Lev 10:6; 13:45. As Jesus' first ministry act, he accepted a leper; would he, in the course of the narrative, also accept the high priest?

13. Following the last miracle in the narrative, the resurrection, the author's attention was once again diverted to the machinations of Jerusalem. Does this help us to understand Matthew's intention?

14. παῖς can be translated either way. Hagner, *Matthew 1–13*, 201.

Perhaps this was why Matthew made no reference to any Jewish participation in the miracle. The centurion in Luke was not exceptional in his belief that Jesus could heal, but only in his faith that he had "authority" to command at a distance. Matthew's literary/theological interest in this episode was framed in such a way that no Israelite could gain a commendation as a result of it. Further, the Lukan incident would suggest that Jesus was coerced to take action by the entreaty of the upstanding Judeans. Matthew very rarely portrays Judeans as noble in his narrative, with the exception of a few outstanding characters like John and Joseph.

This story has a connection with the healing of the Syro-Phoenician's daughter (15:21–28). Jesus expressed, on that occasion, a reluctance to be helpful. There is the hint of that here also, and indeed, it makes the story clearer. Jesus' response to the centurion's request was: ἐγὼ ἐλθὼν θεραπεύσω αὐτόν, which may be translated as a question—"having come, would I heal him?"[15] This translation communicates some reservation on Jesus' part, as was appropriate considering he was on a Jewish mission. The man's insistence then, that Jesus need not come at all but just issue the command, has a distinct parallel with the Syro-Phoenician's persistent faith. In this way, these two Gentile-healing incidents revealed exceptional faith; for both believed Jesus' authority and kindness was so great that even the residue of his bounty was ample. This overt faith was the perfect foil to expose the Jerusalem "priestly" community.

While clearly the indictment of the sons of the kingdom (οἱ υἱοὶ τῆς βασιλείας—8:12), who were to be thrown into the outer darkness, would not be exclusively directed to priests, there is an inference to be made here that does specifically indict them. The first thing to note is that the centurion recognized the authority of Jesus. Matthew's drama revolves around this issue—did Jesus have lawful authority?[16] The crowds[17] recognized that Jesus taught like one who had authority, but ultimately, they backed the authority of the incumbents by calling for the release of Barabbas.[18] The incumbents themselves did not recognize Jesus' authority, as evidenced by the sharp exchange between them (21:23) and their default belief that Jesus was Beelzebub's emissary (12:24). They did not, on the other hand, question the veracity of the miracles. This centurion recognized that Jesus was "under

---

15. Hagner, *Matthew 1–13*, 204.

16. Matt 7:29; 9:6; 21:23; 28:18.

17. Warren Carter profiled the crowd in Matthew and considered them to be neutral and passive concerning Jesus, but distinctly threw their lot in with Jerusalem in the passion narrative. Carter, "The Crowds."

18. Robert Merritt has suggested that the Gospels employed Barabbas as a device to ensure the culpability of the Jews. Merritt, "Jesus, Barabbas," 66.

authority"—as would be expected of the Messiah.[19] His "great faith" was not in Jesus' ability to heal, for that is assumed in the request, but in his statement that he had authority.[20] This is a central issue within the Gospel—who has the authority to represent God on earth? The high priest may legally have had this authority, but Jesus demonstrated it, and the "outsiders" like the Magi, the leper, the centurion, and the Syro-Phoenician woman all recognized it. Jerusalem would not.

The second aspect to this harsh indictment expressed against the Hebrews may have specific implications for the priests, once the context is carefully assessed. The Gentile was a man under authority, and the manner in which he used this authority was damning of Jerusalem. He used it to make an entreaty to Jesus for the welfare of the one under his authority. This was clearly a commendable use of authority, an application that had not been considered by the priests. Even if there were doubts about Jesus, there were no doubts that he removed diseases that made Jews ceremonially unclean. Why didn't the priests, then, avail themselves of the opportunity to have their flock cleansed by Jesus—even if they could not do it themselves? The centurion was not merely commended for his faith, but also for his virtue. His faith had moved him to act wisely and compassionately for the one who was in his house. The priests, on the other hand, did not serve those who dwelt in their "house"; they did not lift a finger to remove burdens (23:4).

Jesus' declaration that the "sons" of the kingdom would be replaced by foreigners anticipated the oracle concerning the destiny of the "heirs." This Roman centurion was from the west, and Matthew had already depicted the homage of the eastern delegation (the Magi), so this statement (8:11) has clear application within the narrative. These foreigners would take their place with the patriarchs, while the descendants would be denied access (literally thrown out violently)[21] to the banquet and their inheritance.[22] The gruesome destiny of these "sons" suggests more than eternal exclusion, if that were not enough; it also implies deep regret and vexation. This statement had drawn the attention of the reader to the most enormous misjudg-

---

19. The Letter to the Hebrews may cast some light on this. Its author emphasized the need for any high priest to be appointed. Interestingly for that writer, the authority came via the declaration of sonship, as has already been noted. Hebrews recorded: "No one takes this honor upon himself; he must be called by God, just as Aaron was. So Christ also did not take upon himself the glory of becoming a high priest. But God said to him, 'You are my Son; today I have become your Father.' And he says in another place, 'You are priest forever, in the order of Melchizedek'" (Heb 5:4–6).

20. Nolland, *Gospel of Matthew*, 355–56.

21. Ibid., 357.

22. The saying functioned to provide additional warning of judgment against Israel. Bird, "Who Comes from the East and the West?," 445.

ment imaginable—Israel was in danger of missing its eschatological destiny because it failed to acknowledge Jesus as this Roman had. This motif, and plain emphasis, was integral to the Letter to the Hebrews. The writer's insistence that "Today, if you hear his voice . . ." emphasized the urgency and the unrepeatable nature of the salvific moment that came with Jesus.

## He Took Up Our Infirmities

The healing of Peter's mother-in-law gave Matthew another opportunity to convey the notion that Jesus was healing many individuals and that none were being denied.[23] Jesus healed these people with "with a command . . . emphasizing Jesus' unquestionable authority."[24] To this phenomenon Matthew applied the reference from Isa 53:4, which in turn suggested to Matthew's readers that Jesus was the "suffering servant" of God. This Isaiah reference not only gave a prophetic perspective to Jesus' healing ministry, but also set the theological parameters of the next four chapters, which amplified the rejection of Jesus (the suffering servant).[25] These chapters would show that the benevolence of Jesus would lead to the following conclusion: "He was despised and rejected by men, a man of sorrows, and familiar with suffering. Like one from whom men hide their faces he was despised, and we esteemed him not" (Isa 53:3). This reference also gave the readers a glimpse of the coming passion narrative, and provided the theological wherewithal to interpret the events. The reader could from this point expect that Jesus' end would come—"By oppression and judgment he was taken away. And who can speak of his descendants? For he was cut off from the land of the living; for the transgression of my people he was stricken" (Isa 53:8). Such are the implications of connecting Jesus to the "suffering servant" of Isaiah.

## Jesus Creates a Storm

The calming of the storm (8:23–27) served three theological purposes in Matthew's narrative. Firstly, it was one of a series of revelations demonstrating that the disciples were, during Jesus' time, not part of the solution, but part of the problem. They, in fact, were not very different from the people

---

23. A curse associated with disobeying "the Lord, your God" was fever (Deut 28:22). Peter's house has the fever removed; therefore, Peter could not be disobeying God's commands by following Jesus.

24. France, *Matthew*, 321. Matthew's readers were mindful that God merely spoke in doing his work; Matthew may have intended a connection here.

25. Seen here is the image that the Suffering Servant relieves suffering. Ibid., 322.

around Jesus, who lacked faith and were part of the "evil and perverse generation" (17:17), did not understand and even opposed Jesus' salvific agenda (16:23), and despised him at the critical moment (26:75). This programmatic negative portrayal of the Twelve could only serve Matthew's theological intention to show that Jesus alone was profitable to God, and that the disciples could only be sustained by divine election and mercy.

The second theological point that Matthew may have sought to make concerned the divine nature of Jesus. This section connected Jesus to YHWH, who stilled the tempest and the waves (Pss 65:7; 89:9; 107:29).[26] The inclusion of a portion of Psalm 7 is warranted to amplify the strong connection Matthew made with the YHWH of the Psalms:

> Others went out on the sea in ships; they were merchants on the mighty waters. They saw the works of the LORD, his wonderful deeds in the deep. For he spoke and stirred up a tempest that lifted high the waves. They mounted up to the heavens and went down to the depths; in their peril their courage melted away. They reeled and staggered like drunken men; they were at their wits' end. Then they cried out to the LORD in their trouble, and he brought them out of their distress. He stilled the storm to a whisper; the waves of the sea were hushed. They were glad when it grew calm, and he guided them to their desired haven. Let them give thanks to the LORD for his unfailing love and his wonderful deeds for men. Let them exalt him in the assembly of the people and praise him in the council of the elders (Ps 107:23–32).

The third implication is to be found in the disciples' final declaration, "What kind of man is this? Even the winds and the waves obey him!" This may have been intended to connect this incident to the previous miracles by alerting the readers to the source and extent of Jesus' authority. The readers, by this question, are invited to consider the options themselves—who is this Jesus and what kind of authority does he have?

## The Demonic Witness

Jesus' identity and authority to deal with the raging sea was restated and recast by the next incident concerning the demoniacs. These demonic occupants of the two men immediately recognized Jesus as "the Son of God"

---

26. Nolland, *Gospel of Matthew*, 370. Nolland also made note of the strong connections with the sea voyage and storm experience of Jonah. Jonah slept and was woken to call on his god. Hagner, *Matthew 1–13*, 220.

that, when the context is considered, was synonymous with authority and judgment. The text allowed the reader to infer that Jesus' arrival was anticipated by demons as the end of an era; their freedom within the covenantal homeland was now terminating or at least in serious jeopardy.[27] Jesus brought a new epoch, according to this paradigm, and this was the demonstration of the kingdom's eschatological arrival. Later within the narrative, Jesus would make this very point; the demonic removal was the significant demonstration of the kingdom's presence (12:28).

This episode provided opportunity for Matthew to emphasize his Christology, and by contrast, impugn the incumbents by implication.[28] Jesus was the expected judge, and this would have been intended to instruct the reader about the nature of Jesus' messianic role. Matthew's recollection of this incident differed from the other accounts in that there were two demon-possessed men mentioned. The most interesting distinctive, however, is Matthew's complete indifference to these two men. In Luke and Mark, Jesus had a pastoral discourse with the delivered soul, who was shown to be in a normal condition. Matthew's interest was not in the possible redemptive implications to be had as the result of the deliverance, but in the disclosure of Jesus' identity and the emphatic denunciation of demonic activity by the new Messiah. Jesus was able to decisively control[29] what had formerly been uncontrollable and was symbolic of the "living death" (people living among tombs prematurely) that could be encountered throughout the territories.

The reception that Jesus received from the disturbed locals warrants a few comments. Matthew did not identify the ethnicity of the region; however, it would be a mistake to assume that these were Gentiles because of the local pigs.[30] Matthew did not fail to portray Gentiles in a positive light, and even the hapless Pilate is shown as attempting to make a right judgment. The belief of the local community that they were better off without the messianic presence would be replicated across all the towns of Israel (10:16).

---

27. The statement of the demons that Jesus was dealing with them "before the appointed time" suggests that the forces of darkness were aware of the time and the hour. The arrival of Jesus had signalled the horrifying "eschatological judgment of all evil" (Nolland, *Gospel of Matthew*, 375). The "supernatural world" was testifying to the arrival of the Messiah Judge, and this should have given further evidence of impending judgment for Matthew's readers. Ibid., 46.

28. France, *Matthew*, 343.

29. The request of the demons to inhabit pigs which were then destroyed served two purposes. It made it clear that the demons were not able to just roam around the countryside and return, as depicted in the parable (12:43–45); and it also gave the clear impression that the death of the pigs was also the termination of the demons.

30. Nolland is persuaded that the townsfolk were Gentiles. Nolland, *Gospel of Matthew*, 376.

Matthew's narrative relies on the Gentile encounters as foils to the Hebrew intransigence. If this was a Gentile town, Matthew had strategically avoided mentioning it. Therefore, it should not be assumed that it was a Gentile town because of the pig farming and disdain for Jesus; these would prove to be inconsequential crimes considering the future "passion" atrocities. Jesus' arrival disturbed Jerusalem, and the Gadarenes were not different. For whatever reason, Jesus was not welcome in Matthew's Israel.

The sobering message that this episode contained for pre-existing authorities was that the kingdom of heaven was dismissing whatever did not conform to its transformational agenda. These demons controlled the graveyard men and were displaced and judged by Jesus' arrival. The people lamented the loss of the pigs, and were not grateful for the loss of the demoniacs. The swine were welcome; Jesus was not. This pattern would be repeated throughout the northern cities and eventually in Jerusalem—the unclean was desirable, the holy was unwelcome. Matthew's Jesus had a destiny with Jerusalem; this Gadarenes encounter was a prophetic glimpse of the Messiah's authority to judge decisively, and of the national rejection of him.

## Matthew's Compulsory Acquisition

Matthew had to this point given a preview of Jesus' authority over the elements, spiritual opponents, and sin. These incidents, in fact, could cast Jesus within the wider narrative as proto-ruler, proto-judge and proto-priest; the calling of Matthew incident may well have been cast as the proto-banquet (9:9–13).[31] The "unseemly" gathering at "the house"[32] was the first glimpse of Jesus in a social and celebratory setting; the image of Jesus at ease with "tax-collectors and sinners" presented a potent prophetic glimpse of kingdom celebration. The eschatological preview was made all the more pertinent by the Pharisaic questioning of the moment.[33] From their point of view,

---

31. "Jesus' action in 'reclining' with sinners was much like serving the figurative hors d'oeuvres of the messianic feast and foreshadowing exactly who would be vindicated in the renewed Israel that he was creating around himself" (Bird, *Jesus and the Origins*, 105).

32. The house could be Jesus' house or Matthew's house in this Gospel, although Luke states that the event took place in Levi's house. France, *Matthew*, 352. This feast is followed by Jesus' demand to "follow me." That being the case, Matthew may have intended to give the impression that Jesus was the host. Nolland, *Gospel of Matthew*, 385. If this is the case, Matthew wanted to develop the theme that sinners were invited into his "house," and, by contrast, they were not welcome in Jerusalem.

33. The Pharisees asked the disciples why Jesus conducted himself this way. France, *Matthew*, 354. It may be that they were, at this early stage, trying to win the disciples away from Jesus.

Jesus' willingness to dine (if not celebrate) with the underclass was a great misjudgment that the Pharisees were unlikely to imitate.[34] Their interest in Jesus could not be pursued for fear of contamination. This had effectively denied them access to the teacher, and the only way to share in the meal was to break custom and have table fellowship with "outcasts." Jesus had come for such as these, and the ceremonially "pure" could gain no admittance. The dilemma was palpable: to gain acceptance one must be unclean, or be prepared to become unclean because of the contemptible contacts. According to Matthew the event should have served as a proof that John the Baptist was a truthful prophet who ought to be believed (21:32). In the narrative, however, it was evidence that Jesus could not be a righteous man, according to the Pharisees.

For Matthew's part, he was either the object of celebration or the host of Jesus' first reception. Matthew's election to the service of Jesus was as unique and irresistible as the calling of the four fishermen. He did not ask for the privilege, but instantaneously left his former life, via the image of leaving his accounting booth and "following" Jesus. The way Matthew portrayed the irresistible calling of the disciples was best understood by the Matthean contrast found in the previous chapter. In that short pericope, two men sought to follow Jesus on their own initiative. When confronted with the discomfort of "not having anywhere to lay his head" (8:20),[35] and the immediacy implied with "let the dead bury the dead" (8:22), the prospective recruits were challenged to reconsider. The disciples, on the other hand, neither initiated the request, nor took time to consider—they were under divine compulsion.

This account of Matthew's inclusion and proto-reception could only serve to strengthen the internal claim of the narrative to divine mandate. Its author, Matthew (at least to its first readers), was divinely acquired and therefore as capable and as obligated to tell Jesus' story as any other of the chosen twelve. The divine call on Matthew was as compelling as that on any former prophet, and therefore his writing should not be considered inferior to what went before. The reader could even have considered that Matthew's role as a disciple involved placing this account of Jesus' story on the public record. As such, the Matthean document was given a sense of divine

---

34. It was one thing to accept fishermen into a new religious fraternity, but accepting Matthew was unthinkable. France, *Matthew*, 353. Separation from "sinners" was integral for Pharisees if they wished to maintain ritual purity. Nolland, *Gospel of Matthew*, 386.

35. Casey noted that Jesus had suggested that creatures were amply provided for, but his followers would struggle to meet their needs. Casey, "The Jackals," 22.

imprimatur by virtue of the internal cues given when one reads the account of Matthew's election.

The connection between this celebratory banquet comprising covenantal outcasts and the eternal banquet was not lost on Matthew, who did not hesitate to make the connection in the next short pericope. John's disciples, who had committed themselves to the strict asceticism depicted by John, were intrigued by the feasting practices of Jesus' disciples. Jesus responded with an allusion to the coming banquet by evoking the bridegroom/wedding celebration metaphor. By doing this, Matthew was able to portray the happy gathering as a preview of the blessed eschatological feast.

If this connection between Matthew's banquet and the question about fasting were sustainable, it would be plausible to interpret the following two pithy parables in the same light. The new wine was only suitable for new wineskins, as was the new patch for the new garment (9:16–17). Both allusions, naturally enough, are intended to illustrate the covenantal shift that was taking place. The old wine and garments were of the former era, for the new had come. What is particularly pertinent, however, is what constitutes the new wine and the new wineskin.

As the overwhelming message of Jesus is the kingdom advent, it is reasonable to assume that the new wine/patch is a metaphor for this grand theme.[36] The new wineskin/new garment within this analogy may well be the formerly discarded community, which had now become the nucleus of Jesus' new community.[37] The new kingdom, therefore, would be poured into the new community of "sinners and tax-collectors"—the old community was not compatible with the new kingdom. Jesus' disciples had to celebrate, for the kingdom had now appeared among Matthew's fraternal underclass. This kingdom belonged to them; however, the kingdom would also destroy the old, in the same way that the new wine/patch would destroy the old wineskin/garment.[38]

---

36. Most commentators have made the connection with the Holy Spirit as the new wine. The Spirit, though, within Matthew, was not as prominent as it is in John's gospel. John made little use of the Synoptics and their theology. Stein, "The Matthew–Luke Agreements."

37. Luz also conjectures: "In my judgment the double saying thus most likely emphasizes the fundamental incompatibility of the old Israel, represented by the enemies of Jesus the scribes, Pharisees and disciples of John with Jesus and the community of disciples" (Luz, *Matthew 8–20*, 37).

38. Matthew uniquely adds that the new wine is poured into the new wineskin so that both may be preserved (Matt 9:17).

## The Gospel Critiqued

Interspersed through the healing narratives was the preliminary critique by Israel's intelligentsia. The standout opposition to Jesus, throughout Matthew, was provided by the Pharisees; however, Matthew integrated and marshaled opposition through a variety of quite distinct religious groupings. The combinations of Herodians, Sadducees, scribes or teachers of the Law, the elders of the people, the chief priests and the Sanhedrin are portrayed by Matthew as a seamless entity that was united in opposition to Jesus.[39] Matthew's inspiration may have come from the heavily attested messianic Psalm 2, which commences, "Why do the nations [peoples] conspire and the peoples plot in vain? The kings of the earth take their stand and the rulers gather together against the LORD and against his Anointed One" (Ps 2:1–2). The Pharisees were dominant in this fraternity; nonetheless, their machinations are best interpreted as representative of Jerusalem, in Matthew, rather than distinct from it.

The Pharisees and teachers of the law were the first on the scene with an explanation of Jesus' ministry. There is no suggestion in Matthew that the miraculous acts of Jesus were viewed as fraudulent; the controversies revolved around the source of his power. There were no prohibitions concerning healing or deliverance in the Law; therefore, any evidence concerning the source of Jesus' suspected illegitimate authority would have to be found in his teaching or practice. A clear breach of the Law would be sufficient evidence that Jesus' authority came from a source other than YHWH. This evidence, however, was hard to come by. So it is against this backdrop that the early critiques of Jesus' ministry should be understood.

The first of these encounters was a secret charge of blasphemy. Jesus was approached by several men carrying a paralytic (9:1–7); Jesus observed their faith and, without invitation or request, forgave the sins of the wretched man. Matthew depicts Jesus as having perceived the thoughts of the scribes, and challenged them by asking them to determine what would constitute an easier claim, forgiveness or total healing. This secret accusation of blasphemy would prove to be the ultimate accusation of Caiaphas (what would be spoken in secret would be made public). He unlawfully believed that such a charge against Jesus did not require a trial (26:65). The claim that Jesus was the "Son of Man" of Daniel's apocalyptic (26:64) and this incident of forgiveness (9:6) were practically synonymous as far as Jesus' opponents were concerned. Jesus' implicit and explicit claim was to be God's representative on earth. This claim had clear implications for the Jerusalem ruling

---

39. Anderson, "Double and Triple Stories," 86.

class, who understood that their tenure would have expired if this claim were true.[40]

When Jesus was finally in the Sanhedrin's dock, Matthew made it clear that there was no legitimate charge that could be brought against Jesus. From this the reader can conclude that the periodic charges made against Jesus could not be sustained under the Mosaic legislature. Certainly it was possible for a human to have authority to forgive sins and even claim to be the human in Daniel's vision; but how could a particular individual prove that he was that apocalyptic "anointed" judge/priest? So although the scribes could not disprove Jesus' messianic claim, Jesus could give a substantial proof of it—the complete healing of the paralytic.[41]

The second challenge was subtle and expressed by an unexpected source, the disciples of John. John's disciples were certainly not portrayed in Matthew as opponents of Jesus; they did, however, have a different modus operandi, which could be cunningly exploited by an increasingly hostile community. The Pharisees, whose similar concern was betrayed by the question, were probably the initiators of this incident. The question had little accusatory power, as rigorous fasting was not a legal requirement for pious Jews. It was, however, an indicator of spiritual discipline and earnestness. The only objective of this incident was to bring clarity for John's community, and possibly to create a slur concerning Jesus' casual approach to asceticism.[42]

The last accusation in this section was the claim that Jesus' authority to cast out demons had come from the lord of the demons (9:34). The people marveled at the deliverance of a mute, whose tongue was loosened (9:32). This marvel was explained by the Pharisees in the only way that they could concede: Beelzebub was Jesus' authority. Matthew's Jesus did not respond to this accusation, as it would receive attention in chapter 12. It is sufficient here to note that they did not require any evidence to come to this conclusion, and therefore it was nothing more than slander. The encounter did, however, set the stage for the next pericope, within which Jesus lamented the leadership void that existed among God's people. The noteworthy incompetence of the Pharisees to discourage the people from putting their faith in Jesus was an obvious illustration that Matthew could exploit.

---

40. Carter, "Matthew's Gospel," 431.

41. John's Nicodemus asserts the necessity of God's blessing in such supernatural acts—"Rabbi, we know you are a teacher who has come from God. For no one could perform the miraculous signs you are doing if God were not with him" (John 3:2).

42. Later in the narrative, similar slurs would be addressed to Jesus' lax approach to cleanliness (15:2). This incident was no doubt also an attempt to impugn Jesus with guilt concerning his selection of celebration partners.

## Priming the New Shepherds (9:35-38)

Jesus' reflection concerning his ministry and travels through the northern region led him to lament that the Israelites were leaderless and vulnerable (9:36). This was a surprising assessment considering that the pericope was introduced by a statement confirming Jesus' resounding success—"Jesus went through all the towns and villages, teaching in their synagogues, preaching the good news of the kingdom and healing every disease and sickness" (9:35). All the towns heard the good news and experienced freedom from sickness and oppression. Why then would this statement be followed by an expression of sympathy and despair?

Jesus' sympathy was not elicited by the people's immediate needs, but by their failure to develop the critical faculty that would enable them to understand who he was. As we noticed in the previous pericope the custodial administrators (shepherds) were muddying the waters with questions of Jesus' legitimacy; rather than encouraging the crowds to think rightly about Jesus, they were leading the community to think of Jesus with suspicion. The Jerusalem leadership would ultimately hold sway over the people, who would unanimously insist that Jesus be "cut off."

Clearly, the compassion of Jesus and his exhortation of the disciples is an implicit indictment—Israel's leaders, though abundantly present, are negligent.[43] Jerusalem's representatives were well established and integrated throughout the community, as evidenced by their constant cameos in Matthew's story. And yet the people were without guidance. The sheep were ἐσκυλμένοι καί ἐρριμμένοι—tormented and thrown to the ground.[44] The reader would be likely to ask how YHWH's sheep had become so oppressed and neglected. The answer was obvious: they were "sheep without a shepherd," a well-known prophetic observation and indictment against Israel's leaders. Before Israel went into Canaan, YHWH insisted that his people would not be like "sheep without a shepherd" (Num 27:17). The prophet Micaiah also told Ahab to send the roaming Israelites home, for he saw that they were "sheep without a shepherd" (1 Kgs 22:17). Ezekiel's indictment against Israel's shepherds was predicated upon their neglect; the sheep "were scattered because there was no shepherd" (Ezek 34:5). This neglect of

---

43. The compassion that Jesus expressed in Matthew may be intended to link the passage to Zechariah 10, where God's anger burned against the shepherds (Zech 10:3) leading to his response to care for them because "I have compassion" on them (Zech 10:6). Nolland, "The King as Shepherd," 135. "Jesus is the positive counterpart to the disastrous shepherd of Zech. 11:16 . . ." (ibid., 137).

44. Luz, *Matthew 8-20*, 64.

Israel's priests and prophets would bring their tenure to an end. The indictment read:

> Therefore, you shepherds, hear the word of the LORD. As surely as I live, declares the Sovereign LORD, because my flock lacks a shepherd and so has been plundered and has become food for all the wild animals, and because my shepherds did not search for my flock but cared for themselves rather than for my flock, therefore, O shepherds, hear the word of the LORD. This is what the Sovereign LORD says: I am against the shepherds and will hold them accountable for my flock. I will remove them from tending the flock so that the shepherds can no longer feed themselves. I will rescue my flock from their mouths, and it will no longer be food for them (Ezek 3:7–10).

This indictment was à propos for Matthew's purposes.[45] By raising the specter of the "shepherdless sheep," Matthew had connected his narrative to the significant indictment within Ezekiel, and its implications for the first-century Judean priestly community would have been plain enough. The worthless shepherds were to be held to account. God had placed himself under oath to remove them (Ezek 34:8–10), according to Ezekiel's prophecy, and in this way he would rescue his flock. This paradigm was important to Matthew's next section, where the disciples were sent out as "sheep among wolves"; the "wolves" would persecute, flog, pursue and even kill the body. It was from the likes of these "worthless shepherds" that God would rescue his sheep.

This indirect reference to Ezekiel had clear implications for indictment in our author's story; however, in a manner that is uniquely Matthean, he had managed to weave in another prophetic implication from Zechariah, a prophet that received extensive midrashic treatment from Matthew. Zechariah wrote:

> The idols speak deceit, diviners see visions that lie; they tell dreams that are false, they give comfort in vain. Therefore the people wander like sheep oppressed for lack of a shepherd. My anger burns against the shepherds, and I will punish the leaders; for the LORD Almighty will care for his flock, the house of Judah, and make them like a proud horse in battle (Zech 10:2–3).

---

45. "It is likely that Matthew intends an oblique criticism of the Jewish leaders here" Nolland, *Gospel of Matthew*, 407. A more plain assessment is made by Chrysostom: "Jesus' words are a 'charge against the rulers of the Jews, that being shepherds they acted the part of wolves. For so far from amending the multitude, they even marred their progress" (Davies and Allison, *Matthew: A Shorter*, 146).

From this prophecy, the Lord was to provide the solution to the people's predicament. Then, according to Zech 10:6, God would rescue both Judah and the house of Joseph (Ephraim), for he has compassion (רחם) on them.

So clearly this little pericope was designed to elicit the messianic connections found in these earlier writings; it would reveal to the readers the intention of Christ to be the Shepherd of Israel (Ps 23:1) who had compassion on the sheep, and it also exposed the negligent incumbents and their impending removal. All this could only heighten the drama of Matthew's story, which introduced Jesus as ruler and shepherd—"out of you [Bethlehem] will come a ruler who will be the shepherd of my people Israel" (2:6).

The exhortation of Jesus to beseech the "Lord of the harvest" was a prayer that would soon be answered; the disciples (twelve only in Matthew) were commissioned to do the work that should have been performed by other shepherds—proclamation of the good news about Jesus. The disciples' understanding of the "Great Commission" would be shaped by this pericope. They understood that their task was to teach about Jesus, teach what Jesus taught and baptize into Jesus. The correct application of these duties would equip them to be the "new shepherds" of the new community.

Notwithstanding the possibility that this pericope had specific implications concerning the negligent character of Israel's stewards, there is another even less palatable interpretation of this passage, which would reinforce the judgment paradigm against the nation. To observe this motif, it is necessary to suspend the presumption that Jesus' reference to a ripe harvest was only for a positive evangelistic purpose: there is a less benign possibility. The prophet Joel may have contributed to this euphemism:

> Swing the sickle, for the harvest is ripe. Come, trample the grapes, for the winepress is full and the vats overflow—so great is their wickedness! Multitudes, multitudes in the valley of decision! For the day of the LORD is near in the valley of decision. The sun and moon will be darkened, and the stars no longer shine (Joel 3:13–15).

This harvest for judgment in Joel was anticipated as a feature of the Day of the Lord, and there can be no doubt that the Israelites stood in the valley of decision. The negative outcome of this mission was fully anticipated by the following passage, which foretold rejection—"I tell you the truth, it will be more bearable for Sodom and Gomorrah on the day of judgment than for that town" (10:15).[46] It was, in fact, this negative outcome that was

---

46. The rejection of God incurs his final judgment. France, *Matthew*, 387. "Gentile cities, notorious in Scripture for their corruption, will encounter more leniency at God's last judgment than unrepentant Israel" (Westerholm, *Understanding Matthew*,

ultimately confirmed; rather than receiving a messianic blessing, the first mission resulted in a messianic curse (11:21–24). The book of Revelation also depicted a harvest for the purpose of judgment (Rev 14:15–20). That apocalyptic harvest was gathered and thrown "into the great winepress of God's wrath." Could this harvest also have that character? In view of the "Day of YHWH" reading of Matthew's Jesus, this interpretation cannot be ruled out.

Without wishing to labor this point, there is a further connection that can be made here. Matthew 9 made reference to Hos 6:6, with the exhortation—"go and learn what this means" (9:13). Consider then the context of this text,

> What can I do with you, Ephraim? What can I do with you, Judah? Your love is like the morning mist, like the early dew that disappears. Therefore I cut you in pieces with my prophets, I killed you with the words of my mouth; my judgments flashed like lightning upon you.
>
> For I desire mercy, not sacrifice, and acknowledgment of God rather than burnt offerings. Like Adam, they have broken the covenant—they were unfaithful to me there. Gilead is a city of wicked men, stained with footprints of blood. As marauders lie in ambush for a man, so do bands of priests; they murder on the road to Shechem, committing shameful crimes. I have seen a horrible thing in the house of Israel. There Ephraim is given to prostitution and Israel is defiled. Also for you, Judah, a harvest is appointed. Whenever I would restore the fortunes of my people, whenever I would heal Israel, the sins of Ephraim are exposed and the crimes of Samaria revealed (Hos 6:4–7:1).

Jesus' appearance in the northern towns was an act of mercy; an opportunity to restore lost fortunes. But God's mercy only exposed the people's crimes/sins, and the atrocities of the priesthood. In this context, a harvest of blessing is unlikely for Judah, and possibly this further advanced Matthew's understanding of Israel's "ripe harvest." Israel may have been at the beginning of harvest; without faith, there would be no redemption, but only condemnation. Jeremiah's haunting lament may have an echo here:

> The harvest is past,
> the summer has ended,
> and we are not saved (Jer 8:20).

---

65). These towns are the "quintessential model of pagan perversion and wickedness" (Bird, *Jesus and the Origins*, 63).

## The Naming of the Twelve

The prelude to the naming of the disciples was the observation by Jesus that the crowds who followed him were "helpless and harassed, like sheep without a shepherd." This observation was followed by a call to action—the disciples were commanded to ask God to send workers into his harvest. This short pericope served Matthew's intention to show that there was a leadership void among the Hebrews that required filling. The priests, whose primary responsibility was to safeguard the people, were not only negligent of their duties, but also obstructionist toward any who would seek to address their unfulfilled duties. The burden that Jesus placed upon the disciples was a natural connector to this first commission that they had received, and it also served as an echo of Isaiah's request to God that he be sent to the recalcitrant Hebrews (Isa 6:8).

Both the first commission here in chapter 10 and the final commission (28:18–20) were issued to the Twelve (without Judas in the latter instance). This first commission was for the house of Israel alone, while the latter was indiscriminate.[47] There is a sharp distinction to be observed between the two commissions: Jesus was particularly pessimistic about the first mission's outcome, but not the second. This was not to say that the second universal commission was going to be unchallenged or unopposed, but that it would not be completely rejected—as it seemed to be in Matthew's first commission account.

The naming of the Twelve was immediately preceded by their calling and conferral of authority: "[Jesus] . . . gave them authority to drive out evil spirits and to heal every disease and sickness" (10:1). The twelve were introduced here for the first time, and all but five are unknown within Matthew's account.[48] Matthew and the first two sets of brothers have already received recognition within the story, and Judas (the last named) would loom large as the narrative progressed.[49] By introducing the disciples at this time, Matthew was able to show the importance of this mission, having disclosed the specific emissaries sent to complete the task. Unlike Luke (10:1), Matthew

---

47. It is important to note that Matthew's final commission does not reject Jews as recipients of the gospel; however, they were no longer the exclusive beneficiaries of Jesus' offer.

48. The narrative introduced seven disciples here but they were probably all previously known to Matthew's readers.

49. Judas Iscariot's role was important for Matthew's paradigm in order to fulfill Scripture: Judas was the "enemy within," yet he too would testify to the innocence of Jesus.

did not mention any other appointments (the seventy) to the task; it was only the Twelve that were sent.

## The Recipients of the Mission

The objects of this mission were the covenant people alone—"Do not go among the Gentiles or enter any town of the Samaritans. Go rather to the lost sheep of Israel." The very specific "fence" placed around this mission emphasized its relevance to the historic covenant that had been made particularly with the natural descendants of Abraham, Isaac and Jacob. Unlike the latter mission (28:18–20), this mission was restricted; as such, it was integral to Israel's story—unfinished family business.

Perhaps the best way to understand this exclusive mission is by the parable that emphasized the exclusive invitation to Israel. "The Parable of the Wedding Banquet" (22:1–14) portrayed a feast long anticipated. The invited guests were particularly chosen and only they were expected; in the first instance, there was no inclusiveness to this feast. These guests, however, were uninterested and either turned to do their mundane activities or turned to assault and slaughter the host's emissaries. Following this rebuttal, the feast was thrown open to anyone who was interested—but the former invited guests were no longer welcome. The invited guests proved that they were not worthy (οὐκ ἦσαν ἄξιοι). It is in this context that worthiness would be imputed during the mission. Those within Israel who accepted the emissaries would prove to be worthy (ἄξιος). The disciples were to stay where they were received, and condemn the community where they were not welcome.

The instructed recipients were not just Israelites, but the lost sheep of Israel. This may cause some contextual complications as earlier (at Matthew's reception for Jesus) Jesus had made a distinction between the "healthy" and "sick," as well as the "righteous" and "sinners." Within this pericope, however, it is critical to accept that the "lost sheep of Israel" is a reference to all Jews, and not those who are lowly or outcast. If this were not a designation for all Jews, the passage would have some consistency problems; for all seemed to hear the disciples' message and receive their beneficent signs. If "lost" in this instant was an attribute of the "lowly," it would be most peculiar that there would be a widespread condemnation on all those who had benefited the most (11:20).

Further, as all Israelites are revealed as lost sheep (no doubt connecting with 9:36), it is clear that Jesus considers them to be in peril. As such, the mission must have a general redemptive context, but this will not exhaust the full intention of the mission. Like the parable, it was an invitation to something greater, or the last chance to escape the indictment and imminent condemnation. The mission was a life-saving exercise, but its rejection would prove to bring greater calamity to those who were indifferent to Jesus' messianic claim.

## The Mission's Message

The simple primary message that the disciples were to proclaim was: "the kingdom of heaven is near." The message had not changed; John's warning of the impending kingdom was being passed on to the disciples. The exhortation to repent, as a consequence of the kingdom's imminence, was the only thing missing, though it is clearly implied by the wider context.[50] The main verb κηρύσσετε (preach) was amplified by the subordinate imperatives attached to the signs, i.e., heal, raise, cleanse and drive out. Therefore, the signs were integral to the message. They were proof of the kingdom's power. Although the signs could only be perceived as blessings, a wise person would have seen a frightening demonstration of the kingdom's power: who would want to oppose a kingdom as mighty as this?

## The Signs of the Mission

The directions given for the mission were very specific, and the signs were to accompany the message. The disciples were required to replicate the ministry of Jesus: they could heal sicknesses, cleanse skin disorders, cast out unclean spirits and raise the dead. These disorders could have rendered any Hebrew unclean. Certainly death, skin disorders and unclean spirits were all factors which made an Israelite unclean and, therefore, ineligible to participate in the religious life of God's covenant community. Even sickness of other sorts and disabilities could render a person less than acceptable before God; priests, for instance could not serve the temple with any physical deformity (Lev 21:18). This issue will receive a fuller treatment in chapter 7; it is sufficient here, however, to note that the ministry of the disciples was to replicate Jesus' cleansing ministry. The infirmities that made Hebrews unclean, according to the Law, were removed. In effect, the unintentional transgressions of Israel were removed, leaving the individuals and villages with only the sins of their choosing. As a consequence of this

---

50. According to the narrative, any reasonable human, even a Gentile, would have repented as a consequence of the miracles (11:25).

healing/cleansing function, it is possible to recognize the apostolic ministry as fulfilling a priestly office, even though priests were not expected to heal.[51]

The one significant function of Jesus that was absent from this commission was the forgiveness of sins. Those that rejected the mission would not be forgiven: in fact, it would be the basis of the most damnable of indictments. Forgiveness, no doubt, was available for the penitent, and the disciples were obligated to give it on God's behalf (6:13–15); however, it was not on public offer as was the physical deliverance from covenantal impurities. Matthew's Jesus could forgive all sins, but that was not the essence of this mission. The mission's rationale was surprising, and this is why Jesus had to instruct the disciples about the true intention of the outreach.

## The Enigma of the Mission

A traditional interpretation of this mission as a benign gracious invitation does not tally with what the disciples were told to do and expect (10:11–36). Donald Hagner expressed the widespread confusion that this passage brings to those who fail to understand the prophetic nature of Matthew's narrative. Hagner wrote:

> The strangeness of this new emphasis on the persecution, suffering, and even death of the very ones who proclaim the fulfillment of the promises, the good news of the kingdom, is remarkable. There is a sharp incongruity, which no doubt impressed itself on the disciples. How could a message of such joy and power, if it were true, be compatible with the things the disciples are now told to expect?[52]

If there are any doubts concerning Matthew's indictment plotline, they will be starved of oxygen in this sequence of threats. There was the possibility that the disciples could warmly bestow blessings; however, it was quickly lost in the expectation of Jesus—which was profoundly negative. Jesus fully expected persecution and rejection; his reason for this was the

---

51. By attributing priestly function to the mission of the disciples, it is proposed that this is a new, higher order priestly community. Previous priests could only declare a healed person cleansed; these new priests, however, demonstrated the power of God to remove the causes for ritual impurity. In the same way that the Law could only declare a sinner guilty and offer little prospect of redemption (Heb 10:1–4), the Aaronic priesthood could only declare a person unclean, with no heavenly power to make the afflicted clean.

52. Hagner, *Matthew 1–13*, 280.

treatment that he had received—"All men will hate you because of me" (10:22; 10:24–25).

The harsh logic of the passage is evident. Jesus' disciples would not have success in their faith-building exercise. Having received the miracles and testimony of YHWH, the recipients were rendered far more culpable than if they had not been evangelized at all. They were now in a more parlous state than the wretched cities of the Hebrew narrative—Sodom and Gomorrah (10:15). These cities were the ultimate expression of God's wrath: cities of total desolation. The shaking of dust (10:14) has resonance with Malachi, which speaks of the ashes of the burned cities sticking to the sole of one's feet (Mal 4:3). This may contribute to the narrative the notion that the evangelized cities were already under God's wrath, which could be made worse by the ministry of the disciples. There is a Deuteronomic connection with this morbid outcome:

> Your children who follow you in later generations and foreigners who come from distant lands will see the calamities that have fallen on the land and the diseases with which the LORD has afflicted it. The whole land will be a burning waste of salt and sulphur—nothing planted, nothing sprouting, no vegetation growing on it. It will be like the destruction of Sodom and Gomorrah, Admah and Zeboiim, which the LORD overthrew in fierce anger. And the answer will be: "It is because this people abandoned the covenant of the LORD, the God of their fathers, the covenant he made with them when he brought them out of Egypt" (Deut 29:22–25).

It is likely that Matthew had this curse in mind when retelling this account. The Sodom and Gomorrah reference was incorporated to establish the crimes of Israel as breaches of covenant; the destiny to befall Israel was the specific penalty of the Law.

The recipients of the mission were described as wolves, a peculiar term in view of the previous designation, "lost sheep." This designation, however, is probably intended to refer to the leadership of the people who would make the disciples unwelcome. A prophet criticizing the inept character of Jerusalem's leadership described them this way: "Her officials within her are like wolves tearing their prey; they shed blood and kill people to make unjust gain" (Ezek 22:27).[53] From this point on the instructions for surviving the mission implied that the disciples would be in direct conflict with the

---

53. Zephaniah also identified the priests/leaders as wolves: "Her officials are roaring lions, her rulers are evening wolves, who leave nothing for the morning" (Zeph 3:3).

stewards of Israel. These people would persecute the disciples in every way, according to Matthew's Jesus, even betraying them to Gentile governors.

## The Requirements of the Disciples

In the introduction of this book, reference has been made to Jesus' command that the disciples expose the crimes of Jesus' enemies (10:26–28). The passage includes the strongest possible exhortation to the disciples not to fail or falter in their task. They were to fear the one who could destroy their soul, and if they were to fail to testify concerning Jesus, they in turn would be without an advocate. The disciples were to make their mission and calling an absolute priority, with no earthly compromise (10:37–39). The disciples, however, were to take comfort concerning their standing before God—they were more valuable than many sparrows (10:31). Jesus was assuring them of their preservation; their demise would be only at God's discretion.

There are significant prophetic traditions that this passage (10:21–39) recalled that ought not be overlooked. Matthew's narrative drew from Micah and Isaiah in this section, and once again, the context of the imported prophecies further illuminates the intention of Matthew. Micah wrote:

> The best of them is like a brier, the most upright worse than a thorn hedge. The day of your watchmen has come, the day God visits you. Now is the time of their confusion. Do not trust a neighbor; put no confidence in a friend. Even with her who lies in your embrace be careful of your words. For a son dishonors his father, a daughter rises up against her mother, a daughter-in-law against her mother-in-law—a man's enemies are the members of his own household (Mic 7:4–6).

Matthew's use of the specific divided house motif found in this passage contributes information that may already be known; the mission was integral to the indictment of the "watchmen" and it could undoubtedly be classified as a confusing mission, for the gracious gifts given by the disciples would only result in an escalated accountability and condemnation before YHWH. To this we can add the Isaiah reference:

> The LORD Almighty is the one you are to regard as holy, he is the one you are to fear, he is the one you are to dread, and he will be a sanctuary; but for both houses of Israel he will be a stone that causes men to stumble. And for the people of Jerusalem he will be a trap and a snare and a rock that makes them fall (Isa 8:13–14).

The juxtaposition between those who fear YHWH and those who do not was highlighted by their respective destinies. To the disciples, YHWH is a sanctuary, but to the nation, particularly Jerusalem, he will be a snare and a rock that makes them fall. It is not necessary to import the context, as these notions were discernible from within Matthew's narrative. The prophetic context, however, is further confirmation of Matthew's indictment paradigm.

The last section of the mission instructions emphasized the merciful nature of the project. Reception of the disciples would be calculated as a reception of Jesus, and by implication, an acceptance of YHWH. This would be greatly rewarded. Even a cup of water given to the disciples would enact a blessing from God (10:42). With such an ending, Matthew implied further that YHWH was ready to bless those who would show even a modicum of gratitude; however, if there was anything to bless after the mission, Matthew had failed to mention it. The mission followed the negative and anticipated script: the towns where the disciples evangelized were cursed as a consequence of their rejection of Jesus (11:20–24).

The "lens" through which these first mission directives has been read has little in common with the lens used in the majority of commentaries on Matthew. For instance, the declaration of Jesus that he had "not come to bring peace, but a sword" (10:34), has been interpreted in ways significantly at odds with this reading. Davies and Allison believe that the sword represents "personal strife and public persecution, and extends to the thought of martyrdom."[54] It is odd that they should interpret the sword as being Jesus' action toward the disciples. Luz ruled out that Jesus wanted to bring "a political rebellion against Rome," and concludes that the sword was intended to bring "familial and societal" division.[55] Nolland agrees with Luz, while conceding that the normal implication of the "sword" is "destructive hostility."[56] For France, Jesus' message is peace, but not peace that avoids conflict; the disciples are, therefore, being encouraged to engage society with "robust controversy" that will in turn lead to division.[57] Hauerwas advances this notion a little further. Quoting Bonhoeffer, he concludes that the cross creates division and controversy in households.[58] Harrington also cannot conceive of this statement as being "(eschatological) warfare," as this would be at odds with the beatitude for peacemakers. He also opts for

54. Davies and Allison, *Matthew: A Shorter*, 167.
55. Luz, *Matthew 8–20*, 111–12.
56. Nolland, *Gospel of Matthew*, 440.
57. France, *Matthew*, 408.
58. Hauerwas, *Matthew*, 108–9.

the sword being division.⁵⁹ Hendriksen was caused to "startle in shocked disbelief" at the sight of this reference.⁶⁰ He does get over this initial reaction, however, to conclude that Jesus said this provocative statement to "stop a person short and make him think."⁶¹ Hagner also agrees that the sword pertains to family conflict, while conceding that "Luke 12:49 has a statement similar in structure to the present passage (πῦρ ἦλθον βαλεῖν ἐπὶ τὴν γῆν, 'I came to bring fire upon the earth'), but this is probably an allusion to eschatological judgment."⁶² This cross-section of commentators is fairly representative. Many admittedly acknowledge that there is a dissonance between what they believe the Gospel is saying and what Matthew's Jesus is actually recorded as saying. To deal with this, the sword reference is understood to only apply to the two successive verses, and not the whole discourse.⁶³ Yet, Jesus' statement of bringing a sword is not at odds with any part of the discourse; rather, it is complementary. Jesus anticipated opposition, and the northern communities were wolfish in character. Jesus had not anticipated any positive outcome from the whole mission. Rather than interpret the sword as applying to households only, it should be understood that the judgment would be so comprehensive that even families will be infused with hatred and division. The divided households are evidence that "The day of your watchmen has come, the day God visits you. Now is the time of their confusion" (Mic 7:4). Therefore, the household conflict points to the imminent judgment of the watchmen/priests. The sword that Jesus brings is his "sharpened flashing sword" that was intended to be used on the day that "the LORD will judge his people."⁶⁴

## The First Fruits of the Mission

Following the elaborate instructions and preparation given through chapter 10, it would have been meaningful for Matthew to inform his readers of the mission results. This he did. The first feedback from the mission, however, would come from an unexpected source—the imprisoned John (11:1–6). This pericope has been considered at length in chapter 4, so only a few contextual observations will be made here.

59. Harrington, *Matthew*, 150.
60. Hendriksen, *Matthew*, 474.
61. Ibid.
62. Hagner, *Matthew 1–13*, 291.
63. Matthew's Jesus believed that his role was "to initiate the coming eschatological judgment" (Bird, *Are You the One*, 112).
64. Deut 32:36, 41.

Jesus' "northern mission" had become public knowledge; John the Baptist was even aware of it from his prison cell. The mission had elicited a question from John that had caused him to wonder about Jesus' wrathful agenda, for Jesus was clearly performing acts of kindness wherever he went, which was a contradiction to the expectations and declaration of John. Jesus' response to John was to quote two verses from Isaiah, which would confirm that programmatic blessings were integral to the "day of vengeance and retribution" as disclosed by Isaiah (Isa 35:4; 61:2). The two apparently irreconcilable realities were taking place, as Isaiah wrote: "For the day of vengeance was in my heart, and the year of my redemption has come" (Isa 63:4). Matthew's Jesus had reminded John of the messianic realities attached to this "Day of the Lord."

This correction and instruction to John gave Matthew the opportunity to affirm the authenticity of John's credentials and launch a scathing critique of the towns where Jesus preached. The mission report found that the communities were fickle, childish, unrealistic, unappeasable and damnable.[65] This section commenced with a question, "To what can I compare this generation?" (11:16), and ended with an assessment of its lamentable condition—"That is how it will be with this evil generation" τῇ γενεᾷ ταύτῃ τῇ πονηρᾷ (12:45).[66] The lengthy passage is interspersed with comparison, condemnation, summary appeal, a prayer of thanksgiving, conflict, prophetic approbation, accusation, and the offer of a sign. The passage is complex, but maintains a unifying indictment theme, which appears to pull together a series of events encountered on the mission.

## An Unappeasable Generation

The blessings and good news that accompanied the mission did not end with the report of great joy as found in Luke 10:17; nor did it end without comment as in Mark 6. Matthew's account confirmed what Jesus expected before he sent the disciples out—they were not accepted. This rebuttal of Jesus initially came via the churlish marketplace cry of "this generation"; John was too sober for them and therefore had a demon, Jesus was too informal

---

65. Wendy Cotter has observed the strange juxtaposition of children "sitting" in the "marketplace" (ἀγορά). Those seated in the marketplace are magistrates (Acts 16:19); therefore, it is possible, even likely, that ἀγορά signified a court. It was the highest stratum of the society that was acting with such immaturity. Cotter, "The Parable of the Children," 299.

66. The Lukan version compares this generation's foolish children with the children of wisdom (Jesus, John and their disciples). Linton, "Parable of the Children's Game," 177.

for them and therefore was a drunkard. What was fully expected in the mission instructions was now made clear—this people could not be appeased. There was no act of kindness, offer of amnesty or manner of approach that would satisfy "this generation." It would seem that they had made their stand against both Jesus and John, having critiqued them as not being good enough. The people had shown themselves intransigent in their willingness to remain unreconciled. No amount of kindness and no miraculous signs could convince them to make peace.

## A Damnable Generation

The excursus that followed (11:20–24) was nothing other than a divine denunciation in the prophetic tradition. The communities that had received the most abundant demonstration of Jesus' authority were astonishingly unimpressed, and, therefore, indictable with a severity not formerly known. Bethsaida and Korazin did not repent. Yet Matthew's Jesus considered that the ministry that he had performed among them would have been sufficient to bring about repentance in the neighboring Gentile cities (11:21). Similarly, Capernaum, the base of Jesus' operations, was also unmoved. Sodom would have been impressed and still existing if it had witnessed the substantial evidence placed at Capernaum's disposal (11:24). As a consequence of the rejection of Jesus, the Gentile towns of Tyre and Sidon and even the abominable Sodom were poised for less wrath on the day of reckoning. The indictment could not be more severe; to be more pitiable than the exceptionally evil Sodom was to place these towns in the worst possible standing with God. In short, it could not be worse.

This dire assessment of the mission's results for Israel could only amplify the true nature of the mission; Jesus anticipated that his message would not be accepted, and having now rejected it, the towns were now in the most indictable position imaginable. The mission had escalated their intransigence, and provided clear evidence that the towns of the north were unwinnable. Although they had hosted Jesus, there was indifference to his claims and offer of amnesty. Their refusal to repent highlighted the mission's intention—to turn the Israelites from their catastrophic opposition to YHWH. To this degree, the mission had failed; however, the kingdom's purpose was not simply benign, for it had been violently advancing (11:12).[67] The northern towns could not be in worse condition after the mission, but

---

67. For France this could not be the kingdom that was violently advancing, but the opposition to it. France, *Matthew*, 430. So it was unclear, for France, how exactly "these violent people 'plunder,' 'ravage,' or 'seize' the kingdom of heaven" (ibid.).

worse was yet to come; for Jerusalem not only rejected the message and messengers, it also killed those sent to her (23:37).

## The Offer of Amnesty

Following the harrowing indictment was this offer to the "weary and heavy-laden" (11:25–29). The placing of this winsome appeal is peculiar after the condemnation of the cities, and it can only mean that some could still respond and be accepted. It may also be in some way a summary of the good news appeal that was being made on the mission. The election motif is strong in this appeal, and once again the revelation of Jesus, that was integral to receiving rest, was only made at the Father's discretion. Jesus' thankfulness that it was made to the children was intended to reveal the disciples as the recipients.[68] In the same way that they alone were privy to the kingdom's "secrets" (13:11), they were beneficiaries of the Father's benevolence. Rest came to those who came to Jesus to find it; the Father had made Jesus known to the disciples and Jesus thanked him for the disclosure of the "secret." So while apocalyptic judgment was underway, there was also mercy being shown.[69] Most, however, according to the larger context, were hardened to Jesus as a consequence of the mission.

## The Unquarrelsome Servant

Jesus' authority to give rest was soon challenged by the Pharisees. The encounter in the cornfields and the healing of the withered hand led to Matthew's disclosure of the plot to kill Jesus (12:14). It was now becoming clear within the narrative that the opposition to Jesus was not borne of simple indifference or ingratitude, but hatred. This was a case in point. Jesus' miraculous sign (12:13) did nothing to trigger repentance or even astonishment: rather, it produced greater enmity and disgust with the new "Christ."

The next section had Jesus withdrawing and many people following (12:15–21). The healings also continued, and presumably the tense conflict at the synagogue was left behind. This gave Matthew the opportunity to insert another "proof text" of Jesus' messianic credentials. Matthew's portrayal of Jesus' messiahship was once again directly connected to Isaiah's disclosure of the "suffering servant." The benign portion of Isaiah inserted

---

68. The commissioned disciples were referred to as "little ones" by Jesus in their commissioning (10:42).

69. Nolland acknowledges the Sabbath inference in Jesus' offer, but denies that this is likely to mean eschatological rest. Nolland, *Gospel of Matthew*, 476.

here served two purposes: it revealed Jesus' programmatic fulfillment of Isaiah's Messiah, and it provided a wider context within which the indictment paradigm could be understood. Matthew quoted the first four verses of Isaiah 42 (12:18–21); the preceding three, however, were of particular relevance to the quoted texts. They read:

> I was the first to tell Zion, "Look, here they are!" I gave to Jerusalem a messenger of good tidings. I look but there is no one—no one among them to give counsel, no one to give answer when I ask them. See, they are all false! Their deeds amount to nothing; their images are but wind and confusion (Isa 41:27–29).

This desperate view of Israel's condition was pertinent to Matthew's depiction of Jesus' mission. The "good tidings" were met with no response; all were found to be false and unprofitable. Apart from Jesus, there were no good tidings—for the incumbent "forerunners" were worthless.

### Could This Be David's Son?

In typical Matthean form, the healing of the mute and blind man from demonic oppression was passed over in record time in order to resume the dominant feature of the narrative, the ongoing conflict and the depiction of Jesus' adversaries (12:24–37). This particular healing triggered a realization among the people, which was posed in the bewildering question, "Could this be the son of David?"[70] This inquiry, and even hope, was quickly snuffed out by the Pharisees who brought their own assessment to the attention of the people—"It is only by Beelzebub, the prince of demons, that this fellow drives out demons" (12:24). In this way, Matthew was able to demonstrate the obstructionist agenda of the Pharisees, who were determined to ignore the evidence in pursuit of their prejudiced self-interest.

Jesus' response to the Pharisees was to implicitly and explicitly indict them. First, there was an appeal to reason—Satan could not logically oppose himself (12:26). The question (12:27) that this passage raises is whether there was an active ministry of exorcism being performed by the Pharisees or their wider religious network; if there had been, then they would probably know that exorcism opposed Satan. If this were the case, their own exorcists would testify against the Pharisees. Consequently, Jesus was able to find witnesses that would condemn the Pharisees, even from their own community.

---

70. Kingsbury observes that Matthew's use of "Son of David" was restricted to Jesus' public standing; however, the disciples did not use this title for Jesus. Kingsbury, "Title 'son of David,'" 592. The disciples referred to Jesus as Lord. Kingsbury, "Title Kyrios," 255.

Alternatively, if Jesus' challenge concerning the source of their exorcisms was tongue in cheek, they were not able to cast out demons at all. This would be a comfortable fit with the parable; for their inability to cast out demons would be perceived as proof that they were on the same team as Satan, who could not oppose himself. Jesus, on the other hand demonstrated that he was opposed to Beelzebub by casting out Beelzebub. Contextually, this makes far more sense. The reason Jesus can cast them out is because he is their opposition, whereas the inability of the incumbents was due to their intrinsic unity with the "evil one." Matthew's assessment of Jesus' exorcisms was that this was clear evidence of the coming of the kingdom (12:28).

This comment was then followed by several other proverbial indictments. The first of these was the binding of the strong man as a prerequisite to the plundering of his possessions. This has (rightly) been generally understood as a metaphor for binding Satan; however, in Matthew's narrative there may be more to this statement. There is the possibility that the strong man who is preventing the departure of his "possessions" was in fact Jesus' human opposition. These opponents were, naturally enough, acting in concert with Satan. And within the context of their obstructionist program, which dismissed any possibility that Jesus could be the son of David, they were safeguarding their possessions. There is also a connection that can be made with the enigmatic character at the wedding feast, who was not wearing the correct clothes (22:11–13), who was bound, hand and foot, and then cast out. Matthew may have connected this unwelcome guest to the high priest by virtue of the Zechariah 3 connection. Should this be a legitimate correlation, the strong man that was to be bound was synonymous with the high priest, who guarded his house (Israel) against intruders (John and Jesus) who sought to plunder his possessions (Abraham's offspring). This will be considered at greater length in the next chapter.

The next pithy proverb clarified the lines of demarcation between those who were part of the kingdom program and those who were opposed to it. Matthew's inclusion of the saying, "He who is not with me is against me, and he who does not gather with me scatters" (12:30) was not accompanied by its Synoptic counterpart—"for whoever is not against us is for us."[71] The Pharisees were not only against Jesus; clearly they were scattering. So this proverb could only have been utilized to accentuate an already distinct divide.[72]

The challenge was then issued concerning the rejection of the Holy Spirit. Jesus had cast out demons and this power, according to the Matthean

---

71. Mark 9:40 and Luke 9:50, with a slight variation.

72. Luz and France both concede that Matthew's Jesus may have the Pharisees in mind here. Luz, *Matthew 8–20*, 209. France, *Matthew*, 482.

account, was by the Holy Spirit. The Pharisees had claimed that Beelzebub had driven out the demon. Whereas the Pharisees' slanderous accusations against Jesus may be forgiven, these opponents had inadvertently blasphemed the Holy Spirit—God. Therefore, they were now beyond any hope of forgiveness. From this point on their enmity was irreversible.

This platform provided Matthew's Jesus the opportunity to launch another tirade against the Pharisees. As they were bad trees, it was impossible for them to produce good fruit. After recalling the invective of John (brood of vipers), Jesus judged that they were evil (12:33–37), and therefore, they were only capable of producing evil.[73] The basis of their impending judgment would be their own words, presumably those that cast the slur upon the Holy Spirit.

This then leads us to the conclusion of the mission assessment. After the multiplicity of miracles and exorcisms, Jesus' opponents asked for a sign. After describing the scribes and Pharisees, along with those that they represented, as an "evil and adulterous generation," Jesus proposed that the sign be that of Jonah. Jonah unwillingly spoke to Nineveh, a godless and cruel city, and it immediately repented and avoided YHWH's wrath. Nineveh received no impressive miracles or kind words, and yet it repented. Israel, on the other hand, could not repent. Later in Matthew's narrative we will witness the priestly community receive reliable and first-hand testimony of Jesus' rising from the earth (just like Jonah's "resurrection" from the fish), and still be unmoved and impenitent.

This afforded one last opportunity to line up the witnesses for the prosecution. Nineveh would condemn "this generation," as would the enigmatic Queen of Sheba (12:42). The end for Israel would be far worse than what went before. Jesus' demonic cleansing would only result in a sevenfold rehabitation of the evil presence (12:43–45). The people are damnable now, but they will be seven times more damnable in the near future—all because they have rejected the mission of amnesty that Jesus offered. And so, that is how it will be with this generation (12:45).[74] In this long and arduous way, Matthew answered the question ("To what can I compare this generation?" 11:16) that was asked at the beginning of this mission summation. His account of the mission served to escalate the notion that Israel had reached the point of no return, and was now under the impending wrath of God.

---

73. Bear in mind the Lord's Prayer—"Deliver us from the evil one."

74. "The generation is being likened to those sent into exile" (Nolland, *Gospel of Matthew*, 510).

## Summation

This chapter has progressed through an extensive and complex set of engagements, discussions, mission experiences and reflections. The net result of the exploration was that Jesus could not broker peace; and this in turn made Israel, and particularly the priestly community (who were represented by their ubiquitous foot soldiers, the Pharisees),[75] vulnerable to judgment of the worst Matthean kind. This passage may yield other motifs, but few will be as strongly supported as the thread of prophetic indictment that this chapter has sought to expose.

---

75. "All the sub-groups (Scribes, Pharisees, Sadducees, Herodians etc.) are portrayed as representatives of the Jewish establishment" (Anderson, *Matthew's Narrative Web*, 98). They are a monolithic group, opposed to Jesus. Stanton, *Interpretation of Matthew*, 180.

# 6

# Parables as Principal Indictment Tool

> *The Teacher of Righteousness is one "to whom God made known all the mysteries of the words of His servants the Prophets."*
>
> (1QpHab VII)[1]

THE SYNOPTIC TRADITIONS ALL testify to the widespread use of parables by Jesus in his public ministry.[2] The reason for Jesus' use of parables has excited considerable debate and conjecture. The uniform testimony of the Synoptic Gospels as to why Jesus used parables[3] has not satisfied some scholars, who note the internal purpose statements concerning parables, but quickly move on to find other explanations—presumably unsatisfied with the severe Synoptic statements of intentionality.[4] "In the modern era few have found it [Jesus' explanation for using the parables] to have significance for actual interpretation."[5] Perhaps the reason for this is that most students of Matthew read it with a lens that is less compatible with the author's actual intention. Matthew's parables are clearly intended to be instruments

---

1. Vermes, *The Dead Sea Scrolls*, 286.
2. "Parables are *prophetic instruments*, the language of OT prophets, which occur especially in contexts of judgment and indictment" (Snodgrass, *Stories with Intent*, 159).
3. Matt 13:11–15; Mark 4:10–12; Luke 8:9–10 all connected Jesus' parables to Isaiah's indictment (Isa 6).
4. See McComiskey, "Exile and the Purpose." Also consider John Crossan for another approach: the parables were an expression of Jesus' religious experience. Crossan, "Seed Parables," 266.
5. Hultgren, *The Parables of Jesus*, 461.

of indictment, a consistent component of a book written to be a prophetic indictment. In pursuit of Matthew's literary intention, an examination of the author's selection, placement, embellishment and explanation of Jesus' parables will be profitable.

Certain observations concerning the use of parables need to be made at the outset. According to the Gospel traditions, the disciples were puzzled by Jesus' parables, and questioned why they were used at all. This militates against any suggestion that the use of parables was the "cutting edge" teaching method of the day, or that it was even widely used by other sects or religious leaders. It should also not pass our attention that the New Testament documents do not record that the Apostles employed this teaching method, either during, or after the time of Jesus, or instructed others to do the same. As a disciple was expected to emulate his or her "master," this would seem peculiar.[6] Lastly, as the prime motivation for using the parables publicly was plainly enunciated in each of the Synoptic Gospels, it would be remiss of any inquiry to neglect this principal explanation, which draws richly from a historical context foreshadowing judgment through exile.[7]

In light of this, it becomes plain that the author intended to revive in his readers' minds the horror associated by recommencing the Exile narrative by using the very words that launched it in the first place (Isa 6:9–10). Assuming that this casts some intelligible light upon Matthew's perception of Jesus' parabolic method, a number of parables will be revisited, in order to ascertain whether they can be recast as indictment tools, in a prophetic tradition. Consideration will be given to Matthew's choice and placement of parables, and the additional features found in the recasting of some, which may suggest that these parables had a specific and unique prophetic intention. The "lens" will also be applied to these parables, to determine whether there is a profitable interpretation that can be made by viewing them against the priesthood replacement motif, as well as a concluding chapter to the Tanach.[8]

---

6. It may be a mistake to assume that the parables had some common heritage with rabbinical allegories. The parables of Jesus were grounded in a prophetic tradition, and, as such, were intended to disclose mysteries—but not to all their hearers.

7. While this has been recently noted by Doug McComiskey, it is not necessary to conclude that the Exile was still in force as a spiritual condition for those who did not believe Jesus' message. It may not be profitable to understand exile in anything other than geographical terms; otherwise it would be necessary to assert that Israel was almost never out of exile. McComiskey, "Exile and the Purpose," 59–85.

8. A previous work has examined these parables by asking: "What if the parables of Jesus were neither theological nor moral stories but political and economic ones? What if the concern of the parables was not the reign of God but the reigning systems of oppression that dominated Palestine at the time of Jesus?" (Herzog, *Parables as Subversive Speech*, 7).

### The Sower and Matthew's Explanation of the Use of Parables

The Synoptic Gospels uniformly present the Parable of the Sower as the first of Jesus' parables, and attach the disciples' inquiry regarding Jesus' use of parables between the parable proper and its seemingly allegorical explanation.[9] Without wishing to spend disproportionate space on sources or primacy, it is immediately obvious that Matthew has seized the source materials and applied them with greater emphasis, incorporating doublets, amplification and immediate application. So while all the Gospels make reference to the Isaiah indictment, and can therefore be considered to carry a prophetic indictment motif, Matthew capitalizes on the implications far more than the other Gospels—which may suggest that Isaiah's indictment is more than a peripheral issue for Matthew.

Incorporating the explanation for the use of the public parables alongside the first designated parable suggests several things. As Jesus was asked why he taught using parables, it seems reasonably clear that the Parable of the Sower was not Jesus' first parable, even though it is the first appearance of the word "parable" in the Synoptic tradition. Secondly, placing the explanation for using parables within the context of this first recorded parable would suggest that Matthew's intention would be that all ensuing parables, particularly those of chapter 13, should be read in the light of Jesus' explanation. And finally, the fact that the Gospel writers all attached the Isaiahanic explanation to this specific parable must be significant. For this reason, any exegetical treatment of this parable must heavily rely on the broader contextual issues that are interspersed within the pericope.

Without the explanation for using the parable, the Parable of the Sower would hardly be remarkable. It presents a familiar agrarian scene, where for some reason the sower indiscriminately disperses the seed in various locations, with only one of these locations, the "good soil," being profitable. The specific explanation for this parable in Matthew specifies that the seed that is profitable as a consequence of falling into the "good soil" is comparable to the person who receives the word (a common feature of all hearers) and also understands it.[10] The Matthean Jesus' entire explanation begins: "When anyone hears the message about the kingdom and does not under-

---

9. It is distinctly possible that Jesus used allegories as well as parables. Allegories are word pictures that have symbolic representation which are intended to be understood in making a point; parables, though having allegorical applications, had much more to do with the revelation of Jesus and the destiny of the nation of Israel in Matthew's paradigm.

10. The parable is more a focus on the soils, rather than the sower or the seed. France, *Matthew*, 503.

stand it, the evil one comes and snatches away what was sown in his heart" (13:19). Matthew, clearly, wants the emphasis to fall upon comprehension. The one who understands is blessed, while those who only receive the word are not; indeed, whatever short-term benefit they derive from receiving the "seed" will be snatched away—a recurrent theme in Matthew's paradigm of judgment (25:29).

This judgment motif (taking back the little that some have) is a feature of many Matthean parables. This notion was further amplified, so as to establish its crucial function, by the explanatory statement, "Whoever has will be given more, and he will have an abundance. Whoever does not have, even what he has will be taken from him" (13:12). From this it appears that the word of God, considered in the light of the broadest definition possible, will have two eschatological outcomes for its recipients. Those who hear the word and fail to understand it have all prior benefit or privilege revoked, whereas those who hear the word and comprehend its true meaning keep what they have and are given even more.

Unlike the other Synoptics, Matthew wishes to leave no doubt as to what constitutes correct understanding of the seed/word. To understand the word was to comprehend the identity and significance of Jesus. As Matthew records, "For I tell you the truth, many prophets and righteous men longed to see what you see but did not see it, and to hear what you hear but did not hear it" (13:17). The narrative is not clear as to how the parables are intended to disclose Jesus' identity and glory, apart from Jesus' self-identification in the two that he explains;[11] perhaps this is not a function the parables naturally perform. In the light of Matthew's inclusion here of what the prophets and righteous ones longed for, it is a safe assumption that Matthew intended the parables to define, at least in part, the identity and role of the Messiah.[12]

## Explanation for the Use of Parables

Each of the Synoptic Gospels answers the question of Jesus' use of parables in slightly different ways, but they are consistent concerning the main point. Matthew's version of Jesus' response, "The knowledge of the secrets of the kingdom of heaven has been given to you, but not to them," like the other

---

11. In the Parable of the Sower Jesus' identity is not directly revealed. However, as the seed is disclosed as the word or the "message of the kingdom," it is clear that this refers to the message that Jesus brings, commencing from the time of John (11:12).

12. Concerning the parables, Bruce Chilton noted: "The aspect of divine self–disclosure is clearly an element held in common with the Isaiah Targum, but in Jesus' preaching it is much more emphatically a personal self–disclosure . . ." (Chilton, *A Galilean Rabbi*, 62).

Synoptics, proposes that parables are intended for the exclusion of those on the "outside," who, through parabolic teaching, are being denied "the secrets of the kingdom." Many have disputed this clearly contentious idea, but there are no substantial exegetical or linguistic grounds to challenge this explanation provided by the Gospels for why the parables were used.[13] The universal rationale for denying the "secrets of the kingdom" to the majority of Israelites is the quotation taken from Isaiah 6. As the Isaiah passage is the primary referent for parabolic usage, it is likely that Matthew considered the thrust of Isaiah's message to be both relevant and abiding for Jesus' public ministry.[14] In fact, the Isaiah quotation is prefaced by an explicit reference to Isaiah's relevance to the first-century Hebrew audience: "In them is fulfilled the prophecy of Isaiah." This additional statement, not found in the other Synoptics, goes some way to demonstrating that Matthew does not want the connection between Isaiah and the parables to be overlooked. Considering Matthew's overall emphasis on fulfillment, this could hardly be insignificant. According to Matthew, Isaiah's words were being fulfilled in the generation that heard Jesus; the parables were instruments of this fulfillment, and there is even a suggestion that this could be the greatest moment of Isaiah's prophecy—first-century Judea was the truly intended audience of Isaiah's indictment.

## Isaiah's Prophecy

Isaiah[15] was commissioned somewhere around 739 BC, "in the year that King Uzziah died." As recorded in Isaiah 6, Isaiah encountered the Lord of hosts through a terrifying vision.[16] Through this vision, it became clear that Isaiah, as well as the kingdoms of Israel and Judah, were under threat of imminent judgment. Following Isaiah's restoration through God's initiative,

---

13. "God has chosen some people to be enlightened and has deliberately left others in the dark, and the parables are designed to reinforce this divinely appointed separation" (France, *Matthew*, 508).

14. John (12:37–40) uses the Isaiah reference as the basis for the Jews not accepting the miracles of Jesus, further making the point that Jesus' ministry to Israel, according to the Gospel writers, was significantly influenced by the prophecy of Isaiah 6.

15. Over twenty copies of Isaiah were found at Qumran. Isaiah was of particular interest to the Essenes, whose first commentary/midrash was of the prophet, composed around 100 BC.

16. John asserts that Isaiah saw Jesus and witnessed about him (John 12:41). According to John, then, the words of indictment were first spoken by Jesus and given to Isaiah. If this were Matthew's view also, Jesus would not be repeating Isaiah's words, but his own.

Isaiah requested to be God's spokesperson and was commissioned with a message that was both peculiar and disturbing. He was told:

> Go and tell this people:
>
> "Be ever hearing, but never understanding; be ever seeing, but never perceiving. Make the heart of this people calloused; make their ears dull and close their eyes. Otherwise they might see with their eyes, hear with their ears, understand with their hearts, and turn and be healed" (Isa 6:9–10).

What makes this prophecy particularly disturbing is its finality: YHWH is speaking to "this people," but not with salvific intent. God's determination was that Israel and Judah be judged. He intended to further facilitate their recalcitrance by denying them the visual and auditory means by which they may have come to their senses and appealed for mercy. Judah had reached the place of no return and Isaiah's message made this point clear. Rather than being a trigger for repentance, the preaching of Isaiah was intended to escalate Judah's intransigence, and withhold the possibility of favor. God would ensure that the eyes, ears and hearts of the covenant nations would continue on their path toward destruction.[17]

Isaiah made no appeal for mercy or reconsideration. It was immediately apparent that this condemnation was justified and non-negotiable. Isaiah's only question was "how long?" The response was as plain as the prophecy itself:

> Until the cities lie ruined and without inhabitant, until the houses are left deserted and the fields ruined and ravaged, until the LORD has sent everyone far away and the land is utterly forsaken (Isa 6:11–12).

With this further clarification, it was apparent that both Israel and Judah were destined for destruction and exile, which were the ultimate penalty for covenantal crimes.[18] And so it was. Samaria was destroyed shortly after in 721 BC. The ten tribes that inhabited the northern kingdom were deported by Assyria, never to return. The southern kingdom of Judah endured two waves of exile to Babylon, which concluded with the destruction of Jerusalem and its temple by Nebuchadnezzar.

---

17. Isaiah's indictment expresses "a common theme among the prophets: Israel is too far gone and judgment is already decreed" (Snodgrass, *Stories with Intent*, 159).

18. Deut 28:21, 63; 29:28; Lev 18:25–27.

Judah's history from Isaiah's prophecy to 586 BC demonstrated the determination of God to "stay the course" of destruction.[19] Hezekiah and Josiah, both exemplary and reforming kings of Judah, were unable to restore Judah's standing with God, even when Josiah undertook covenantal renewal (2 Kgs 23). Judah's infrastructure was destroyed and the majority of its inhabitants remained in Babylon permanently; others returned approximately 70 years later, according to the biblical record.

The returnees from Persia, according to one account, numbered 42,360 (Ezra 2:64).[20] This was a miniscule percentage of those who had departed. However, according to Ezra and Nehemiah, the renewed Judah had reason to be confident concerning its future. God was clearly portrayed as the instigator of the resettlement through extraordinary Persian favor (Ezra 1), and the reconstruction process of temple and city were nothing short of remarkable. The return from Babylon marked an end to YHWH's former competitors. The post-exilic prophets do not refer to Israel's former pantheon (Baal, Asherah, etc.); on this issue, it would seem, the newly established Israel was truly reformed. There was a new zeal for the Law, purity, and the prescribed national identity markers. Fully sanctioned temple practices were re-established through the preservation of authentic Levitical priests. Judah continued this way for half a millennium, even being preserved from global Hellenization and its bloody aftermath. It appeared that Israel had been punished through exile and destruction, but now the reconstituted Judea had been substantially restored. The post-exilic community could feel confident of its standing with YHWH; it did not hear Isaiah's dire prophecy again until the first century. It is in this context that Jesus' restatement of Isaiah's prophecy must be understood.

## Fulfillment of Isaiah 6 in the First Century

YHWH's foreshadowed judgment in Isaiah 6 appears to come in two phases. The first of these judgments specifically points to the destruction of Samaria and Jerusalem, and their ensuing exiles. The second phase of judgment, however, is not so clear. It reads:

---

19. Jonah's prophecy of destruction to Nineveh warrants a mention for two reasons: it revealed that God was amenable to mercy toward Gentiles in contrast to his attitude to the covenant nations; also, showing mercy to Assyrian Nineveh was strategic for the destruction of Samaria by the undiminished Assyrian Empire.

20. This number is subject to some controversy. Williamson, *Ezra–Nehemiah*, 36.

> And though a tenth remains in the land, it will again be laid waste. But as the terebinth and oak leave stumps when they are cut down, so the holy seed will be the stump in the land (Isa 6:13).[21]

This verse is difficult to interpret due to its brevity, its allusions, its place in the wider context and its possible reference to secondary judgment, tinged with a glimmer of hope.[22] What is pertinent here is whether there is the possibility that Matthew considered Jesus to be YHWH's last and final wave of judgment.

It is difficult to ascertain whether Matthew's Jesus considered the prophecy included two distinct judgments. On the other hand, it is difficult to understand how Matthew's Jesus could raise the specter of this judgment again, specifically implicating the first century generation (13:14), if he believed the prophetic indictment of Isaiah had already run its course. Clearly, Matthew's Jesus believed that Isaiah's indictment was unfinished business, for there were ample other indictments that could have been invoked which did not have such a clear historical fulfillment.

Matthew may have intended Jesus' public ministry from Matthew 13, largely expressed through the use of parables,[23] to be understood as the final and unavoidable judgment prophesied by Isaiah.[24] Isaiah 6:13, on this reckoning, may have been awaiting fulfillment, which could be anticipated on the "Day of the Lord." Matthew's apocalypse (Matt 24) does not foreshadow any future exile, but only destruction.[25] In fact, the wise (those who are able to hear) are advised to exile themselves by fleeing before the impending day (24:16).

---

21. "The MT, although difficult, remains still the most plausible: 'It will again be laid waste, like a terebinth or an oak, whose stump is left over even when felled'" (Childs, *Isaiah*, 58).

22. Ibid., 57.

23. Though Matthew connects Isaiah 6 directly with Jesus' public teaching ministry, it is apparent throughout the Gospel that Israel is not only incapable of hearing; it is also incapable of seeing. The miracles are unconvincing for the first century audience of Jesus, even though the miracles are convincing enough for everybody else; even Sodom would still exist if it had seen what the Israelites had witnessed (11:21–24).

24. Joseph Alexander suggests that "the tenth will return and be for a consuming." He concluded that "The prediction was not fulfilled once for all, but again and again" (Alexander, *Isaiah*, 154).

25. Walter Brueggemann translated Isa 6:11–13 in this way: "until the failure of cities, houses, land; until the land has profound massive abandonment; until only 10 percent remain, and then fire, and then only a stump." The prophecy, according to Brueggemann, would end with the nullification of Israel, "a ceasing to be in the world. The burden of the oracle is that God has given up on this beloved people and will no more protect them, but will actively intervene to undo them" (Brueggemann, *Isaiah 1–39*, 61–62).

It is natural enough to try and avoid the implications of the Isaiah prophecy and try to soften the impact of its disproportionately negative words. Klyne Snodgrass, for instance, believed that Mark's version intentionally omitted "Make the mind of this people dull, and stop the ears, and shut the eyes, so that they may not look . . . and listen . . . and comprehend . . . and turn and be healed" in order to soften the implications.[26] Matthew has, however, also exercised some liberty here. By inserting "For this people's heart has become calloused" (3:15), Matthew is avoiding the notion that the parable is intended to make the heart calloused, for it is already the case that the "outsiders" are afflicted with this condition.[27] However, here lies the critical failure of interpretation of this indictment apart from its narrative context. These "outsiders" in Matthew are already subject to the curses that followed the conclusion of the mission (11:20–24). They had rejected Jesus, and he had now decreed their end. The leaders had committed the "unforgivable" sin (12:31) and even Jesus' closest relations (who stood "outside") have become alienated from the Messiah's mission (12:46–50). Prior to this, Jesus taught the disciples, but the crowds could also hear (7:28). The crowds were able to see ample signs, even in their hometowns (Matt 10). This privilege, however, was now to end. Open teaching was replaced with parables and miraculous signs would be replaced by the "sign of Jonah" (12:38). "Hearing and seeing" had, effectively, come to an end. The disciples were now to receive private instruction (13:10), even within the house (13:36). It is plain that the progression of the narrative is all-important in interpreting this loaded pericope.[28] The parables are presented by Matthew as the first expression of the judgment/curse of God/Jesus on a people who have rejected Jesus.

Matthew also used another reference point for Jesus' use of parables (13:33). The Psalm 78 reference establishes that Jesus' parables were not completely without salvific value; Jesus, according to Matthew, was disclosing "secret things hidden since the creation of the world." This by no means negates the former explanation for parabolic usage, for it was only the disciples who accessed these "secrets"; the parables were meaningful for those who could understand them. Within these parables Matthew presented a clear and high Christology and an eschatology that would shape

---

26. Snodgrass, *Stories with Intent*, 159.

27. Matthew uses ὅτι, which suggests "because"; Mark uses ἵνα, which suggests "in order that." For Mark, the parables are instrumental in this hardness, whereas for Matthew, they are a consequence of the hardness.

28. "For Matthew, Isaiah's words find close correspondence in the rejection of Jesus noted in chaps. 11 and 12" (Hagner, *Matthew 1–13*, 374).

the church's views for 2000 years.[29] So while parables were revelatory for the disciples of Jesus, they were not so for the crowds who were now on the outside. Matthew wanted Jesus' ministry to be understood as the completion or fulfillment of Isaiah's ministry.

## Early Parables: Matthew 13

Matthew 13 contains seven or eight parables, depending on how the last statement of Jesus (13:52) is understood. This group of parables is considered to be the third of Jesus' five discourses in Matthew. This particular discourse is in the center of the manuscript, thus pointing to its centrality in understanding the whole document. The other Synoptics report the Parable of the Sower much earlier, and do not attach the parabolic set that is found here in Matthew. So, without doubt, Matthew considers the Sower, along with its complementary set of parables and the extended explanation for using the parables, to be integral in portraying the mission of Christ.

As a prelude to this discourse, Jesus confronted the Pharisees and teachers of the law concerning their desire for a sign. His refusal to give them a sign, other than the sign of Jonah, set the backdrop for understanding the parables of Matthew 13. Nineveh repented at the preaching of Jonah, and the Queen of Sheba came a great distance to hear the wisdom of Solomon (12:41–42). The point being made by this is that Gentiles of that time required no sign, but the contemporary wicked and perverse generation did. Jesus' teaching, which is greater than the wisdom of Solomon, is now to be heard. The hearers must listen to Jesus if they are to have any reprieve from their condition, which is condemnable. Indeed, Nineveh and the Queen of Sheba would be called as witnesses to testify to Israel's recalcitrance. Following this, Matthew also recorded the allegory of the exorcism as a prelude to the chapter. Once the demon was cast out, the cleansed "house" became suitable for seven demons, and was thus entirely corrupted. Indeed, Jesus was casting out demons and healing the sick; this, however, was not translating into faith or understanding. On the contrary, Jesus' ministry appeared to compound the problem—even being a catalyst for the establishment's conspiracy to destroy him. Signs, then, are unprofitable: "ever seeing they do not see." This prepared the scene for the parables, where the same phenomenon can be observed. Although faith comes by hearing, *ever hearing*

---

29. By these seven parables Matthew portrayed Jesus as universal judge, the possessor of the world, and the one who owns and commands angels. The doctrines of the last day's separation and the notion of hell are primarily drawn from Matthew's document, and first explicitly cited in this set of parables.

this generation *does not hear*. And in this way, the narrative prepares its readers for the central discourse on parables.

The first of the parables, the Parable of the Sower, described the profitable person as one who heard the word along with everyone else, but, unlike the majority, also understood it. This has been considered in brief. The fate of the other seed was to become unprofitable, its recipients having been fickle, preoccupied with worldly concerns or lacking in perseverance. Each of these examples of seed, although intrinsically good, achieved little as they were not accompanied by a ruthless and steadfast dedication. The benefits that Jesus' hearers received from his teachings were short-lived; they did not translate into permanent and abundant blessing. Like the temporarily cleansed house, the recipients of the word in the parable did not benefit for long; their final state was worse than before they had received the seed. Apart from the seed that fell in the good soil, which represented those who understood, all other seeds produced a false start and disappointment.

The second parable was the Parable of the Weeds. It, along with the next five parables in this set, began with the formulaic, "the kingdom of heaven is like." By commencing these parables this way Jesus would have caught the interest of the audience, who had an acute interest in the kingdom of heaven and the possibility of its imminence. The hearers would have had every reason to believe that Jesus was teaching them something of great importance, which could be of significant benefit to them. Although there was no deception on Jesus' part, without intimacy with the teacher the message of the parables would remain superficially pleasing and simple, yet fundamentally obscure and with an unattainable meaning. This is the very message contained within the first parable of the set, the Parable of the Sower.

In the Parable of the Weeds, good seed was sown, which produced wheat. The enemy then sowed weeds among the wheat.[30] The wheat and weeds grew together and were clearly distinguishable, but allowed to coexist until the Day of Judgment. On the final day a separation would occur, resulting in the weeds going to the flames and the wheat being collected for the barn.[31] This parable was later explained at the disciples' request when they were alone with Jesus. Having already established that his preferred designation was the "Son of Man," the person who sowed the "good seed" was revealed to be Jesus; the "enemy" was the devil. The harvesters were Jesus' angels. With further elaboration, Jesus emphasized the end of both the

---

30. The sinister nature of the enemy is emphasized by his actions while the farmer was sleeping—he works under cover of darkness (secretly). Hendriksen, *Matthew*, 563. Jesus, on the other hand, did his work in the open and during the day (26:55).

31. Later in the narrative the Pharisees will be identified as the plants that have not been planted by God and will be pulled out by the roots (15:13–14).

good seed and the weeds—blessedness and damnation. This parable also bears the judgment motif of the separation of the good from the bad, which is the purpose of YHWH's coming, according to Malachi (Mal 3:17–18).

This parable, which was only clarified to the disciples in the "house," portrayed Jesus as the source of every human who is acceptable for the kingdom. This extraordinary explanation revealed what was not known to the parable hearers, that is, that Jesus had planted and preserved all who enter the kingdom. Did the disciples understand the implication of this explanation? Did they also understand that those who were uncommitted and indifferent to Christ, along with his enemies, were the offspring of the devil and destined for the flames? Whatever Jesus planted was good; the rest were intended to be strategic to the devil's obstructionist agenda.[32]

This parable was intended to demarcate the universal battle lines, and so reveal a worldview that, under normal circumstances, would be considered paranoid and conspiratorial.[33] Its explanation should have enlightened the disciples concerning Jesus' view of himself, and helped them to understand why he was in constant conflict with the leaders of Israel. Further, as the field was defined as the world, Jesus was not casting himself as exclusively the sower of blessing for Israel, but as the universal redeemer and judge.[34]

What, however, would those "on the outside" have made of this parable? The natural presumption within Israel was that the Jews had God's favor as a consequence of the covenantal privileges that they enjoyed. Why would the hearers assume that they were anything but the planting of the Lord in the world, convinced of their good standing with God and their blessed destiny? Jesus informed the disciples that this was not the case—otherwise "they would turn and be healed."

Placed between the Parable of the Weeds and its private explanation are two parables that fundamentally develop the same idea as each other. The Parable of the Mustard Seed and the Parable of the Yeast both describe something small, which, in due course, became totally pervasive and dominant. Again, these were descriptive of the kingdom of heaven. The neatest way to understand this pair is to observe that the kingdom will initially appear small, grow incrementally and intentionally, and finally be the largest

---

32. Kingsbury's view of this parable is that it is a call for separation from the synagogue. In due course, God would separate the church from Judaism. Snodgrass, *Stories with Intent*, 204.

33. This is a feature of Johannine theology also; believers are the offspring of God, unbelievers are the offspring of Satan (John 8:43; 1 John 3:10).

34. Robert McIver considers the parable to be a call for tolerance within the church community; that is, the need to put up with imperfection till the return of Jesus. McIver, "The Parable of the Weeds."

and most pervasive of all kingdoms. Intuitively, this would be a ludicrous way for a kingdom to come. Kingdoms that sought dominance and control came on a grand scale with significant military might. This kingdom, however, was "forcefully advancing" (11:12), and through these illustrations of Matthew's Jesus, nothing would hinder its progress and ultimate dominance over all things, not even the "gates of hell" (16:18).[35] Although the metaphors of a harmless mustard plant and a lump of dough would scarcely be seen as awful apocalyptic images, in reality that is how they were intended to be understood. In many parables, the folksy and whimsical character of the central illustration was both disarming and disturbingly understated. Jesus and the kingdom that he had inaugurated would become the only redemptive hope of many, and the certain destruction of most.

These two parables, unlike the first two, were not interpreted. Perhaps Matthew's intention was to establish a hermeneutic for understanding the parables that could then be applied to all the parables. Should this be the case, the first interpretive guideline for these parables, as well as all the others, is that they disclose the Matthean Jesus' fundamental worldview; he is the central causal character of world history and his role has universal and permanent applicability. What was disclosed, therefore, did not have regional or time-bound relevance alone: it purports to be the metanarrative of Jesus revealing the way history would play out. This is an audacious claim by any measure. In view of this, the one who planted the mustard seed and the woman who added the yeast are together portrayals of Jesus' own role in this metanarrative. He is the founder, sustainer and possessor of the kingdom of heaven, and the world is his field.

An aspect of the parables that requires some attention is Jesus' use of distasteful or politically incorrect terms in the Synoptics. In many parables within the Synoptic tradition, Jesus used illustrations that would have been provocative to his hearers. Commending the dishonest manager (Luke 16:1–15), caring for "unclean" ravens (Luke 12:24), and comparing his own future return to "a thief in the night" (24:43) must all have created some disquiet amongst the Hebrew audience. These particular parables were also suggestive and probably confronting. The mustard tree became

---

35. The prophet Joel depicted the Day of YHWH as a day of invasion. YHWH would lead an army as large as a locust plague, an organized, powerful, unbeatable army that would enter the window like a thief and burn everything before it. "Before them the earth shakes, the sky trembles, the sun and moon are darkened, and the stars no longer shine. The LORD thunders at the head of his army; his forces are beyond number, and mighty are those who obey his command. The day of the LORD is great; it is dreadful. Who can endure it?" (Joel 2:10–11) Is this how the forceful advance of the kingdom of heaven should be interpreted? "The term βιάζομαι can mean 'occupy a territory by force'" (Balabanski, *Eschatology*, 152).

a haven for the birds of the air, who, should the metaphor be extended, would have been the natural enemy of the mustard seed that produced the tree. The birds of the air, which benefited from the security provided by the tree, presumably, as the metaphor goes, were also welcome within the kingdom of heaven. As these birds were not identified, and in view of the fact that Peter objected to eating certain "birds of the air" because they were "unclean" (Acts 10:12–14), it may be the case that this parable is referring to Gentile inclusion.[36] Similarly, and more substantially, yeast/leaven for Jews may have been synonymous with sin and impurity.[37] God commanded that all celebrations in Israel be conducted without yeast in bread or anything else. It was not even to be found within the national borders (Exod 13:7) and those who breached the ordinance, on particular days, were to be "cut off" (Exod 12:15). In view of this, it is peculiar and highly provocative to assert that the kingdom of heaven is like "yeast." Why this metaphor is used is not explained, and it would have made Jewish hearers less amenable to Jesus and his kingdom message.

The fifth and sixth parables in the set also make a similar or identical point to each other. The Parable of the Hidden Treasure and the Parable of the Valuable Pearl are only found in Matthew, and advance one of Matthew's recurring themes. Both parables centered on the discovery of items of supreme value. The treasure in the field may have been accidentally found, although this was not necessarily the case. Whether it was found as the result of an active search, or simply stumbled upon, the point is that the discoverer knew its value and was prepared to abandon everything else to secure the treasure. The merchant was specifically looking for special pearls; when one of supreme value was found, he too abandoned everything that he formerly possessed, in order to possess this one pearl.

These parables immediately remind the reader of the total commitment that Jesus insisted was necessary for kingdom attainment. Self-mutilation (5:29, 30), total dispossession (18:21) and familial abandonment (10:37, 38) are all possible, if not required, in order to attain the prize that Jesus had come to inaugurate. The disciples are portrayed as having "left everything"

---

36. Paul considered that a significant mystery (secret) of the gospel was Gentile inclusion. He wrote: "This mystery is that through the gospel the Gentiles are heirs together with Israel, members together of one body, and sharers together in the promise in Christ Jesus" (Eph 3:6). See also, Bird, *Jesus and the Origins*, 72–77.

37. There has been a traditional understanding that leaven/yeast was indicative of evil and the mustard tree was a noxious plant. This has been recently challenged by Ryan Schellenberg, who has found no historical evidence to suppose that these were deemed to be sinister or undesirable. Schellenberg, "Kingdom as Contaminant?"

to follow Jesus (19:27).[38] These two parables entrench this aspect of Jesus' teaching as central to Matthew's soteriology—perhaps the only salvation that was available under the Law. Some clarification of this point is essential.

Without wishing to attempt a thoroughgoing reconstruction of Matthew's understanding of the Mosaic covenant, it is necessary, at this point, to propose a solution, which must heavily rely on the theology of Paul. Paul considered that those who were bound by the Mosaic covenant were effectively under a curse (Gal 3:10). Paul's rationale for this was that the Law required absolute obedience continually in order to attain the blessings that were available to those under this covenant. Matthew, at every point within the Gospel, upholds the tenets of Torah and even affirms an extremely rigorous interpretation of it, as can be plainly seen in the Sermon on the Mount. Rather than negate Pauline theology, Matthew affirms Paul's view of the Law's rigorous demands and binding requirements—even to the *yod* and *tittle* (5:18). Matthew did not portray Jesus as abandoning any of the Law's requirements or relaxing its demands on anyone, even on the disciples. In view of this, Jesus' soteriology, as recorded by Matthew, necessarily imposed the exacting and onerous requirements of the Law; no other system could be taught or advised. Jesus was under the Law, which required that the Law be taught without contradiction. Within Matthew's paradigm, those who had appropriated faith, and so attained to a blessed state in spite of their personal failings, did so as a consequence of God's revelation and instigation, not through Christ's personal tuition (16:17). Jesus did not instruct people to have faith; however, he actively searched for faith and greatly rejoiced when he observed that God had shown this kindness.[39]

These parables of the discovered valuable items can be interpreted in two different ways. As Jesus was the primary human subject of all the former parables, it would be appropriate to consider that Jesus was the one who absolutely denied himself in order to attain the prize of the kingdom of heaven, which, as Matthew records at the conclusion of the Gospel, was given by the Father (28:18).[40] In this case, these parables testify that the only one who attains the treasure is the one who is prepared to pay the ultimate cost. The parables could also be interpreted as the obligation placed upon every Israelite who wants to attain the kingdom's treasure—namely Christ. This, however, would be the least likely interpretation; for even the disciples were shown by Matthew to be slow learners and occasionally faithless

---

38. France, *Matthew*, 539.

39. Matt 8:10; 9:22; 11:25; 15:18; 16:17.

40. Matthew clearly intends his readers to make the connection with Dan 7:14, where "one like a Son of Man" was given an everlasting kingdom and all authority.

(17:17–20). Matthew's final assessment concerning the disciples conforms to the unchallenged perspective presented in the church's Epistles: their selection and appointment was based on grace alone.

The last parable, the Parable of the Net, reiterated the teaching of the first kingdom parable, the Parable of the Weeds, within the set.[41] The net harvested the produce of the sea indiscriminately. The fishermen then selected the good fish and threw the rest away. This parable was immediately explained thus: the wicked are separated from the righteous. What is striking about this explanation is that the destiny of the righteous was not mentioned; Matthew's interest here was in the destiny of the wicked—Jesus' angels would "throw them into the fiery furnace, where there will be weeping and gnashing of teeth" (13:50). In a similar way, the Parable of the Weeds also spent more time disclosing the destiny of the "weeds." This may go some way to enlightening us in regard to Matthew's particular intention for this third discourse. The judgment of the wicked was possibly more pertinent to Matthew's agenda than the destiny of the righteous. If so, this set of parables, particularly in view of the stated rationale for their use, were intended to foreshadow the end that Jesus' audience were to expect. Rather than representing future possibilities or options, the parables are veiled indictments, made explicit to the disciples, who alone became privy to the terrifying implications.

## The Last Mysterious Parable/Allusion

Following these parables Jesus tested the disciples' comprehension by asking: "Have you understood all these things?" (13:51).[42] Many commentators view their positive response to this question with some cynicism, and rightly so.[43] Matthew had no qualms about portraying the disciples as being slow learners (15:16). Although they were advised concerning Jesus' death several times, the message was never understood. They are set in contrast with, of all people, a Gentile woman, who had not been privy to the teaching of Jesus. She understood, and was consequently considered to have "great

---

41. France has pointed out that the OT background to this parable has all but been ignored. "Hab. 1:14–17 views God as having made people like fish and Babylon as being allowed to catch them in nets and then sacrifice to his nets. Ezek 32:3 says God will throw a net over Pharaoh and haul him up in his dragnet" (Snodgrass, *Stories with Intent*, 488). The first of these is particularly interesting, especially if the kingdom is being presented as comparable to an invading empire that brings judgment.

42. France acknowledges the incomplete character of the disciples' understanding, but believes that they are on the road to greater understanding. France, *Matthew*, 544.

43. Hagner, *Matthew 1–13*, 401.

faith" (15:28). Within Matthew, the disciples' awareness of who Jesus was did not surface till later in the document (Matthew 16); even then Jesus rebuked Peter for not understanding the program. What then should be made of the conclusion of these parables: "He said to them, 'Therefore every teacher of the law who has been instructed about the kingdom of heaven is like the owner of a house who brings out of his storeroom new treasures as well as old'" (13:52)?

This statement, which rounds off the pericope, must reflect on the whole discourse. By its placement, it would seem to be crucial in understanding the parables within this set. So it is certainly important to understand what it means. A few suggestions have been made: the preferred views are that the disciples became these "teachers of the law," or that such learned Christians existed in the Matthean community that they naturally fell into this category.[44] Another suggestion is that Matthew himself may have been such a scholar, and this was an attempt to strengthen his credentials in the early community.[45] What is particularly interesting is that a number of commentators believe that γραμματεύς referred to a Christian scribe. There has even been an attempt to reconstruct the sentence to read everyone "discipled to be a scribe."[46] The problem with these various proposals is that they do not give due consideration to the force of γραμματεύς (teacher of the law/scribe) within the total document. Jesus was always referred to as διδάσκαλος, never γραμματεύς. Why then, would his disciples ever be given the institutional foes' designation, unless they were such before they had met Christ?[47]

---

44. Ibid., 402.

45. It has been suggested that this scribe is Matthew himself. Senior, "Between Two Worlds." Also, Hannan, *The Measure and Demands*, 121. If indeed Matthew was the author of this document, he was not interested in advancing any personal standing. For one thing, by making no mention of authorship it would appear that the author was not driven by a self-disclosure agenda. Assuming Matthean authorship, Matthew demonstrates considerable humility. When the disciples fail in understanding or conduct, no exception is made, even for the author. Also, following the record of Matthew's inclusion (9:9), Jesus' comments concerning his mission to save "sinners" and the "sick" must surely reflect poorly on Matthew. As a tax collector, Matthew was the antithesis of the establishment, which was typified by the teachers of the law. Matthew was their outcast; therefore, it would be highly unlikely that he would confuse the issue by taking their discredited standing (γραμματεύς) and applying it to himself. None of the disciples, to our knowledge, were trained interpreters of the Mosaic Law, which is the usual definition of scribe. France, *Matthew*, 544.

46. Nolland, *Gospel of Matthew*, 569.

47. Don Carson notes that the construction only works one way; that is, scribes who become disciples. Carson, "The Jewish Leaders," 171.

Teachers of the Law, in Matthew, are scholars of the Torah who lawfully sit in the seat of Moses (23:2). Mark (Mark 2:16) and Luke (Acts 23:9) both identify teachers of the law as Pharisees, though clearly these designations are not synonymous in Matthew. In Matthew, they are specifically the theological directors of first century Judaism,[48] and as such, are Jesus' main opposition along with the other Pharisees.[49] In Jesus' protracted indictment (chapter 23), they are the primary objects of his wrath. Many of these scholars/scribes would have been drawn from the highest priestly ranks.[50] So it would be highly unusual that this designation would be used in place of the normal designation given to Jesus' chosen followers—the apostles. There is the possibility, however, that this designation was intended to identify an apostolic individual who was not part of Matthew's story.

There is no doubt that Pharisees, and consequently, teachers of the law, were significant participants in the life of the early church (Acts 15:5). The first ingathering of converts was likely to have included many of the Jerusalem teachers. The first message of Peter was in Jerusalem, and most probably in the temple precincts. An address of this type, which resulted in mass conversion, must have had the attention of the ubiquitous priestly caste within the walls of Jerusalem. Peter's instruction to those who perceived the implications of his message was that they should repent and be baptized (Acts 2:38). In Luke's paradigm, the Pharisees and Sadducees did not repent, and therefore, they were not baptized along with the majority of Judeans (Luke 7:30). This being the case, Luke's Peter may well have been instructing the "recent" converts to do what John had previously implored them to do. The baptism of the Holy Spirit was the bonus that would be added to these post-resurrection proselytes (Acts 2:38). Should it be Matthew's intention to affirm this community of Christian Pharisees, there is every possibility that they would have been well represented within Matthew's theological fraternity.[51]

---

48. Theological literacy was beyond the scope of most Hebrews, who were dependent upon an elite educated community that interpreted and disclosed the Torah's requirements. The function of "scribe" in the post-exilic community took on special significance when Ezra, the first high priest after the Exile, was primarily designated סֹפֵר (scribe)—implying official or administrator. Many priests were regional scribes in the post-exilic community. Leuchter, "'The Levite in your gates,'" 433.

49. Not all teachers of the law were against Jesus; at least one even sought to follow him (Matt 8:19).

50. Matthew has five categories of leadership in Israel: chief priests, teachers of the law, Pharisees, Sadducees and elders of the people. Apart from the Sadducees, these leadership groups were used in interchangeable combinations by Matthew, and they never appeared to be in conflict with each other within this narrative.

51. Bird considers that Matt 23:15 may be a reflection on the Judaizers who followed

There is another possibility, which builds on the same premise. In recent scholarship, Matthew has been regarded, by some, to have a significant contra-Pauline agenda.[52] Such verses as "many will say Lord, Lord . . ." have been interpreted as a denial of a fundamental Pauline doctrine.[53] There is the possibility, however, that the conclusion of the third discourse anticipates and affirms a teacher of the law who, having been discipled into the kingdom, would bring out[54] of his treasury understanding of both the old and the new. While all converted Pharisees could be cast in the light of this affirmation, there is the possibility that this conclusion to the parabolic set was an affirmation of a particular Pharisee, Paul.[55] It may be that Matthew sought to endorse the "latter apostle's" ministry[56]—particularly at a time when Paul was being so easily dismissed by Christian and non-Christian Jews in Jerusalem.[57] As this possibility has not been canvassed in any of the background material consulted for this reading, a brief case will be made for the contention, which, if viable, would appear germane to understanding Matthew's theology and intent.

---

the Christian mission to advocate law-keeping among Gentiles. Bird, *Crossing Over Sea and Land*, 68.

52. Sim, "Matthew 7.21–23." On the other hand, David Wenham had made a case for the similarity of Matthew's and Paul's soteriology. Wenham, "The Rock."

53. Rom 10:9; 1 Cor 12:3.

54. Peter Phillips notes that the verb ἐκβάλλει may not mean "bring forth," but "cast out." So he argues that the call may be for the scribe to jettison the new and old to make way for the kingdom's treasure. Phillips, "Casting Out the Treasure." Perhaps, however, ἐκβάλλει works just as well when the disciple is constrained to declare the "new and old."

55. The proposition that Matthew may have had Paul in mind when referring to the "teacher of the law discipled into the kingdom" could be considered unjustifiable if others had not previously argued similarly from Matthew 7:14–30. David Sim believes that Matthew had Paul and his community in mind as those who falsely claimed to be serving Christ, and consequently, were the objects of Matthew's severe eschatological censure (workers of lawlessness). Further, Weiss, Loisy and Taylor have also proposed that the cameo in Luke and Mark of the unauthorized and accepted exorcist was a veiled endorsement of Paul who was not acceptable within the Jerusalem "inner-circle." Sim, "Matthew 7.21–23," 325–43. Therefore, there is precedence for believing that a cameo of Paul may exist in Matthew.

56. It is plain from New Testament documents that Paul's apostolic credentials were not obvious to all; hence the necessity for Paul's robust defense of his calling (1 Cor 9:1–2).

57. While Matt 13:52 declared that "every teacher of the law. . ." This would not negate the possibility of there being one particular person who fitted this description in Matthew's estimation. At the very least, it must certainly be conceded that Paul unmistakably fits this description and function better than any other NT character, even if there were many other candidates.

It is probable, in view of the flow of Matthew's narrative, that the disciples did not have a clear grasp of what Jesus was telling them concerning the parables. The "secrets" were given to them, but they had only the most rudimentary of insights as a consequence. Given that they affirmatively answered Jesus' probing question without being totally persuaded by, or conversant with, Jesus' worldview and eschatology, it would be odd if Jesus were ready to describe them as teachers of the significant treasure. Jesus' parables, and his hermeneutic of them within this set, proposed a significant paradigm shift from existing second temple theology. In brief, Jesus proposed that:

- He was the steward of God's word, who uttered mysteries previously hidden—by implication, the teachers of the law were not;
- He was the judge of Israel and the world;
- He would send his angels to facilitate final judgment;
- He was the object of longing of former prophets and other righteous individuals;
- Judgment would be based on correct conduct as opposed to former covenants or racial divides;
- Gentiles would enter his kingdom;
- The kingdom of heaven would relentlessly advance and dominate all kingdoms;
- The devil was the origin of those who were indifferent or opposed to Jesus;
- Isaiah's indictment was fulfilled in that generation.

These "secrets" were most certainly not fully understood by the disciples at that time, even though they were disclosed.

Paul, on the other hand, considered that he was given insight into and stewardship of the mystery (μυστήρια) of God.[58] The author of 2 Peter considered that Paul spoke with God's wisdom, and that his epistles were Scripture, which the unstable distorted to their own destruction (2 Pet 3:15). Paul's particular "mystery" was to do with the identity of Christ, final judgment, and the inclusion of the Gentiles. These three themes are intrinsically incorporated into the discourse of Matthew 13, and also disclosed as μυστήρια.

---

58. "Although I am less than the least of all God's people, this grace was given me: to preach to the Gentiles the unsearchable riches of Christ, and to make plain to everyone the administration of this mystery" (Eph 3:8–9). Also, Col 1:26–27; 2:2; 1 Cor 2:7; 4:1; 15:51; Eph 1:9; 3:3–4; 6:19; Rom 16:25.

According to Acts, the Jerusalem Council met to consider the issue of Gentile inclusion, an issue that was primarily championed by Paul. Paul's rebuke of Peter, recorded in Galatians 2, revealed that Peter had not been fully convinced of the mystery of Gentile inclusion, even though he had indicated otherwise to Jesus, at the end of this passage in Matthew.[59]

Another possible reference to this issue in Matthew is found at the end of the indictment of chapter 23. These "woes," concerning the teachers of the law and the Pharisees, culminate with the indictment that would make them responsible for the shedding of all righteous blood. Jesus sent them prophets, wise men and teachers of the law (γραμματεύς); some would be killed and crucified, flogged in their synagogues and pursued from town to town (23:34). This vilification happened before or at the time of the writing of Matthew. Although the description has general apostolic relevance, it fits none better than Paul, whose journeys and persecutions recorded in Acts, along with his own letters, confirm the total disdain that many had for Paul, both within and outside the church, and particularly in Jerusalem.

The suggestion is this: without Paul's insights and writings, the secrets may not have been clarified to the early church. Paul testified to receiving the secrets, and championed them in spite of relentless persecution. No other apostle described his ministry as a stewardship of the μυστήρια. The set of parables in Matthew 13 are a disclosure of the "μυστήρια of the kingdom" (13:11). Paul alone, among the primitive Christian community, could be classified as a scholar and teacher of the law—à propos Matthew's designation. As perhaps the highest profile member of the early church, Paul had attained almost universal disapproval;[60] therefore, it is not impossible that the writer of Matthew would afford him a "cameo," and therefore, an "apostolic" endorsement.

Though it is by no means proven, a veiled reference to Paul, such as may be possible here, would be pertinent to understanding Matthew's theology. Matthew, more than any other Gospel writer, presented and defined righteousness (δικαιοσύνη) as the goal of God's people.[61] Paul also considered that righteousness was the goal of both Judaism and Christianity.[62]

---

59. This whole discussion assumes two things of Matthew, apart from an early dating. The first assumption is that Matthew was aware of Paul's reputation, teachings and claims at the time of this record. Second, it assumes that Matthew was aware of the movements and theology of Peter during and after the time of the Jerusalem Council.

60. Acts 19:26; 24:5.

61. Jesus' hardline view of salvation under the Mosaic dispensation in Matthew reaches a palpable and disturbing climax when the disciples cry, "Who then can be saved?" (19:25).

62. Paul uses the word δικαιοσύνη twenty-nine times in Romans alone.

Matthew explicitly[63] taught that righteousness was a matter of conduct and correct adherence to Torah,[64] while Paul taught that God justified sinners, and therefore considered them righteous, by faith alone—apart from works.[65] This sharp conflict continues to present difficulties for the faith community, which historically has been divided by the two views of attaining righteousness.[66]

An implicit reference to Paul may do two things to resolve this issue and help us understand Matthew's document. It would suggest that Matthew's "righteousness" was in agreement with Paul, who also believed that those under the Law gained their righteousness by keeping the Law.[67] Secondly, and most importantly for this reading, it would appear that Matthew was not concerned to develop a thoroughgoing doctrine of new covenant soteriology; its primary concern, it seems, was to clarify the binding requirements of the Mosaic covenant as the basis of completing God's demands, and thereby gaining righteousness. As righteousness was not attainable by anybody who did not greatly exceed the best and most rigorous righteousness of the day (5:20), it is clear that nobody can attain it, and consequently, all would be removed from covenant with God. This testifies to Matthew's broad intention—to communicate that Jesus came to fulfill God's longstanding indictment against Israel. Nonetheless, redemption is available to those who are privy to the private teachings of Jesus—the disciples who are in his "house."

## Central Parables: Making the Message Clear

The parables of chapter 13 within Matthew were intended to show that the public hearers of Jesus did not receive anything more than interesting

---

63. Matthew also implicitly teaches salvation by belief in Jesus. Matthew's Jesus said to them, "I tell you the truth, the tax collectors and the prostitutes are entering the kingdom of God ahead of you. For John came to you to show you the way of righteousness, and you did not believe him, but the tax collectors and the prostitutes did. And even after you saw this, you did not repent and believe him" (21:21–32).

64. Matt 5:20.

65. Rom 3:21–24.

66. "The noun 'righteousness' is not found in Mark and it occurs only once in Luke (1:75). But in Matthew it is used seven times, and in every case the evangelist has almost certainly introduced the word himself. This is one of Matthew's most important and distinctive theses. Whereas Paul uses the word to refer to God's *gift* of grace or salvation by which man is enabled to stand in a right relationship with his Creator, in Matthew the word refers to the righteous conduct which God *demands* of disciples" (Stanton, *The Gospels and Jesus*, 69–70).

67. Gal 3:12.

stories, while the disciples were given the keys to understanding them. Without the explanation of the parables, the crowd would have had no reason to believe that Jesus was illustrating the concept of judgment against them.[68] Final judgment, which divided the "good" from the "bad," was standard second temple eschatology;[69] those who were not in covenant relationship with God (Gentiles, sinners and tax collectors) would experience YHWH's wrath. Indeed, if post-exilic theological reflection had taught Israel anything it was that separation from sinners and Gentiles was integral to maintaining covenantal legitimacy and remaining in the land (Ezra 9:1–15). Therefore, without the explanation of the parables, most of Jesus' stories could be reconciled as consistent with the mainstream conservative view—that a pure and separate Israel was safe from God's wrath. This was of particular concern to the Essenes who exercised widespread influence.[70]

The latter parables, however, are different from the former; for while judgment was obscured in the former, it was unmistakable in the latter—"When the chief priests and the Pharisees heard Jesus' parables, they knew he was talking about them" (21:45). These parables, within Matthew's narrative, become triggers for an escalation of conflict (21:46) and contribute a clear historical and eschatological framework that clarifies the covenantal breaches of Jesus' opponents. Some of the parables under consideration are uniquely Matthean. Other parables, which were also recorded in Luke or Mark, are substantially different, though usually in similar order.

The Parable of the Unmerciful Servant (18:21–35), which is one of two parables found in the fourth discourse, was directed toward the disciples for their instruction. The whole discourse centers on two issues: acceptance of the lowly and forgiveness. The question that is answered by these parables is "Who is the greatest in the kingdom of heaven?" (18:1).[71] As a prelude to this parable, Peter asked Jesus how often it was necessary to forgive. Jesus' response, "seventy times seven," is reminiscent of Lamech's boast that his wrath brought about vengeance of "seventy fold seven" (Gen 4:24). Lamech, who was portrayed as the apex of boastful vindictiveness in the prediluvian world, was the antitype of kingdom graciousness. This set the scene for the parable, which required little explanation.

---

68. Keener, *Matthew*, 128.

69. As it is a point of inconsistency for some, it needs to be noted that the prospect of a violent final judgment in Matthew is not inconsistent with the ethical dimension of nonviolence for Jesus' disciples. See Reid, "Violent Endings."

70. Harrington, *The Impurity Systems*, 261. For influence of the Essenes see Stegemann, *The Library of Qumran*, 138.

71. Snodgrass, *Stories with Intent*, 65.

The servant within the parable had an astronomical debt, one that was clearly beyond the means of any human to repay.[72] This man and his family were to be sold into slavery, and all his possessions confiscated. Even this would have been insufficient to repay the debt; it was, however, a provision within the Law that debts be recovered this way.[73] The master did not consign a time frame for repayment, so it is safe to assume that the conditions and obligations of the Law would be met; the man and his family would be released after seven years. However, this was not greatly relevant, as the man pleaded for mercy and received it. The forgiven servant then found a man who owed him a relatively small sum, about three months' wages. This second debtor, after being assaulted by his creditor, pleaded for more time. Rather than receive forgiveness, he was placed in incarceration, a provision not made by the Law, until "all the debt be repaid." The master heard of this hypocrisy and ingratitude and had his servant cast into prison, until the unpayable debt be paid.[74]

This parable picks up a favorite Matthean doctrine, one that was first proposed in the Sermon on the Mount. Those who are forgiven are those who in turn forgive (6:12–15). This forgiveness is administered only to those who request it; it is without limitation and no works or sacrifices are required. This parable, along with Jesus' teaching on forgiveness, is difficult to reconcile with later apostolic views of forgiveness once they are examined carefully. Firstly, the Law made no provision for the forgiveness of capital offenses and required that violators be "cut off"—a euphemism for being put to death. As Jesus did not come to "abolish the Law," how are his views to be reconciled with the Law? Also, it seems that only those who are capable of forgiving debt, according to the Matthean formulations, will be forgiven.

Certainly there is an element of preparing the disciples for the new kingdom in Jesus' teaching and parables. And perhaps this affirms the view of some that Matthew's primary intention was to provide a catechetical tool. It is likely, however, that the doctrine espoused by Matthew has some implications for the Mosaic legislation as it operated prior to AD 70. It appears from the Synoptic tradition that those who were designated "sinners" or "tax collectors" represented two classes of people who existed outside acceptable covenant society. Sinners, who are typified by prostitutes and lepers, are those who are permanently outside the mediatorial system by virtue of the fact that they had become permanently "unclean." The tax collectors

72. Possibly around 60,000,000 denarii—164,000 years of labor. Ibid., 66.
73. Lev 25:39; Deut 15:12.
74. It has been proposed that the intention of the parable was to exhort the readers not to inform on "unforgiving servants," which in turn would make each debtor vulnerable to judgment. Scott, "The King's Accounting," 440.

were those who were in the same category of alienation as sinners, but for different reasons—they had become complicitous with Rome and therefore were natural enemies of Israel's eschatological hopes. The irony here was that Jerusalem had a profitable symbiotic relationship with Rome's administrators, but cast out those who performed the duties of Rome. Many of the sinners (prostitutes) were likely to be the product of a system that allowed easy and obligation-free divorce, which is, coincidentally, the topic covered in response to the Pharisees immediately after this parable.

It is proposed here that this teaching about forgiveness was not intended to undermine Mosaic teaching, but to indicate the day when the king settles his accounts. Once again, the forgiveness of the community is contingent on its ability to be a conduit for God's mercy. The community must forgive if it wants to be great in the kingdom. This, then, is a warning to the disciples; if the "house" should stop administering appropriate forgiveness, it would, in turn, have its own forgiveness revoked. The "system" that Matthew's Jesus confronted in the first century, neither advocated the death penalty (as Jerusalem could not implement it under Rome), nor did it provide the means for covenantal restoration. It did not know mercy or justice (12:7). The forgiveness granted to the servant in the parable was withdrawn, with penalties reimposed and significantly escalated. As such, this cannot be the forgiveness that is made available through the new covenant (Heb 8:12), which assures its members that their sins are forgiven and forgotten.[75] This is in itself a huge issue, which requires extensive treatment not possible here.

The Parable of the Workers in the Vineyard (20:1–16) was also presented to the disciples. It revolves around one basic concept, which brackets the parable—"But many who are first will be last, and many who are last will be first" (19:30; 20:16). In this parable the workers commenced work at various times of the day; however, they are paid in reverse order, and (contentiously) the same amount. Two points are immediately apparent from this illustration. The owner of the vineyard (YHWH) was not obligated to extend any provision beyond the primary agreement (the Mosaic covenant). However, this agreement/covenant did not limit the owner's generosity, which he chose to extend to the latter laborers. According to the premise of this parable, which is found in the prelude to it (19:28–29), Jesus' disciples would be given primary stewardship over Israel. As such, the "last" within this metaphor would have been the "first" appointed stewards—the teachers of the law and the Pharisees, who lawfully sat in Moses' seat (23:2). They, necessarily, would need to be dethroned.

---

75. Forgiveness in the Tanach was never permanent or complete, according to Matthew; if it were, Jesus could not justly hold his opponents responsible for all the righteous blood shed from Abel (Matt 23:35–36).

In relation to the question that introduced these parables, "who is the greatest in the kingdom,"[76] this parable could be instructive to both inform the disciples that they, as the new stewards, are greater, but also to serve as a reminder that they did nothing to deserve their privilege, other than miss the heat of the day. They are also implicitly advised not to treat "latecomers" (possibly incoming Gentiles) as inferior.

The theme of replacement of existing stakeholders with apparent "nobodies" is developed further in Matthew's next three indictment parables, which were directed to his hostile opponents. Their response to these parables was telling, as it provoked a determination to have Jesus destroyed (21:45), and led to their first attempt to imprison him by trapping him in his own words (22:15).[77] These parables are a set, and make the indictment of the hierarchy, which had already been alluded to throughout the document, palpable. The three parables portrayed Israel as a nation that was disobedient to God and indifferent to any claims that he had upon it.

This set of three is found in a section of Matthew (21–26) that heavily relied on Zechariah's prophecy.[78] The entrance into Jerusalem by Jesus on a donkey was heralded as the fulfillment of Zechariah's vision (Zech 9:9). Further, Zerubbabel was to bring out the capstone, for he would lay the foundation of the temple and complete it (Zech 4:6). In this account, Jesus referred to the rejected capstone, which became the undoing of those who rejected it (21:42–44). There is also the reference to the striking of the shepherd, as a precursor to the scattering of the sheep (26:31; Zech 13:7). The last significant reference in Matthew to Zechariah was concerning the thirty coins that were paid and returned to the temple (27:6–10; Zech 11:12–13).[79] This is important as these three parables may also be heavily influenced by Zechariah's prophecy.

76. This "parable of the last judgement . . . functions as a warning against boasting or presuming oneself to be among the first" (Davies and Allison, *Matthew: A Shorter*, 329).

77. The chief priests and Pharisees initially tried to use lawful means to subvert Jesus. Through these questions, they attempted to ensnare Jesus in some statement which would contradict Moses. The first question was from the Pharisees and the Herodians, the second from the Sadducees. With this construction, Matthew was able to portray all existing stakeholders, including Herod, as a united force that opposed Jesus.

78. Matthew's dependence on Zechariah for Jesus' script is well recognized. Wright, *Victory of God*, 588–600.

79. This composite reference, attributed to Jeremiah in the narrative, is likely to be an amalgam of Jeremiah 19 and Zechariah 11. The Jeremiah reference spoke of the destruction of Jerusalem and Judea, and more pertinently, the Zechariah reference spoke of the termination of the Covenant that God had with all the peoples (presumably the houses of Israel and Judah). It was on that day that the union of Israel was dissolved and God ended the national covenant.

The first of these parables, the Two Sons (21:28–32), presented a simple question to the chief priests and the representatives (elders) of the people. Again, the scene was a vineyard, and the sons are told to work in the vineyard. The first refused but later did his father's bidding, while the second agreed to his father's demand, but failed to do the work. The question ("which of these two sons did the father's will?") was answered, using the only plausible response.[80] Unlike the former parables of the third discourse, the secret was not withheld for long—prostitutes and tax collectors were, by inference, doing God's will, while the "righteous" leaders were not. John the Baptist did not convince the establishment, nor were they convicted by the throng of "rabble" that was replacing them in God's kingdom. The charge, laid at the feet of the chief priests, was that they did not repent and believe John.[81] This demonstrates that, in Matthew's gospel, John provides a foundation for belief in Jesus and consequently, for right conduct towards God. Further, Matthew proposed that certain phenomena being witnessed across Judea (the ingathering of the spiritual underclass) constituted irrefutable proof concerning Jesus, proof that warranted repentance and belief (21:32). And so, the "obedient sons" (prostitutes and tax collectors) escalate the considerable indictment, and testify to the unreasonable intransigence of Israel's stewards.

A possible connection with Zechariah's prophecy is the notion of two sons, or, in Zechariah, two anointed ones (Zech 4:14). In the prophecy, Joshua was given the commission and crown to do the bidding of God (Zech 6:11). Joshua's perpetual appointment was dependent on his conduct, which required obedience to Torah and, significantly, mercy and compassion (Zech 3:7; 7:9). It would be Zerubbabel, however, who would build and complete God's house (Zech 4:9). Following the mention of the two anointed ones, a flying scroll was sent forth that would bring judgment (a curse) upon the house of robbers and upon those who swear falsely. The prophecy continued, "I will send it out, and it will enter the house of the thief and the house of him who swears falsely by my name. It will remain in his house and destroy it, both its timbers and its stones" (Zech 5:4). As this extended Jerusalem pericope in Matthew identifies the temple as a den

---

80. "In a 'paradigmatic legal decision' they [the leaders] pronounce judgment on themselves" (Luz, *Matthew 21–28*, 30). Wendell Langly dealt with the complexity of both sons being partially good and partially bad. He believes that the force of the indictment can be found when a hypothetical third son, not mentioned in the parable, fails to honour the father with neither words nor deeds. This son is fully and unambiguously culpable; and so, Langly argues, were the high priest and the elders. Langley, "The Parable of the Two Sons."

81. "The message of John the Baptist . . . now becomes the focal point of salvation" (Longenecker, *The Challenge of Jesus' Parables*, 157).

of robbers (21:13), and the priests are exposed as perjuring their testimony (26:59), the connection may be made between the dismantling of the temple (24:2) and the conduct of the disobedient "anointed" son.

The second parable of the set, the Tenants (21:33–41), intensified the rhetoric and made clear Jesus' understanding of Israel's history and destiny. This parable was recorded in all three Synoptics with little variation. Its hearers immediately understood the story; in Luke, the crowd protested crying "May this never be" (Luke 20:16), and in Matthew, the postscript made it plain that the chief priests and Pharisees knew he was talking about them. The story was an encapsulation of the nation's history, for Matthew's Christ perceived that Israel (via its leadership) was unwilling to give God his due, having beaten all who came to remind them of their obligations.[82] The son, the last and greatest of the emissaries, was murdered by the tenants. Johannes De Moor has observed that the Targumic background to this parable revealed that Israel was the vineyard, and therefore not culpable. Moor concludes from an intertextual reading of the Targum that it was the chief priests who were the negligent "tenants" and at odds with the prophets.[83] This point can be inferred, however from the immediate context.

The story was followed by a citation from the Psalms: "The stone the builders rejected has become the capstone; the Lord has done this, and it is marvelous in our eyes" (Ps 118:22–23). There could be no ambiguity here. Jesus was the son and the last emissary. After his murder, wrath would follow and worthy tenants would be installed. Though rejected by the "builders" (this must imply the priestly leadership) as a stone not compatible with their edifice/house, Jesus would still be the centerpiece, completion and authority over God's permanent temple. This parable presented Jesus as the last witness: his great standing should have elicited respect and a change of mind. The escalated violence and intransigence of the tenants, however, testified to the entrenched adversarial relationship that they had with the vineyard's owner. Their destruction and removal, according to the parable, was the only remaining option, and eminently justifiable.

At this point it is necessary to make an observation that reveals Matthew's strong interest in establishing that Jesus fulfilled Isaiah's indictment. All the Synoptics place the Parable of the Tenants in a vineyard. Matthew, however, has to this point placed three consecutive parables in a vineyard

---

82. J. R. C. Cousland suggests that the priests and Pharisees are represented in Matthew as "knowingly and selfishly resisting God and his purpose . . ." Cousland, *The Crowds*, 285. This parable, therefore, should not have taken them by surprise.

83. De Moor, "The Targumic background of Mark," 70, 73. De Moor also noted that the winepress was a euphemism for altar, and the watchtower was a euphemism for the temple. See also Balabanski, *Eschatology*, 178.

setting (20, 21), which were strategically placed in order to make an Isaiah connection. Following chapter 22, where Jesus told the banquet parable and successfully avoided the traps set to indict him, Matthew recorded the seven woes of indictment against Israel's leaders. Lastly, Matthew recorded Jesus' prophecy concerning impending doom (chapter 24), which would be experienced in the lifetime of his audience. Matthew appears to have taken the template for this indictment progression from the prophet Isaiah.

Isaiah's allegory (Isa 5) described a vineyard that was loved and well cared for; yet it produced no fruit for its owner—the Lord.[84] Israel and Judah were the vineyard. This was followed by six woes of indictment, which in turn led to the irreversible judgment that would not end until all was destroyed (Isaiah 6). Matthew's use of Isaiah's metaphor for Israel (vineyard), followed by the indictment and apocalyptic, acted in concert to establish another unmistakable connection with Isaiah's ministry and writings.[85]

This does not, however, negate a reference to Zechariah also. Matthew was masterful in his ability to weave prophetic strands together simultaneously to further strengthen his fulfillment paradigm. Zechariah witnessed authority going to the house of Aaron (via Joshua) after the Exile,[86] which in effect denied the crown to David's offspring, Zerubbabel (Zech 6:9–11).[87]

---

84. Hagner, *Matthew 14–28*, 620. The detailed description of the setting up of the vineyard, although realistic in itself, is based on the LXX text of Isa 5:2, where each of Matthew's first four clauses, beginning with ἐφύτευσεν ἀμπελῶνα "he planted a vineyard," and including reference to the hedge, wine press, and tower, is found in almost exactly the same language (although the order of the clauses in the LXX is 2, 1, 4, 3). Horne, "The Parable of the Tenants," 113.

85. John Kloppenberg denies any connection between this parable and Isaiah 5; however, he still acknowledges that the temple's demise was as a consequence of the crimes of its stewards. Kloppenborg, "Isa 5:1–7 LXX." Allan Martens disagrees: "The parable is obviously an allegory based on the Song of the Vineyard in Isa 5:1–7 where the vineyard represents Israel" (Martens, "Produce Fruit," 158).

86. Michael Segal examined Zechariah 3 and found that Joshua's appointment was conditional; he was required to walk in YHWH's paths, and to act as judge/governor of YHWH's house. Zech 3:7, then, was a commission to "strengthen/reinforce my house." The commission to Joshua was extended to the maintenance of the courts and precincts of the temple. Segal, "The Responsibilities," 724.

87. There is some difficulty in reading Zechariah 6. It appears in the text that Joshua receives the crown and with it the designation of "the branch." However, this is complicated by the previous reference to Zerubbabel as the one who would build the temple (Zech 4:9). It has also been understood that the "branch" was a reference to the Davidic promise, and would therefore be a designation for Zerubbabel rather than Joshua. The real issue is: Did Zechariah identify Zerubbabel as the messianic king and expect the new age to begin in his lifetime? Or did he say that the time is coming when the branch or shoot of David (the Messiah) will come and be both king and priest? Joyce Baldwin holds the latter view. She says, "The symbolic coronation and the enigmatic term 'Branch' referred to a future leader, who would fulfill to perfection the offices of priest

Joshua, however, may not have been given the crown of authority permanently, as it was to be placed in the temple. Marko Jauhiainen has argued that the crown was to be kept for Zerubbabel, who was also referred to as "the rock" or "the branch" (6:14).[88] "Joshua's role is both to stand in for Zemah [branch] and, together with his fellow priests, to be a living sign of the coming restoration by walking in the ways of Yahweh and keeping his charge."[89] If this is the case, Joshua would know the right time for the crown to be transferred by the sight of the king "coming to Jerusalem, riding on the donkey" (Zech 9:9). It may be then that the rightfully installed king was therefore destined to be a king and priest; both offices would exist within the one title. Zechariah would then have been recording the future of Zerubbabel when writing: "It is he who will build the temple of the LORD, and he will be clothed with majesty and will sit and rule on his throne. *And he will be a priest on his throne.* And there will be harmony between the two" (Zech 6:13). The priests, should this be a correct reading of Zechariah, were only temporary stewards of the authority, but not the possessors of it. Consequently, their authority would need to be surrendered to the one who was both the son and permanent high priest; however, it appears in the parable that the wicked tenants believed that they would become the heirs should the son be destroyed. Presumably, by destroying Zerubbabel's line, God would have no other "anointed" option but the Aaronic line.

The last of the three in this set, the Parable of the Great Banquet, was also transparently obvious in its intention, and spoken to the leaders of Israel. Luke records this parable much earlier in his account, and the setting is in "a prominent Pharisee's house" (Luke 14:1). Matthew appears to present this whole set of parables in the temple precincts (21:23) where the tension

---

and king, and build the future temple with all appropriate splendour (Hag 2:6–9). In this way the priestly and royal offices will be unified. The old interpretation that Messiah is meant has not been displaced. Nowhere else in the OT is it made so plain that the coming Davidic king will also be a priest. It is for this reason that the passage has occasioned so much questioning" (quoted in Smith, *Micah–Malachi*, 136–37). Perhaps Baldwin is overzealous in defending the old messianic interpretation. At one stage of the tradition the prophet probably thought of both Zerubbabel and Joshua being co-rulers. "The 'counsel of peace' between the two of them means that they would not only work together harmoniously, but they would execute the counsel of God which would be peace (שָׁלוֹם) indeed. However the text says that the crown was to be put on the head of Joshua as a sign of the branch. It was then to be put in the temple as a reminder of God's promises" (Smith, *Micah–Malachi*, 218). Smith may be correct here; however, if Joshua's entitlement were dependent on his conduct, as Michael Segal has argued, then the crown would have been taken from the Aaronic line with Christ's judgment upon it. Either way, the Aaronic line seems temporary, while Zerubbabel's line is permanent.

88. Jauhiainen, "Turban and Crown."
89. Ibid., 511.

had escalated considerably. In Luke's version of the parable, it is a "certain man" who was holding the banquet, and only a single invitation went to the guests. Matthew records that it was a wedding banquet for the king's son. There were two messages sent in this account, perhaps emphasizing the natural incredulity a king would have when his invited guests would be indisposed. The most significant and telling variation in this parable is the response of the king to the guests. In Luke they are simply no longer welcome; in Matthew, however, the invited guests were destroyed and their "city" burned (22:7). This additional information is almost universally accepted by scholars as pointing to the destruction of Jerusalem.[90]

A further development in Matthew's version is the appearance of a guest who was not suitably attired.[91] This person was harshly treated and cast out—"Tie him hand and foot, and throw him outside, into the darkness, where there will be weeping and gnashing of teeth" (22:13). This aspect to the story can be explained by the propensity of early Christians to liken righteousness to being correctly adorned or "clothed."[92] This could have been a veiled warning that only those who are adorned by the bridegroom are chosen; hence the follow-up explanation—"For many are invited, but few are chosen" (22:14). Understood another way, no other righteousness would be acceptable—not even that of the priestly caste.[93]

This enigmatic unwelcome figure at the kingdom banquet may have a specific connection with the judgment that was destined to fall on the high priest.[94] As this section in Matthew relied so heavily upon Zechariah, it may be reasonable to make a connection with the inappropriately dressed high priest of Zechariah 3.[95] Zechariah's vision witnessed the reestablishment of the Aaronic priesthood.[96] Joshua had become unclean by virtue of his

---

90. This parable can "only refer to the destruction of Jerusalem, which was viewed as having been caused by Israel's rejection of God's messengers, particularly the nation's rejection of Jesus" (Martens, "Produce Fruit," 164).

91. It may be that by wearing inappropriate clothing the "guest" had dishonored the host. Bauckham, "The Parable of the Royal Wedding Feast," 488. Snodgrass has also noticed a Zephaniah connection in the punishment of officials who are wearing foreign attire (Zeph 1:8). Snodgrass, *Stories with Intent*, 312.

92. Gal 3:27; Col 3:10; Rom 13:14. See also, France, *Matthew*, 827.

93. The whole of Exodus 28 describes Aaron's garments (including undergarments) which are holy.

94. Bauckham believes a case can be made that the first invited guests are the leaders of Israel. Bauckham, "The Parable of the Royal Wedding Feast," 488.

95. Daniel Olson has also made a connection for much of this parable with Zephaniah 1, and this is a compelling case. This latter part, however, he considers may be derived from 1 Enoch. Olson, "Matthew 22:1–14 as Midrash."

96. Vanderkam states that the new "splendid garments" of Joshua (Zech 3)

foreign sojourning, and the replacement of his filthy garments was symbolic of his recommissioning to the high priestly office. This entitled him, and his descendants, to have a place in the heavenly council (Zech 3:7).[97] The high priest, therefore, by virtue of his position, was metaphorically entitled to be in the divine presence.[98] This parable, however, may have revealed that such would not always be the case, and that anyone who was not clothed by the King's son would be cast out. So while God was willing to extend grace to Aaron/Joshua following the Exile, there was a distinct conditionality ("If you will walk in my ways and keep my requirements," Zech 3:7) attached to it, a phrase derived directly from Deut 28:1. Should the high priest fail to be adequately dressed for the kingdom a second time, however, there would be no certainty of grace.[99] Hence this may be a reference to the termination of the Aaronic priesthood.[100] It was clear that nobody would access the kingdom who did not honor the Son; Matthew ensured that his readers would understand that Jerusalem did not honor Jesus.[101]

## The Latter Parables

The final discourse in Matthew ends with another parabolic set of three, two of which are uniquely Matthean. These parables echo themes found in the earlier parables, as well as the Sermon on the Mount. In a literary sense, these parables have a difficult role to fill; they follow an extremely intense and climactic indictment, first spoken through clearly understood parables,

---

"symbolize the restoration of a proper relationship between the Lord and his people . . ." and the dawning of a "new age." Vanderkam, "Joshua the High Priest," 553–70. If this was the case, what would the casting out of Aaron/Joshua mean for Israel?

97. Segal, "The Responsibilities," 729.

98. Min Suc Kee believes that the tabernacle was the earthly counterpart of the heavenly council where YHWH assembles with the sons of God. Kee, "The Heavenly Council," 270.

99. "Tie him hand and foot, and throw him to utter darkness" has a correlation in 1 En. 10:4. In that reference it was *Azazel* (leader of the fallen angels) who was cast out. Olson, "Matthew 22:1–14 as Midrash," 450. Also, France, *Matthew*, 827. This has some resonance with the "strong man" (12:29), who must be tied up before his possessions are plundered. The suggestion has already been made that this could refer to the high priest; the possibility, however, that *Azazel* (the scapegoat referred to by this name) could also be implicated, may connect this even more closely with the temple stewards.

100. The Hebrews writer made a similar suggestion: "We have an altar from which those who minister at the tabernacle have no right to eat" (Heb 13:10). The absence of Aaron from Hebrews 11 is also telling: why would Aaron be left of a list of God's faithful people when he is spoken about throughout the letter?

101. In this parable Jesus referred to the unwelcome guest as friend. It should be noted that Jesus also referred to Judas as friend at the betrayal.

direct denunciation, and grief over the refusal of Jerusalem to accept Jesus' longstanding mercy and love. This was then followed by the distressing apocalyptic chapter, and the realization that Jerusalem would be destroyed, its temple never to be rebuilt.[102] Anything placed between all of this and the passion narrative must be critically important; however, it also runs the risk of being redundant, in the literary sense—"filler" material allowing the readers to catch their breath. These latter parables are primarily directed to the conduct of the leaders of the "two houses." They anticipate a final judgment based on correct conduct, and only one community will survive that judgment and be commended.

The first of these parables, the Ten Virgins (25:1–13), is the most enigmatic and allegorized of all Matthean parables.[103] Interpretations of the parable have exercised considerable theological imagination over two millennia, and with this in mind, it may be unwise to propose yet another possibility. The "lens" used in this reading, however, does open up further interpretive prospects.

This interpretation of the Ten Virgins is drawn from the immediate context of the parable and some historical connections with the allusions contained in it. The context is an admonition to the disciples, which is premised by a challenging question—"Who then is the faithful and wise servant, whom the master has put in charge of the servants in his household to give them their food at the proper time?" (24:25). The apocalyptic passage had made clear that difficulties were coming, and rather than simply telling the disciples that they were on safe ground, Jesus issued this challenge followed by further significant threats. This parable, like the two others in the set, echoes the earlier theme of separation to either reward or punishment, based on doing the will of Jesus—the master coming to make ultimate recompense (24:46–51). The disciples were favored, prepared and blessed, but now they had to demonstrate the fruit that the former leadership had failed to produce. This paradigm enables an interpretation of the parable that makes reasonable contextual sense.

One of the features of the Parable of the Ten Virgins that makes it particularly obscure is the female subjects. Just as the Lost Coin parable in Luke justifiably presents God in the guise of a female character, so this parable disarms its readers by using female images, which may symbolize male leadership—the stewards "whom the master has put in charge."

---

102. Matthew did not consider the temple to be unjustified: it only became untenable as a consequence of its corrupt stewards. Gurtner, "Matthew's Theology of the Temple."

103. Snodgrass, *Stories with Intent*, 511.

An issue that may be relevant to this parable is an aspect of the high priest's ministry, which no doubt, accounted for rigorous effort and timetabling in the first century, when Mosaic instructions were followed so precisely. The first duty of Aaron and his sons, from the outset of the Law, was to keep the menorah (the lamp) burning through the night: "In the Tent of Meeting, outside the curtain that is in front of the Testimony, Aaron and his sons [5 in total] are to keep the lamps burning before the LORD from evening till morning. This is to be a lasting ordinance among the Israelites for the generations to come" (Exod 27:21).

So the menorah burned through the night, a high priority and a demanding priestly function, probably in anticipation of the coming of the Lord.[104] Further, Solomon commissioned ten such lamps to be made for the temple, five placed on the left and five placed on the right[105] of the entrance to the inner sanctuary (1 Kgs 7:48). This image of the entrance to the inner sanctuary, adorned with the ten golden lamps, would have been a standard recollection to Hebrews nostalgic for Solomon's great temple. Consider, also, that it has been noted that the tabernacle/temple had strong near-Eastern parallels with royal bridal chambers,[106] where relationships were metaphorically consummated; therefore, there exists a distinct historical context to apply to the parable.[107] Like the excluded wedding guest, these virgins are excluded from the banquet, because they had failed to honor the bridegroom.

The interpretation of this parable, when these historical and contextual issues are considered, could be understood with a hermeneutic that can be applied to all three parables in the set. The leadership of the disciples would be tested, as would the leadership of Israel. They both existed to wait for the Lord, and the lamp with its oil reveals to us their priestly function, or commitment to the assigned task.[108] The faithful ones are those that are

---

104. The importance given to tasks within the temple is highlighted by the death of Aaron's first two sons, who offered unauthorized fire and incense (Lev 10:1), which was forbidden in Exodus 30. They were then carried outside the camp.

105. Matthew also used separation of sheep and goats, those on the right and those on the left, within this set.

106. The Gospel of Philip, probably third century, made reference to the temple in these terms: "There were three buildings specifically for sacrifice in Jerusalem. The one facing west was called 'the Holy'. Another facing the south was called 'the Holy of the Holy'. The Holy of Holies is the bridal chamber."

107. YHWH is often described as a bridegroom coming to his bride. Jer 3:14; 31:32; Ezek 16:32; Hos 1:2.

108. Like David and Saul, both the priests and the apostles were anointed by God for a season. As was the case with Saul, God alone would denounce and remove the unfaithful leadership. Until then, the high priest still had the respect of the apostles, if not their obedience.

able to keep the lamps burning all night, as required by the Law, for they do not know when the master will return; they obey the command to watch (24:42). The master was entitled to delay, as the bridegroom does in the parable. Delaying had the effect of separating those who were willing and able to welcome him from those who had not made this a priority. And so, those who were not waiting were excluded from the celebration; their failure to be doing their assigned task when the master returned (24:25) is proof that he did not know them, and by inference, they did not know him.[109]

The Parable of the Talents (25:14–30) is recorded in Matthew and Luke. The differences between the versions suggest completely different sources, although they both make similar concluding points. Luke's version is uncharacteristically unrestrained, with servants receiving one talent and, and in one instance, turning that talent into ten. As a reward, the newly appointed king assigned that particular servant with ten cities to administer. Matthew's version is much more restrained: the servants each receive a sum, which, when doubled, attracted the master's approbation, while the servant who had one talent and gained no return was condemned—his meager coin assigned to the richest servant. Luke's version seems more intent on the notion of a returning king, who was not the choosing of his countrymen. These reluctant citizens of his kingdom were slaughtered in front of him. Matthew's interest was quite different.

Matthew's parable recorded that the servants were each given talents in keeping with their ability.[110] Therefore, it was reasonable to expect a return from each of them, albeit proportionately small or large depending on the servant. The master was not harsh as the last servant implied; even the bank interest would have met the master's requirement, as is also recorded in Luke. The unprofitable servant was crippled by his attitude toward the master. His negative assessment of the master determined his uninspiring conduct, which was classified in Matthew as lazy and evil.

The last servant's conduct with the talent may not have appeared evil, but his disdain of the master had blinded him to any positive response to the trust shown to him.[111] The master "entrusted" these servants with privilege, was exceedingly generous to those who honored him, and called them to enter his joy. The story presents the master as being kind and good, recalling

---

109. Noted earlier was the failure of Jerusalem to welcome the Messiah in Bethlehem.

110. Ben Chenoweth believes that the talents connect back to the "secrets" given to the disciples. Chenoweth, "Identifying the Talents."

111. Luke's version makes it obvious that the failed servants resented the master/king intensely.

an insight that was given to Jeremiah: those who know the Lord know that he is kind.

> This is what the LORD says:
>
> "Let not the wise man boast of his wisdom or the strong man boast of his strength or the rich man boast of his riches, but let him who boasts boast about this: that he understands and knows me, that I am the LORD, who exercises kindness, justice and righteousness on earth, for in these I delight," declares the LORD.
>
> "The days are coming," declares the LORD, "when I will punish all who are circumcised only in the flesh—Egypt, Judah, Edom, Ammon, Moab and all who live in the desert in distant places. For all these nations are really uncircumcised, and even the whole house of Israel is uncircumcised in heart" (Jer 9:23–26).

Fundamentally, the servant did not know the master; otherwise he would have attempted some achievement, knowing that grace was available; low regard for the master had determined the servant's inactivity. This disobedience left the servant with no excuse. The master believed that he was capable of the trust given and did not overburden the servant beyond his ability.[112]

This parabolic set defined the conduct of the faithful and wise servant, and conversely, the unfaithful and foolish servants. This parable identifies both types of servant, in the same way as that of the Ten Virgins. The issue concerned who was doing the master's bidding when he returned. The evil servant violated the trust given him, and was cast out as a consequence. The little he had was given to the one who had the most, a repeated and popular theme in the Matthean narrative; and so, failure to do the master's bidding resulted in the withdrawal of any former privilege. The implication for the disciples, having been given stewardship of the new community, was that their work would be tested—even as the former leaders' work was tested.

The last parable in the set, also last in the document and unique to Matthew, is the parable of the Sheep and the Goats (25:31–46).[113] Notably, this last parable portrayed the king as a shepherd, whose task was that of separation or judgment.[114] This concluding parable divides the inhabitants

---

112. The judged servant in this parable has been interpreted by some to be the leaders of the post-exilic community, who made allegations against YHWH that he was negligent and mean-spirited. Snodgrass, *Stories with Intent*, 529, 761. See, for instance, the questions in Mal 1:2, 6, 7 and 2:17.

113. Not all agree that this is a parable. "This unit is not truly a parable. It is an apocalyptic discourse with a parabolic element in 25:32b–33" (Hultgren, *The Parables of Jesus*, 310).

114. Jesus' last parable presented the Son of Man as king and shepherd, which reflects

of the world into two categories: those who acted kindly to the group who belonged to Jesus and those who did not. The "sheep" were destined for blessing, for unbeknownst to them, their kindness to Jesus' people was acknowledged by Jesus as a kindness to him. For the "goats," the converse was true; their failure to show kindness to the least of Jesus' brothers was interpreted as indifference to him. This judgment is universal, implying that all would be judged by their attentiveness to the needs of Jesus' brethren, and therefore to Jesus. This does not, however, negate the increased responsibility placed upon the leaders who administer the mission of the church or Israel.

This final parable has given currency to the belief that Matthew advocated a soteriology of works.[115] This view, however, fails to appreciate the context of the "set." These parables cannot be understood without acknowledging both the question that makes them meaningful and its answer: "Who then is the faithful and wise servant, whom the master has put in charge of the servants in his household to give them their food at the proper time? It will be good for that servant whose master finds him doing so when he returns" (24:45–46).

These parables, it is proposed, were intended to be contextually interpreted, and historically meaningful. The "faithful and wise" were administrators, whose task was to ensure that the members of the household had food at the proper time—they had responsibility for the physical and spiritual wellbeing of God's people.[116] Failure to meet the needs of the poor within

---

back to the first designation of Jesus in this Gospel (2:6)—"a ruler who will shepherd . . ." Nolland, *Gospel of Matthew*, 1034. Hauerwas, *Matthew*, 210. There is an emphatic connection made here between Jesus as the Danielic judge, the ruling shepherd. Also, "with all his angels" is a direct quote from Zechariah (LXX) which speaks of the coming of the Lord, "with all his angels"(14:5). Hultgren, *The Parables of Jesus*, 311.

115. This parable is made more difficult by various interpretations being placed upon it in recent times. Are the "least brothers" all needy people, needy Christians, Jews or those who propagate the Christian faith? There are similar questions about the identity of all the nations. Snodgrass, *Stories with Intent*, 551–52. Snodgrass concludes that this parable, when taken as a narrative, simply emphasizes charitable works as an expression of faith—not as a means to faith. It is simplest to assume that the "least brethren," who receive kindness as surrogates of Jesus, should be understood as believers in Jesus. In Matthew, a cup of water given to such as these will result in a reward (10:46); this parable is likely to be conveying no more than an extension to this notion. This reading undertaken here, however, has its focus upon the "two houses," their common destiny (AD 70) and the outcome of separation foreshadowed in Malachi (3:18)—where God declares, "you will again see the distinction between the righteous and the wicked, between those who serve God and those who do not." So this final parable seems to connect seamlessly to Malachi, as would be expected if Malachi was a significant oracle through which the story was advanced.

116. Friedrichsen, "A Note on και διχοτομησει αυτον."

the Hebrew community, as well as failure to properly instruct, is a regular accusation throughout the prophets. This background was integral to Jesus' indictment against Israel's leaders in Matthew—the temple was intended to be a house of prayer (request), not a place of exploitation. Isaiah made the point well enough,

> The LORD enters into judgment against the elders and leaders of his people: "It is you who have ruined my vineyard; the plunder from the poor is in your houses. What do you mean by crushing my people and grinding the faces of the poor?" declares the Lord (Isa 3:14–15).[117]

Isaiah believed relief for the poor was to be had when the Messiah would come—"The Spirit of the Sovereign LORD is on me, because the LORD has anointed me to preach good news to the poor" (Isa 61:1). Jesus' repeated pronouncement revealed what God's requirement was: "I desire mercy, not sacrifice" (9:13; 12:7). And only those who do the will of the Father enter the kingdom of heaven (7:21). The temple stewards were charged with the responsibility of meeting the needs of the poor on YHWH's behalf (Deut 26:12–13).[118] This was clearly not evident from the Matthean image of the first-century temple practices.

Historically, the disciples did demonstrate an acute awareness of their stewardship responsibility. From the earliest accounts in Acts, the needs of widows and the poor were at the forefront of apostolic action. The severe famine throughout the Roman world (Acts 11:28) enabled the church to demonstrate the qualities that Jesus sought, with widespread financial redistribution to meet the needs of the church in Judea. Could it be that the primitive church's correct response to the test brought the promised blessings, while the failure of the temple administration continued in fulfillment of these Matthean parables, resulting in its destruction by Rome in AD 70?

With regard to Matthew's metanarrative, this parable makes a strong connection with a fundamental proposition that this reading is attempting to demonstrate—the replacement of the existing shepherds in favor of a shepherd who would act as a discerning judge: "As for you, my flock, this is what the Sovereign LORD says: I will judge between one sheep and another, and between rams and goats" (Ezek 34:17).[119] Having cast Jesus as a shepherd from the outset (2:6), and having described the lost sheep of Israel as the

---

117. It is unlikely that religious people stole from the poor; however, they had other means of manipulating the meagre possessions of the poor away from them—an accusation found in Matthew 23.

118. Stevens, *Temples, Tithes and Taxes*.

119. France, "On Being Ready," 190.

"sheep without a shepherd . . . helpless and harassed" (9:35), it is fitting for Matthew to end the parabolic ministry of Christ with this separation parable. The unfit shepherds would soon be candidly exposed as marauding thugs, who would have no hesitation to cruelly assault the sheep (26:67).

## Summation

Matthew's parables cannot be understood using simply one template. Each set of parables has its own context and purpose within the overall structure. Every parabolic set in Matthew includes a question, which is answered within the parables. The key to understanding the parables in Matthew, then, starts by understanding the question, for that is where they derive their meaning.

The parables of the third discourse were intended to obscure the truth being taught by Jesus, for the purpose of completing Isaiah's indictment against Israel. With these parables, Jesus changed his mode of operation. Prior to chapter 13 Jesus did not speak in parables; he spoke openly and plainly. After the curses and condemnations found in chapters 11 and 12, the parables were used as a means of reactivating Isaiah's unfinished indictment (Isa 6). The question ("why do you speak in parables?") was answered with the rubric through which these parables were to be interpreted. The central parables were not difficult to understand. The five that have been considered are in two categories: those spoken to the disciples for their instruction, and the latter three to the leaders of Israel as a clear reproach and denunciation. The last set of parables foreshadowed the basis upon which future judgment would be made—and thus naturally flowed out of the apocalyptic passage (Matt 24). These were addressed to the disciples, and did not presuppose that their success was certain or assured. The question that these parables answered was: "Who then, is the faithful and wise servant?"

Matthew's parables are strategically chosen and often unique. Their nuanced presentations and distinctive groupings significantly contribute to the sense that Matthew's intention for this document was to indict the Jerusalem incumbents. Without doubt, the severest images of future punishment found in the Christian Bible are attached to these Matthean parables. Therefore, if Matthew's narrative simply intended to convince Jews of the virtue of Christianity or to be a liturgical aid, the choice of parables, the versions chosen, the explanations given and the violence depicted within them would appear to defy any meaningful explanation. It is proposed, then, that the parables contribute significantly to the assertion that Matthew's gospel is, among other things, a prophetic indictment that would justify YHWH's rejection and dismantling of the temple within the lifetime of that ultimate generation.

# 7

# The Universal Priest and the Judge of Israel

> *See, O Lord, raise up for them their king, the son of David,*
>
> *In the time which thou knowest, O God, to reign over Israel thy servant; and gird him with strength to shatter the unjust rulers . . . He will possess the nations, to serve beneath his yoke.*
>
> (Psalms of Solomon 17:23)[1]

THE QUESTION OF THE identity and purpose of Christ in the view of the Gospel writers is of fundamental importance in understanding the Synoptic tradition. A significant unifying feature of the Gospels and other New Testament writings is the view that Jesus was the Christ, or Messiah—meaning "Anointed One."[2] This identity was established at the outset of all the Gospel documents apart from Luke, which allowed its readers to make their own assessment according to the history that the writer sought to document. Each Gospel read as the unfolding history of the Jesus event to the point where it became obvious, according to the writers, that Jesus was the Messiah that Israel was to expect. Matthew is no exception: Jesus' identity was the Christ, of Abraham and (most significantly) of David.[3] The no-

---

1. Bruce, *Jesus and Christian Origins*, 79–80.

2. Jesus was understood to be "the Christ," which "became almost a proper name" (Carson, "Christological Ambiguities," 100).

3. David is noted six times in the opening chapter and provides the centerpiece and highpoint of Israel's pre-exilic history.

tion of Messiah cannot be extracted or isolated from its historical context, which, according to the Gospels, indicated one who would somehow both resemble David his forefather, and also be David's historical terminus—his fulfillment and his eternally enthroned son. For this reason, most students of the Gospels have rightly asserted that Jesus was the long-expected and final king of Israel. Is it possible then, that the concept of Messiah can mean anything else? Could Jesus' opponents have understood Messiah differently, a view which would have set the parameters for the conflict, and ultimately for the crucifixion?

A significant component of this reading is to view Matthew as a concluding document that envisaged the termination of the Levitical system. Although this is not the traditional reading of Matthew, this approach reads the narrative in order to explore the possibility that Matthew wove a priestly subtext throughout his document as the backdrop to Jesus' ministry and his struggles. A Hebrew community that was intimately acquainted with the cultic ordinances of the Torah would have understood this subtext.[4] The confrontation between Jesus as Messiah priest and the incumbent priesthood should, consequently, be understood as the reason for the ongoing conflict within the narrative, which would conclude with the denunciation of Israel's leaders. Matthew identified Jesus as a king (27:11) and a prophet (21:11) within his narrative, by Jesus' own admission and by the observation of others; the title of Messiah may have meant either of these two functions, but this need not exhaust the possibilities. Messiah may have meant something altogether different in the first century, and without the explicit references by the Hebrews writer to Jesus as the High Priest, the priestly role of the Messiah may have completely eluded the modern reader.[5]

What is being proposed here is that Messiah, in Matthew, might have been heavily laden with priestly meaning.[6] At no stage did Matthew explicitly claim that Jesus was a priest.[7] Yet Jesus' healing ministry and his

---

4. This may not have been a subtext to the first century community who understood that authority was ultimately vested in the high priest. However, for modern readers, who are not dependent upon or surrounded by priests, a priestly narrative or subtext may be more elusive.

5. Crispin Fletcher-Louis has produced a comprehensive treatment of Jesus' priestly messiahship as found in Mark's gospel. Fletcher–Louis, "Jesus as the High Priestly Messiah: Part 1"; Fletcher-Louis, "Jesus as the High Priestly Messiah: Part 2." There is significant overlap of these themes in Matthew's gospel. Jesus' priestly office is also apparent in John's gospel. Heil, "Jesus as the Unique High Priest."

6. The lens being used for this reading assumes that the theology of Hebrews may have been consistent with the theology of Matthew.

7. David was also never referred to as a priest, and yet, as will be seen, he had an unmistakable priestly ministry.

challenges to the leaders of Israel presented what appears to be a clear claim to priestly efficacy—a claim that may well have been understood by the Jerusalem establishment of the first century. Jesus' messianic role, in Matthew, was heavily shaped by his connection to David, who was unique among kings. David functioned as a priest prior to his coronation. This issue may be critical in understanding Matthew's Jesus.

Apart from statements in the Epistle to the Hebrews, no specific priestly designation for Jesus would exist. Jesus as the Great High Priest was set in juxtaposition to the Aaronic priesthood throughout that epistle.[8] The fundamental theme of the letter is that Jesus was an effectual priest, while Aaron was limited to the point of being ineffective. Matthew may be presenting the same theology, expressed in the form of his "historical" narrative. Jesus had authority to heal/cleanse and forgive, while the priestly community neither forgave nor healed; their administration was demonstrably bereft.[9] Matthew's presentation of social and spiritual outcasts, unchallenged demonic freedom, and the helpless condition of the unclean (the dead, lepers, those with bleeding and Gentiles) all testified to the failure of the priests, whose responsibility was to purify YHWH's people. It seems, then, that Jesus was presented as an alternative priest—one with demonstrable authority that was able to meet the needs of the people.

The role of the high priest is strikingly prominent in Matthew. All Synoptics depict Jesus standing before the high priest in the passion narratives; Matthew, however, unfolds his narrative as a protracted conflict, which ultimately draws out of the shadows the true and final antagonist—Caiaphas.[10]

---

8. This same motif has been identified in Matthew and called the "two shepherds schema" by Chea, who has recognized the Ezekiel subtext. Chae, *Jesus as the Eschatological Davidic Shepherd*, 380.

9. It may be argued that it is inappropriate to claim that the Levitical priesthood is deficient if it operates within its natural limitations. Aaron and his descendants were not able to remove illnesses and impurities, and these maladies could render an Israelite ceremonially unclean. This same approach, however, is taken in Hebrews. The writer of that Epistle made the point that the limitation of the priesthood was a significant failing, for it could not bring "perfection" (Heb 7:11). This resulted in the termination of the Aaronic tenure. The superior priest displaced the inferior priest. The author of Hebrews writes: "For the law appoints as high priests men who are weak" (7:28). Priests represent humans before God. If a human has an illness that makes her unclean, and the priest cannot deal with it, he cannot be fully effective, even if this achievement is beyond his ability. A competent priest is one who is able to save to the uttermost, forgiving sins, and removing uncleanness completely. This is the priesthood that Jesus has, according to Hebrews (Heb 7:26–27). See also Ladd, *Theology of the New Testament*, 625–28.

10. Unlike Matthew, John's gospel emphasized the temporary nature of Caiaphas's tenure by stating that he was the high priest that year (John 18:13). Heil, "Jesus as the Unique High Priest," 730.

Caiaphas is uniquely depicted in Matthew as hosting the conspiracy (in his house) to deceitfully arrest and kill Jesus (26:3).[11] He unjustly drew the trial to a close without having established just grounds for indictment (26:65).[12] The chief priests, of whom Caiaphas was the leader, convinced the crowd to reject Jesus (27:20),[13] and then they were depicted as mocking him at his death (27:41).[14] They bribed Judas to betray Jesus (26:15), and then ignored his statement that Jesus was innocent (27:4).[15] The chief priests broke Sabbath to collude with Gentiles (27:62).[16] After they heard the testimony of their own guards that Jesus had risen (28:11), they did not repent; rather, they colluded to perpetrate an enduring public deception (28:12).[17]

In order to make the case that an underlying message of Matthew is that Jesus came to remove the old priesthood and establish a new priesthood, it will be necessary to consider the prominence given to the high priest in the Law. In doing so, it will be shown that the Anointed (Messiah) has more to do with the priestly functions of propitiational mediation and judgment, than with the functions of king or prophet.

## The Role of the High Priest

From Israel's inception following the Exodus, the fledgling nation was characterized by the presence of God in the midst of the community. Israel was essentially a theocracy—a nation that was governed by its God. Moses' role in the development of the nation, according to the Pentateuch, was central,

---

11. "According to Exod 21:14 crimes committed with evil intent (δόλῳ) are not pardonable. Thus the whole Sanhedrin decides to commit a capital crime!" (Luz, *Matthew 21–28*, 332).

12. "Only on the basis of the already assumed impossibility of Jesus' being the Messiah can Jesus' statement mean that there is no need for further witnesses" (Nolland, *Gospel of Matthew*, 1133). Nolland believes that they are genuine in their belief that Jesus is not the Messiah; however, Matthew portrayed them as convinced that he actually was the Messiah. Even if they were not convinced at this point, the resurrection was certainly compelling evidence; yet, Matthew portrayed Jerusalem as resolute in their antagonistic trajectory toward Jesus and YHWH.

13. Nolland, *Gospel of Matthew*, 1173.

14. France, *Matthew*, 1071.

15. France observes that Ahithophel betrayed King David by siding with Absalom and took his own life. 2 Sam 17:23 (LXX) is echoed in Matthew's "he went off and hanged himself" (ibid., 1041).

16. Nolland, *Gospel of Matthew*, 1235.

17. This was to be a "well-kept secret" between the priests and the guard. Hagner, *Matthew 14–28*, 877. Matthew placed this secret deal on public record. It was declared from the rooftops.

and yet undeserved and dispensable. Moses' reluctance to speak on God's behalf (Exod 4:14) led to the appointment of Aaron, Moses' older brother. How this transfer of responsibility took place is unclear, for Moses continued to be the primary leader and judge of Israel. What is clear, however, is that the rod/staff of authority was assigned to Aaron, and Israel would only exist as a theocratic and viable identity as long as one of Aaron's descendants represented the nation as its priest.

The importance of the high priest in Israel cannot be overstated. The books of Moses give greater attention to Aaron's garments (Exod 28) than to instruction regarding the conduct of a king (Deut 17:14–20). The king was instructed not to consider himself better than his countrymen (Deut 17:20), whereas the high priest wore a gold plate on his forehead, which read "holy to the Lord" (Exod 28:36). When a ruler sinned unintentionally, he was dependent on the high priest to restore his covenant status through sacrifice (Lev 4:22). The high priest, however, was responsible for his own sin and represented himself. His sin brought guilt upon the whole nation, which could be punished for the priest's sin (Lev 4:3). Ordination of Aaron and his successors was to take a period of seven days (Exod 29:35), whereas kings were anointed spontaneously for as long as it took to empty a horn of oil (1 Sam 10:1; 16:13). In short, Israel could and did exist without a king for all but four hundred years of its history. The anointed priest, however, was indispensable. Without the priest, no atonement could be made and Israel would be without its cultic ruler, who provided access to God.[18]

## The Function of the King in Deuteronomist History

The importance of the priesthood to Israel, from a modern perspective, seems secondary to that of the king. The Deuteronomic story appears to be focused on the emergence and history of the kings of Israel and Judah. Priests rarely get mentioned through these accounts, and they seem peripheral to the main story. Consequently, the messiah role has normally been associated with the king rather than with the priest. This has shaped the popular view of Jesus' identity; however, it seems obvious that Jesus did the work of a priest, prior to his installation as king.

In this section a case will be made that the Deuteronomist[19] was primarily interested in the emergence and role of the king, with a view that the

---

18. Such was the high priest's standing that blaspheming God and cursing the priest were considered synonymous (Exod 22:28). This was a law that even Christians were mindful of before AD 70 (Acts 23:5).

19. For the purpose of this reading, it is accepted that there was probably a school or

success or failure of kings, from Moab to Exile, would depend on the king's attitude to the priesthood and the cultic life of Israel. Saul, for example, showed contempt for Levitical priests, even to the point where he had them put to death (1 Sam 22:18). Further, Saul did not seek to restore the Ark of the Covenant to Israel or give it an enduring home. David, conversely, restored and protected the priesthood (1 Sam 22:22; 2 Sam 8:17), restored the ark and desired to build the temple.

Following Joshua's conquest of the land, tribal divisions and the occupation of designated lands resulted in the effective splintering of Israel. The book of Judges records a period of tribal isolation and self-interest, horrendous moral apathy and the resurgence of Canaanite superiority in the land (Judg 1:27–36). Over the nearly 350 years of Judges "history," judges periodically surfaced to free various tribes from their humiliating subjugation. The book provided the crucial apologetic for the appointment of a king, signaled by the recurring editorial comment "In those days Israel had no king; everyone did as he saw fit" (Judg 17:6; 18:1; 19:1; 21:25).

Judges not only justified the need of a king; it also gave legitimacy to Judah's claim to the title. The natural heirs to monarchical rule in Israel were Ephraim and Judah—the prophetic blessing of Jacob/Israel was the basis of this (Gen 49:8–12, 22–46). It is not surprising then that these two tribes produced Joshua and Caleb—the two representatives of the twelve tribes that successfully entered the land.

Concerning Joseph, whose blessing was to fall upon Ephraim his second-born, Jacob had said: "Your father's blessings are greater than the blessings of the ancient mountains, than the bounty of the age-old hills. Let all these rest on the head of Joseph, on the brow of the prince among his brothers" (Gen 49:26). Joseph's rise in Egypt, along with his own dream concerning his supremacy over his brothers and parents, was vindicated by Jacob when he placed Ephraim as firstborn over Israel, in the stead of the cursed firstborn sons Reuben, Simeon and Levi.[20] Ephraim inherited the largest and most central portion of Canaan. Reuben, on the other hand, took his place on the east of the Jordan, while Simeon and Levi were denied any substantial holdings, both scattered. Joshua the conqueror, Samuel the transitional priest and kingmaker, and the first king of the Northern Kingdom, Jeroboam, were all Ephraimites. Ephraim's monarchical claims were certainly substantial.

The book of Judges, however, portrayed the tribe of Ephraim as weak and surly. Its primary judge, Deborah, was a woman who recruited Barak

---

redactor that shaped the Hebrew narrative from Deuteronomy to 2 Kings.

20. Wenham, *Genesis 16–50*, 487.

from Naphtali to free the tribal states from their oppressor Jabin, the king of Canaan (Judg 4:4–24). The obvious implication for Ephraim was that it was incapable of producing a male warrior king to protect Israel. Ephraim did produce another judge, Abdon, whose only recorded attribute was a multitude of donkey-riding progeny (Judg 12:13–15). The Ephraimites were not successful in battle. In the first chapter Judah's success in all but defeating the Canaanites, even in the hills of Ephraim, is starkly contrasted by Ephraim's dismal epithet—"Nor did Ephraim drive out the Canaanites living in Gezer, but the Canaanites continued to live there among them" (Judg 1:30). Ephraim's surly conduct when others succeeded also portrayed the tribe as having a strong but mistaken belief in its own entitlement. Its attempt at civil war with the lowly Jephthah from Gilead was a significant humiliation (Judg 12:1–7).[21]

Judah was also accorded monarchical privilege or destiny with Jacob's blessing—"The sceptre will not depart from Judah, nor the ruler's staff from between his feet, until he comes to whom it belongs and the obedience of the nations is his" (Gen 49:10). Judah, unlike Ephraim, was enhanced by the critique of Judges. Twice within the narrative God was sought and on each occasion he advised that Judah should lead Israel (Judg 1:2; 20:18). They had the greatest military successes and produced profitable judges.

The only other tribe that could legitimately make a claim to the monarchy was Benjamin. The redactor of Judges left no doubt as to the possibility of a perpetual Benjamite dynasty with the book's conclusion. Israel's dysfunctional history during the time of the Judges climaxed with the brutal rape and murder of a Levite's concubine, which almost concluded the history of Jacob's last son (Judges 21). The person sinned against was a Levite,[22] from Bethlehem—David's town of birth. The violators were Benjamites, who lived in the town of Gibeah—Saul's hometown.

The final verse in Judges, "In those days Israel had no king; everyone did as he saw fit" (21:25), reveals the disdain of its author for the conduct that Israel displayed with respect to the Levitical priesthood. Levi was not

---

21. This was not the first time Ephraim was shown to be pathetic. After Gideon had secured victory over the Midianites and was continuing pursuit of them, Ephraim tried to intimidate Gideon for not giving them a bigger role in the victory (Judg 8:1). The one role Ephraim did have (to seize the waters of the Jordan to stop the invaders crossing the Jordan—Judg 7:24), they dismally failed to do. As in the situation with Jephthah, Ephraim thought it could gain acclaim by challenging the judge who was weary after securing Israel's peace. Gideon pacified them with flattery; Jephthah called their bluff and slaughtered them. This is not an impressive performance for a tribe that hoped to produce the king of Israel.

22. The concubine was, of course, the greatest victim, but under the Law, she was the possession of the Levite.

sinned against through the Gibeah incident alone, for Israel went on to break its national vow by violating the "festival to the Lord," where the ark of the covenant was present at Shiloh (21:19). This same lament of disdain was first recorded by the author of Judges in relation to the appalling event in Ephraim, when Micah recruited a mercenary Levite to serve a shrine that he had built to his plethora of gods (Judg 17).

Judges, through its narrative, ascribed legitimacy and even nobility to Judah, while showing Ephraim to be insubstantial, and Benjamin so evil that it was worthy of destruction. During this Judges period, Israel was constantly in violation of Torah, particularly with respect to the precepts regarding priests and their central function in the life of the nation. It is probable, then, that Judges advocated the need of a king who would unite the nation and centralise and safeguard the high priestly office. The books of Samuel unfolded the history of how the right king came to office and gave further information concerning how the priestly office in Israel had become morally and terminally bankrupt.

After the demise of Eli's priestly dynasty (1 Sam 4:12), Samuel adopted the priestly and prophetic role in an interim capacity—although it could be argued that his presentation to Eli made his priestly functions legitimate as an adopted son.[23] The rise of Saul, and then David, are the themes that occupy these books. With the priestly "anointed one" or messiah now deposed, the experiment with kingly messiahs commenced. Though interpreted as a rejection of YHWH (1 Sam 8:7), Saul's installation became a primary catalyst for national unity. His tenure would, however, be terminated with his life; David was destined to be the new and permanent "messiah" through his offspring according to the promise (2 Sam 7). Saul made no attempt to enquire of the ark (1 Chr 13:3), or relocate it during his royal tenure. David, however, brought the ark back from exile in Kiriath Jearim (2 Sam 6:13–14), where it was tended by non-Israelites (Gibeonites) from the time of Eli's demise. David did this in two stages: the first was unsuccessful, and the ark remained for three months with the Gittite, Obed-Edom. The second attempt was led by David, who was wearing the priest's ephod[24] in the company of 30,000 Israelites. A bull and a fattened calf were sacrificed after six steps. Clearly, David functioned as a priest under whose ministry God

---

23. "In 1 Chronicles, however, Samuel is classified as a Levite" (Klein, *1 Samuel*, 6). "The divergence between Levitic and Ephraimite ancestry has been explained harmonistically: though from the tribe of Ephraim by birth, Samuel was attached to the tabernacle as a Nazirite and 'almost automatically drawn by Levitic tradition into family attachment to the tribe of Levi' (Albright, *Prophetic Tradition* 161)" (ibid.).

24. "The linen cloth was, apparently, a priestly garment" (Anderson, *2 Samuel*, 105).

returned to Israel. Exile (of the ark) occurred under Levitical priesthood, while restoration took place under David.

According to the Deuteronomist history, Saul was a failure. His greatest offenses were his presumptuous and unlawful sacrifice (1 Sam 13:11–14) with which he sought to enquire of the Lord, and the slaughter of the priestly community at Nob (1 Sam 22).[25] David, however, was a great success. He preserved the priests and saved the life of Abiathar (1 Sam 22:20). He installed high priests after his enthronement and earnestly desired to build the sanctuary.[26]

This was not the end of the story or of the comparison, for David is an enigma within the Deuteronomist record, one that would challenge the letter of Torah by being an unauthorized and yet effectual priest/king. David supported and preserved the Levitical/Aaronic dynasty, yet David showed no hesitation in wearing the priest's ephod (1 Sam 23:9), approaching and ministering before the ark (2 Sam 6:14), eating consecrated bread (1 Sam 21:6) or offering sacrifices (2 Sam 24:24)—actions that did not incur God's wrath, but blessing. So David functioned as an effectual priest, even before his enthronement. Was this the messianic template for David's descendant, Jesus, who would become the significantly greater priest/king? This will be a primary consideration in our examination of Matthew's depiction of Jesus' messianic self-identity.

In brief, then, apart from the period when David exercised priestly and kingly rule, the Deuteronomic narrative depicts a lawless and fragmented Israel, that failed to honor the extensive requirements of Torah concerning Levitical status and function. The king was, in part, a solution to this problem—for he would be able to unite the nation, as Saul did, and if he had understood God's plan, as David did, he would establish, centralise and pay homage to the Aaronic succession and its mediatorial role as stipulated in Moses as a lasting ordinance (Exod 28).

## The Meaning of Son of Man

The Synoptic Gospels' primary designation for Jesus was the Son of Man, Christ's self-disclosed title.[27] Nothing could be more significant to any quest

---

25. Saul could not coerce an Israelite to slaughter the Levites, so the task was assigned to Doeg the Edomite. Saul, it seems, was the only Israelite who was capable of such an act.

26. Much of David's wealth was assigned to the temple's construction, even though he could not do the task himself (1 Chr 22:14).

27. John Collins, in a review of Sigmund Mowinckel's classic study of messianism

for Jesus' self-awareness, and possibly his mission, than this loaded and enigmatic designation. Unfortunately, the meaning and implications of the title have proven elusive, or at least unsatisfying. "Son of Man" may have a clear allusion to Dan 7:13, which was subsequently quoted at the time of Jesus' Sanhedrin interrogation (26:64). Matthew extracted the fullest meaning of the designation found in its Daniel context, particularly in the Great Commission: "all authority in heaven and earth has been given to me" (28:18). How this title has influenced our understanding of messianic function is significant; it has generally been accepted as the foreshadowing of the Messiah's royal reign over heaven and earth. There is no doubt that Matthew's Jesus, via this Daniel connection, was established as a true regent over God's creation, but to what extent did the first-century community confirm this particular christological interpretation?

Some observations need to be made at this point. A Jewish king would not have been unwelcome in Judea—particularly one that would sanction the full operation of legislative Torah and reestablish judicial privilege to the priestly class, as David did. A king represented the only way that Judea could operate as an independent theocracy; Gentile control was anathema and a hindrance to any hope that Judea had to reform and move toward its eschatological completion. Clearly, a long-standing vacancy existed for such a king in Israel, though the choice of candidate was restricted by prophetic and genealogical constraints. Jesus was a viable candidate, even if his connections and pedigree were poor (son of the carpenter). Nonetheless, the Jerusalem establishment were alert to the possibility that Messiah might come. It knew that the time for such a king was right, and it was also aware of the role of Bethlehem, the city of David's offspring (2:4). Like Herod, Jerusalem was disturbed by the report of Messiah's arrival (2:3). Matthew's portrayal of the symbiotic relationship between the Jewish rulers and Herod may have been the catalyst for this concern, for things appeared to be progressing reasonably well; Herod was a sympathetic patron of the temple, and perhaps even capable of moral reform.

The Son of Man title, however, was charged with symbolism and challenge to Jesus' opponents. Jesus' unambiguous use of the title when questioned by Caiaphas, in its direct prophetic context of Daniel 7, left no doubt that Jesus had uttered blasphemy and deserved the death penalty (26:65). What then could be so blasphemous about this title, which was not hidden by Jesus from the people of Judea and beyond, that warranted open violation of Torah and due process by the chief priests in the pursuit of Jesus' destruction?

―――――――――

(*He That Cometh*), acknowledged the correctness of Mowinckel's view that "Son of Man" was a "transcendent, universalist strand of eschatology as superior to national messianism" (Collins, "Mowinckel's *He That Cometh* Revisited, 14).

While the title "Son of Man" has been traditionally accepted as some kind of messianic designation, the notion has been challenged by a generation of scholars. Barnabas Lindars has argued forcefully for an idiomatic usage of the Aramaic *bar enasha* (son of man), which he noted, "simply means "a man.""[28] This was no doubt the case; however, others have suggested that pre-Christian Jewish tradition had already adopted the idiom and refilled it with messianic significance.[29] The debate is yet to be resolved.[30] Nonetheless, Vermes takes comfort, in his most recent discussion on the debate, from a Spanish translation that has appropriated the complexities of the discussion, by using "est Hombre" (this man) for *ho huios tou anthrōpou* as a self-designation.[31] There is no doubt that Jesus was referring to himself by the designation, and it may not have been intended to carry a specific messianic implication. But the Jesus of the Synoptics did use it as a canvas upon which his function and purpose could be disclosed.[32]

Within Matthew's narrative the Son of Man may have been intended to be ambiguous.[33] This ambiguity was also integral to the identity of the enigmatic Son of Man in Daniel's vision. Referring to the Danielic vision, Morna Hooker observed concerning its usage in 1 Enoch,

> The Son of Man is not introduced as a well-known, recognizable figure, but as an enigmatic one that needs explanation: the explanation which follows is certainly an explanation—or reinterpretation of Daniel, and the author possibly intended it to be regarded as such by his readers.[34]

This ambiguity of Daniel is matched by the ambiguity of Matthew.[35] The story itself makes it clear that Jesus was intended to be understood as the

---

28. Lindars, *Jesus Son of Man*, 3.

29. Vermes, *Jesus and the World of Judaism*, 95.

30. However, it has been recently argued that there is no evidence that *bar enasha* was used as a generic term for "man." Owen and Shepherd, "Speaking up for the Qumran."

31. Vermes, *Jesus In His Jewish Context*, 90.

32. "The phrase is used as a cipher for the eschatological mission that surrounds [Jesus'] mission" (Bird, *Are You the One*, 98).

33. Vermes, *Jesus and the World of Judaism*, 91. Vermes makes the point that this designation was "expected to entail ambiguity."

34. Hooker, *The Son of Man in Mark*, 44.

35. Lindars acknowledges that Matthew appears to think that the Son of Man was an apocalyptic title. He considers, however, that this may be denied by the question concerning Jesus' identity. If the "Son of Man" meant Messiah, why would Jesus inquire who the disciples thought he was? Lindars, *Jesus Son of Man*, 115. Perhaps Lindars has not taken into account the unfolding narrative, which presented a dawning realization

"man" of Daniel's vision. The climactic conflict between Jesus and Caiaphas makes this clear (26:64), which is the last time the designation was used in the Gospel. Within the judgment pericope of chapter 26, Caiaphas had emerged as the true enemy of Jesus, and Jesus emerged as the appointed messianic judge.[36]

The "Son of Man" in Daniel was, considering the company of the peculiar creatures described in its context, a most unexpected figure. The depiction of various beasts that represented kingdoms of authority were clearly contrasted with the "humanness" of the Son of Man; perhaps even driving the point that the eschatological human will be the only true and ultimate human.[37] The beasts all had power and authority for a season, with which they terrified the creation (Dan 7). Each one in turn was destroyed or stripped of its power. It was then that the Son of Man was given eternal power and entitlement,[38] unlike any of the beasts, that had all their authority withdrawn. Therefore, at the very least, the Matthean Jesus' reference to himself as the Son of Man in Daniel's vision showed that Jesus believed himself to be the final and enduring head of an eternal kingdom—the kingdom of God. All nations would worship him, and he would have sovereign rule over them. The one "like the Son of Man" is endued with the rights and privileges of "the Ancient of Days"—even worship (Dan 7:14). The person in Daniel's vision would necessarily be the god/man—and this was the blasphemy, according to Caiaphas, attached to Jesus' claim. The ambiguity attached to Daniel's Son of Man, and Matthew's Son of Man, is removed when Jesus declares that he will come on the clouds, and have God's authority (26:64). It is appropriate that this declaration was made to Israel's high priest.

The revulsion of Caiaphas in the face of Jesus' claim was not without self-interest. Israel's Law and history had determined that the one who could "draw near" to God was the high priest. His majestic garments, which included God's seal upon his head as an exclusive possession of YHWH and the twelve tribes emblazoned upon his breastplate, qualified the high priest, more that any other, to be the eternal appointment and the enduring god/man.[39] Like God, the high priest was holy, and therefore unique amongst

---

as to the identity of Jesus. It is proposed here that the direct Danielic reference ultimately informed the enigmatic self-designation in Matthew's account. It provided the unveiling of Jesus.

36. John's gospel asserts that judgment belongs to Jesus because he is the Son of Man (John 5:27).

37. The natural weakness of the human is contrasted with the forcefulness and natural strength of the horned beasts. Goldingay, *Daniel*, 168.

38. "The sovereignty he is given is like God's own" (ibid.).

39. The Law required that Aaron's garments be made with purple, blue and scarlet

Israelites. As the designation "Son of Man" had never been applied to any individual other than the prophet/priest Ezekiel, it may be that this designation had specific priestly connotations.

Further to this, it has been noted that the Daniel image of the Son of Man had a specific cultic resonance.[40] The high priest could approach God on one day of the year, the Day of Atonement. The slaughter of beasts was the necessary prelude to the Day of Atonement, and having been stripped down to his basic linen ephod and undergarment, Aaron's successor could enter "the most holy place" to perform the ultimate priestly duty. Before entering behind the veil, it was necessary for Aaron to create a cloud of smoke,[41] in order to conceal the atonement cover. The cloud was to be the one barrier the priest could not traverse; exposure to YHWH, via the atonement cover, would result in Aaron's death (Lev 16:2). The image, then, of slaughtered beasts, with the Son of Man entering through the clouds and coming before YHWH, is unmistakable priestly imagery.[42] The Son of Man went where Aaron could not go, and received an enduring title and authority, the like of which was the eschatological aspiration of the high priestly office. Jesus' designation, therefore, may have pointed to his priestly identity. Caiaphas' fury, in this case, was therefore understandable.

There was another implication that may be drawn from Jesus' apocalyptic stewardship in Matthew: all previous authority was stripped and destroyed. Jesus' suggestion to Caiaphas that he would witness this heavenly coronation necessarily placed the high priest around the throne and in the company of beasts—all stripped and humiliated.[43] On the one occasion that Jesus spoke to Caiaphas, he made clear that he was the Messiah and the Son of God,[44] and that Caiaphas would witness his exaltation. There is a distinct

---

linen. This was identical to the material required for the temple curtain, which essentially "veiled" God (Exod 26–28). If nothing else, this image of God and Priest veiled in the same material would suggest that the Priest was the son of God. Also of interest is the image of Christ in Revelation dressed in a robe "dipped in blood" (Rev 19:16). Jesus was the real priest, truly doused in the blood of his offering. Aaron is the "copy"—just an ineffectual imitation, as was the temple he served in, according to the Hebrews writer (Heb 9:24).

40. Fletcher-Louis, "The High Priest as Divine Mediator."

41. Matthew's magi brought incense as a gift. Aaron alone uses incense in the atonement proceedings.

42. "Moses enters the theophanic cloud in Exod 24:18" (Goldingay, *Daniel*, 170). However, this was on earth, not in heaven.

43. This may be what Paul refers to in Col 2:15 "And having disarmed the powers and authorities, he made a public spectacle of them, triumphing over them by the cross."

44. Donald Verseput considers the designation "Son of God" to be a means of

echo here of Mordecai's exaltation and the humiliation/demise of Haman, which is an example of Hebrew theodicy.

## Interpreting Davidic Precedence in Matthew

On two occasions in the Synoptics Jesus referred to David to solve a difficulty that was drawn to his attention and to clarify his own status to those who opposed him. The choice of David, and not of a patriarch or Moses, is quite telling. First, Jesus is asserting the legitimacy of Davidic precedence for his own activity, and therefore confirming the popular belief that he may be the expected Davidic offspring. Furthermore, David appears to have offered sacrifices (2 Sam 24:25)[45] in a manner that could be interpreted as Mosaic violation (Lev 17:1–9). As David was under the Law, he was required to keep its requirements, particularly as they pertained to cultic ordinance.

On the first of these occasions Jesus was confronted in a Galilean field; the disciples were caught red-handed picking and consuming grain (12:1). Preparation of food was permitted on the Sabbath, but not collection (Exod 16:26). The Law made provision for Israelites to eat grain from neighbours' fields (on six days) as they travelled through them, so there was no violation there. Nonetheless, Sabbath-breaking was a capital offense and the first post-Mosaic violator was put to death for collecting sticks (Num 15:32). The Pharisees who brought the charge must certainly have been keeping Jesus' troop under surveillance, which of itself may have brought a similar Sabbath-breaking charge. This did not exonerate Jesus, who could not be killed for Sabbath-breaking under Roman occupation, but the violation would certainly have contributed to any prosecution's case that sought to establish Jesus as an unrighteous fraud. As this incident was not mentioned

---

defining the individual who perfectly expressed the will of God on earth. Verseput, "The Role and Meaning," 549. Interestingly, however, he did not consider that God's will on earth was always intended to be expressed primarily through the office of the high priest.

45. It should be noted that this last statement of 2 Samuel must be significant as the books of Samuel commence with the appointment of Samuel and the demise of Eli's house. In this way David may have been presented as a superior priest to Eli. David, according to 1 Chr 22:1, declared that the house of the Lord was to be on the site where he offered this sacrifice. Consequently, there is the possibility that David offered the first sacrifice of the temple, before it came to be. Roddy Braun also notes that the Chronicler informs this incident with previous sacrifice imagery. Divine acceptance of the sacrifice is reminiscent of Elijah's sacrifice, the sword of the angel is reminiscent of Josh 5:13 and its implications for holy ground, the purchase was an echo of Abraham's purchase of Machpelah's field to bury Sarah, and the threshing floor recalls Gideon. Braun, *1 Chronicles*, 218.

again, or even appeared to be an issue at Jesus' trial, it is safe to say that Jesus' response adequately dealt with the charge.

Jesus' defense did not deny the charge, but appealed for special provision based on Davidic precedence, as already mentioned.[46] David and his companions, when hungry, ate consecrated bread that only the high priest's family could eat (1 Sam 21).[47] Why David was allowed to eat the bread is unclear; the only stipulation placed upon its procurement was the sexual abstinence of David's men[48]—not necessarily of David. David not only ate the bread, but also took it out of the sanctuary to consume it—an act that was forbidden, even for the high priest.[49] The compliance of the high priest, Ahimelech, was to cost him his life at the hands of Saul (1 Sam 22:18). How is it that David, who was not even a king at the time, was permitted to eat the bread and not die as a consequence of it? Did David have this special standing in Israel?

Certainly Samuel had anointed David as God's choice (1 Sam 16:13) and a priest would certainly have been aware of the prophecy concerning the

---

46. There have been various attempts to understand this incident. They range from Jesus re-informing the priorities of Sabbath to his casual disregard for the stipulation because David also transgressed in a similar way. Kazen, *Jesus and Purity Halakah*, 58–60. This incident, as well as the hand-washing accusation, has led Thomas Kazen to conclude: "Although remaining somehow within the framework of the purity paradigm, Jesus disregards impurity in a way which may threaten the whole concept and cause its breakdown" (Kazen, *Jesus and Purity Halakah*, 347). Casting Jesus in this light challenges the notion that the least of the commands were inviolable (5:18), and casts him as a passive resister of the Law of God. There is no breach of Torah with the hand-washing incident, but there is most certainly a Sabbath breach to be found in Jesus' action in the grainfield.

47. "This bread is to be set out before the LORD regularly, Sabbath after Sabbath, on behalf of the Israelites, as a lasting covenant. It belongs to Aaron and his sons, who are to eat it in a holy place, because it is a most holy part of their regular share of the offerings made to the LORD by fire" (Lev 24:8–9).

48. Abstinence from sexual relations is required of those who will meet with God (Exod 19:15).

49. Westerholm believes that the Davidic precedence points to a more relaxed interpretation of the letter of the Law: "David's action, though contrary to the letter of the law, is countenanced by Scripture; it thus cannot be the intention of the divine lawgiver that the terms of Torah be interpreted rigidly and every deviation from such an interpretation be condemned" (Westerholm, *Jesus and Scribal Authority*, 98). There are difficulties with this line of argument. David's avoidance of the death penalty could also, on this reckoning, suggest that God did not intend capital punishment. The exception cannot be used to undermine the explicit requirements of Torah. Law must be legalistic, or it cannot be law. There are also other examples where God extracted exact penalty for transgression, even though it could be argued that there was human need involved (Num 15:32–36). So this line of argument can only point to the arbitrariness of God—another solution needs to be found.

clan of Judah's eternal ascendancy (Gen 49:10). Added to this, the fact that Goliath's sword (taken by David) was kept by the high priest in the sanctuary may raise some distinct possibilities concerning David's standing. Aaron's staff, some manna and the tablets of the Law were specifically kept by the ark as specified by God (Heb 9:4). The sword would certainly have been a valuable adornment for a king, and the shortage of military hardware during Saul's reign would have made it a useful possession (1 Sam 13:22). The sword was wrapped beside the sacred garment (1 Sam 21:9). For these reasons it is reasonable to speculate that the sword of Goliath had some sacral meaning, perhaps as a symbol of the rise of Israel's Messiah.[50] David's standing, then, could well have been understood as having a distinct priestly component, which is why Abiathar, Ahimelech's sole successor, had no hesitation in giving David the high priestly ephod (1 Sam 23:9).[51] Further, it is interesting to observe that David appointed his sons to be priests (2 Sam 8:18).[52] So, clearly, David must have had some sense of his priestly entitlement.

In the grainfield incident, Jesus also mentioned the non-violation of Sabbath by priests on duty (12:5). This additional statement would have no relevance at all but for the point that is made by the previous analogous situation. Jesus is a priest on duty, like David.[53] His companions, like David's, are sanctified for priestly task by virtue of association with the "high priest" whom they serve.[54] The official high priest must break Sabbath within the confines of the temple and eat consecrated bread there. However, a greater priest was then present, one whose ministry was valid, even in a grainfield—doing the will of God. Jesus' answer to the accusation must have been either an acceptable response to the charge, or unusable by an accuser in an ad-

---

50. Klein, *1 Samuel*, 214.

51. There is speculation that Judah and Levi intermarried to such an extent that David had a natural connection to the priestly office. Adler, "Exodus 6:23." However, this was not considered to be a possibility by Jesus' questioners in Matthew or according to the Hebrews author (Heb 7:14).

52. "No indication is given as to whether or not the priestly function of David's sons was different from that of Zadok and Ahimelek (or Abiathar)" (Anderson, *2 Samuel*, 137).

53. Kingsbury believes that the title Son of David incorporated the sense of a healer rather than a king in Matthew. Kingsbury, "Title 'Son of David,'" 591–602. Yet there seems to be no record of an incident where David healed anybody, although he did avert God's wrath.

54. There is an interesting twist to the story of the five loaves in John's gospel (John 6:9). Dallas Roark made a connection between these five loaves and the sacred five loaves that David secured from the high priest in 1 Sam 21. This may have foreshadowed the eucharistic meal, which was then distributed to feed the multitude. In Grassi, "Five Loaves." So it may be that the priestly function of Jesus exists as a subtext of all the Gospels.

versarial examination. For to raise the issue would demand further Davidic comparison and assessment of Jesus' priestly bona fides, which were clearly evident to any priest.[55] This is also why Jesus was not charged with unlawfully forgiving sin—something only God can do, through the human agency of his choice.[56]

The conclusion of this section is succinct and theologically explosive. Jesus claimed to be greater than the temple (12:6),[57] claimed that the Pharisees condemned the innocent (12:7), and asserted that he was "Lord of the Sabbath."[58] Jesus' assertion to the Pharisees of his greatness contributes further to the Matthean paradigm that his opponents were not "in the dark" concerning Jesus' identity. Their own research findings and Jesus' profession were not ambiguous to them. Secondly, another feature of the escalating indictment was put in place: the Jerusalem establishment was not averse to condemning the innocent.[59] The context of Hosea's prophecy ("For I desire mercy, not sacrifice, acknowledgment of God rather than burnt offerings," Hos 6:6) revealed that acknowledgment of God through Jesus' deeds was essential to covenantal well-being. The covenant-breakers in Hosea were "a band of priests" who sought to ambush and murder (Hos 6:9)—a pointed and particularly apt comparison. The last, and intuitively provocative, assertion is hard to understand. Could the high priest, who regulated Israel's cultic life of "Sabbaths," have been known as the Lord of the Sabbath? There is a distinct possibility, though there is no clear evidence. At the very least, claiming

---

55. "Jesus justifies his disciples' breach of the Sabbath because he claims to be a sacral king and high priestly Son of Man. Where *he* is, in that place there is the transcendent liturgical space and time of the true temple in which his disciples can legitimately act as priests for whom Sabbath prohibition against work does not apply" (Fletcher-Louis, "Jesus as the High Priestly Messiah: Part 2," 77).

56. Collins, "The Charge of Blasphemy," 397.

57. "Given the great importance of the temple, the place of God's presence and the performance of the cultus, this statement is utterly astonishing in its significance" (Hagner, *Matthew 1–13*, 330).

58. Jesus' claim to be "Lord of the Sabbath" may well have been a challenge to the existing high priest, who was lord of the cultic requirement; cultic atonement was regarded as a Sabbath (Lev 23:32).

59. The mercy that God desired within this context was to administer justice, rather than let the guilty go free. The leaders did not love mercy, so they condemned the innocent. Mercy, in its Hosea context, was an expression of covenant loyalty to God. France believes that Jesus had declared "that needy people who pluck grain to eat on the Sabbath are guiltless" (France, *Matthew*, 485). This, however, would be a clear breach of the Law, in spite of its ethical appeal. Jesus made no appeal for exemption of the Law's demand based on his impoverished condition.

Lordship of Sabbath must have strong inference for covenantal oversight, for the sign of the Mosaic covenant was the Sabbath (Exod 31:13).[60]

Jesus' second Davidic reference was the last encounter that Matthew describes with the community of Pharisees (22:41–46). Jesus' provocative question concerning David's relationship to his Lord provoked no further questioning from his opponents, who had tested Jesus three times in quick succession—the second instance in the document where Jesus was tested three times. The three cleverly devised tests were intended to trap Jesus in a compromising statement, which would directly contravene Mosaic covenant Law.[61] Jesus' question tested the Pharisees, and they refused to reply.

With this question Matthew's Jesus reflected on David, once again, by referring to Psalm 110 and, consequently, identifying himself as David's lord. It was not customary, in Hebrew understanding, that the father be exceeded by his offspring.[62] David, however, knew that his offspring would be greater than himself. In this way, Jesus claimed to be greater than David. The quoted psalm also included the Son's exaltation through God's commitment to subdue his enemies under him (Ps 110:5–6). At this stage of the proceedings, there can be no mistake as to the identity of Jesus' enemies: David's prophetic psalm revealed that the leaders of Israel had unwittingly made God their enemy when they made the Son their enemy. Their destined condemnation was in this way assured, and it set the foundation for the complete indictment of seven woes and the abandonment of the temple.

These are not the only inferences to be made from this psalm. The enthroned Messiah was clearly portrayed as an eschatological judge who would ruthlessly crush all his enemies. And lastly, and perhaps most disturbingly, the exalted Messiah and David's Lord is declared to be an eternal priest, who has no connection to Aaron. The only biblical threat to Aaronic/Levitical tenure and entitlement within Scripture was the enigmatic

---

60. "Jesus is said here to be the 'Lord of the Sabbath' in the sense that he has the sovereign authority to decide what loyalty to the Sabbath means" (Hagner, *Matthew 1–13*, 330). On this basis, can there have been any doubt that the high priest would have believed himself to be the "lord of the Sabbath"?

61. The first challenge was regarding taxes, which financed the Roman occupation of Judea. Jesus' response neither negated Roman entitlement nor contravened Moses, who forbade images. Otherwise, why did Jews keep coins at all? The second test was issued by the Sadducees, who attempted to demonstrate from Moses how ludicrous the notion of resurrection was. Jesus exposed them as ignorant of Scripture, as the Patriarchs are not dead, according to YHWH's self-introduction to Moses. The third test was an attempt to compromise Jesus by pressing him to choose which law was important and, by implication, which law was not.

62. Hagner, *Matthew 14–28*, 651. Nolland, *Luke 18:35–24:53*, 974. Further support for this contention is in Davies and Allison, *Matthew: A Shorter*, 385.

priesthood mentioned in Psalm 110. The possible emergence of a priest who, like Melchizedek, came from nowhere and was far greater than Abraham, may have been a deep concern for a smugly complacent priestly upper class. This psalm pointed to a Messiah who would unseat all others in his exaltation, and Jesus made it clear that the time for this priestly kingdom to commence had arrived. With this question Jesus indicated what authority he had to do these things, a hitherto unanswered question (21:23), but now a terrifying prelude to the divine rapprochement and indictment of the Jerusalem priestly aristocracy.[63]

## The Priestly Challenge in Matthew 21

The challenge to the Pharisees concerning Jesus' legitimate stakehold in David's promise was no doubt pre-empted by Jesus' messianic claims, reception and conduct on this first visit to Jerusalem in Matthew's account. Jesus had not escaped the attention of the Jerusalem establishment from his humble beginning in Bethlehem. Any serious messianic claim could not be made in regional areas of Judea or Galilee alone; like any king of Judah, the king had to be heralded in Jerusalem. Jesus' mode of entry, riding on a donkey, signalled such a claim, and the fickle community responded affirmatively to the obvious nonverbal proclamation (21:9).

The donkey and its colt were a direct reference, according to Matthew, to Zechariah's prophecy[64] and exhortation to Jerusalem:

> Rejoice greatly, O Daughter of Zion! Shout,
> Daughter of Jerusalem!
> See, your king comes to you,
> righteous and having salvation,
> gentle and riding on a donkey,
> on a colt, the foal of a donkey (Zech 9:9).

The symbolism of the donkey and colt, however, does not end there. The Anointed One of Judah was described in Jacob's prophecy: "He will tether his donkey to a vine, his colt to the choicest branch" (Gen 49:11).[65] In another instance, when Israel's leadership was being usurped by Adonijah, David had Solomon sit upon his mule as a sign that the rightful power had been trans-

---

63. Matthew intended to provoke his readers to recoil at the figure of Jerusalem. Verseput, "Jesus' Pilgrimage," 120.

64. Matthew was the only synoptic that made direct reference to Zechariah.

65. Nolland believes the Gen 49:11 connection is reenforced by the Zechariah connection. Nolland, *Gospel of Matthew*, 833.

ferred to him (1 Kgs 1:33).[66] Jesus did not have a king to succeed; however, the narrative made clear that the donkey and colt were the possession of the Lord (21:3). As such, the donkey was holy.[67] Jesus' appropriation of the donkey was certainly a messianic declaration, and it may have been understood as having some priestly implications by the Jerusalem priestly class.[68]

The response of the crowd to Jesus' entry into Jerusalem followed the script of Psalm 118 perfectly. The throng with branches in hand welcomed the one whom the "builders rejected." YHWH, according to the psalm, is the savior, and they cry, "Blessed is he who comes in the name of YHWH" (Ps 118:22–27). As a result of the commotion and the heightened expectations created by Jesus' arrival the whole city was disturbed, literally shaken (21:10). The events that followed were unexpected and spectacular.

The cleansing of the temple precincts (21:12–17) was probably a metaphor for exile.[69] Matthew's scriptural reference for the action, taken from Jeremiah 9, formed part of the escalating indictment of Jerusalem which would end with YHWH abandoning the covenant. What Jesus did that day was remove impurity from the temple courts, a function assigned through sacramental right to the high priest, normally performed on the Day of Atonement (Lev 16).[70] This action of judgment, therefore, may have emphasized Jesus' credentials as an effective priest, in the midst of the legitimate and yet impotent priests. They correctly asked Jesus to explain the source of his authority to do what Mosaic legislation exclusively assigned to the Levitical community. Jesus did not answer the question until the following day, before the final indictment.

---

66. Evans, "The Two Sons of Oil," 574. David's use of a donkey may have also demonstrated obedience to the Law which limited the possession of horses (Deut 17:16).

67. The Law required that firstborn colts were to be redeemed with a lamb, or have their necks broken (Exod 34:20).

68. Another, though remote, possibility is that the forceful acquisition of the donkey was a prelude to the curses of Deuteronomy 28. "Your donkey will be forcibly taken from you and will not be returned" (Deut 28:31).

69. The original exile was the removal of the first humans from the garden of Eden, where relationship with God and eternal life was possible. Similarly, exile from the land was more than loss of property—it was removal from access to the temple. This explanation for the Exile was clarified by the Deuteronomist in 2 Kgs 17:22–23: "The Israelites persisted in all the sins of Jeroboam and did not turn away from them until the LORD removed them from his presence, as he had warned through all his servants the prophets. So the people of Israel were taken from their homeland into exile in Assyria, and they are still there."

70. Nolland believes that this action may have been connected to Mal 1:10 as a symbolic shutting down of the temple. Nolland, *Gospel of Matthew*, 844. As such, Jesus may be responding directly to YHWH's desire that someone shut down the temple and its contemptuous priesthood.

The responsibility to maintain the temple precincts and manage its affairs was the responsibility of the high priest and the Levites who were given to him for his various duties (Num 1; 3:6).[71] Their failure to preserve these precincts highlighted their incompetence to understand their duty, or perhaps revealed the presumptuous attitude that they had to the cleansing requirements. The temple trade was no doubt profitable and probably dishonest; exploitation of pilgrims is well known.[72] The Law did make provision for trade to assist pilgrims who had a long distance to travel (Deut 14:24–27). There is no suggestion in the Law, however, that this should have been taking place in the sanctuary precincts. It should be plainly obvious to any student of the Law that the courts were for priests to carry out ministry, and not for trade. The human presence in the temple area was the reason why Atonement had to be made. The Day of Atonement was a ritual sacrifice which purified the tent and holy place from human contamination.[73] In view of this, it was obvious that the priestly class was required to treat the precincts with the greatest respect; not to do so was both presumptuous and contemptuous of Israel's holy place.

No matter what prompted or justified the temple trade and traffic, it was clearly abhorrent to Jesus.[74] The Jeremiah reference, which was directly

---

71. "If Joshua [Zechariah 3] ensures that the temple remains in good condition, then God in turn commits to passing along his position to his progeny" (Segal, "The Responsibilities and Rewards of Joshua," 731). The visitation of the temple by Jesus (the embodiment of YHWH) was in order to critique the Aaronic stewardship. This was a sound basis for termination of the Aaronic/Levitical tenure.

72. See Evans, "Jesus' Action in the Temple."

73. "He [the high priest] shall then slaughter the goat for the sin offering for the people and take its blood behind the curtain and do with it as he did with the bull's blood: He shall sprinkle it on the atonement cover and in front of it. In this way he will make atonement for the Most Holy Place because of the uncleanness and rebellion of the Israelites, whatever their sins have been. He is to do the same for the Tent of Meeting, which is among them in the midst of their uncleanness" (Lev 16:15–16).

74. In Matthew these events happened on the same day. Luke incorporated Jesus' indictment in the same pericope, which is otherwise found in Mark 13 and Matthew 23–24. Luke's indictment is succinct and pointed: "As he approached Jerusalem and saw the city, he wept over it and said, 'If you, even you, had only known on this day what would bring you peace—but now it is hidden from your eyes. The days will come upon you when your enemies will build an embankment against you and encircle you and hem you in on every side. They will dash you to the ground, you and the children within your walls. They will not leave one stone on another, because you did not recognize the time of God's coming to you'" (Luke 19:41–44). Luke therefore portrays Jesus' entry as a "last chance," whereas there is no hint of this in Matthew. Nonetheless Luke, like Matthew, made a clear connection between Jesus' rejection and the events of AD 70.

drawn from the LXX, contributed further evidence that Israel was in peril of YHWH's imminent wrath.[75]

> Has this house, which bears my Name, become a den of robbers to you? But I have been watching! declares the LORD.
> Go now to the place in Shiloh where I first made a dwelling for my Name, and see what I did to it because of the wickedness of my people Israel. While you were doing all these things, declares the LORD, I spoke to you again and again, but you did not listen; I called you, but you did not answer. Therefore, what I did to Shiloh I will now do to the house that bears my Name, the temple you trust in, the place I gave to you and your fathers ... (Jer 7:11–14).

Restating the "den of thieves" (21:13) analogy for the temple practice must have also invoked its associated judgment, which resulted in the first destruction of Jerusalem and its temple in 586 BC.[76]

Matthew's Jesus, through these two incidents, was portrayed as a wrathful priest, who was also a prophet with monarchical rights and destiny. Interestingly, such a profile was given to Melchizedek in the Dead Sea Scrolls; he was expected to come as the eschatological judge of righteousness. Paul Kobelski notes that Qumran literature made much of the reemergence of Melchizedek as an apocalyptic judgment against Belial/Satan.[77] He considered that "the similarities between Psalm 110 and 11QMelch are too numerous to be coincidental and suggest that the Melchizedek presented in 11QMelch was consciously modeled after the person addressed in Ps 110:1."[78] Kobelski suggests that Melchizedek is portrayed as both a heavenly and historical figure and as God's agent of judgment; this, he believes, heavily influenced the New Testament perspectives on both the "Son of Man" concept in the Synoptic tradition and Hebrews' presentation of Christ's priestly appointment.[79] Geza Vermes considers the Qumran literature

---

75. Sim, *Apocalyptic Eschatology*, 174; Bird, *Are You the One*, 127.

76. According to Psalm 78, the tabernacle was destroyed at Shiloh and the priests put to the sword by God. The ark did not return to Israel until brought to Jerusalem by David—Israel's true shepherd.

77. Kobelski, *Melchizedek and Melchirešaʿ*, 134, 181.

78. Ibid., 134.

79. There is no shortage of interest in Melchizedek in the intertestamental period and the first century. "Sources include Philo, (a) *Congr.* 99, which discusses the literal and allegorical significance of the tithe; (b) *Abr.* 235, a non-allegorical account similar to Haggadic midrash; and (c) *Leg. All.* 3.79–82, which is predominantly allegorical; ... (3) two passages from Josephus, *War* 6.438 and *Ant.*1.180, which may reflect earlier traditions in addition to Gen. 14" (Ellingworth, *Hebrews*, 352); Kobelski, *Melchizedek*

(11Q13) to be a midrash that proclaims liberty to captives (Isa 61:1) and the fulfillment of key covenant concepts: jubilee (Lev 25:13) and freedom from debts (Deut 15:2).[80] Vermes also sees Melchizedek as an eschatological and heavenly judge who defeats Belial.[81]

The dual tasks of Melchizedek in the Q11 literature appear to be identical to the portrayal of Matthew's Jesus. Hartmut Stegemann has recognized the distinct implications for priesthood entailed in the arrival of an end time priest like Melchizedek. He notes:

> The first week of years of the tenth and last epoch of world history is portrayed by the *Melchizedek Midrash* as a great "Year of Release," in which Melchizedek fulfills the promise of Isaiah 61:1 that "release" will be proclaimed to prisoners. This act is interpreted to be a general amnesty of the pious in Israel for all their sins thus far committed. The conclusion of the tenth epoch consists of a "Day of Atonement" (Lev 25:9), on which Melchizedek proclaims the "Year of Favor from the Lord" and presides over the Last Judgment in the form of a judgment of punishment upon all the evil in the world.[82]

The anticipation by the Qumran community[83] of the imminence of a messianic priest, who would bring both end time judgment and amnesty (good news), parallels the reappearance of Elijah in John. As Elijah/John was anticipated by former prophets (Isaiah, Malachi), so Melchizedek was anticipated by the king/priest David. By drawing his readers' attention to Psalm 110 as the last "civil" encounter Jesus had with his executioners, Matthew invoked the Melchizedek/Jesus connection. The wrath of Jesus was understandable within this messianic expectation.[84]

---

and Melchireša, 136–37.

80. Vermes, *The Complete Dead Sea Scrolls*, 500.

81. Ibid.

82. Stegemann, *The Library of Qumran*, 119.

83. Stegemenn proposes that the Qumran community was nothing more than a "publishing house" for the widespread Essene community that had its headquarters in Jerusalem. Though this hypothesis has challenged formerly held views concerning the small fringe sect, it does make reasonable sense. Qumran caves contained far more manuscripts than would be needed for a community that has been estimated to be between 50–300 people. Stegemenn argues that the absence of mundane documents at Qumran (letters, balance sheets, membership rolls, etc.) is irrefutable proof that Qumran was not the Essenes headquarters. Their influence was widespread and their vision was for national unity. Ibid., 138.

84. Zech 5:1–4 describes a flying scroll that will remain in "the house" and then destroy it, both "timbers and stone." Meredith Kline observed that the measurement of the scroll was that of the inner chamber of the temple, and that the flying scroll was

While in the temple precincts, Jesus healed both the lame and blind. As these particular types of healing are mentioned here there may be some narrative implications, particularly as healing was a routine part of Jesus' ministry at its commencement. The particular healings chosen, though not unknown in healing accounts in Matthew, present an interesting possibility within the context of temple ministry. No diseased persons, lepers or demoniacs were restored, for clearly, they would not be permitted into the temple precincts. However, certain crippled and blind people could enter this area and be provided with food. Levites with physical disabilities, the blind and lame, could not serve as priests, or they would "desecrate the altar and sanctuary" (Lev 21:16–23). These Levites could not draw near in service, but they could eat the temple food, which had to be eaten in the temple courts. It may be the case, then, that these healings were specifically of maimed Levites, and this would have been an extraordinary proof to the Levitical community that a superior priest than Aaron, who could not restore his kinsmen, had come to the temple.

When the chief priests and the teachers of the law witnessed this along with the exalting cry of the children,[85] "Hosanna to the Son of David," they did not rejoice, but rather, were offended. They then challenged Jesus for not being disturbed by such adulation, and no doubt, by the cry of praise to David's son. Jesus' reply from Psalm 8 drew no further response from his enemies in Matthew's account. The reason why God ordained praise from children was to "silence the foe and avenger" (Ps 8:2).[86]

## Miracles and Priestly Function

Miraculous healings are an unmistakable testimony to Jesus' authority in all the Gospels. The Synoptics catalogue many of the same miracles; any attempt to discern the individual author's view of why Jesus used miracles must examine the order and context in which the supernatural incidents are found. Matthew had a particular use for the miracles: to escalate Israel's culpability and demonstrate her recalcitrance, and secondly, to reveal Jesus' priestly competence.[87] It is this latter use that will be considered here.

symbolic of covenant termination, resulting in a curse (Zech 5:3). Kline, *Glory in Our Midst*, 178–79.

85. παῖς can also be translated servant or attendant. It may be the case that the lesser priests, who were still in the temple after its cleansing, were the ones giving praise to Jesus.

86. See France, *Matthew*, 789.

87. Jesus did not remove physical impurities as the consequence of his prophetic role, but as a demonstration that he had authority to forgive sins on earth (priestly role).

Mark's and Luke's first recorded miracle was Jesus' healing of the demoniac in the Capernaum synagogue. Matthew's first recorded miracle is the cleansing of the leper.[88] This incident, recorded in all three Synoptics, pointed specifically to Mosaic legislation, which accorded the high priest (or his sons) the responsibility of declaring a person clean once the disease was removed (Lev 13). The leper was not favored under Moses; he was destined to be a pariah outside of the community, issuing a warning to all concerning his unclean status. He must cover his face and live beyond the fringe of the covenant community, make no attempt to groom himself and must only wear torn clothes (Lev 13:45–46). This is the antithesis of the high priest, who was the centre of the community, who was always required to be well groomed and who could never tear his clothes (Lev 21:10). Exclusion from the covenant community was an exclusion from the possibility of divine grace, and therefore, a hopeless situation. By giving priority to this miracle, Matthew went straight to the heart of the Levitical law; the Law said nothing about demons.

It is difficult to understand the rationale of the Mosaic legislation. The regulations centered on a person's ability to be ceremonially clean, which enabled an Israelite to fully participate in the life and privileges associated with being a community of YHWH. A person in Israel could have one of three standings. The first and most profitable was to be ceremonially clean and therefore able to participate in the sacral life of the community, within given limitations.[89] The high priest, for instance, had access to the most holy place once a year. A woman, on the other hand, would never be permitted in the tabernacle precinct. A person's gender, tribal standing and nationality would determine the level of access and privilege they could enjoy in the system; this is on the assumption, of course, that one is ceremonially clean. Then there were those who had forfeited all opportunity to be covenantally restored through priestly representation. These people were, in effect, those who had committed capital offenses, sins that the sacrificial law could not amend—they were to be "cut off,"[90] a euphemism for being

---

See Collins, "The Charge of Blasphemy."

88. Leprosy is recorded five times in the Old Testament. Moses' hand was made temporarily leprous (Exod 4:6). Miriam, Moses' sister and deliverer, contracted it and was healed (Num 12:10). Naaman the Aramean was also healed (2 Kgs 5), while Uzziah, king of Judah died with the disease (2 Chr 26:21). The only other incident is the curse placed upon Joab's house by David.

89. It has been argued that most Jews were in a state of corpse impurity, which was only dealt with when they went to the temple. Poirier, "Purity Beyond the Temple," 251.

90. The majority of these, though not all, are found in the chapters following the instructions concerning the Day of Atonement (Lev 16).

put to death.[91] The third category, which also applied to the leper, effectively required self-exile (Lev 13:46), or in the case of bleeding or discharges, sufferers must exist free of human contact (Lev 15). Unlike the penalty for capital offense, however, these restrictions were often temporary. Once the offending condition was healed, a person could be covenantally restored by declaration of the priest following the prescribed sacrifice. These conditions included leprosy, bodily discharges, emissions of blood including the menstrual cycle, childbirth, contact with dead humans or other creatures and some minor moral offenses.[92] Non-capital offenses, such as theft, made one no more unclean than childbearing. Such were the Law's requirements.

Leprosy, though outside of a person's control, was sin, which required cleansing and forgiveness through sacrifice (Lev 14:19). Once a person was healed, he was eligible for forgiveness, although it was not automatically bestowed. The sacral requirements were lengthy and complex (Lev 14:1–31). Giving the "gift" that Moses commanded could take several weeks and considerable expense, plus a considerable amount of work on the high priest's part.[93] Perhaps fortunately for the high priest, he would not have normally expected to see a case of cured leprosy during his whole tenure. Through this first miracle in Galilee, Matthew had intended his readers to deduce that Caiaphas had become aware that Jesus was cleansing lepers in his jurisdiction. The testimony to the priests that would result from the leper's ritual cleansing has two components. It testifies to the validity of the Mosaic requirements and Jesus' adherence to the same, and it also testified to the failure of the existing order of priests.[94] Like the healing of the blind and the lame in the temple precincts, this would be a humiliation and offense; rather than this being a testimony to them, it was in reality a testimony

---

91. Israel's priests had no right to take life under Roman law. Capital offenders were "cut off" without being put to death. These covenantal exiles were the sinners and tax collectors.

92. Should a person refuse to undertake ritual purification within the prescribed time he must be "cut off" (Num 19:13).

93. The cleansing rite and declaration of purification had to take place at the temple in Jerusalem. Many Jewish sects considered that there could no longer be uncleanness if the temple did not exist. Poirier, "Purity Beyond the Temple," 362. This optimistic outlook demonstrates that the temple was integral in the decontamination or purification process. The logic is that if God did not supply a temple, he must not require cleansing.

94. Jesus' healing ministry implicitly testified against the incumbents. "Jesus' activities among the crowd thus echo YHWH's indictments against Israel's false shepherds who neither seek nor heal (Ezek 34:1–16)" (Chae, *Jesus as the Eschatological Davidic Shepherd*, 211).

against them—an early contribution to an escalating indictment against Caiaphas in Matthew.[95]

The unidentified leper's proposal to Jesus ("if you are willing, you can make me clean," 8:2) demonstrated confidence in Jesus' ability, but did not presuppose his willingness to show the kindness. Could it be that any priest, entrusted with the care of Israelites, would be unwilling to relieve an Israelite's burden? Jesus' summary indictment of the Jerusalem establishment made it clear that they were unwilling—"They tie up heavy loads and put them on men's shoulders, but they themselves are not willing to lift a finger to move them" (23:4).

In defense of the high priest, he was required by legislation to avoid any situation that could contaminate his fragile purity.[96] He was prohibited from being exposed to any contagious disease, or coming into contact with the dead. The superiority of Jesus' priesthood in Matthew, however, enabled him to remain clean following contact with the unclean or dead, a point that Matthew ensures is not lost on the reader. Matthew recorded that Jesus came into physical contact with the leprous (8:3), the bleeding (9:20) and the dead (9:25). He even entered a house with a dead person in it (9:23), an action expressly forbidden for the high priest (Lev 21:11).

Jesus' contact with contagious diseases was a legal dilemma for his opponents and a complexity for modern students of Matthew.[97] As the Law expressly forbids such contact, particularly when undertaken deliberately, how was Jesus able to remain "clean" while apparently breaching the Law? Further, any contaminated person who did not undertake ritual cleansing was to be "cut off." Clearly, no purification took place, as Matthew's Jesus did not go to Jerusalem till much later in the narrative. How then can Jesus' covenantal standing have been preserved? What options are possible?

---

95. Helen Bond is mistaken when she asserts: "As far as the Synoptic writers were concerned, the precise identity of the High Priest was irrelevant . . ." (Bond, "Caiaphas," 184). Bond, however, appears to have modified this position, having identified what may be called a "two-house" hypothesis. Referring to the naming of Caiaphas, "The effect of this is to set up a parallelism between the two scenes: Jesus, the hero, surrounded by his disciples, contrasted with the high priest, the archvillian [antichrist?], surrounded by Jewish leaders" (Bond, *Caiaphas*, 124).

96. "The high priest, the one among his brothers who has had the anointing oil poured on his head and who has been ordained to wear the priestly garments, must not let his hair become unkempt or tear his clothes. He must not enter a place where there is a dead body. He must not make himself unclean, even for his father or mother, nor leave the sanctuary of his God or desecrate it, because the anointing oil of his God has dedicated him. I am the LORD" (Lev 21:10–12).

97. See, Kazen, *Jesus and Purity Halakah*; Harrington, *The Impurity Systems*; Klawans, *Impurity and Sin in Ancient Israel*; Harrington, *The Purity Texts*; Schwartz et al., *Perspectives on Purity and Purification*.

There are four possibilities. The first possibility is that Jesus was not bound by Mosaic legislation because of his divine standing. This is enormously problematic, however, as that would mean that Jesus was not under Law, a proposition the early community was quick to deny (Gal 4:4).[98] Another possibility is that Jesus simply abrogated cleanliness regulations.[99] There is no suggestion of this in Matthew; Jesus' personal mission statement included the resolve that every *yod* and *tittle* of the Law would remain in force (5:18), and Matthew was careful not to include any statement that may have given the impression that Jesus had altered Torah for Israelites, such as was the case in Mark ("In saying this, Jesus declared all foods 'clean,'" Mark 7:19).[100] The third possibility is that Jesus simply broke the Law.[101] Like the former possibility, this would fundamentally contradict Matthew's view that Jesus was blameless (27:4, 19). The Law does not give exceptions: ritual impurity is the product of touching the unclean.[102] The last option, the one favoured here, is that humans were cleansed or raised at the instant that Jesus touched them. In other words, he did not touch a leper or a dead person. His relationship with God was such that God would not let Jesus be polluted, in the same way that David was confident that God would not allow "his holy one see decay" (Ps 16:10). The Father and the Son acted in concert; no time lapse could be observed, in Matthew's account, between the touch and the healing, therefore, it is a distinct possibility that these people were not unclean at the instant that Jesus touched them. Although this cannot be proven, it is disturbing how little attention is given in the literature to the

---

98. In Luke 2:24 Luke also noted the sacrifices made by Jesus' family at the temple. The two doves were required for a sacrifice of atonement for the woman who had given birth (Lev 12). One could argue, therefore, that if Mary was unclean according to the Law for giving birth to Jesus, then the Law still applied to the "holy" family.

99. For instance, France believed that Jesus set aside all Levitical laws pertaining to food and contagion defilement. France, *Matthew*, 583. And also, Nolland, *Gospel of Matthew*, 621.

100. There is a difference between declaring that what goes in cannot make one unclean and actually declaring that the Law is annulled. In the case of menstruation, clearly this did not make a person unclean; however, the Law declared that a woman is unclean at the time of menstruation. While these laws were all annulled following Jesus' resurrection, it cannot be said that they were annulled incrementally by statements that Jesus made. Even the Mark statement should not be interpreted as a change of the Law, but a revelation for the early Christian community that could not conceive of a world where unclean foods did not actually cause personal impurity.

101. Kazen develops this line. He believes that contact impurity was significant in the first century, and cannot be downplayed. His conclusion as to how Jesus could avoid such contamination is that Jesus was "relatively indifferent" to the laws. Kazen, *Jesus and Purity Halakah*, 164.

102. Bird, "Jesus as Law-Breaker," 16.

question of how Jesus remained clean, while doing what the Law specifically forbade. Perhaps this is a consequence of not recognizing that the Gospels are Hebrew literature, written to extend the existing narrative.

The legal quandary that Jesus' contact with contagions posed for his accusers should be obvious. They could not accuse him of being ritually unclean, for the "ritually unclean" were healed when touched by Jesus. To make the case that he was unclean, the lawyers ran the risk of exposing Jesus' ability to sanctify "sinners," a notion that was better buried than exposed. For this reason, it is proposed, the healings performed by Jesus in Matthew were not presented at his trial as an instance of covenantal breach compounded by his non-pursuit of Mosaic purification—a crime punishable by death (Num 19:13). To make these healings a tribunal deliberation would have resulted in the necessary discussion concerning the authority of Jesus' clearly effectual priesthood.[103]

We are not able to consider all the healings specifically, as this would require more space than is available in an overview to examine Matthew's authorial intent. All of the physical healings, to varying degrees, bear out the intention outlined in our discussion concerning the leper. Matthew's other use of miracles, to make obvious Israel's intransigence to Messiah, has previously been considered. Exorcisms, which often resulted in physical healing also, will be dealt with in a later section of this chapter. At this stage, greater consideration will be given to the Mosaic concept of illness and disability—handicaps that rendered Jews ceremonially unclean.

## The "Sin" of Sickness and Disability

Matthew presented Jesus' healing and exorcism ministry as a fulfilment of Isaiah 53: "He took up our infirmities and carried our diseases" (8:33). The intention of these healings, however, was not simply to make life easier for the multitude.[104] Sickness, disabilities, certain charitable activities (caring for

---

103. The sandwiching of the incident of the woman within the incident of the ruler's daughter deserves some attention. Matthew's Jesus knew the law concerning ritual impurity. Therefore, having contact with a contagious woman on the way to the ruler's house made him unclean until evening (Lev 15:27). By raising the girl on the same day, Matthew may have been demonstrating that Jesus could not be made unclean.

104. This is the subject of extensive discussion. Most commentators seem to be satisfied by dividing uncleanness into two categories, moral and societal, or moral and ritual. Himmelfarb, "Impurity and Sin," 37; Klawans, *Impurity and Sin*, 156. However, "moral" is not a category found in the Law, even if there are different consequences for different types of uncleanness. Moral and societal categories are modern constructs that attempt to differentiate between culpable uncleanness and accidental uncleanness. Jay Sklar notes that there is no differentiation in the treatment of the Law between

the sick and dead), particular unclean foods and even normal bodily functions could render a Hebrew ceremonially unclean for anything from a day to a lifetime. To be unclean had implications for drawing near to God and contact with other Israelites. A husband, for instance, could have no physical contact with his wife during her menstrual cycle, and intercourse at that time was a capital offense (Lev 18:19, 29). A woman was unclean during and seven days after her menstrual cycle. Anything she touched was also unclean (Lev 15:20–23).[105] A woman who had protracted bleeding or a woman who had given birth were ceremonially unclean; they were required to offer sacrifices to cleanse them of their sin[106]—"In this way he will make atonement for her before the LORD for the uncleanness of her discharge" (Lev 15:30).[107]

As previously mentioned, physical handicaps and blindness also had an impact on a person's ability to draw near to God. Levites could not offer

---

unintentional sins and uncleanness as the consequence of ritual defilement. Both require purgation and ransom. Sklar, "Sin and Impurity." Bird also observes that Judaism "did not always know a rigid distinction between ethics and purity or belief and ritual. Moral and ceremonial impurity were not always distinguished" (Bird, "Jesus as Law-Breaker," 21).

The Hebrews writer made a clear distinction between sins of ignorance and deliberate acts. The atonement ritual specified in Hebrews 9 (the Day of Atonement) only enacted purgation of "unintentional sins" and that was the extent of the Levitical mediation. This may have included all sins that did not irretrievably breach the covenant stipulations (the capital offenses). However, sin could not be removed without both purgation, and the termination of the offensive behaviour or medical condition. Spadaro, "An Examination of the Relationship."

Therefore, the Law had made sufficient provision for a demarcation to exist between sins of a "high hand" and sins of ignorance, which could be associated with ill-health or even natural processes, such as giving birth. It is not helpful to introduce concepts of moral and societal when these categories are alien to the text. This is an emotional issue for some and it may be difficult to separate the modern views of readers from that of the ancient world of the Mosaic stipulations. "We would do well on an individual basis to ask ourselves if our methodological choices, terminological decisions, and historical reconstructions may be too closely aligned with our own ideologies. We may do well to identify and bracket those issues we feel we cannot deal with dispassionately" (Klawans, "Methodology and Ideology, 95).

105. "The Torah is insistent that ritual impurities must be purified (Num 19:20) before the impure individual can participate in temple worship" (Harrington, *The Purity Texts*, 10).

106. Apart from the leper in Matthew's narrative, no one was required to return to the priest and fulfill the Mosaic requirement. Matthew may have intended his readers to assume that the same requirement was placed on all who had been covenantally unclean. On the other hand, Jesus' declaration of salvation to the woman with bleeding revealed her to no longer be a "sinner," and therefore, this constituted the priestly declaration necessary for full absolution in heaven. These people, however, may have remained outcasts within the "covenant" community.

107. Also Lev 12:6–7.

service with disabilities, for they would desecrate the holy things (Lev 21:23). Death was also a contagion; anyone who contacted a dead person was unclean. Aaron could not attend his parents' funerals (Lev 21:11), for their bodies were unclean. Though the Law makes no reference to demons (unclean spirits, 10:1), clearly they too rendered a person unclean. The point of all this is to show that the Law did not view sickness as amoral—it had covenantal and moral implications, which required atonement to be made by the priest for the individual, or through the corporate cleansing Day of Atonement (Lev 16).

## Healing As Forgiveness

In view of the Law's teaching on sickness and diseases, it seems reasonable to place their removal within the realm of priestly function. There is no general history of priests removing sicknesses—their task was to identify the disease and declare whether a person was clean or unclean. Atonement could not effect forgiveness or "cleanness" for a person still beset by sickness or disease. The Aaronic priesthood's limitation was clearly apparent. It had authority to restore fully those who had been healed; however, the "heavy-laden" could find no respite in Jerusalem.

Apart from particular cleansing procedures, such as those for cleansed lepers and individuals subject to bleeding, the main instrument for community cleansing was the Day of Atonement (Lev 16; Heb 9:7). This annual sacrifice was able to atone for the involuntary violations described in the five chapters that precede Leviticus 16, and possibly some undetected minor moral transgressions. Volitional sins of a serious nature incurred the death penalty; many of these transgressions are listed after the Day of Atonement account. Sins that did not incur the death penalty, such as theft, careless oaths, contamination, not testifying when witnesses were called and unwitting violations of a minor category (Lev 4–6), all needed to be atoned for through sacrifice by the priest for the individual transgressor. The major function of the Day of Atonement, however, was to cleanse the "holy things" (the temple precincts) of Israel's contagion, in order for God to remain among them.

The point is that the high priest could not remove the imperfections that resulted in ritual uncleanness, and, therefore, the covenantal alienation remained on those who had these involuntary burdens.[108] Jesus, by contrast,

---

108. This view of atonement is not widely accepted. Many Leviticus scholars believe that the Day of Atonement was an effectual annual cleansing of all violations. The following is representative: "This rite of sprinkling the blood cleanses . . . the Holiest

removed these burdens for all who came to him. Jesus healed all who came in every place; very few, though, had their sins forgiven for the purpose of kingdom entry. The lack of faith in communities such as Korazin and Bethsaida, which had experienced widespread healing and deliverance, was a cause for indictment, as has been previously noted. Although Jesus did occasionally forgive sin, this was relatively rare. So Matthew's Jesus was effectively removing the burdens that caused involuntary alienation; by these miracles, Jesus was forgiving unintentional sins by removing their causes. This was, therefore, a direct challenge to the priestly competence of Caiaphas (and all who went before him); he is indicted for failure to be a shepherd and burden-remover for his people (Ezek 34:4).[109] Having removed the involuntary transgressions of the nation, Jesus, in effect, left the whole nation culpable and indictable; for the people's only remaining offenses were the ones they chose to have. Even these sins, however, could be forgiven and removed. To this end Jesus issued an invitation to all who were unable to bear their burden.

## Invitation to Enjoy Sabbath

Preceding the Sabbath controversy and the ensuing debate of chapter 12, Jesus issued a universal invitation to the covenant community:

> Come to me, all you who are weary and burdened, and I will give you rest. Take my yoke upon you and learn from me, for I

---

Place from the impurities (טמאת) of the Israelites' transgressions that have penetrated into the Holiest Place. All cases of uncleanness of the people (chaps. 11–15) pollute the sanctuary to some measure. For the sanctuary to function effectively and for it to continue to abide in the midst of the people, it must be cleansed annually. In addition, this rite cleanses the Holiest Place from the פשעים, 'acts of rebellion,' and from the חטאת, 'sins,' of the Israelites. The choice of these terms recognizes that the people sin not only accidentally and out of ignorance, but also willfully. The term פשע, 'act of rebellion,' stands for any acts that were intentional violations of God's law" (Hartley, *Leviticus*, 240). This, however, was not the understanding of Matthew, who recorded Jesus' indictment that all the righteous blood shed from Abel to Zechariah would be visited upon his obstructionist opponents (23:35). Such a curse would have no validity if sins were indiscriminately absolved on an annual basis. Within the limitations of this project, the Hebrews perspective has been adopted as part of the "lens" in this reading. Previous research in Hebrews has concluded that the Day of Atonement, as understood by that writer, had very limited to no efficacy in removing sin; "for it is impossible for blood of bulls and goats to take away sin (Heb 10:4)" (Spadaro, "An Examination of the Relationship").

109. If healing the paralytic was proof that the man's sins had been forgiven, what constituted proof that Jerusalem's priests had effectively removed sin?

am gentle and humble in heart, and you will find rest for your souls. For my yoke is easy and my burden is light (11:28–30).[110]

This invitation was compatible with Jesus' mission statement ". . . the Son of Man did not come to be served, but to serve, and to give his life as a ransom for many" (20:28). This is a clear messianic claim, for who could offer rest to all? What kind of Messiah, however, could issue this invitation and make such a claim: a Messiah king or a Messiah priest?

The demand for a king by Israel led God to issue a solemn warning through Samuel (1 Sam 8:10–17). The thrust of the warning was that a king would impose intolerable burdens, the like of which would cause the people to cry out for relief. The Israelites would carry the king's load and ensure he had a life of leisure. He would take the best of all the people's possessions, and their children would make his food and his perfume, as well as run ahead of his carriages (1 Sam 8:10). In short, kings were not intended to relieve burdens. David and Solomon were no exceptions.

The high priest, however, was to be the servant of the people—"Moses and Aaron and his sons were to camp to the east of the tabernacle, toward the sunrise, in front of the Tent of Meeting. They were responsible for the care of the sanctuary on behalf of the Israelites" (Num 3:38). This service role was extended to the whole Levitical community, who were ". . . to perform duties for him and for the whole community at the Tent of Meeting . . ." (Num 3:7). Aaron and his sons were to represent Israel before God, offering sacrifices and offerings on the people's behalf, and ritually cleansing community impurities.[111] Aaron was required to bear the guilt of the community before the Lord (Exod 28:38); Jesus, like Aaron, was destined to be a sin bearer: ". . . my righteous servant will justify many, and he will bear their iniquities" (Isa 53:11). Unlike Aaron's mediation, Christ's offering and representation were acceptable to God.

Jesus' claim to offer inward rest was not an untested boast of a hopeful Messiah. Just as Jesus was able to prove that he had priestly authority to forgive sin by removing unintentional uncleanness (sicknesses and diseases), so his offer of Sabbath was confirmed through the universal provision he was able to provide. Feeding the multitudes (15:29–38) was a fulfilment of temple function. Jesus had demonstrated his capacity to meet the needs of Israel's multitudes outwardly, which also testified to his capacity to bear the

---

110. "'You will find rest for your souls' echoes the Hebrew text of Jer 6:6 (LXX has 'purification' instead of 'rest' . . ." (France, *Matthew*, 450). Could it be that rest and purification were in some way synonymous in Matthew's culture?

111. Jesus' servant role was best symbolized by the foot-washing incident in John—a distinctly priestly metaphor.

burdens of all in Israel.[112] As such, Jesus' function was not simply as a priest, but also as a temple (12:6). The prophet Malachi foreshadowed judgment on the nation that robbed God by not tithing (Mal 3:8–9). God's house/temple was to be a place of provision; God's "storehouse" was intended to be "full of food" (Mal 3:10): a place of blessing that would have flowed to the whole land. Matthew's Jesus, by feeding multitudes of people, testified to his authority to function as the center of Israel's physical and spiritual life.

Jesus' offer of universal service was a clear messianic claim, yet it bore no resemblance to any kingly precedents. Kings were not the servants of Israel, but the served. The high priest, though invariably a recipient of the greatest privilege and esteem, was intended to be the servant of the Lord. Jesus' invitation was, therefore, a challenge to the high priest's exclusive claim to be Israel's representative and burden-carrier. This contributes to the emerging picture of Jesus as a priest in Matthew, as a prelude to his sacrifice and eternal enthronement.

This offer of rest, when read in Old Testament context, may also inform us concerning Matthew's "prophetic" advancement of the Hebrew story:

> Flee for safety, people of Benjamin! Flee from Jerusalem! Sound the trumpet in Tekoa! Raise the signal over Beth Hakkerem! For disaster looms out of the north, even terrible destruction. I will destroy the Daughter of Zion, so beautiful and delicate. Shepherds with their flocks will come against her; they will pitch their tents around her, each tending his own portion (Jer 6:1–3).

> This is what the LORD Almighty says: "Cut down the trees and build siege ramps against Jerusalem. This city must be punished; it is filled with oppression. As a well pours out its water, so she pours out her wickedness. Violence and destruction resound in her; her sickness and wounds are ever before me. Take warning, O Jerusalem, or I will turn away from you and make your land desolate so no one can live in it" (Jer 6:6–8).

> To whom can I speak and give warning? Who will listen to me? Their ears are closed so they cannot hear. The word of the LORD is offensive to them; they find no pleasure in it. But I am full of the wrath of the LORD, and I cannot hold it in. From the least to the greatest, all are greedy for gain; prophets and priests alike, all practice deceit (Jer 6:10–13.)

> This is what the LORD says: "Stand at the crossroads and look; ask for the ancient paths, *ask where the good way is, and walk in*

---

112. The multitude of Matthew 15:30 should be understood as Jewish and not Gentile. Cousland, "The Feeding of the Four Thousand."

*it, and you will find rest for your souls."* But you said, "We will not walk in it" (Jer 6:16, emphasis mine).

The offer of amnesty and rest would not find a welcome in Jeremiah's Jerusalem, and it was unlikely to find much acceptance in Matthew's Israel either.

## The Healing Garments

The healing/forgiveness narrative flows seamlessly through accounts of Gentile healing, demoniac deliverance, the forgiveness of the paralytic, the acceptance of the long-term outcast Matthew, through to the raising of the ruler's daughter, which is interrupted by the unplanned healing of the "unclean" woman. The healing of the woman with the persistent bleeding is sandwiched within the story of the ruler's request and the healing of his daughter. Unlike Mark, who recorded that the daughter was sick initially, Matthew goes straight to the crux of the story: Jesus was to go into a house with a dead person within and touch the corpse (9:18). Jesus, in this account, knowingly proceeds to a situation forbidden for priests—a house of contagion.[113] That story ended with Jesus advising the mourners that she was only asleep; and perhaps she was, raised by the Father so as to maintain Jesus' ceremonial cleanness. Interesting as this possibility may be, the focus here is on the woman and the garment she touched.

As an unclean woman, any contact with a clean person was a considerable inconvenience; as has been mentioned, casual contact would make the ceremonially clean unclean till evening. Her approach from the rear, and (in other Gospels) the pressing crowd, were intended to conceal her desperate audacity. Certainly if this had occurred to the high priest the woman would have been publicly rebuked at best. Jesus wished to assure her that she was not simply healed, but also affectionately accepted, with the designation "daughter"—quite a homecoming for a long-term outcast.

In this incident, and elsewhere in far greater numbers (14:36), the garment's edge was touched as the contact point for healing. A person was no less polluted by an unclean person who touched his garment than a touch to a part of the body. The garment is a key to understanding Jesus' self-identity, and even public perception of him. The priest's garment was not simply some kind of conduit from person to person, but was itself clean and sacred (Exod 28:21). Aaron's garments could not be removed from the temple, for fear of contamination. They were dedicated as exhaustively as

---

113. Contact with a corpse automatically "incurred a seven-day impurity" according to Numbers 19. Kazen, *Jesus and Purity Halakah*, 196.

Aaron was (Lev 8:30). Further, the Psalmist records the episode of ultimate blessing: the oil of anointing running down Aaron's beard and down his garments (Ps 133).

Jesus' garments in John's gospel included a seamless undergarment/ephod—the type worn by high priests (Exod 28:6–8). In John's crucifixion account, the integrity of the garment was preserved. (Matthew did not mention this incident.) The high priest was expressly forbidden from tearing his garment, a sin committed by Caiaphas, according to Matthew, as he accused Jesus of blasphemy (Lev 21:10).[114] Of note also, Jesus' garment was transfigured with him on the mountain in Matthew's account (17:2). As little prophetic precedence for healing through garment tassels is recorded in Scripture, the only referent for these incidents is the high priest's holy garment, which, like the high priest himself, was more contaminable than helpful. The recording of such healings, therefore, could only further strengthen the possibility of Matthew's subtext—that Jesus was an indestructible priest with authority (Heb 7:16).

## Forgiveness of Sin

If Jesus' priestly posture in Matthew has, up to this point, required some careful attention to the Levitical requirements, it certainly becomes more transparent when accounts of his forgiveness of sins are considered.[115] The first and obvious instance of forgiveness was toward the paralytic, whose friends

---

114. Bond also makes this connection. Bond, *Caiaphas*, 126.

115. It may be argued that Jesus forgave sin as a function of his divine prerogative rather than his priestly role. Adela Collins points out that the "Who can forgive sins but God" reference is not a reference to who forgives, but who has authority to make such declarations. "The implication is that Jesus is inappropriately acting as God's agent" (Collins, "The Charge of Blasphemy," 397). This works equally well in Matthew's account. The point, however, seems to be explicit within the text. Jesus' appeal is not to his divine identity, but his earthly one: "But so that you may know that the Son of Man has authority on earth to forgive sins . . ." (Matt 9:6). The necessity for Jesus to be a priest to perform this function is reenforced by the Hebrews writer, who goes to lengths in making the case that Jesus was fully human in order to be a priest who could act on behalf of humans: "For this reason he had to be made like his brothers in every way, in order that he might become a merciful and faithful high priest in service to God, and that he might make atonement for the sins of the people" (Heb 2:17). Jesus did not become human, according to the Hebrews writer, just to be a sacrifice, but also to be a priest. Even though there are irregularities in Hebrew narrative concerning the declaration of the forgiveness of sins (consider Nathan for example—2 Sam 12:13), these should not be pressed as examples that forgiveness was not restricted to priestly function. No one can be certain if Nathan, for instance, had any priestly connection, or that his declaration was anything more than information, rather than an absolution of sin.

showed such faith in Jesus (9:1–8). Matthew omitted much of the detail of the story, but true to his commitment to the conflict narrative and Jesus' priestly prerogative, the essential challenge of the incident remained intact.

Without any request for forgiveness, Jesus gave it to the totally dependent paralytic on the basis of his friends' faith. Granting such a blessing without sacrifice or cleansing requirements, and, most notably, no reference to the temple and its stewards, was nothing short of a declaration of the ultimate authority. By sending such a clear message to the lawful guardians, Jesus' action was intended to be plainly provocative in Matthew's narrative. The proof that he did have authority to forgive sin was then clearly demonstrated to his "priestly" detractors by the miraculous healing. In all this the healed man (affectionately called "son") and his friends said nothing.

Matthew's interest was not focused on the recipient's response to the events, but on the horrified contingent of Pharisees. The healing was presented as a proof to these opponents that Jesus had authority that they could not have imagined.[116] It should be remembered that physical disability was generally perceived as being a by-product of personal sin (John 9:2). The Pharisees' thoughts, in Matthew, were classified as evil (9:4), for they considered Jesus' absolution of the paralytic's sins as blasphemous. Without doubt, the healing account was intended to demonstrate Jesus' mercy, and prove that "the Son of Man has authority on earth to forgive sins." Therefore the Son of Man, first introduced here as having authority to forgive sins, and later, as Lord of the Sabbath, casts the Son of Man as a priest, for what king or prophet ever claimed the authority to forgive sins? Up until now, there had been one possible source of forgiveness on earth; this incident was a declaration that Jerusalem's under-utilized monopoly had come to an end, and that it could not compete with the new dynamic priest.

Though this account seems to overtly reveal Jesus to be a merciful and effective priest, this mercy was also implicit in his wider dealings; a point demonstrated most acutely by Matthew's own calling (9:9). Matthew was a tax collector, and, as such, was an outcast who could never be seen among acceptable Hebrews again. Matthew could not make himself acceptable to his countrymen, for he, even more so than the leper, was a permanent pariah. His only community was the other outcasts. Together they were an unforgivable and lost society—the community the effective priest would embrace and make holy. Matthew's immediate departure from his life and trade at the invitation of Christ revealed that Matthew was a man who longed for a way back to God. Jesus' acceptance of Matthew presupposed a

---

116. Luz sees this as divine prerogative, while France identifies this with the earthly assignment of the Danielic Son of Man. Luz, *Matthew 8–20*, 28; France, *Matthew*, 347.

forgiveness that the high priest could not provide. Further, Matthew would be recast as a shepherd of the new community that had power to forgive, without the use of ritual sacrifice or cleansing. This set the parameters of the new community: one that did not rely on the oversight of those with impeccable heritage, sheltered privilege and physical perfection, but on the new priest, who could exalt sinners like Matthew.

## Demonic Testimony in Matthew

Any modern reading of the Synoptic accounts and their demonic explanation for some afflictions is perplexing. Demons, and their wretched influence on Judean society, are a feature of Matthew.[117] Demons were apparently as common as Roman soldiers or merchants within the Gospel accounts—they were surprisingly unexceptional. This is not easily explained. Matthew, like the other Gospel writers, wrote a story that was intended to be a believable depiction of the time of Jesus. The demonic activity in these accounts, therefore, must reflect a common perception for the first-century Hebrew community. To rationalize this emphasis on demons by simply claiming that this was the worldview of an uneducated society fails to observe the wider biblical testimony. There was no other period of Israel's history[118] that had any resemblance to the Judea of the Synoptics. This being the case, why would the Judean society that predated the Gospels have been any more sophisticated? Secondly, it was not the masses alone that recognized demonic activity; it was the discussion of the Jerusalem intellectual class (12:24). To suggest that these scholars were unsophisticated would be a considerable miscalculation.[119] Matthew's record portrays a Palestine that was awash with demons, in the same way other places might experience a plague of rodents or flying creatures. This is difficult to understand and cannot be easily dismissed. Pertinent here, however, is not how or why or even if demons existed generally, but what their role was in the Matthean narrative.

In Matthew, demons are not simply an inconvenience; they are critical to the Jesus story and contribute to the development of Israel's indictment. They too, testify (8:29). Demons testify concerning Jesus' identity and

---

117. Kazen has presented two explanations for Jesus' ability to exorcise demons. They are his dynamic purity, which destroyed them (Bruce Chilton) and his offensive purity, which conquers them (Klaus Berger). Kazen, *Jesus and Purity Halakah*, 300.

118. Saul's tormenting spirit was the outstanding demonic precedence recorded by the Deuteronomist.

119. For a good treatment of the intellectual sophistication of the scribes, see Gale, *Redefining Ancient Borders*, 87.

priestly efficacy (12:28); they also prove the ineptitude of the incumbent administration, which was charged with the responsibility of purifying the nation, lifting burdens and subduing evil.[120] Jesus gave an explanation for why Israel was infested by evil spirits.[121] The priestly community and theologians believed that Jesus was the devils' Lord, a position that Jesus asserted was untenable for obvious reasons (12:26). The demons, like Rome, had occupied Judea. Arguably, there was little that the high priest could do about Rome; but he was left without a valid excuse for why the covenant people had become so oppressed and polluted under his tenure.

Jesus explained the exile of demons as proof that the kingdom of God had come (12:28). Their removal was by the "Spirit of God." The "kingdom of God" and the "Spirit of God" were historically and theologically significant. Luke's gospel variant of the "Spirit of God" gives some insight into the allusion made by the connection. Luke recorded: "But if I drive out demons by the finger of God, then the kingdom of God has come to you" (Luke 11:20). This reference to the "finger of God" recalled the testimony of Pharaoh's magicians, who were incapable of replicating the gnat plague.[122] This third judgment on Egypt produced life from the dust (Exod 8:16); it could only be done by "the finger of Elohim"—the Hebrew God. Though Matthew supplants the term "finger of God" with the Spirit of God, the meaning remains the same: only YHWH deals decisively with evil. Hence, when evil is driven out, YHWH's kingdom has come.

The reason why Matthew used the term "spirit," rather than "finger," in this instance is not certain. However, the possibility exists that he wanted to revive the memory of Saul and David. This could well be a key for understanding how Matthew used demonic exile as integral to the indictment narrative. David was given the Spirit of God when anointed by Samuel (1 Sam 16:13). Saul at that time had been abandoned by God's Spirit, who was replaced by an evil spirit. This precedent fits Matthew's paradigm reasonably well. Matthew, unlike the other Synoptics, portrayed the religious

---

120. "The demonic aspect of impurity is also evident in several rites belonging to the Israelite cult, and it is probably at the root of the purification offering (*hattat*) and cultic expiation (*kipper*)" (Kazen, *Jesus and Purity Halakah*, 338). That being the case, there were attempts to remove evil spirits, and Jerusalem may have failed in this undertaking.

121. Demonic impurity could be overcome by the holy status of the exorcist. Therefore exorcism should be understood against the backdrop of purity legislation—the function of priests. Ibid., 338–39.

122. Ted Woods has made a comprehensive study of the "finger of God" reference in Luke and established its Old Testament origins to be specifically Exod 8:19 and 31:18. Woods, *The 'Finger of God'*, 243.

leadership of Jerusalem as evil (12:34).[123] The "brood of vipers" metaphor was used uniquely by Matthew's Jesus for the Jerusalem representatives; and this reinforced their sinister standing to the document's readers.[124] Matthew, therefore, intentionally portrayed Jesus' adversaries as legitimate and yet evil, in the same way that Saul was legitimate and evil. Jesus, who attracted heavenly approbation when filled with the Spirit (3:16–17), was to replace the discredited and evil incumbent as David displaced Saul. According to this scenario, the demonic infestation was indicative of the priestly disposition—the rise of the true and permanent Messiah drives out the evil steward and the oppression that characterised his administration.

The verbal joust concerning the authority that the protagonists employed to deal with demons may suggest that both were capable of removing them. However, Jesus' exorcisms were permanent.[125] The analogy that Jesus drew in Matthew was with a dispossessed evil spirit who would reinhabit its former residence, along with seven less desirable colleagues (12:43–45). Thus it would be for the "evil and perverse generation."[126] Whatever improvement is bestowed upon them, either by Jesus' national exorcism ministry, or by the devices of the priestly order, the end result would render the generation worse than before the intervention. Depending on how this is interpreted, two possibilities present themselves. If the exorcisms were performed by Christ, who temporarily "cleansed" his generation, the net result would have rendered the nation more culpable and infested than before.[127]

---

123. "The notion that 'evilness' is the root trait, or fundamental quality, characterising the Jewish leaders is in full accord with the tenor of Matthew's story" (Kingsbury, "The Developing Conflict," 60).

124. It has already been noted that vipers were known in the ancient world as creatures that consumed their parent. More pertinently, this also made reference to the Hebrew metanarrative, which anticipated Messiah to crush the head of the serpent's offspring (Gen 3:15).

125. The demon-possessed men in the Gadarenes are an interesting test case (8:28). The demons anticipated an eschatological judgment by Jesus (the Son of God). The implication of their request was that they had certain freedoms, prior to "Judgment Day," under the current administration. The request to be sent into the pigs also may indicate that the demons could not return to their former habitations, unlike the returning demon of Matthew 12:44.

126. "The demons, as we saw, would return, and the last state of the 'house' would be worse than the first" (Wright, *Victory of God*, 334).

127. This may appear to be inconsistent with the previous notion of permanent demonic exile. However, a rejection of Jesus the exorcist would also be a rejection of his ministry—thus rendering the Judean community susceptible to an escalated reinfection. In this instance, reinfection would be a judgment brought upon the recalcitrant people; it is not the result of priestly ineptitude or limitation. The Pharisees, on the other hand, could not maintain demonic deliverance under any circumstances.

If, on the other hand, it was the exorcism ministry of the incumbents, they are shown to be the primary source of Judea's demonic plague; any attempt they make to "cleanse" the nation actually makes it more putrid.

Matthew's account does imply that Jerusalem had some exorcism capabilities.[128] The wretches that Jesus would turn away in the final judgment included those who could claim the ability to exorcise (7:22). And the question Jesus asked concerning the source of the Pharisees' authority implied some efficacy on their part (12:27). Jesus and the Pharisees could not both be casting out demons by Beelzebub, for then they would be deriving authority from the same source as each other, which would constitute division within Satan's realm. Jesus, however, could prove that the kingdom of God had come, as demons were definitively cast out by the "Spirit of God." Two kingdoms are therefore set in juxtaposition: God's and Beelzebub's. Jesus' authority came from God, as did his kingdom; the antithesis, along with its clear implication concerning his opponents, was plain enough.

The exorcism debate in Matthew forms a critical component of the escalating indictment narrative. Within this discussion, the issue of the unforgivable sin was foreshadowed as a criterion for permanent judgment. The one who does not gather with Jesus is opposed to him (12:30). What had already been made clear was that two kingdoms were operating at cross purposes with different sources of authority. The Pharisees' testimony was that Jesus worked as Beelzebub's emissary; however, it was the Spirit of God on display when demons were exiled by Jesus, according to Matthew. As the Spirit of God was casting out demons, any suggestion that another source was responsible was unforgivable blasphemy. Evil comes from evil hearts (12:35); so evil conduct exposed the guilt of the sinner. Final judgment would be made on the basis of a person's words (12:36). The Pharisees' words were that Jesus' exorcisms, which could only be executed by the Holy Spirit, were the work of Beelzebub. Therefore, their words would eternally indict them, for they had committed the unforgivable sin.[129]

---

128. It has also been argued (by Shirock) that the "sons" who drive out the demons may be a reference to Jesus' own disciples. Nolland, *Gospel of Matthew*, 499. This has considerable appeal textually. These sons will judge the Pharisees, and clearly, Jesus was commissioning the disciples to be the judges of Israel (19:18). If purity was a prerequisite for casting out demons, Jesus' disciples had somehow been made clean.

129. Nolland believes that by attributing Jesus' work to Beelzebub, the unforgivable sin was being committed as it excluded people from participating in the "forgiveness project" of Jesus. It is their obstructionism that is unforgivable. Ibid., 505. Contextually, however, it is the naming of Jesus as evil (Beelzebub's emissary), rather than as Lord, which is instrumental in their judgment.

## The New Shepherd in Matthew

The final section of this chapter will consider a key identity marker of Jesus in Matthew—as the Shepherd of his people. Of the Synoptics, Matthew alone introduced Jesus as a shepherd (2:6). This motif instructed Matthew's readers as to the role that Jesus played in Israel's final days. Two distinguishing verses, which are only found in Matthew, emphasized Jesus' priestly mission.

Joseph, as the adoptive father and source of Jesus' legal status, plays a much bigger role in Matthew than in the other Gospels. Matthew is much more concerned with the issues that directly pertain to Mosaic precedence and requirement. Jesus' identity, therefore, is primarily made known to Joseph in this account of Jesus. Joseph was told in a dream, "She will give birth to a son, and you are to give him the name Jesus, because he will save his people from their sins" (1:21). From the first introduction in Matthew, Jesus was introduced as a Messiah who could remove sin from his people—the eschatological priest.[130] Of interest, by contrast, was Luke's disclosure of priestly ministry in his infancy narrative. Luke presented John as a Levite and, more particularly, a legitimate heir to the priestly ministry. John's ministry in Luke entailed forgiveness of sin, a role not attributed to him in Matthew (Luke 1:77; Matt 3:3). Matthew's John heard confession, but did not absolve sins (3:6). Luke, in fact, implied that people turned to Jesus if they had been cleansed by John, recording that,

> All the people, even the tax collectors, when they heard Jesus' words, acknowledged that God's way was right, because they had been baptised by John. But the Pharisees and experts in the law rejected God's purpose for themselves, because they had not been baptised by John (Luke 7:29–30).

So Luke, it seems, portrayed John as a kind of priest, anointed from the womb; he cleansed the people through baptism and absolved them of sin.[131] This prepared them to recognize and follow Messiah. On the basis of this paradigm, John was the priest who brought people to Christ. John was a virtual and proper priest—a possible rival for Caiaphas. Ministering away from the temple, he maintained ritual purity and dietary asceticism, forgave sin and cleansed the contrite of the nation through baptism. Matthew did not develop this perspective, but reserved any notion of priestly function for Jesus and his followers.

---

130. The identity of "his people" was ambiguous and could only be understood as the narrative unfolds. Claiming that these people are exclusively Israel generally does not fit comfortably with the gospel story. Repschinki, "For He Will Save," 265.

131. Nolland, *Luke 1:1–9:20*, 84.

The understanding that Joseph received concerning his child's destiny in Matthew was ambiguous concerning the beneficiaries of his priestly redemption. The question of who his people would become is a major theme in Matthew's account. The chief priests also knew whom to expect. The Messiah was to be born in David's city: Bethlehem—"in the land of Judah, are by no means least among the rulers of Judah, for out of you will come a ruler who will be the shepherd of my people Israel" (2:6). His task, as far as they could ascertain, was to govern the covenant community. The composite quote that Matthew attributed to them is not directly influenced by Micah; its attendant disclosure of messianic function was taken from 2 Sam 5:2—a reference to David as shepherd of Israel.[132] While many significant characters in Israel's history were shepherds,[133] no one was more associated with the title than David and his eschatological offspring. This expectation concerning Messiah, which is placed in the corporate mouth of "all the chief priests and teachers of the law," demonstrated Matthew's interest in revealing the Jerusalem priestly intelligentsia as expectant of the Davidide, who would shepherd the people. Their disturbance by Jesus' arrival could well have been driven by the same motive as Herod; Jesus was a threat to Herod's aspirations, and he was also a threat to the tenure of the temple stewards.

While John's gospel also shared Matthew's interest in Jesus as shepherd, Mark and Luke did not consider this Christological identity critical to their accounts. In Matthew, Jesus as shepherd was crucial to the paradigm, and through its contextual application, it seems to make clear that shepherd was synonymous with priest.

An aspect of prophetic fulfilment that Matthew sought to connect to Jesus' ministry was the Ezekiel indictment against the shepherds of Israel. To this end, Matthew recorded "When he saw the crowds, he had compassion on them, because they were harassed and helpless, like sheep without a shepherd" (9:36). As previously noted, this well-used metaphor[134] could only indict the priestly house of Caiaphas, as Israel had no other legitimate leadership. While David was designated as a shepherd for God's people, it was not a standard expectation for kings to be their carers and sustainers. David delivered Israel, not simply through military conquest, but also through effective sacrifice.[135] Ezekiel's indictment affirmed the replacement of priests with the shepherd David—"I will place over them one shepherd, my servant David, and he will tend them; he will tend them and be their

---

132. Hagner, *Matthew 1–13*, 29.
133. Abraham, Jacob and Moses were also shepherds.
134. Num 27:17; 1 Kgs 22:17; 2 Chr 18:16; Ezek 34:5.
135. 2 Sam 24:18–25.

shepherd. I the LORD will be their God, and my servant David will be prince among them. I the LORD have spoken" (Ezek 34:23–24).

## The Importance of Matthew's Messianic Priest Theme

The priestly connection that can be deduced from the Matthean subtext may be critical to understanding Matthew as a prophetic advancement of Israel's story. The preparation of the disciples through teaching, temporary commission, prophesied future ascendancy and the final great commission, was shaped by the contrast between "shepherd-like" leaders and the impure, self-interested incumbents. From the Sermon on the Mount to the last commission, Jesus guided his disciples to be a leadership of a different order. The twelve disciples were not to be like the "hypocrites," Jesus' standard designation for Israel's leaders in Matthew, which was used, perhaps coincidentally, twelve times throughout his account.

The ministry of the disciples in Matthew had several dimensions. They were clearly trainee/apprentices and their inability to learn at times caused both exasperation and astonishment on Jesus' part. They also functioned in a vice-priestly role, undertaking Jesus' ministry throughout the "parishes" (chapter 10). This ministry was intended to legally inform all Israelites that the kingdom age was dawning. As a demonstration of this reality, the disciples were given the priestly power of Jesus, with the significant exception of forgiveness of sin. The intentional poverty that was attached to the task warranted generosity by the villagers as an expression of acceptance. Their rejection was fully expected, as was clear in the commissioning (10:22). In this instance, dust was to be shaken off the disciples' feet, which was a prophetic statement concerning the destiny of the ungrateful towns—"'Then you will trample down the wicked; they will be ashes under the soles of your feet on the day when I do these things,' says the LORD Almighty" (Mal 4:3). Lastly, they were prepared to understand their destiny as it pertained to Israel. The apostles would be the tribunal of condemnation or vindication (Matt 19:28)—a task formerly consigned to the old order priests.[136]

By drawing attention to the harassed and helpless condition of the covenant people (9:36), Jesus was preparing the disciples to be the shepherds who would effectively shepherd God's community.[137] By implication, the "harvest" was the covenant community that had been badly serviced by its negligent shepherds; the "workers" that the disciples were encour-

---

136. The Sanhedrin was the tribunal of judgment of Israel in Jesus' time. Their authority was derived from Deut 17:8–13.

137. Paul considered that the proclamation of the gospel is a priestly duty (Rom 15:16).

aged to beseech God for, were, according to this context, shepherds. Had the "harvest" been managed well, Israel would have been devoted to Jesus, thus rendering to God the thanksgiving that was rightly expected.[138] While the Israelites were happy to enjoy the immediate curiosity that Jesus aroused, profound and meaningful faith was not common.

The immediate and short-term commission that followed this exhortation was to replicate Christ and his message throughout Israel. The specific exclusion of any of the towns "outside of Israel," at this point, revealed that the covenant was restricted and binding upon Israelites alone. The miraculous dimension to this commission was not intended, within Matthew's paradigm, to convince the Israelites with regard to Jesus, or inaugurate standard apostolic and Christian practice; it was a means of escalating indictment. Having been legally informed of the impending kingdom and witnessing its power, Israelites were without excuse and fully culpable. This theme will be developed further in chapter 8.

The final commission in Matthew is substantially different in character from the former short-term commission of chapter 10. In this final commission, Jesus' disciples were given the task of discipling[139] the first covenant community, baptizing (cleansing) and teaching Christ's Torah. In effect, they were commissioned as a community that would continue the priestly function of Christ.[140] Though this commission is substantially different from the former, which emphasised miraculous signs, but did not mention baptizing or teaching, the disciples in both instances are being "little christs"— their authority to do what they did was a consequence of their functional connection to the high priest Jesus. In this way, the disciples functioned as the house of Levi to the Aaronic priesthood; it multiplied and extended his work.

---

138. Nolland referred to his commentary on Luke in noting that "Harvest here is not exactly an image of (eschatological) judgment as in Mic 4:11–13; Isa 63:1; Jer 25:30–31; Joel 3:13 . . ." (Nolland, *Gospel of Matthew*, 408). No reason for this is given, which is peculiar considering that all Matthew's harvesting images have to do with eschatological judgment.

139. This function has much more to do with making judicious decisions on behalf of the covenant community than the role of personal mentoring.

140. This should not be understood as a Roman Catholic or sacramentalist apologetic; the disciples did not have authority to forgive sins or offer sacrifices in Matthew. Their functions were to communicate what the high priest had achieved (rather than enacting the high priest's ministry), and to identify and admit/exclude those who would be eligible for the new community. John's gospel testified that the disciples were commissioned to exercise forgiveness (John 20:23), though in practice they did not become confessors.

## Peter and the Apostolic/Priestly Function

Peter's commissioning to the position of "gatekeeper" in Matthew is problematic (16:13–20). For now, however, the traditional Protestant interpretation will be defended. The revelation that Jesus was the messianic appointment of YHWH was the significant insight necessary for the disciples to be given the blessing and ministerial standing that followed. Contextually, Peter answered on behalf of the Twelve,[141] and the appointment to be little christs/foundations, as an extension of Jesus' universal and supreme messianic/foundational role, was an acknowledgement of the oversight role they would exercise in the new community. The new community was not simply a gathering, but the new temple;[142] those who became part of this temple would have the same testimony as Peter, the first small rock incorporated into the new structure.

Peter and the disciples were to function in a judicial role in Matthew, as was emphasised by what followed their principal declaration about Jesus. This key and unique apostolic function within Matthew, which translated into an ongoing feature of Christian leadership, was to "bind and loose on earth." In the same way that Matthew recorded two commissions, this mandate was repeated twice for emphasis—"whatever you bind on earth will be bound in heaven, and whatever you loose on earth will be loosed in heaven" (16:19; 18:18). Any assertion that this role was specifically Petrine must be dismissed by its second occurrence, which was directed to all the apostles, and even to the wider Christian community.

There is much conjecture as to what is meant by "binding and loosing," and it is difficult to ascertain what constitutes the "whatever" that could be bound or loosed.[143] It has become popular to consider that this is a reference to the ministry of exorcism;[144] however, the context gives no support for this interpretation. An obvious possibility, which is favored by the Roman Catholic Church, was that Peter would have a primary role as gatekeeper for the church. This option cannot be ruled out altogether, apart from the more inclusive application of the text in chapter 18. If this text did assign Peter, or even the Twelve, the exclusive right to forgive and not forgive, there would be no lawful place to be accepted in heaven apart from their

---

141. France, *Matthew*, 617.

142. Paul used this symbolism (1 Cor 3:16; Eph 2:21), as did the author of Peter (1 Pet 2:4–5).

143. Richard Heirs undertook a rigorous analysis of the possibilities. Hiers, "'Binding' and 'Loosing.'" What is proposed here is not dissimilar to later rabbinical usage concerning the admission or placing of bans.

144. This is not without some support. Nolland, *Gospel of Matthew*, 678.

ministry. Further, such a ministry would necessitate an office that was hereditary and permanent, much like the Aaronic high priestly institution. Within Matthew's wider context, however, this proposition would appear to be untenable.

As previously mentioned, the one priestly ministry that was not assigned to the disciples prior to their mission in Matthew was the forgiveness of sins. Certainly, Jesus forgave sin (9:2). He did, however, instruct all kingdom aspirants that they would be forgiven proportionately according to the measure of forgiveness they applied to others (6:12). So it could be argued that all Jesus' followers were under obligation to forgive offenses against themselves, not against God. Therefore, to interpret "binding and loosing" as an apostolic ministry for the hearing and forgiving of sin generally must be viewed with suspicion—such a critical function would require a directive with much greater clarity, and some clear historical data that would indicate that this was what the apostles understood by the commission. The ambiguity left by the text itself, and its context, along with the absence of any declaration by the apostles in Acts that they had forgiven sin/s, militate against this being Matthew's intention, interesting as it may initially appear.

The view being proposed here is that this task is very closely aligned to forgiveness, without actually being identical to it. The context of the second appearance of binding and loosing was connected with a judgment that the new community of Jesus, and not just the apostles, was to make. In this instance the community was to act as God's judiciary. Its task was to "exile" recalcitrant sinners. In making a determination to either restore or exile, the church was in effect binding and loosing. Contextually, then, the church neither forgave nor denied forgiveness; its task was to determine whether a person was forgiven or not based on his/her conduct.[145] Like the high priest of Israel, her task did not make a person clean or unclean; the church's task was to make a judicious declaration based on an individual's conduct, or profession. Returning, then, to the former context of this priestly responsibility, the rock upon which judgment was to be made was the profession that Jesus was Lord (16:16–18). Profession of Jesus as Christ cannot be accompanied by unwillingness to heed the community discipline; therefore, deliberate defiance and refusal to ask for and acknowledge the need for forgiveness would render the person a covenant breaker. Exile, similar to that applied to "a pagan or tax-collector," was the decreed penalty (18:17).

This is not the whole meaning of the "binding and loosing" assignment. There is a historical viewpoint, expressed within another New Testament document, which may elucidate what "binding and loosing" means.

---

145. Derrett, "Binding and Loosing," 116.

The Hebrews writer presented a view of the sacrificial system that may have been a widespread perception among Jewish Christians. The Hebrews writer believed that the Aaronic ministry had no heavenly efficacy. Aaron's work, even on the Day of Atonement, only cleansed externals,[146] and not the conscience (Heb 9:9–10). Aaron's work was performed in the earthly "copy" of the true tabernacle, which exists in heaven (Heb 8:1–5). The logic of Hebrews, which had resonance with the Platonic understanding of the relationship between the seen and the unseen, was that heavenly efficacy required heavenly propitiation (Heb 7:26; 8:1–2). Aaron's ministry could not inwardly cleanse, nor was it acceptable in heaven. It was temporal, external and earthly. Forgiveness in heaven required a heavenly priest—one "like the Son of Man." The Law appoints Aaron/Levi to function as priest on earth; therefore, Jesus' ministry can only be valid on earth if undertaken in a "higher" place—heaven (Heb 8:4). Thus the heavenly priest had entitlement on earth by virtue of his superior "melchizedekian" standing—he is able to save "completely" (Heb 7:25). The converse was not true; Aaron had no efficacy in heaven, only on earth (Heb 9:9).

This Hebrews perspective comfortably shapes the Matthean priestly assignment, for the new order of "priests" could make judgments based on what heaven accepted, which had been made known through Jesus' teaching. So a person accepted by the community on earth was acceptable in heaven. The converse would also be true—a person acceptable in heaven would be acceptable to the church. The high priest, on the other hand, could cast out Matthew (a prime example), as a permanent covenantal pariah, yet heaven paid no attention to "Aaron's" pronouncement. Heaven, rather, made Matthew a judge of Israel and leader of the new community, in Caiaphas' stead (19:28). The reason for this was Matthew's unreserved acceptance of Jesus—the greater High Priest. Should it be the case that Hebrews does relate to the Matthean text this way, the assignment to "bind and loose" has much more to do with efficacy than specific function; "heaven and earth" have entered a cooperative and causal relationship for Jesus' "sanctified" ones. This concept may be the key to understanding this peculiar commission: the church had attained an efficacy not available to Israel's lawful, yet discredited and ineffectual priesthood.

---

146. This limitation of Aaronic cleansing to the "externals" explains the derogatory description assigned to the Pharisees by Jesus—"whitewashed sepulchres" (23:27).

## Summation

This chapter has attempted to demonstrate that the subtext of Matthew presented Jesus as the Priest of God. Jesus' ministry, teaching, identification, miracles, audacious claims, and instruction to his disciples all point to a ministry that had come to displace a thoroughly corrupted and inept Aaronic line. The new order of "priests" was not restricted to the temple: they, like David, could minister with freedom and efficacy. Jesus was not an immediate and direct threat to Herod, but to Caiaphas; this was the devastating truth that was fully apprehended by Jesus' opponents in Matthew. The appointment of the disciples as the new priests was an integral part of the deposition of the former priesthood, and a critical component of the denunciation of Israel's shepherds in Ezekiel 34.[147] It is concluded, therefore, that the Messiah Priest subtext within Matthew is both central and critical, for it clarified the nature of the indictment and the instrumentality it sought to condemn.

---

147. An interesting paper by David Mathewson made the point that the twelve foundations of the New Jerusalem in Revelation 21 were identified by names of the apostles imbedded on precious stones. Mathewson, "A Note on the Foundation Stones." As the high priest of Israel was adorned with twelve precious stones, with the names of the twelve tribes engraved upon them (Exod 28:21), this must surely constitute further evidence that the early church perceived that Jesus' disciples are the new community and Jesus the new high priest.

# 8

# Subpoena, Trial, Execution, and Vindication: The Termination of Aaron

> *The wicked watches out for the righteous, and seeks [to slay him. The Lord will not abandon him into his hand or] let him be condemned when he is brought to trial.*
>
> (4Q171: IV; commentary on Ps 37:32–33)[1]

MATTHEW'S GOSPEL CONCLUDES WITH Jesus' entry into Jerusalem and the final conflict that awaited him there. These dramatic concluding chapters are consistent with the preceding vehement polemic, for they portrayed Jesus as the innocent and righteous Messiah who suffered gross injustice at the hands of the Jerusalem priestly aristocracy. Jesus' opponents could not be cajoled in his territory of Galilee; they would hardly be persuadable in the theatre of their own authority. In Matthew's presentation, Jesus did not come to Jerusalem with an olive branch, nor did he come to be an accidental victim. The demeanor of Matthew's Jesus, along with the author's editorial comments, elevated this plausible Judean conflict, trial and execution to such eschatological significance that the reader would be left with no doubt that this was the divine strategy intended to change both Israel and the world.

    This Jesus came to the Holy City through the "front door" with public adulation and unhesitating acknowledgement of his divine and Davidic prerogative. Rather than attempt to win over Jerusalem's influential citizenry following his arrival, he rebuked and condemned their practices and

---

1. Vermes, *The Dead Sea Scrolls*, 292.

beliefs—even physically disrupting their courts with violence (21:12). Matthew's Jesus was not captured against his will; rather, he had the power to control these events with angelic battalions (26:53), but chose to submit to the unscrupulous authorities.

Lastly, in the final extraordinary twist of this dramatic theodicy, the innocent and rightful Messiah's coronation, along with the overthrow of his enemies, would be an outcome of the high priest's malevolence. In like manner to the epic theodicy in Israel's story, Matthew echoed the exaltation of Mordecai in this Christ drama, along with the permanent demise of his conspiratorial adversary—Haman/Caiaphas. The plot to kill Jesus would result in the demise of its instigator. Jesus was "cut off," only to be exalted and vindicated by God via the resurrection; Caiaphas, however, would be Matthew's ultimate villain and the catalyst for the demise of Aaron's successors. Through Jesus' death, according to Matthew, the Aaronic dynasty, along with the temple within which it served, had lost its tenure to represent humans before YHWH. Jesus' new community had now become the locus of God's presence and authority, even to "the very end of the age."

In this final chapter, the Jerusalem events (chapters 21–28) will be considered with a view to exposing the author's use of the passion traditions to advance his belief that Jesus' death was a judicial action against the Levitical priesthood, which in turn led to the termination of the Mosaic administration. In this section of Matthew, the reader encounters some unique and enigmatic material, which can best be explained by the paradigm of indictment that has been seen throughout the document. This is further accentuated by Matthew's presentation of the only Roman representative in his passion narrative, Pilate. The governor was disturbed by Jesus' predicament, and, being convinced that he was innocent, made every attempt to secure his freedom. Further, Matthew also uniquely described the apprehension of the governor's spouse, which was the consequence of her quasi-revelation, as well as Pilate's hand-washing episode. This portrayal of Rome's unwillingness to participate in the mock trial could only serve to further implicate the malicious and unrelenting vehemence of Jesus' accusers.

Due to the brevity of this survey, many reflections on the narrative must be judiciously avoided. Some of this material has been considered in earlier chapters on the parables and the priestly subtext. Still other parts of this narrative, such as the woes of chapter 23, are so obviously indictments against Jerusalem's stewards that an extensive treatment may not be warranted. What will follow is an observation of Matthew's sequence of events, his unique material and the particular manner in which common source material was used, in order to expose a pattern of editorial intent which suggests that this Gospel may have been intended to conclude Israel's Mosaic narrative, and, therefore, constitute a legal polemic that presented a clear case that there was "just cause," on YHWH's part, to terminate the temple and the office of its mediatorial stewards.

## The Return of the King

There is no shortage of material that has attempted to elucidate the implications of the various accounts of Jesus' entry into Jerusalem (21:1–11). The common features of the traditions include the description of the use of the donkey and the adulation of the crowd that declared, "Blessed is he who comes in the name of the LORD!" Matthew is distinctive at several points: Jesus was designated the son of David,[2] both the donkey and its colt are mentioned, the Zechariah prophecy is explicitly incorporated, the controversy about Jesus' identity is mentioned, and there is just the slightest hint that this event was not simply a positive prelude to a tragic execution.

Starting with the last of these distinctives, Matthew has here echoed his earlier concern that Jesus was *persona non grata* in Jerusalem. Matthew uniquely summed up the response of Jerusalem to Jesus' arrival thus: ἐσείσθη πᾶσα ἡ πόλις—the whole city was shaken (21:10). When Jerusalem first heard the news of a Messiah in Bethlehem, Matthew recorded that ὁ βασιλεὺς Ἡρῴδης ἐταράχθη, "King Herod was disturbed," and πᾶσα Ἱεροσόλυμα μετ' αὐτοῦ, "all Jerusalem with him" (2:3). It may have been possible to argue that Jerusalem's concern in the birth narrative had to do with some apprehension the city may have felt about Herod's response to the news of a new king. However, Matthew dispels that notion with his "entry" narrative, for Herod and his successor are nowhere to be seen in Matthew's passion narrative, leaving Jerusalem to be still shaken for its own reasons when Jesus arrived.

The question concerning Jesus, τίς ἐστιν οὗτος—"who is this?" may not be a quest for information, but an indignant rejection of the Galilean's pretensions, which were communicated by the manner of his arrival. It would be surprising at this stage of the narrative if the Jerusalem rulers were unaware of Jesus or his claims. The crowd was not responding to the question raised, but fuelling the indignation of Jerusalem's stewards with their assertion that Jesus was the prophet.[3] What was meant by the crowd's assertion that Jesus was the prophet from Galilee is unclear. It may be that they believed he was

---

2. Mark also makes a Davidic connection with the crowd's declaration "Blessed is the coming kingdom of our father David!" (Mark 11:10).

3. There was another prophet who rode a donkey and intended to curse the Israelites (Num 22–24). Unlike Balaam, however, Jesus was not prevented from the task.

a special Galilean, or it may be a Matthean allusion to the long anticipated prophet spoken of by Moses: "The LORD your God will raise up for you a prophet like me from among your own brothers. You must listen to him" (Deut 18:16). In any case, the crowd's adulation of Jesus was the likely cause for the disdainful response by the beleaguered Jerusalem hierarchy.

Matthew also managed to let slip, once again, a direct reference in this passage to Jesus' Davidic heritage. One cannot help but wonder if Matthew was interested in making some veiled connection with David's own entrance and capture of Jerusalem recorded in 2 Samuel 5. That passage is noteworthy for its clear implication of Davidic entitlement, and the reference to the lame and the blind, who according to the overconfident Jebusite incumbents, would be able to ward off any Davidic advance. Jesus' own apparently harmless, but soon to be seen as militaristic, advance on the city was to be characterized by the restoration, or even the removal (via healing), of the lame and blind.[4] Matthew's use of the Davidic connection here may have been intended to further develop his paradigm of fulfillment, by demonstrating Jesus to be an individual who exercised divine prerogative. Matthew's Jesus entered the antagonistic city with the same fearless enterprise displayed by his "priestly" forebear David.[5]

Some have noted the use of the donkey along with its colt, which is only mentioned in Matthew, with some concern; for it has been suggested that Matthew (the most Jewish Gospel[6]) had failed to observe the Hebrew parallelism implicit in the Zechariah source. Perhaps there is another explanation. It may be that an original Hebrew version of this Gospel also incorporated the parallelism of Zechariah, which, when translated into Greek produced the peculiar reading in final Matthew. Apart from this minor observation, it is important to note the arrival of Jesus on an unbroken donkey on such an auspicious occasion. Humanly speaking, a person would be foolish to try this stunt if they wanted to make a "grand entrance." Perhaps implicitly, this action was of itself a demonstration of divine authority—even over animals.[7]

---

4. Matthew alone recorded the healing of the lame and blind, who were likely to be Levites within the temple precinct.

5. Though kings may not have ridden donkeys routinely (Solomon was well known for his horses and stables), it is notable that David did, which was of such significance that Solomon's use of it was a sign of his rightful ascension to the throne (1 Kgs 1:33). Further, the messianic symbolism concerning the rise of Judah included the role of his donkey (a colt) which would be tethered to the finest branch (Gen 49:11).

6. Hare, "How Jewish?"

7. Jesus' action against the fig tree and the calming of the waters also revealed the divine control motif in the Synoptics.

Concerning the reference agreed to by all Gospels, "Blessed is he who comes in the name of the LORD," it may be profitable to glance at its context within Psalm 118. All Synoptics use this reference along with a previous reference from this Psalm, "The stone the builders rejected has become the capstone; the LORD has done this, and it is marvelous in our eyes" (Ps 118:22–23). The rejected capstone metaphor was also used by all in connection with the Parable of the Tenants, by way of indictment. This connection should not go unnoticed, as it also may explain one of the more enigmatic verses in the Gospel tradition that is found in connection with the cursing of the fig tree:

> Jesus replied, "I tell you the truth, if you have faith and do not doubt, not only can you do what was done to the fig tree, but also you can say to this mountain, 'Go, throw yourself into the sea,' and it will be done. If you believe, you will receive whatever you ask for in prayer" (21:21–22).

The rejected capstone, the rejected fig tree and the overthrow of the apparently indestructible mountain are implicitly connected. This can be seen from Matthew's heavy reliance on Zechariah, which prophesied the rise of Zerubbabel:

> What are you, O mighty mountain? Before Zerubbabel you will become level ground. Then he will bring out the capstone to shouts of "God bless it! God bless it!" Then the word of the LORD came to me: "The hands of Zerubbabel have laid the foundation of this temple; his hands will also complete it. Then you will know that the LORD Almighty has sent me to you" (Zech 4:8–9).

This weaving together of Hebrew narrative in the retelling of the Jesus event seems integral to understanding Matthew's gospel, if not all the Gospels.[8] The basic schema is that Jesus was rejected because he was not considered integral to the Hebrew cultic system: the glory of the temple, its capstone, was rejected. As a consequence, the nation received a curse, as was previewed by the definitive action against the fig tree.[9] In such a way, the impossible (i.e., the removal of what was a major impediment to true religion) could be achieved for those who believe—faith is the means of

---

8. An editorial comment found in John reveals that these events had a dawning relevance for the disciples. John wrote: "At first his disciples did not understand all this. Only after Jesus was glorified did they realize that these things had been written about him and that they had done these things to him" (John 12:16).

9. Jesus' curse, in Matthew, took place immediately. Nolland, *Gospel of Matthew*, 852.

removing the demands of the monolithic and oppressive system that had little currency in heaven.[10] Faith in the "capstone" would displace the Mosaic impediment to YHWH.

## Jerusalem's Concerns Were Justified

Matthew seamlessly moved from the popular reception of Jesus to his condemnation of the temple practices (21:12–17). By way of variation, Mark has this account on the following day (Mark 11:12), and Luke accounts for this event after the lamentation of Jesus over Jerusalem (Luke 13:34). Matthew does not imply that the temple "indictment" was immediate, but the narrative reads in such a way as to appear that this is the next event in a tumultuous day. Though this event has routinely been called the cleansing of the temple, there is more going on than simply cleansing; this event was intended to weave together several interrelated prophetic strands. As the reader has come to expect in Matthew, this event was also loaded with prophetic precedence and significance.

As a cleansing, this action of Jesus was an attempt to redress the illegitimate practices of the temple in order to safeguard its integrity and sacramental role in the life of the nation. This, in recent times, has been challenged by E. P. Sanders, who believed that it was an act of divine judgment in order to terminate the system that purported to redeem through the purchase and surrender of beasts.[11] This proposition was well refuted, in part by Craig Evans, who believed that Sanders' critique did not give due consideration to the necessity of commerce to facilitate the system that God had implemented and which was integral to the Mosaic legislation.[12] This is defensible. However, there remains a distinctly prophetic component to Jesus' action that has a distinct echo to the beginning of the Hebrew narrative with its emphasis upon Israel's tenure in the land.

Existence within the land was critical to Israel's identity, not because of the particular real estate that it occupied, but because of the presence of YHWH in its midst. Exile should therefore be interpreted as having its precursor in the exclusion narrative of the first parents, Adam and Eve. God walked in the garden, and their expulsion denied them the routine access and privilege associated with being in his domain, which included access

---

10. Keener connected the removal of the mountain to Zechariah 4, making the point that the mountain that needed to be overthrown was the "reformation of the Jewish religious system" (Keener, *Matthew*, 505).

11. Evans, "Jesus' Action in the Temple," 237.

12. Ibid., 257.

to the Tree of Life (Gen 3:24). Similarly, Israel was a constituted theocracy with assurances of the existence of YHWH in the land/temple; this had been formerly pledged to Solomon (1 Kgs 9:3). Exile, in these terms, carried the notional implication that YHWH had suspended or terminated covenantal relationship with Israel. The action that Jesus took, therefore, may have had a prophetic component that the nation would be dislodged from its privileged proximity to YHWH.

It may be that the theological significance of the temple-storming was multifaceted, for the institution was not terminated until a later time.[13] However, there is a distinctly punitive component to this action that foreshadows the judgment that Sanders described. The implications of the action surely fell most heavily upon Aaron's successor, Caiaphas. He was charged with the maintenance and purity of the temple (Zech 3:7). The central sacrament in the life of Israel, the Day of Atonement, established the high priest as the only person responsible to remove the impurity of the human presence from the temple (Lev 16:19). How much more then, it could be argued, was it his responsibility to ensure righteous conduct and fair arbitration in its precincts, as requested by Solomon at the temple's dedication (1 Kgs 8)?

The prophetic precedence for this particular event is found in several places. Matthew's relatively succinct retelling of this account may suggest that he expected that the primary accusation would import the contexts of its biblical antecedents. Zechariah ends with the statement that the Day of the LORD will be characterized by the absence of Canaanites/traders in the House of the LORD (Zech 14:21). Malachi noted, as the final indictment against the priests, that their practices constituted theft from the Almighty. Tithing was clearly being practiced, but the tithe was not being brought into the House for the provision of food for God's people (Mal 3:8–9). It is reasonable to presume then that the priests were in the habit of using their cultic responsibilities as the avenue of their personal enrichment, rather than the public good. Perhaps the Parable of the Tenants is an allusion to this event—the stewards of the vineyard had withheld the owner's due entitlement (21:33).[14]

The most direct reference to this incident, however, is found in Jeremiah 7. The prophet recorded God's horror at the sight of his holy place having become a "den of robbers" (Jer 7:11). YHWH's responded to this with the following indictment:

---

13. There is a growing consensus that the rending of the curtain was the moment of YHWH's abandonment of the temple; this will be considered later. Bolt also supports the view that the "cleansing" was a portent for judgment. Bolt, *The Cross*, 30.

14. God receives his due, it seems, when his poverty-stricken people are cared for (25:31–46).

> Go now to the place in Shiloh where I first made a dwelling for my Name, and see what I did to it because of the wickedness of my people Israel. While you were doing all these things, declares the LORD, I spoke to you again and again, but you did not listen; I called you, but you did not answer. Therefore, what I did to Shiloh I will now do to the house that bears my Name, the temple you trust in, the place I gave to you and your fathers. I will thrust you from my presence, just as I did all your brothers, the people of Ephraim (Jer 7:12–15).

Jeremiah's indictment proceeded to this climactic condemnation:

> Cut off your hair and throw it away; take up a lament on the barren heights, for the LORD has rejected and abandoned this generation that is under his wrath (Jer 7:29).

The implications of the accusation that the temple had become a "den of robbers" are unambiguous; God wiped out Shiloh for the wicked conduct of Eli's house and effectively suspended the Aaronic mediation system until it was reestablished by David.[15] Therefore, he would not hesitate to judge Jerusalem's wickedness in like manner—with destruction. This connection was not lost on Matthew. In the same way as the Isaiah 6 indictment was invoked upon "this generation," so was the Jeremiah indictment recommissioned. However one chooses to look at the temple incident, it is hard to avoid its key elements of indictment and judgment.

## The Fig Tree's Demise

The seemingly unjustified fig tree condemnation (21:18–22) is another of the enigmatic incidents found in the Gospels. The consensus concedes that this act is something of a prototypical or prophetic judgment directed to the house of Israel.[16] Within Matthew, with its close proximity to the "den of robbers" remark, it would be remarkable if Matthew had not intended the Jeremiah context to be applied here also.[17]

Following the verses from Jeremiah quoted above, there was a series of indictments that drew their authority from the covenant at Moab (Deut

---

15. Eli's sons were abusing their role and extorting dishonest gain (1 Sam 2:16). God broke Eli's neck like the unwanted dedicated donkey (1 Sam 4:18).

16. Martens, *The Challenge of Jesus' Parables*, 154.

17. Mark's gospel noted that it was too early in the season for figs (Mark 11:13). This would have made a connection with the Micah indictment "What misery is mine! I am like one who gathers summer fruit at the gleaning of the vineyard; there is no cluster of grapes to eat, none of the early figs that I crave" (Mic 7:1).

28:30). Jeremiah records: "Therefore I will give their wives to other men and their fields to new owners. From the least to the greatest, all are greedy for gain; prophets and priests alike, all practice deceit" (Jer 8:10). On this Day of Judgment, the following would also take place: "'I will take away their harvest,' declares the LORD. 'There will be no grapes on the vine. There will be no figs on the tree, and their leaves will wither. What I have given them will be taken from them'" (Jer 8:13). Therefore, the fruitless fig tree, followed by its withering demise, should be understood as a fulfillment of divine wrath.[18] Israel's inheritance, according to Matthew's restatement of Jeremiah's prophetic indictment, was to be revoked.

## Jesus' Authority

Following the temple incident, Jesus was questioned regarding the source of his authority (21:23–27). The temple officials, and, no doubt, the high priest, could not find fault with Jesus' actions, and they were astonished by his power. This presented a dilemma for them, for Jesus was clearly at odds with them; however, as a priestly class it would have been imprudent for them to act in a way that would appear unrighteous to onlookers. Their first approach was to ascertain the source of Jesus' authority and the time when this authority was bestowed upon him (21:23). Jesus chose not to answer them, but to challenge them regarding John's authority. This encounter was used by Matthew to expose the pragmatic hypocrisy that was pervasive in the conduct of Jesus' priestly opponents. They were not interested in the truth; they simply wanted to avoid the indignity of giving a response that made them vulnerable (21:25–26). The upshot of the incident was that Matthew's Jesus was both indifferent to their authority and without fear of them. Jesus' questioning of them also showed how important John was to the messianic claims of Jesus. John's message was that Jesus was heaven's ultimate representation (Matt 3). The priests could not accept John, because they could not accept Jesus. Jesus made no attempt to charm these rulers or pacify their malicious intent; the stage was set for the final conflict between them.

## The Parabolic Indictments

The questioning of Jesus' authority was followed by a full frontal assault on his opponents who understood plainly that they were the targets of

---

18. This connection is also made in Mark's gospel. Chance, "The Cursing of the Temple." This same point is, however, denied by others. Esler, "The Incident."

these specific parables (21:45). These parables, in fact, were instrumental in provoking them into action. Matthew recorded: "When the chief priests and the Pharisees heard Jesus' parables, they knew he was talking about them. They looked for a way to arrest him, but they were afraid of the crowd because the people held that he was a prophet" (21:45–46). Matthew's editorial revealed this priestly community as being both cowardly and petulant. Their desire to arrest Jesus was borne out of their personal grievance; it had nothing to do with transgression of the Mosaic or Roman laws. They were, in Matthew's estimation, motivated by self-interest. Jesus had humiliated them by his effectual ministry and his unambiguously scathing critique of their history and practices.

These parables have been given detailed treatment in chapter 6, and it will be sufficient here to visit them in the broadest possible terms. The parable of the Two Sons implicated the leaders in the crime of claiming to do their Father's will, while being totally negligent. John the Baptist, by contrast, was diligent. His labors had secured the ingathering of the wretched community comprising prostitutes and tax collectors; these were gaining entrance to the kingdom, whilst the willing but delinquent priesthood/son was failing to enter.

The Parable of the Tenants was extremely pointed, and had implicated these opponents of Matthew's Jesus as being the products of and participants in the longstanding rejection of YHWH's prophets. Their determination was to kill the son, who was the last of a long line of heavenly emissaries. This was used to make a clear statement of their historical animosity to God and their cynical attitude to their binding covenantal obligations.

The last parable exposed them as being thoroughly uninterested in participating in the eschatological celebrations. The people who had received the wedding invitation to the King's banquet had better things to do. Naturally enough, this was a blatant insult. The mundane activities of life were of greater value to these recalcitrants, and they had no interest in being guests of the King. Their destiny was to be outcast, destroyed and even to have their city burned (22:7).

## Jesus' Jerusalem Testing

The parables of indictment were followed by three questions posed by various configurations of Jesus' enemies who sought to provoke a Torah transgression (22:15–39).[19] The first of these was made plainly obvious by

---

19. It has been argued that Matthew did not appreciate the differences between Sadducees and Pharisees based on 16:12. Meier, *The Vision of Matthew*. This does not

the accompanying editorial comment: "Then the Pharisees went out and laid plans to trap him in his words" (22:15). The plan was to avoid a direct challenge to Jesus, but to trap him with a question from younger members of the Pharisaic and Herodian community. The disciples of the Pharisees asked Jesus about paying homage to Caesar through taxes. Part of this ploy was to flatter the teacher and emphasize his uncompromising and fearless virtue. They prepared Jesus with these words: "'Teacher,' they said, 'we know you are a man of integrity and that you teach the way of God in accordance with the truth. You aren't swayed by men, because you pay no attention to who they are'" (22:16).

Matthew is unambiguous concerning the intent of the questioners; "Jesus knew their evil" (τὴν πονηρίαν αὐτῶν). Both Mark and Luke recorded this same encounter, but their accounts managed to avoid this severe designation of the younger Pharisaic adversaries.[20] The inclusion of Herodians may have been sufficient to demonstrate the evil character of this delegation. It can be seen from this account that, whatever may have been the social and political divisions between the various factions in Jerusalem, Matthew's intention was to weave them into a single and purposeful unity. The chief priests and the Pharisees were, in Matthew's estimation, looking for a way to arrest him (21:46). A plan was consequently devised by the Pharisees (22:15), which was implemented by their disciples and the Herodians. This test was followed by the Sadducees,[21] who thought they had an imponderable dilemma that would force Jesus to deny any heavenly schema. This would make a mockery of any claim he had made to heavenly authority. The Pharisees heard about the failure of their traditional adversaries (22:34), and decided to test Jesus again with a challenge designed to trap him into denying the unity of the Law.

It is not necessary to reflect a great deal on the individual tests; the first was intended to corner Jesus by forcing him to denounce the "lordship" of Caesar, or, by affirming the practice of paying taxes, to be seen as a capitulator to Rome, thus denying Israel's eschatological hopes. Jesus' answer did neither; he effectively showed disdain for the currency which belonged to the one engraved upon it. Why would any righteous Hebrew wish to keep such coins at all? Jesus' exhortation to his opponents was to give God what belonged to him. This retort brought them back to the indictment found within the Parable of the Tenants; for they had failed to render to YHWH what belonged to YHWH.

---

recognize Matthew's interest in the unity of opposition to Jesus.

20. Hagner, *Matthew 14–28*, 634.

21. The ruling priests, including Caiaphas, were Sadducees.

The Sadducees' farcical attempt to ensnare Jesus ended with a biblical theology class. The question of which of the seven grooms would possess the single wife in the resurrection age was intended to point out that life beyond its earthly and temporal dimension was untenable. Any claim that Jesus was an eschatological Messiah on this reckoning, therefore, was ludicrous. Matthew's Jesus casually pointed out that YHWH introduced himself to Moses as the God of Abraham, Isaac, and Jacob, five hundred years after they had passed from the earthly reality (22:32). Though the Pharisees were completely at odds with Sadducees historically on this point (Acts 23:8), they would have happily accepted an outcome that humiliated Jesus and exposed him as a king of the non-world. Matthew does not point out the division between them, and the reader is left to observe this as the second temptation in a trilogy of temptations.

The last of these testing questions had a benign quality to it, yet Matthew intended his readers to view it as malevolent. This question was not prompted by the legal expert's quest for knowledge; rather, its intent was to test Jesus (πειράζων αὐτον). Unlike Mark's account, Matthew recorded no plaudits for a question well asked from a fellow son of Abraham. Mark's Jesus, in fact, commended the questioner who was clearly enamored by Jesus' response (Mark 12:34). For Matthew, this encounter had malicious intent and functioned, therefore, as the last of the entrapment questions.[22]

There can be little doubt that Matthew intended these three temptations to remind his readers of the devil's temptation trilogy in chapter 4. The tempters were evil (22:18).[23] Interestingly, in Matthew the devil was not actually categorized as evil.[24] By implication, evil resides in the humans who oppose the new community.[25] The important and particular intention of Matthew in placing these three "tests" together was to show the audacity of

---

22. Following the three questions, they had depleted all their courage, and asked no more. Jack Kingsbury in Stanton, *The Interpretation of Matthew*, 193.

23. It should be noted that Luke and John had a specific role for Satan—the possession and actions of Judas. (Luke 22:3; John 13:27). Mark gave Satan minor coverage and he did not connect him with Judas, nor did he use any literary device to suggest Satan's reappearance. Matthew's account gave greater significance to Satan, portraying him as Jesus' definitive opponent early in the narrative. Satan's failure to "reappear" in person in Matthew's account was intended to imply that Satan would use alternative means to thwart YHWH's program in Jesus. Even Peter, who opposed the purpose of God, was regarded as a satanic representative (16:23). How much more would the "evil" opponents in Jerusalem rightly bear the epithet?

24. This is not to say that Matthew considered that the devil was not evil; rather, it is to point out that evil was substantially personified in Jesus' opponents. These may even be the ones who planted the weeds in his field (13:38).

25. See Matt 5:11, 39, 45; 12:35.

the community that did not hesitate to undermine Jesus, who, in Matthew's estimation, was YHWH coming to the temple.[26] This was the very point of the next pericope, when Jesus audaciously challenged his opponents to recognize the superiority of David's offspring. But before turning to this, there is historical relevance attached to the testing of YHWH that needs to be considered.

The Davidic admonition that was significantly dwelt upon by the Hebrews author, "Today, if you hear his voice, do not harden your hearts as you did at Meribah, as you did that day at Massah in the desert, where your fathers tested and tried me, though they had seen what I did" (Ps 95:8–9), was a central indictment concerning Israel's conduct in the wilderness.[27] Israel had attempted to test YHWH, and in David's assessment, they paid a heavy penalty for it (Ps 95). It would soon be seen, in Matthew's narrative, that Israel would once again be severely rebuked for testing YHWH through his earthly representative, Jesus.

## David's Son

Jesus' provocative question concerning the identity of David's son ended the attempts to trap Jesus;[28] from that point on, any means would be enlisted to bring about the demise of the messianic pretender. This section received some treatment in the previous chapter, so it will be sufficient to briefly touch on the significant theological point that Jesus was making.

The prophetic ascension of a priest that was not from the Aaronic/Levitical dynasty would not have passed the notice of the priests in Jerusalem. The single most potent threat to the permanent tenure of the Levitical high priesthood was the declaration found in Psalm 110. The psalm contains the DNA of Matthew's Christology: David's son and LORD would be exalted to the right hand of YHWH, who would then proceed to subdue the son's enemies.[29] This son would be given authority to rule the earth,

---

26. "[Jesus] projected the notion of (Daniel's) evil empire on to the present Jerusalem regime" (Wright, *Victory of God*, 598).

27. It is of interest that Moses noted that the testing at Meribah and Massah had specific reference to Levi, the priestly caste: "About Levi he said: 'Your Thummim and Urim belong to the man you favored. You tested him at Massah; you contended with him at the waters of Meribah . . .'" (Deut 33:8).

28. "No one could say a word in reply, and from that day on no one dared to ask him any more questions" (22:46).

29. Son of David was somehow associated with the notion of judgment; therefore, this discussion took place before the indictment sequence of chapter 23. Loader, "Son of David."

and this function was intrinsically connected to his permanent high priestly appointment, which would be sealed by YHWH's oath, in the order of Melchizedek. This was to be followed by the unsurpassed terror attached to the appointment—"The LORD is at your right hand; he will crush kings on the day of his wrath. He will judge the nations, heaping up the dead and crushing the rulers of the whole earth" (Ps 110:5–6). It is no surprise then, that no one would dare ask him a question (22:46) after Jesus' provocative reference to Psalm 110.

## The Culmination and Fulfillment of Covenantal Transgressions

Matthew is not alone in recording this indictment sequence with its seven woes (23:1–39), but it is more comprehensive and scathing than Luke's version. Luke follows Mark in both sequence and content of what followed after the Davidic reference to Psalm 110; Matthew set his own course with this material and considered that the implications of the ascension of David's priestly descendant was an appropriate opportunity to bring the concluding castigation of the incumbent priestly community and its entourage. These seven woes concluded with the cumulative condemnation of all malicious and self-interested priests/stewards falling upon the heads of those who governed in Jerusalem (23:35). They would be condemned for the rejection and slaughter of all God's prophets, for they had conceded that they were the descendants of those who actually perpetrated the atrocities (they were the offspring of evil—23:33). Jerusalem may have escaped this indictment, had it accepted God's final emissary; but without this penitent act, it was made liable for all of Israel's past indebtedness.

The central allegation that permeated the whole sequence of indictments was hypocrisy—this community was just not what it purported to be. It had acted the part of a righteous mediation community, but had been, in reality, a self-interested group that had used its sacral office for its own prosperity and social standing. This allegation gained currency in the prelude to Matthew's "woes" with the insistence that the leadership be obeyed but not imitated (23:3). Matthew made it clear that the priestly incumbents were not impostors, for they "sat in Moses' seat" (23:2).[30] In this way Matthew rejected the widespread claim, mostly made by the Qumran community,

---

30. The hypocrisy theme was embellished with this statement and its ensuing observation—"So you must obey them and do everything they tell you. But do not do what they do, for they do not practice what they preach." Jesus, on the other hand, taught Torah, but also kept it (7:21). Powell, "Do and Keep," 434.

that the current priesthood was illegitimate.[31] If they had been illegitimate, Jesus' allegations would have led to the reinstatement of the legitimate Mosaic successors; as it was, however, it was the office of priesthood itself that was in jeopardy, for its representatives were truly legitimate[32] and yet thoroughly corrupt.[33]

It has already been noted how this series of indictments is juxtaposed by the righteous expectations of Jesus for prospective kingdom participants in the Sermon on the Mount (chapter 3). There is, however, another connection to be made with this passage. In Malachi, YHWH proposed a series of failings on the part of the governing community that resulted in a pledge by God to bring a curse upon the priesthood (Mal 2:1–2). Their crimes against YHWH were covenantal faithlessness, disrespect (through the offering of blemished animals), failure to instruct the people in the way of their fathers, resulting in the stumbling of many, and finally the robbery of God through the manner in which they withheld the tithe. Matthew's allegations are that the ruling class caused people to stumble by placing obstacles in the way of those who sought to enter the kingdom. They (the Pharisees) made wretched disciples.[34] They considered the gold in the temple to be sacred, rather than the temple itself, thus showing their primary commitment to money and disrespect to God. They tithed minutiae but failed to practice the important matters of justice, mercy and faithfulness.[35] And lastly, they commemorated the prophets, whom their fathers had slaughtered, with elaborate sepulchers. While the two are not identical, the scathing critique found in both documents, and the similarities between them are sufficient, it is proposed, for the conclusion to be drawn that Matthew saw his recorded indictment as the fulfillment of the foreshadowed curse by YHWH in Malachi.

The conclusion of this pericope leaves little doubt that Jesus' condemnatory speech was the terminus of the priestly system. Following the last "woe," Jesus had laid upon that generation the cumulative guilt of every

---

31. Gartner, *The Temple and Community in Qumran*, 4.

32. Gurtner, *The Torn Veil*, 105.

33. Craig found the High Priestly extended household in Jerusalem to be thoroughly corrupt, violent and indecently wealthy—more like a mafia operation than a priesthood. Evans, "Jesus' Action in the Temple."

34. Bird believes that these disciples were more political than spiritual. Bird, "The Case of the Proselytizing Pharisees?"

35. This is critically important to the tithe concept in Malachi. By failing to bring the "whole tithe" into the House of God in Malachi, the priests had failed to fill "God's storehouse." As a consequence, there was no food for the poor. So tithing and mercy were integral to each other. Failure in regard to justice was a key indictment against the Levites also, for they would be judged for "defrauding laborers of their wages, oppressing the widows and the fatherless and depriving aliens of justice" (Mal 3:5).

unrighteous generation before it. Matthew has asserted that Jesus' mission was to fulfill the Law (5:17), and here is the only time that Jesus commanded fulfillment, using an imperative structure—πληρώσατε "fulfill" . . . the measure of your forefathers' sin. This is an echo of the sin of the Amorites—"In the fourth generation your descendants will come back here, for the sin of the Amorites has not yet reached its full measure" (Gen 15:16).[36] Matthew seems to be suggesting that this dire fulfillment on Jesus' particular generation is the terminus of a long and patient outreach on God's part toward an unremittingly obstinate and recalcitrant covenant community. Like the Amorites of the fledgling Hebrew nation's day, Israel too had now found the boundary marker of God's long-suffering patience; once crossed, destruction was imminent.

## Jesus' Lamentation

The concluding lamentation of Jesus following this series of indictments brings the whole passage to a poignant end (23:37–39).[37] Jesus' words here were intended to communicate the long and arduous history that YHWH had endured with a nation that rejected his love. The ultimate cause for the failure of this relationship to endure and be blessed was the unwillingness of its human recipients to desire it. Israel was deemed to have consistently and definitively rejected YHWH's maternal affections. As a consequence of this, they were now left desolate or abandoned.[38]

It is hard to find another passage in Matthew that implicitly identified the author's Jesus as YHWH more prominently than this passage. It was Jesus who had been rebutted and spurned from the beginning of this tumultuous relationship. Jesus longed to gather the recalcitrant nation; it now fell

---

36. By commanding fulfillment of the nation's cumulative atrocities, Matthew's Jesus has demonstrated that the Day of the Lord has come.

37. The connection between the woes, which were directed to the scribes and Pharisees, and the destruction of the temple could only be made if these sects were representative of the priestly community, for administration of the temple was vested in the Levites/priests alone. Block, *Ezekiel: 25–48*, 647.

38. The lament concerning the impending destruction of Jerusalem has profound resonance with Lamentations. This will become more apparent later in the chapter. Noteworthy in Lamentations was the comparison of Jerusalem's destruction to that of Sodom—"The punishment of my people was greater than Sodom, which was overthrown in a moment without a hand turned to help her" (Lam 4:6). Consider then Matthew's indictment (which was not found in Mark's account) "If the miracles performed in you had been performed in Sodom, it would have remained to this day. But I tell you that it will be more bearable for Sodom on the day of judgment than for you" (11:23b–24).

to him to decree its end, not as a prophet of YHWH, but as YHWH himself. The events that followed this agonizing conclusion to the indictment passage were the inevitable fallout of the "divorce." The apocalyptic passage and the passion narrative were the logical consequence of the indictment. If the "woes" passage was the judge's verdict on the state of the relationship, the remainder was the story of the covenant's execution.[39]

Luke's use of this tradition has quite a different trajectory that is not altogether inconsistent with Matthew. Luke records:

> As he approached Jerusalem and saw the city, he wept over it and said, "If you, even you, had only known on this day what would bring you peace—but now it is hidden from your eyes. The days will come upon you when your enemies will build an embankment against you and encircle you and hem you in on every side. They will dash you to the ground, you and the children within your walls. They will not leave one stone on another, because you did not recognize the time of God's coming to you" (Luke 19:41–44).

Luke's version achieves similar ends to Matthew in a far more succinct retelling. The destruction of Jerusalem, for Luke, is the direct outcome of the failure of the Jews to apprehend the importance of the coming of Jesus. Implicitly, for Luke, even at that late hour peace was available had Israel responded appropriately. Matthew's Jesus, however, presented a long history of covenantal failure as the primary cause of the coming desolation. We cannot be certain that Matthew's Jesus had come as a "covenantal" Savior at all. His mission to the outcasts from the beginning looked as though Jesus was gleaning the refuse of the Hebrew nation, while showing almost no interest in persuading "middle" Israel to find redemption and peace with YHWH.

The declaration of Israel's desolation, made immediately pertinent with the abrupt declaration ἰδού ("behold"), was in effect the final curse that would trigger the tragic passion events, which in some form of divine retribution, measured out God's wrathful termination of the Mosaic covenant. The condemnation of the scribes and Pharisees was the catalyst for this lamentation with its somewhat reluctant and gripping concluding curse. What transpired, however, was not altogether unexpected: the destiny of the temple, which was the nerve center of the nation's existence, rested in the hands of its stewards. If the temple/Jerusalem became degenerate, through

---

39. This desolation could only refer to the destruction of Jerusalem and the temple in AD 70. Schnackenburg, *Matthew*, 235.

dishonesty, injustice, lack of mercy and the shedding of innocent blood,[40] YHWH had sworn to ruin it. Such was the warning that Jeremiah recorded:

> This is what the LORD says:
>
> "Do what is just and right. Rescue from the hand of his oppressor the one who has been robbed. Do no wrong or violence to the alien, the fatherless or the widow, and do not shed innocent blood in this place. For if you are careful to carry out these commands, then kings who sit on David's throne will come through the gates of this palace, riding in chariots and on horses, accompanied by their officials and their people. But if you do not obey these commands, declares the LORD, I swear by myself that this palace will become a ruin."
>
> For this is what the LORD says about the palace of the king of Judah:
>
> "Though you are like Gilead to me, like the summit of Lebanon, I will surely make you like a desert, like towns not inhabited. I will send destroyers against you, each man with his weapons, and they will cut up your fine cedar beams and throw them into the fire" (Jer 22:3–7).

Could it be that the unaccompanied arrival of Jesus on the donkey was a direct contrast to the blessed state that Judah's kings were to enjoy when they entered Jerusalem, had it been all that it was intended to be? Regardless of this possible connection, it is clearly likely that Matthew had such a context in mind with this "messianic" declaration of the temple's ruined abandonment. The majestic city with its glorious temple was from that time deserted, as was symbolized by the departure of Jesus (24:1), and in the course of Matthew's prophetic unfolding all would see what had been emphatically declared. The demise of Jerusalem and its house/temple, like the fig tree, was complete once Jesus had condemned the city—for YHWH had come, but was not welcome.

## The Destiny of Jerusalem

The twenty-fourth chapter of Matthew commences with the affirmation of the temple's grandeur, and the direct disclosure and confirmation that its days were at this point numbered (24:2). The naive observation of Matthew's

---

40. This concept of innocent blood is central to understanding the indictment and judgment that would fall upon the city. This important concept will be dealt with later in this chapter.

disciples while leaving the temple was the perfect foil to begin this wide-ranging and perplexing apocalyptic declaration, delivered from the vantage point of the Mount of Olives.[41] Jesus' declaration that the temple would not simply be deserted and besieged, but systematically torn apart, had such a forceful intent that one cannot doubt the anger that precipitated it. Dismantling the temple would be an achievement in its own right, and would require a determined hostility that was inconceivable at the time that Matthew's Jesus uttered the words. With amicable arrangements with Rome in place, at this stage of the narrative this was certainly not a likely or predictable outcome. What followed Jesus' stark revelation was the elucidation of that coming judgment and preparatory advice for those who valued Jesus' instruction.

In Matthew's account, the disciples were concerned to know the timing of the catastrophe (24:3), which was unambiguously disclosed as all but imminent. The very generation that heard the words of Jesus, according to Matthew, would witness the tumultuous destruction of the temple (24:34). This apocalyptic contained a rudimentary guide to assist Jesus' community navigate the impending storm. It contained warnings, information on how the events would unfold, and advice on what to do immediately before or at the time. Unlike previous Hebrew apocalyptic writings, this passage had a strong pastoral emphasis. All that was denied to the disciples was the exact time of the event.

There will be no attempt to carry out a detailed consideration of this passage. For the purpose of this reading, it is sufficient to say that the passage was entirely relevant to the immediate destruction of Jerusalem, as argued by others,[42] and the context makes this view self-evident apart from a particular condition that may be difficult to interpret.[43] Many of the "signs" alluded to in this passage could appear to be fulfilled within New Testament documents, including Matthew's, as well as in the historical events that led up to the Jewish wars.[44] False christs/prophets, rumors of wars, famines, earthquakes, perse-

---

41. "... Zechariah 14 with its stunning representation of Yahweh standing on the Mount of Olives and causing the mountain to split in two 'challenges the reader to consider the eventual destruction of Jerusalem as part of Yahweh's larger purpose...'" (Ham, "Reading Zechariah," 97).

42. Wright, *Victory of God*, 339–68.

43. Brown believes that Matthew 24:1–32 alone is pertinent to the Jewish Wars and the Destruction. Brown, "The Matthean Apocalypse," 3.

44. There is good reason to accept Peter Bolt's view that the apocalyptic in Mark needs to be more fully integrated with the immediate narrative, which leads to a view that the coming events are all found within the passion narrative. Bolt, "Mark 13." These same observations can be made of Matthew. However, it may be that Bolt has not fully appreciated that the justified wrath which was upon Israel's stewards was necessarily upon their "house" also. This would include both buildings and people. This is central

cutions, backslidings and the advancement of the Gospel to the ends of the world (Col 1:23) are all evidently fulfilled in first-century writings.

Within the passage, Jesus' greatest concern was whether his followers would adequately read the signs of the "end," and not be deceived or grow cold. The illegitimate messiahs were the ones cast as the major problem for the church; its nemesis would not be Rome, even though history would show that the church was brutalized by the Empire. Whoever these false "messiahs" would turn out to be, they would take a significant toll on the fledgling community (24:24). They would pop up everywhere, in the desert and in the secret rooms (24:26). Their ability to negate the influence of the Gospel would be formidable, and the nature of their activities would not be obvious. So who were the false messiahs and prophets that Matthew's Jesus was warning of?

Assuming then that Matthew considered this apocalyptic passage to be foreshadowing the destruction of Jerusalem, the author would have had some sense of who comprised this corrupting influence within the primitive church. There is even a hint that the reader would have understood the "abomination that causes desolation" ("let the reader understand" 24:15).[45] Clearly, Matthew had a considerable disdain for Pharisees, and they must have been prime suspects for his consideration in the post-resurrection period. Yet the antagonism between the Pharisees and the disciples of Jesus was such that it is hard to imagine how they would represent a serious theological threat; these "false christs" must have been closer to the Christians theologically than the Pharisees of the Gospels, who most certainly would not have presented themselves in Jesus' name (24:5). The Pharisees depicted in the Gospels would no doubt have been involved in the persecution of the church, but they would not be capable of the subtlety necessary to make the plausible claim of having the "insider" information necessary that could entice the disciples to follow them into the desert or the inner rooms[46]—

---

to understanding God's wrath in full expression as foreshadowed in Deuteronomy 28. It seems that Jesus presented himself as a typology of the temple, rather than as a reality of the temple's typology. So what would happen to Jesus would inevitably happen to the temple. The "willful" and deliberate destruction of Jesus' body was a portent for the temple's demise. The temple would not perish in the same way as every other building; rather, its seemingly indestructible façade, made of enormous sculptured stones, would be deliberately καταλυθῇ ("thrown down") in Mark and καταλυθήσεται ("shall be destroyed") in Matthew.

45. David Wenham believes that a larger section of chapter 24 derives from Daniel. The lawlessness and the abomination may be related. Wenham, "A Note on Matthew 24:10–12." One wonders if there could be a greater abomination occurring in the temple than the cursing, exclusion and physical abuse of YHWH by the high priest of Israel.

46. "Inner rooms" when taken from the Aramaic could have meant assembly or

"to deceive the elect, if it were possible" (24:24). Though there cannot be certainty as to who these messiahs and prophets were, or even whether they constituted a cohesive group, there is every chance that they were the same agitators and law-keepers that Paul had encountered. Coincidentally, the significant faction in Jerusalem, according to Acts, was the party of the Pharisees (Acts 15:5). These were probably the same Christians who were zealous for the Law (Acts 21:20) and exerted strong influence upon James.[47] They would have been a significant influence in both Gentile and Hebrew churches, and were possibly the villains in some of Paul's letters.[48]

## The Survivors of the Cataclysm

Chapter 24 ends with a rhetorical question, introducing three parables that addressed the question of who would survive the cataclysmic event predicted by Jesus. Who would be the faithful and wise servant doing his job when Jesus returns to settle accounts? The designated servant must prove diligent in undertaking the assigned function, which was to ensure that all the servants in the master's house were amply provided for. The faithful leader would be rewarded; the unfaithful leader, who abused his position and burdened the servants of the house, would be cast out with the hypocrites (24:51).[49]

The judgment of leaders was then illustrated further with three parables, which have already received some consideration in chapter 6. Here it is sufficient to say that the parables of the set dealt with issues pertinent

---

Sanhedrin. Hagner, *Matthew 14–28*, 706.

47. Jewett, "Agitators and the Galatian Congregation," 204. Robert Jewett proposes that the Galatian agitators who sought to lead the church to Torah observance were likely to have their origin in Jerusalem/Judea.

48. Should this hypothesis be correct, it would be hard to sustain the view that Matthew's "community" was a Torah–observant sect, for why would he assert that there would be deceivers coming in Jesus' name? In this context, false christs would have to be a reference to those claiming priestly representation on Jesus' behalf. It was in the early church, according to Hebrews, that the legitimacy and efficacy of the Aaronic priesthood was still being contested. Christians were being influenced to accept Mosaic boundary markers, and temple participation where possible. False prophets who advocated false christs, therefore, could well have been a reference to those who would insist that Christians needed to stay faithful to temple practice and consequently committed to Aaronic/Levitical mediation.

49. The destination of the failed leaders was "a place with the hypocrites" (24:51). This place is later called the place prepared for the devil and his messengers (25:41). It may be then that the devil's messengers and the hypocrites, according to this assessment, are the same. This would strengthen the argument that Matthew believed that the "hypocrites" of chapter 23 were the devil's messengers—the offspring of the serpent.

to the discussion of Matthew 24; they covered the issues of waiting and being ready (Ten Virgins), willing and proactive stewardship (Talents), and distribution of resources to the lowly in the community (the Sheep and the Goats). The faithful and wise stewards are those that watch, work and act compassionately. These would continue, while the faithless stewards would have their tenure terminated.[50] These parables, which expound the character of the impending judgment, were pointing to AD 70; the leaders in question were the Aaronic/Levitical leaders (including the variegated groups that form the leadership collective in Matthew) and the new apostolic collective. The disciples would have to be alert and waiting for the cataclysmic event (which is amply testified to in apostolic literature),[51] they would have to be diligent to make use of the deposit/talent that Jesus had given them,[52] and they were to ensure that all believers/servants were adequately provided for in the master's absence.[53]

## The Determined Opponents

Chapter 26 commenced with a declaration that Passover would be the precursor of Jesus' demise (26:2). Matthew's narrative, at this point, turned to the strategy of Jesus' opponents. Matthew was not reticent to make a judgment concerning the actions of the priests and elders; he asserts that they devised a plot to deceitfully arrest Jesus (26:4). By naming the host of this gathering as the leader of the priests Matthew broke rank with other Gospel writers. Ultimate responsibility for the impending injustice, in Matthew's estimation, could be attributed to Caiaphas. Caiaphas was shown to be the ruthless instigator of the process, which would rely on his own judgment to bring a verdict (26:65). Israel's high priest was required by Law to abstain from any action that could make him unclean; a plot within his own home to have an innocent man put to death had no parallel in the history of high

---

50. This seems to address the problem that some have concerning judgment and grace. For example: "It seems to me that the notion of judgment according to works is a theological impossibility . . . But it may be that we, as human beings, need the idea of judgment because, without it, we would be unable to take God seriously as God" (Luz, *The Theology of the Gospel of Matthew*, 132). It is not necessary to propose that the threat of judgment is to coerce "good behavior." It is legitimate, but it has to be understood against the backdrop of AD 70.

51. Rom 13:12; 1 Cor 3:13; Eph 6:13; 1 Thess 5:2; Heb 10:25; 2 Pet 3:10; 1 John 4:17.

52. The Apostles believed they had exclusive stewardship of Jesus' message. Acts 10:41; Rom 1:5.

53. Acts 6:1; 1 Tim 5:3.

priests. No Gospel writer, other than Matthew, was prepared to bring this direct charge against the high priest.

Up to this moment in the narrative, Caiaphas was not referred or alluded to; unlike all the seemingly impotent enemies of Jesus, Caiaphas was decisive, influential and successful. Matthew gave the distinct impression that Caiaphas had influence over all Jesus' enemies. His decisions were implemented and he controlled the deliberations of the Sanhedrin; he was the sinister puppeteer who emerged from the shadows at the critical time, in Matthew's account. It was Caiaphas who led the plan to arrest and kill Jesus (26:4), and he led the Jerusalem posse (via his servant),[54] he presided as judge and he coerced the Sanhedrin/jury (26:65). There could be little doubt that Caiaphas was instrumental in the decision to sway the mob against Jesus (27:20), and also to instigate the "cover-up" following the resurrection (28:12). Unlike the other Gospel writers, who were prepared to distribute the blame or be non-specific, Matthew was prepared to name the prime instigator of these events.[55]

The devotion of the unnamed woman followed in Matthew's narrative. Her role was to anoint the body of Jesus in preparation for his death (26:12).[56] The placement of this incident between the priest's plan and Judas' betrayal appears designed to contrast their hatred with her devotion, but also make the point that these events were not taking Jesus by surprise. His knowledge of how and when these events would unfold was integral to the story. Matthew's Jesus was not fleeing injustice, or appealing against it; rather, he embraced the importance of the events, which were inevitable to his mission. The anointing event was meaningful for Matthew's Jesus, and may have been expected by him. Ironically, her kind and heavenly action was probably what Judas needed to encourage him toward his evil assignment. Matthew's next scene reveals Judas standing before the high priests, receiving the thirty coins for his willingness to betray Jesus.

---

54. It appears that the elders and chief priests did not arrest Jesus—they waited for the delegation to bring Jesus to Caiaphas's court where they were already assembled (26:57). In these circumstances, the representative of the high priest would have led the delegation. It is not surprising then that he would be the focal point of the aggression of the disciples (26:51).

55. Bond asks the question why Caiaphas is specifically named in Matthew's gospel—was it to "emphasize the contrast between the two men, Jesus and Caiaphas?" (Bond, *Caiaphas*, 124).

56. This incident has received particular attention within the previous chapter.

## The Passover Meal

The Synoptics are uniform in the presentation of Jesus' last supper as a climactic Passover event. Its extensive symbolism should not be overlooked. The historical Passover was the prelude to the wrathful destruction of Egypt's offspring. This too was a meal on the eve of a great calamity—the magnitude of which had already been foreshadowed by Jesus in Matthew's narrative. The following day the temple curtain would be torn,[57] as an expression of God's departure, and the permanent termination of Israel's unique form of cultic mediation.[58]

In Matthew's account, the meal was underway when the tense moment of Judas' exposure arrived (26:25). After Jesus declared that a betrayer had infiltrated their fraternity, the disciples, each in turn, canvassed the possibility of his own guilt, until it fell to the confrontation of Judas by Jesus. Hagner notes that Judas addressed Jesus as Rabbi rather than Lord; this was the title given throughout the narrative by those who did not acknowledge Jesus as Lord, while all the disciples called Jesus "Lord."[59] Once Judas was exposed, the reader is left to assume that he departed to enact his crime, allowing the meal and the inaugural sacrament to continue.

The Passover meal was the most solemn celebration in the Hebrew calendar.[60] This celebration seems to have evolved within the Hebrew narrative to become a larger festival that combined the remembrance of the Exodus and a rite that resembled the Day of Atonement. The inaugural Passover was presided over by the head of each household, who prepared the lamb and protected his household with the creature's blood (Exod 12). As the narrative progresses, however, the Passover sacrifice was to be celebrated in the "place he [YHWH] would choose for his name" (Deut 16:5)—Jerusalem. This accounts for the annual pilgrimage to Jerusalem at Passover. The same

---

57. It has been commonly thought that the tearing of the veil facilitated access to God that was formerly denied; see Gurtner, *The Torn Veil*. However, it is possible that the veil preserved Israel who could not see God and live. Therefore the removal of the "safety barrier" could have meant the outbreak of YHWH's long restrained wrath.

58. "The veil to the sanctuary is symbolically rent when Jesus dies on the cross (Mark 15:38). Contrary to Israel's sense of divine election, the Gospels assert that God has rejected Israel for a new covenant people, those who confess Jesus as Messiah" (Perkins, "If Jerusalem Stood," 201–2). Perkins's replacement theology may be questioned, but it is not unreasonable to affirm that the cataclysmic breach that took place was also the commencement of a new order in the minds of the Gospel writers, as a consequence of Jesus' death.

59. Hagner, *Matthew 14–28*, 768.

60. The Israelite who did not celebrate Passover was to be "cut off" (Num 9:13). In spite of this, it is recorded that the Passover was not celebrated from Samuel to Josiah (2 Kgs 23:22; 2 Chr 35:18).

sacrifice, as recorded in Numbers 28, also included the slaughter of bulls and rams, along with other offerings. Rather than being just a remembrance, the event included at this point an element that appears to be atonement ritual performed by the priest. This could not be Yom Kippur, which was not until the seventh month; nonetheless, the Law required that everyone who celebrated Passover be clean, even prior to the Exile (Num 9:6).[61] This may have been the established practice that was enshrined in Hebrew legislation through to the post-exilic community (Ezek 45:18–24; Ezra 6:19–20). The following is a translation of Ezek 45:18–25:

> The Lord Yahweh's message is as follows: On the first day of the first month you are to take an unblemished young bull and decontaminate the sanctuary. The priest will take some of the blood from this sin offering and put it on the doorposts of the temple, the four corners of the altar plinth and the doorposts of the gate to the inner court. You are to do likewise on the seventh of the month, for anyone who sins inadvertently or through ignorance. In this way you are to make expiation for the temple. On the fourteenth day of the first month you should hold the Passover, after which unleavened bread is to be eaten for seven days. The head of state is to provide on that day a bull as a sin offering for himself and all the people in the land. During the seven days of the festival he is to provide as a holocaust to Yahweh seven bulls and seven rams, unblemished beasts, on each of the seven days; also a young goat for a sin offering each day. For every bull and ram he is to provide an ephah as a cereal offering, with a hin of oil to every ephah. At the festival that begins on the fifteenth day of the seventh month he is to make the same provision for seven days, the same sin offerings, holocausts, cereal offerings and oil.[62]

It is against this intertextual background that it is possible to interpret the Passover meal of Matthew's Jesus as both a connection to Exodus and to the atonement for the remission of sins.[63]

---

61. John's gospel specifically refers to Judas as "unclean" (John 13:10–11), and he departs following the bowl-dipping incident which led to his exposure, as is the case in Matthew (John 13:26–27).

62. Allen, *Ezekiel 20–48*, 241.

63. Daniel Block believes that the ritual purgation (resembling Day of Atonement) of the temple was a one-time event, rather than an ongoing practice for the festival period. Block, *Ezekiel: 25–48*, 662–64. However, he also acknowledges that the purgation ritual commencing on the fourteenth day had changed the character of Passover. He wrote: "Whereas the original Passover was apotropaic, to ward off Yahweh's lethal actions, and subsequent celebrations provided annual reminders of that original event,

The final Passover of Jesus, in Matthew, was reconstituted as a new ordinance for Jesus' "house." As previously mentioned, Matthew's account of the Jesus story set in juxtaposition two rival houses—one presided over by the Jerusalem establishment (Aaronic succession) and the other presided over by Jesus. The house upon the "rock" would endure, while the other would be demolished by the impending calamity.

In this way, the new "Passover" ordinance had used the symbolism of the old to convey the notion that Jesus' house was protected against the impending wrath, and that Jesus himself was the Passover lamb that ensured the cleanliness of those within the house.[64] This event, within the early church, would become the memorial of Jesus' death, and its subsequent meaning that his community had escaped YHWH's wrath, through Jesus' shed blood (1 Cor 11). No mention is made in any of the Gospels that Jesus participated in the lamb sacrificed by the priesthood, or that this was indeed the practice of the day. Certainly no lamb is mentioned at this Passover, and the reader is left to conclude that Jesus may be the Lamb of God.[65]

The declaration of the new covenant "in my blood" (26:27) is a direct reflection on the inaugural sacrifice (young bulls) of the Mosaic covenant (Exod 24:8); at that time the blood of the sacrifice was sprinkled on all the Israelites. While the "new Moses" motif is evident throughout the Gospel,[66] it is never more apparent than at this point. It is unlikely that Matthew intended this to be understood as anything other than the new covenant anticipated by the prophets Jeremiah and Ezekiel (Jer 31; Ezek 34).[67] Jesus presided over the "sacrifice," even though he himself was the sacrifice. With this declaration of Matthew's Jesus, it is clear that Matthew had presented

---

in the Ezekielian ordinance the memorial purposes of the Passover are overshadowed by the purgative concern. Thus, while the Passover, the most fundamental of all Israelite celebrations, is retained in Ezekiel's new religious order, its nature and significance have been changed" (Block, *Ezekiel: 25–48*, 666). Leslie Allen does not consider that there is any difficulty with the preceding Atonement Day type activity being an ongoing feature of the new temple. Allen, *Ezekiel 20–48*, 226.

64. Israelites were not protected from the judgment at Passover if they were not in a protected house (Exod 12:13); Judas left the "house" that evening, and by inference, was no longer protected by Jesus' patriarchal act.

65. John's gospel makes Jesus' identity as the Lamb of God explicit (John 1:29).

66. This includes the "new law" from the mount (chapters 5–7), and the five discourses within the narrative, which are routinely considered to be a recasting of, or pointer to, the five books of Moses.

67. The Ezekiel prophecy followed the indictment of Israel's shepherds, and was presented as a Covenant established with a new order of shepherds, presumably not Aaronic/Levitical. The Epistle to the Hebrews also noted that the New Covenant had implications for the termination of Aaronic mediation.

Jesus as a "high priest," capable of removing the sins of many, while also being the offering of his own mediatorial role.[68]

The Last Supper ensured what Matthew had been trying to make clear: the death of Jesus was not simply a horrendous injustice, but also the active decision and work of the Christ. Jesus knew that this event was his destiny and he did nothing to avoid the execution, which was his own self-sacrifice for the preservation of his new community.[69] The theological dilemma attached to this scenario is not explained. The plan is God's, and all concerned follow the script; however, those who participate in the execution, such as Judas, are fully accountable for their actions.[70] Matthew sums up the situation with this Christ statement: "The Son of Man will go just as it is written about him. But woe to that man who betrays the Son of Man! It would be better for him if he had not been born" (26:24).[71] Jesus' priestly act of offering himself could not have been an accident of history, in Matthew's narrative, nor could Jesus actually offer himself without the aid of the enemies.

## The Insubstantial Disciples

The remaining disciples are not opposed to Jesus, in Matthew's gospel, but neither are they of great benefit to him. Back at the Mount of Olives Jesus foreshadowed the backsliding of the disciples, with specific focus on Peter's impending triple denial.[72] His denial will take two forms: Peter will be incapable of complying with Jesus' heartfelt request to support him in prayer (26:38), and then he will publicly denounce his master (26:69–74). What is so striking about this depiction of Jesus is the acceptance of the disciples' failures, and the assurance that their wholehearted abandonment of Jesus would not lead to their permanent demise (26:32). Matthew's Jesus was cer-

---

68. Once again, the Hebrews writer also presented Jesus as both perfect priest and sacrifice (Heb 8:1–3; 9:23–28).

69. France, *Matthew*, 988.

70. Judas exited the story by hanging himself. This, according to Charlene Moss does two things, "it tells the outcome of Judas' act of treachery; and, second, it lays the bloodguilt of Jesus' death at the feet of Jerusalem's religious leaders" (Moss, *The Zechariah Tradition*, 173).

71. This theological assessment of Jesus' death was also set forward in Acts: "This man was handed over to you by God's set purpose and foreknowledge; and you, with the help of wicked men, put him to death by nailing him to the cross" (Acts 2:23).

72. Matthew's use of the number three is important to the narrative; it functions to give strong affirmation of the particular point Matthew sought to make. Of interest, Pilate sought to have Jesus released three times also. This could only further develop Matthew's view of Pilate's innocence in the proceedings. Callahan, "Who Really Killed Jesus?" 88.

tain that they would follow the divine script and that he would meet them in Galilee after all the events had run their course (26:32).

Matthew never mentions grace as a concept within his narrative, but there can be no doubt that this kindness shown to the faulty disciples was intended to be understood as the fullest expression of it. Jesus had identified the "blessed" as the one who does not fall away because of him (11:6). Jesus declared to the disciples that they would fall away because of him (26:31), but not irredeemably; their restoration, and therefore their blessedness, was enshrined in the resurrection event (26:32). Matthew's depiction of Jesus' ability to mediate for and restore even these flawed disciples could only reinforce the existing depiction of Jesus' superior priesthood.

## Confrontation in the Garden

Matthew does not refer to Gethsemane as a garden;[73] however, the name itself suggests that it was probably an olive grove or orchard.[74] The incident is critical to Matthew's narrative in demonstrating that the priestly transaction that was about to take place was not with any earthly identity, but with heaven. Jesus appealed to his Father to find another way, if it were possible.[75] The readers were to presume that the response to the anguished prayer of Jesus was that there was no other way—Jesus was required to do the Father's will.[76] Jesus' own instinct for self-preservation was shown to be subordinate to doing the Father's will. In the following verses it would become clear that Jesus had the legions of angels at his disposal (26:53); however, he had determined to do the will of God. Matthew's Jesus was portrayed as a free agent, even at this critical time.

Jesus' ministry to YHWH was to be rendered without the assistance of other humans (Isa 63:5).[77] This is reminiscent of the work of Aaron and

73. John recorded that this place was a garden (John 18:1, 26).

74. Hagner, *Matthew 14–28*, 782.

75. Jesus' earnest prayers are reminiscent of the heroes of the Hebrew narrative, from Abraham and Moses to Daniel and Jonah. These prayers are in private away from the disciples. As such this episode is in contrast to the chief priests, who have been accused of public prayer, and who avoid any consultation with YHWH during their council deliberations.

76. The Hebrews writer considered that the prayers of Jesus were instrumental to the success of his gruesome mission. He wrote: "During the days of Jesus' life on earth, he offered up prayers and petitions with loud cries and tears to the one who could save him from death, and he was heard because of his reverent submission" (Heb 5:7).

77. The failure of the disciples to support Jesus by passively keeping watch occurs three times, and has a resonance with Peter's active threefold denial.

his successors on the Day of Atonement;⁷⁸ Matthew's Jesus was required to be a solitary mediator. Here at Gethsemane Jesus went ahead or further into the "garden"; this too may have an allusion to the private and sacred high priestly work of Aaron in the holiest place on Yom Kippur. The desertion of the disciples may have been integral to the development of Matthew's priestly subtext, as the high priest was required to enter "the most holy place" alone (Heb 8:1–2).

The "garden" as a place of priestly duty has some metanarrative resonance. Adam, the first failed priest, was excluded from the garden, where previously he had access to God. The "walled" temple may well be the representation of the "walled" garden within which God could be met by the human representative; for the temple was heavily adorned with garden images such as pomegranates, lilies, palm trees, and various creatures. Aaron himself bore pomegranates upon the hem of his robe (Exod 28:33). Luz notes a connection with Abraham's sacrifice and this is apparent by the instruction to the disciples to "sit here," the instruction given to Abraham's servants.⁷⁹

Jesus' betrayal εἰς χεῖρας ἁμαρτωλῶν, "into the hands of sinners" (26:45) was recorded in Mark as well as Matthew. By identifying the high priest's delegation as sinners, Matthew is leaving little doubt as to what the reader should make of the adversaries. Matthew's Jesus drew the attention of the arresting party to the charade of the whole incident; they could have arrested him peaceably while he taught in the temple courts—the armed posse was not necessary (26:55). But for Matthew, once again, this took place specifically to fulfill the Writings (26:56).⁸⁰

## The Final Conflict: The Exercise of Priestly Authority

A central feature of this reading is that Jesus was presented as a Messiah priest in Matthew's gospel, and that his mission included the displacement of the existing Aaronic/Levitical system of mediation. It is against this paradigm that the confrontation between Jesus and Caiaphas is central to understanding Matthew's story as the conclusion of the Hebrew metanarrative.

78. "No one is to be in the Tent of Meeting from the time Aaron goes in to make atonement in the Most Holy Place until he comes out, having made atonement for himself, his household and the whole community of Israel" (Lev 16:17).

79. Luz, *Matthew 21–28*, 395.

80. This whole episode bears echoes of previous significant Hebrew stories. The temptation in the garden and the entrance of evil particularly come to mind. Jesus, however, endured the evil presence and obeyed God. There is also a reminder of the unthinkable test of Abraham with Isaac and the angelic intervention; in this instance, the angels would not intervene, and Jesus would be offered at the behest of his Father.

Though there are no linguistic connections or specific biblical reflections back to the beginning of the Hebrew/human narrative, there is no other passage of Scripture that illustrates so well the proto-embryonic and final conflict of Genesis—"I will put enmity between you and the woman, and between your offspring and hers; he will crush your head, and you will strike his heel" (Gen 3:15).[81]

Jesus' ministry began with the healing of the leper and the instruction to go and be examined by the priest. From that time Caiaphas was aware that there was another priest operating within his jurisdiction. Jesus went on to heal all manner of uncleanness from the Israelites, including bleeding, demon possession and death. Jesus was also prepared to forgive sin, the ultimate priestly prerogative. Jesus was confronted throughout the narrative by roving agents, and it is clear that his life was in danger as a consequence of his ministry (12:14). His destiny with Jerusalem was the climax of the narrative, for it was here that his enemy would condemn him (16:21; 20:18). The ultimate operative against Jesus was Satan, as depicted in the testing account of chapter 4, but now, Jesus would be confronted by his ultimate accuser—Caiaphas.

Matthew's depiction of Israel's highest court in the words "[They] were looking for false evidence against Jesus so that they could put him to death" was as bold an assertion as any found in the whole narrative.[82] The elders and priests, under Caiaphas, had resolved to hear false testimony[83] and to murder Jesus.[84] Their inability to find any plausible testimony, though many false witnesses came forward,[85] forced Caiaphas to take the initiative in the

---

81. There is no doubt that Caiaphas was hostile to Christ; whether Matthew intended Caiaphas, however, to be the representative of God's adversary is based on the flow of the narrative. The book of Revelation, interestingly, describes the adversary of God adorned in garments that strongly resemble the garments of the high priest (Exod 28:6–21; Rev 17:3–6).

82. "According to *m. Sanh.* 4.1 capital trials may not be conducted at night, and they may be conducted only on two consecutive days. Furthermore, no sentences may be passed on the evening before a Sabbath or a festival. Such trials must be opened with the reasons of acquittal. According to m. Sanh. 4.2, in capital trials the voting always begins with the youngest member of the Sanhedrin so that the older members do not influence the younger ones. Thus the voting never begins with the high priest" (Luz, *Matthew 21–28*, 444–45).

83. By describing the witnesses that the Sanhedrin were looking for as "false" or "contrived," Matthew has made it clear that the Sanhedrin knew that there was no legitimate testimony against Jesus, and that he was innocent.

84. No doubt this tribunal was aware of the law: "Do not spread false reports. Do not help a wicked man by being a malicious witness" (Exod 23:1).

85. In Mark, the false witnesses were not actively recruited, as they were in Matthew. Bond, *Caiaphas*, 122.

proceedings over which he was a judge. Having found two witnesses[86] who agreed upon what Jesus had said,[87] Caiaphas challenged Jesus to respond to the charge, but he remained silent.[88] This frustration forced Caiaphas to charge Jesus under oath to answer.[89] Jesus was confronted with a direct question concerning his identity.[90] Jesus' confirmation that he was the Christ, and consequently the Son of God, was developed further by reference to his Son of Man identity and the judgment motif connected with it from Daniel 7.

At this climactic juncture in Matthew's narrative, the perennial question is answered: "By what authority are you doing these things?" Up until now Jesus has not responded; however, with this composite reference to Psalm 110 and Daniel 7,[91] Matthew's Jesus announced that his authority had come from God, and that he had authority to judge in heaven and earth. By so doing, Matthew was able to fully inform the enigmatic self-designation of Jesus; according to Matthew, the Son of Man (Jesus) is the Danielic apocalyptic judge who has permanent authority.[92] Matthew's Caiaphas had understood the implications of the statement, for according to Daniel's prophecy the Son of Man had the exclusive authority of God over

---

86. The testimony that Jesus had said he would destroy the temple was not presented as false evidence in Matthew, but it was in Mark. This strongly suggests that the charge is true. Jesus' words, "I am able to destroy" was a statement that he had authority to judge the temple, rather than a threat to destroy it. Ibid., 125.

87. The testimony was that Jesus had spoken against the temple. Consider Jer 26:11: "Then the priests and the prophets said to the officials and all the people, 'This man should be sentenced to death because he has prophesied against this city. You have heard it with your own ears!'" (Sloyan, *Jesus on Trial*, 60).

88. This was intended to make the Suffering Servant connection again—"and as a sheep before her shearers is silent, so he did not open his mouth" (Isa 53:7). France, *Matthew*, 1024.

89. The Law required testimony of any witness who was charged under oath—"If a person sins because he does not speak up when he hears a public charge to testify regarding something he has seen or learned about, he will be held responsible" (Lev 5:1).

90. David Catchpole, in an examination of Jesus' response in Aramaic, concluded that Jesus had affirmatively, though reluctantly, answered the question. Catchpole, "The Answer."

91. France, *Matthew*, 1027.

92. "The Son of Man becomes the cosmic judge of the world whom Caiaphas will see at the last judgment" (Bird, "The Crucifixion of Jesus," 27).

all things, even over Caiaphas and his temple.[93] Matthew's Jesus, therefore, had claimed to be the judge of Caiaphas.[94]

Caiaphas' response to Jesus' declaration was to tear his garment,[95] and declare that witnesses were not needed to prove the blasphemy of the accused. Caiaphas' response did not allow for the possibility that Jesus was truly the one he claimed to be. It was his responsibility to prove that Jesus was not the Messiah, something that he was unwilling to do, according to Matthew's narrative. The immediate and unanimous verdict, that Jesus was "worthy of death," was followed by what would appear to be an uncharacteristically brutal attack upon Jesus by the otherwise genteel and reasonable assembly (26:67).[96] In this way, Matthew depicted the injustice of Caiaphas as one who presided over the abusive treatment and murder of Israel's true judge.[97] The council was not presented as thoughtful and moderate, but as intemperate and violent; these were the shepherds that God would replace.

## Judas and His Role in the Priestly Indictment

Following the trial, the backsliding of Peter was given some attention before Matthew developed the story of Judas into his narrative. Of all the Gospels, Matthew is the one that portrays Judas most sympathetically.[98] He was still cast as being under perdition (26:24), but his deep remorse and the absence

---

93. It is in this context that Matthew intended his readers to understand the last commission, which makes explicit his authority in both dimensions of existence (28:18).

94. Karl Kuhn, in a recent examination of the Aramaic Apocalypse of Daniel, concluded that it was likely that the "early church's conceptualisation of Jesus' divine sonship developed in dialogue with Jewish apocalyptic traditions announcing a transcendent, eschatological redeemer that go back at least to Daniel 7" (Kuhn, "The 'One like a Son of Man,'" 42). Maurice Casey has also made a case for the reliability and stability of Aramaic sources that were relied upon by the early church in the first century. Casey, "Aramaic Idiom."

95. This was an action expressly forbidden by law (Lev 21:10), and the Law made provision for the priestly ephod to be tear-resistant (Exod 28:32; 39:23). The tearing of the garment, which was of identical fabric to the temple curtain, may have been a prelude to God's termination of the Covenant when the curtain was torn at Jesus' death. Like the garment, it was torn from top to bottom.

96. Although Evans makes a strong case that brutal conduct was a feature of the priestly caste. Evans, "Jesus' Action in the Temple."

97. As they did not understand "I desire mercy, not sacrifice," they had condemned the innocent (12:7).

98. ". . . the figure of Judas seems to emerge more humanly in Matthew's Gospel than it does in Mark and Luke. This is partly due to Matthew's insistence on the guilt of the chief priests and elders" (Conard, "The Fate of Judas," 165).

## SUBPOENA, TRIAL, EXECUTION, AND VINDICATION 267

of direct satanic involvement in his actions is noteworthy. Most importantly, Matthew uniquely made direct reference to Zechariah 11 in connection with Judas and his pivotal role in the drama; it is this prophetic fulfillment that is most revealing about the author's intentionality.

Firstly, some reflection on an earlier portion, left untreated, of this passion narrative is needed. Judas' agreement with the chief priests to surrender Jesus was accompanied by the request for funds. The question was "how much are you willing to give?" (26:15). The priests counted out thirty pieces of silver, the price of an accidental death of a slave (Exod 21:32). Of interest here is the source of this reference: in Zechariah 11 YHWH commanded that the thirty pieces of silver be cast to the "potter," and with some sarcasm, they are described as "the handsome price at which they priced me" (Zech 11:13). Matthew's assimilation of the Zechariah reference suggests that Judas cast the coins into the temple at the behest of YHWH, and that they were given to betray YHWH, who, in Matthew's narrative, was Jesus.

In consideration, then, of chapter 27, Judas is depicted as one who is stricken with remorse at the knowledge of Jesus' condemnation. He acts to fulfill the prophecy, which is so obvious that Matthew deems it unnecessary to attach his formulaic "in order to fulfill . . ." First Judas sought to return the money, and seemingly recanted his testimony; he informed the priests that he had betrayed "innocent blood" (27:4).[99] The priests and elders understood the implication of this and told Judas that it was his responsibility—so he threw the coins into the temple (just as it had been written).[100]

The chief priests collected the coins and agreed the money was tainted by blood, and therefore could not be put in the treasury. The funds, however, were reportedly used to purchase a burial field for foreigners (27:7).[101] The rationale behind this transaction was that blood defiled the land; land

---

99. Judas recanted his testimony and declared that Jesus was innocent and this was met by indifference. "Matthew's chief priests slip into even deeper depravity" (Bond, *Caiaphas*, 122).

100. Early Christian tradition presented Judas's demise as being parallel to the demise of the "wicked priest" in Qumran writings. Rick van de Water writes: "Both the wicked priest and Judas, guilty of shedding innocent blood, are judged by the *lex talionis*, receiving in like kind for their evil deeds [1QpHab 9:1; 12:2–3; Acts 18–19]" (Van de Water, "The Punishment of the Wicked Priest," 417).

101. This may have an interesting twist. Akeldama has been recently excavated to expose that it was not the burial place of foreigners or paupers, but of the Jerusalem establishment. Graves of Herod, Annas and Caiaphas were found there. Akeldama also occupied a portion of the area known as Gehenna. Should this have been publicly known when Matthew was written, it would lend extraordinary currency to texts that referred to Gehenna as the place assigned for hypocrites (24:51). Ritmeyer and Ritmeyer, "Akeldama: Potter's Field." and Avni and Greenhut, "Akeldama: Resting Place." See also, Vanderkam, *From Joshua to Caiaphas*, 424.

purchased by the "blood money" was defiled (under a curse) and therefore only suitable for the "unclean" foreigners.

Moss has observed the similarities between 2 Chronicles 24 and Jeremiah 26.[102] Chronicles recorded the death of the priest Zechariah (to whom Matthew attributes righteous blood—23:35) and its apparent connection with the invasion of Judah and Jerusalem by the Aramean army. Jeremiah advised Jerusalem: "Be assured, however, that if you put me to death, you will bring the guilt of innocent blood on yourselves and on this city and those who live in it . . ." (Jer 26:15).

This theme of innocent blood, which is a Matthean exclusive, is extremely pertinent to the Hebraic sensibilities of Matthew's audience, and Catherine Hamilton has insightfully developed this notion in an article entitled "'His blood be upon us': Innocent blood and the death of Jesus in Matthew."[103] Hamilton makes the point that Matthew tied Jesus' death to the death of Abel and Zechariah.[104] Both Abel and Zechariah were acceptable priests who were slaughtered by unrighteous "priests." Jesus as a functioning priest in Israel will attract the same fate, for he provokes the ire of the ineffectual priests.[105] The blood of the innocent pollutes the land, a concept that is central to understanding Judaism.[106] The point here is that innocent blood cannot be expiated but by the blood of the one who shed it (Num 35:33). Matthew had presented Caiaphas as the responsible agent in the slaughter of Jesus; therefore it was imperative that Caiaphas, and his succession, be "cut off." Whatever course of action was available to Israel, it would either have its priestly line terminated, or the city, which had been polluted by the blood money, would have to be destroyed. Hamilton notes:

> Unexpiated blood renders the land barren; indeed, Jacob Milgrom states, "the land becomes polluted with the consequence that neither God nor Israel can abide there"; the land, defiled with blood, will eventually vomit out the inhabitants (Lev

102. Moss, *The Zechariah Tradition*, 121.

103. Hamilton, "'His blood be upon us.'"

104. Matthew mentions Zechariah, son of Berekiah (the prophet), but describes the death of Zechariah, son of Jehoiada (the priest). Moss argues on balance, that Matthew appears to be merging at least two Zechariahs into a composite character for theological reasons. Moss, *The Zechariah Tradition*, 123. The melding of prophets (as when Jeremiah is referred to while quoting Zechariah) and Scripture (as in "He shall be called a Nazarene") is a difficulty to modern interpreters, but clearly not a problem for Matthew's audience. These served to draw several threads of Scripture together in the minds of Matthew's readers.

105. Twice in the narrative is Jesus noted as innocent/righteous (27:4, 19).

106. The cities of refuge (Num 35:6–34) were established to avoid the possibility of innocent blood being shed as the result of an accident.

18:25–28). Bloodshed thus has a corporate effect: the blood of the innocent shed by anyone within Israel brings blood down on the whole people's head.[107]

In an article that preceded Hamilton's, David Moffitt had observed the textual dependence of Matthew upon Lamentations.[108] Moffitt made note of the textual similarity between Matt 27:39 and Lam 2:15, which was used to support his claim that allusions to Lamentations can be found within Matthew's passion narrative. He observed that the shedding of righteous blood, which was integral to Matthew's story (2:16–18), was the result of the crimes of the religious leadership, resulting in the destruction of city and temple in 586 BC.[109] Lamentations reads:

> The kings of the earth did not believe, nor did any of the world's people, that enemies and foes could enter the gates of Jerusalem. But it happened because of the sins of her prophets and the iniquities of her priests, who shed within her the blood of the righteous (Lam 4:12–13).

Moffitt's observation concerning the Lamentations connection and its explanatory power for the destruction of Jerusalem may be another piece necessary to understand the plot of Matthew. Jesus' death, according to this paradigm, should be understood as an act of judgment upon the city, its temple and its priesthood, rather than just a salvific event. Moffitt's paper went some way to proving this:

> . . . Matthew explicitly draws on Lamentations in his account of the events leading up to the crucifixion in order to portray Jesus' death as the primary act of righteous bloodshed by the hands of religious authorities in Jerusalem that results in the destruction of Jerusalem and the temple.[110]

There can be no doubt that Matthew had a particular interest in the theme of righteous blood spilt; what had not, however, been noted by Hamilton or Moffitt was the particular bloodguilt of Caiaphas, the presiding high priest.[111] He had secured the agreement of "all the chief priests and elders of the people," who in turn coerced the people to share in their bloodguilt

107. Hamilton, "'His blood be upon us,'" 92.
108. Moffitt, "Righteous Bloodshed."
109. Ibid., 306.
110. Ibid., 300.
111. It is possible that Matthew had been influenced by the Qumran commentary on Habakkuk, which anticipates the destruction of the wicked priest (high priest) by divine retribution. Van de Water, "The Punishment of the Wicked Priest," 395.

(27:25).[112] This sequence should leave us with no doubt as to Matthew's programmatic indictment agenda. This is "just cause" for the destruction of Jerusalem and the termination of mediation under the Mosaic covenant.[113] Hamilton acknowledges both the indictment and the salvific agenda of Matthew:

> The temple's desolation coincides with the tombs opening and the dry bones of Israel walking again (27:52). Destruction and re-creation come together in Matthew's vision and in the paradigm of innocent blood. Neither one stands alone. Judgment and forgiveness coincide. Thus far, Matthew's vision is thoroughly Jewish. Matthew's theodicy is the theodicy of the prophets and the rabbis, who see in the city's devastation the expiation of a defiled land and the final mercy of God. What is new is the claim that the history of the land and the covenant people, the history both of bloodshed and pollution and of sacrifice and purification, comes to its climax and end in Jesus. It is a claim made in Jesus' words about his blood at the Last Supper: "this is my blood of the covenant, poured out for many for the forgiveness of sins" (26:28). As the covenant people take defilement upon themselves, the covenant is made again in the blood of Jesus. As the temple is destroyed, the temple cult is fulfilled in Jesus, in the blood poured out for many for the forgiveness of sins. The city is razed, but it is the holy city in which the risen ones will walk. Jesus' blood is poured out not only for the termination of the covenant people and the temple but also for its restoration.[114]

The motif of covenant termination through the death of Jesus may also be supported from the texts that Matthew had so heavily quoted in this passage. The Zechariah context to the thirty coins and their return to the temple are bracketed between the declarations of covenant termination:

> Then I took my staff called Favor and broke it, revoking the covenant I had made with all the nations [peoples].[115] It was

---

112. Some have tried to argue that this cry of the people was to enact the forgiveness of God in keeping with later christological understanding. But this seems untenable. Cargal, "'His blood be upon us.'"

113. "Josephus, who asserts that the people have polluted the temple even with the blood of their fellows (*B.J* 5.9.4 §381, cf. §402; and 4.2.12 §§201–2), asserts that the divinity has abandoned their holy places and stands now with the Romans (*B.J.* 5.9.4 §412)" (Hamilton, "'His blood be upon us,'" 100).

114. Ibid., 100.

115. God had no covenant with the nations (Gentiles). His covenant was with Israel and Judah.

revoked on that day, and so the afflicted of the flock who were watching me knew it was the word of the LORD. I told them, "If you think it best, give me my pay; but if not, keep it." So they paid me thirty pieces of silver. And the LORD said to me, "Throw it to the potter"—the handsome price at which they priced me! So I took the thirty pieces of silver and threw them into the house of the LORD to the potter. Then I broke my second staff called Union, breaking the brotherhood between Judah and Israel (Zech 11:10-14).[116]

It seems, then, that the whole episode of the coins and Judas' participation was intended to have some reference to the context found in the prophetic writings. It would appear from the passage that the covenant was revoked "on that day" (Zech 11:11), which was the day that YHWH was "purchased" and the coins were returned to the potter. In Matthew's narrative, Jesus' death occurred on the day that Judas returned the coins. This provides further evidence of Matthew's intention to show the death of Jesus as the termination of Israel's exclusive covenant.

## The Vindication of Pilate

In all the Gospels Pilate was portrayed as unwilling to crucify Jesus, only proceeding with the execution against his will. Matthew, however, included in his presentation the dream of Pilate's wife (27:19), who was convinced of the innocence of Jesus. Once again Matthew had Gentiles receiving revelation concerning Jesus, the previous being the Magi (2:12). The priests, on the other hand, were neither warned of the impending calamity nor prevented from participating. Pilate's insistence that he had no bloodguilt as a consequence of the handing over of Jesus is unique to Matthew. The cleansing of his hands evoked the legal requirement of cleansing when an Israelite encountered a dead body (Deut 21:1-9). Whether this established the innocence of Pilate or not is inconsequential; Matthew intended his readers to understand that Israel had accepted full responsibility, and in so doing, had relieved both Rome and its representative of the heinous bloodguilt.[117]

---

116. "This one he called 'Pleasant.' It referred to Yahweh's covenant with the nations that they would allow his people to go free. The other staff was called 'Union,' referring to the reunion of the northern and southern tribes of Israel. These were to be the objectives of the new David according to Ezek 37:16-28. But whereas Ezekiel saw the staffs as indicators of saving events, the prophet in Zech 11 sees them as symbols of doom and judgment" (Smith, *Micah-Malachi*, 270).

117. "All the people answered 'Let his blood be on us, and on our children'" (27:25).

Therefore, a case can be made that Matthew was only interested in the bloodguilt being attributed to Jerusalem, and not to Rome.[118]

## The Termination of the Covenant

This reading has proposed that Jesus' death was the moment when YHWH's exclusive covenant with the nation of Israel was terminated in Matthew.[119] Matthew's account of Jesus' death contains unique material, which is pertinent to this paradigm. But there is also common material, which also needs to be considered as part of the termination motif.

In this passage all the Psalm 22 images are present, and, like Mark's account, all the Israelites present hurled taunts at Jesus (27:39). The chief priests are also present (27:41), implicating them in the crime of the evil men who hurled insults at the "righteous one" of Psalm 22.[120] The Synoptics also report the three hours of darkness from midday to mid-afternoon (27:45). The meaning of the darkness has attracted a great deal of conjecture. Darkness as a motif for judgment is ubiquitous in Hebrew literature. Darkness was the ninth plague on Egypt before the slaughter of the firstborn. It was also present when God communicated to Abraham the assurance of the covenant (Gen 15:12).[121] It is not necessary to appeal to only one precedent in the Hebrew narrative for an understanding of this event; any or all may be valid in understanding its theological import. However, this section will canvass three other possibilities.

To develop the hypothesis that Jesus' act on the cross was a priestly act of "self-sacrifice" as Christian reflection was inclined to suggest,[122] then the darkness could be symbolic of the cloud that Aaron was required to create

---

118. Helen Bond sees a much less benign role for Pilate in Matthew. She believed that Pilate manipulated the crowd to achieve the outcome in the Gospel. Bond, *Pontius Pilate in History*, 136. This is a peculiar interpretation in light of his efforts to be exonerated. Bond also failed to mention the acceptance of guilt by the crowd in the place of Pilate, which is a key to both Pilate's and Rome's exoneration in Matthew's account.

119. Bird notes from Mark's account: "The Day of the Lord imagery also implies that the kingdom is manifest. The sudden coming of darkness elicits images of Yahweh's wrath and judgment being poured out (Exod 10:21; Jer 15:9; Amos 8:9). The judgment encompasses humankind in general (v. 33) and Judaism in particular (v. 38). The tearing of the temple veil announces both the triumph of the eschatological king and the declaration of judgment upon an apostate institution" (Bird, "The Crucifixion of Jesus," 30).

120. Bond, *Caiaphas*, 123.

121. Greg Forbes gives the "darkness" incident in the Synoptics a comprehensive and balanced treatment. Forbes, "Darkness Over All the Land."

122. Rom 3:25; Heb 9:25.

and enter on the Day of Atonement, and also the cloud that the Son of Man passed through when approaching the Ancient of Days (Dan 7:13). As such, the darkness may have been a veiling of the high priestly act of Jesus.

Another possibility is the apocalyptic vision attached to the Day of the LORD in Amos:

> Woe to you who long for the day of the LORD. Why do you long for the day of the LORD? That day will be darkness, not light.
>
> It will be as though a man fled from a lion only to meet a bear, as though he entered his house and rested his hand on the wall only to have a snake bite him. Will not the day of the LORD be darkness, not light—pitch-dark, without a ray of brightness?
>
> I hate, I despise your religious feasts; I cannot stand your assemblies. Even though you bring me burnt offerings and grain offerings, I will not accept them. Though you bring choice fellowship offerings, I will have no regard for them (Amos 5:18–22).

Although the prophecy had an immediate context with the deportation of the Northern Kingdom, it may have been used by Matthew to depict judgement in Israel, and not the death of Jesus alone. Amos was even more explicit concerning the darkness on the Day of the Lord, "I will make the sun go down at noon and darken the earth in broad daylight" (Amos 8:9). The darkness in the Synoptics' crucifixion narratives would recall the dread attached to the day when God would visit his people.[123] Further, this day would be as an ultimate loss: "I will make that time like mourning for an only son and the end of it like a bitter day" (Amos 8:10).[124]

The last possibility to canvas is the curse that was invoked by the death of Jesus. We are able to see how his death recalled the ancient prophecy that "cursed is anyone who is hung on a tree" (Deut 21:23).[125] This "cursed state" was also anticipated in the demise of the Suffering Servant (Isa 53), the image of whom Matthew had already invoked in the ministry of Jesus (8:17). The Servant was considered stricken by YHWH, according to the prophecy (Isa 53:4). The possible connection between the manner in which Jesus died and the darkness is found in its Deuteronomic context:

> If a man guilty of a capital offense is put to death and his body is hung on a tree, you must not leave his body on the tree overnight. Be sure to bury him that same day, because anyone who is hung on a tree is under God's curse. You must not desecrate

---

123. Darkness as a sign of YHWH's Day is also noted by other prophets—Ezek 32:7–8; Joel 2:31; Zeph 1:15.

124. Bolt, "Feeling the Cross," 5.

125. Paul made this specific connection regarding Jesus' death (Gal 3:11).

the land the LORD your God is giving you as an inheritance (Deut 21:22–23).

If the darkness constituted the end of the day and continued to Jesus' death, then the land was desecrated by another means—Jesus' body on the tree.[126] This possible connection would reinforce the motif of judgment falling upon Israel as a consequence of Jesus' death. In the same way that unexpiated bloodguilt brought judgment, the darkness may have functioned to reinforce the cursing of the land.

Pertinent to understanding Matthew's theology of Jesus' work are the events that happened at the moment Jesus died.[127] The rending of the temple curtain is common to all Synoptics,[128] but the splitting of rocks and the enigmatic resurrection are distinctly Matthean.[129]

The significance of the curtain,[130] though unexplained by Matthew, is plain—God had left the temple.[131] Hagner notes:

> A remarkable symbolism is involved, which none of the evangelists stops to explain. Clearly, however, the tearing of the veil is a type of apocalyptic sign pointing, on the one hand, to the wrath and judgment of God against the Jewish authorities (10:3) and,

---

126. It is not necessarily the case that darkness constituted the beginning of the night; however, the following reference to Peter's gospel suggests that this was considered to be a factor by some: "Now it was noonday, and darkness prevailed over all Judea, and they were afraid and distressed for fear that the sun had set while he was still alive. For it is written for them that the sun should not set upon one put to death" (Gospel of Peter in Throckmorton, *Gospel Parallels*, 183).

127. Luke's account had the rending of the curtain precede Jesus' death. Dennis Sylva considers that this was a sign of Jesus' discontinued fellowship with the God of the temple, rather than a portent for the temple's destruction. Sylva, "The Temple Curtain."

128. The tearing of the veil "serves as a vindication of Jesus' prophecy against the Temple." It foreshadowed the imminent destruction of the same. Chilton, *A Galilean Rabbi*, 80.

129. Matthew was much less subtle than Mark; the splitting rocks and the opening graves were intended to communicate instant and emphatic vindication. Ibid., 82. This too plays significantly into the courtroom drama; YHWH is making his views known concerning Jesus' innocence. There has been some attempt to demonstrate from wider Hebrew literature that the extraordinary events in AD 30 may have been historical. Plummer, "Something Awry in the Temple?"

130. The curtain was specifically the one that concealed the "Holy of Holies" (Gurtner, "LXX Syntax").

131. "After the death of Jesus, who is God's most important and final envoy in the long series of divine messengers to Israel, God initiates judgment, starting at the temple" (de Jonge, "Matthew 27:51," 72).

on the other, to the end of the temple, where God is no longer present.[132]

Hagner, however, fails to acknowledge that the termination of the temple cultus and the departure of God not only condemned the leadership, but the nation that was implicated in its crime.[133] Watts connects this event in Mark (also applicable to Matthew) with the baptism of Jesus who has come to judge the temple stewards who have aligned themselves with God's enemies:[134]

> ... the voice through the rent heavens at Jesus' baptism declared him to be God's messianic son sent to purge and restore the temple. Here at the climactic moment on the cross, Jesus again reveals his divine authority. His "great cry" rends the hostile temple's curtain thereby both demonstrating and affecting the reality that it, not he, is the one "forsaken."[135]

The earthquake (27:51), with its attendant consequence of opened graves (27:52), was followed by what Matthew believed was some kind of immediate resurrection event.[136] This study is not a test of Matthew's historical accuracy, but a theological reading of the incident. Why did Matthew include this unique material?

The splitting of rocks/earthquake was foreshadowed in the end-time events predicted by Matthew's Jesus earlier in the narrative (24:7). This, however, does not explain its significance, which may be found in Zechariah's prophecy. The prophet foretold the (post-exilic) destruction of Jerusalem and the siege by Gentiles. It would occur when YHWH's feet would touch the Mount of Olives and it would split in two (Zech 14:1–4). Though perhaps not directly connected, the seismic judgment that fell on the priestly house of Korah when it presumed to usurp Moses/Aaron has some resonance with the split ground of Matthew's account. It is remote, though

---

132. Hagner, *Matthew 14–28*, 849.

133. Deirdre Good observed a pattern of hostility that resulted in withdrawal by Jesus throughout Matthew. This being the case, YHWH's departure could be attributed to the hostility of Israel to his Son. Good, "The Verb Anachōreō."

134. Watts, "The Lord's House," 317.

135. Ibid., 322.

136. There is an interesting variation on these events found in the Gospel of Peter: "Then the Jews and the elders and the priests, when they had perceived what great evil they had done to themselves, began to lament and to say, 'Woe for our sin; the judgement and the end of Jerusalem has drawn near'" (Throckmorton, *Gospel Parallels*, 250). So clearly there was a connection made between AD 70 and the death of Jesus, even if the source revealed a desire to show Jerusalem in contrition.

possible, that Matthew sought to recall the priestly face-off in Numbers 16 to suggest the vindication of Jesus.

It is impossible for Matthean students to understand why Matthew made exclusive mention of the enigmatic appearance of Israel's righteous departed (27:52); it is reasonable to concede, however, that there was a theological point to be made by it. It is logical, in view of Matthew's view of Jesus' life-giving efficacy (11:28), that these "ancients" were irresistibly raised by the impetus of the self-giving of the great Messiah. However, Matthew may have an indictment motif attached to this mysterious event, as he has demonstrated at other times in the narrative. An equally enigmatic reference to the resurrection of dry bones in Ezekiel may shed some light on this:

> Therefore prophesy and say to them: "This is what the Sovereign LORD says: O my people, I am going to open your graves and bring you up from them; I will bring you back to the land of Israel. Then you, my people, will know that I am the LORD, when I open your graves and bring you up from them . . ." (Ezek 37:12–13).[137]

The purpose of this resurrection, it would seem from the prophecy, was to bear witness to Israel that YHWH was at work and bringing eschatological fulfilment.[138] These "saints" entered the city and were witnessed by many, according to Matthew.[139] As Jerusalem has already been portrayed as the recalcitrant and hostile city, now under indictment, the saints could only function as witnesses to the legitimacy of Jesus' claims, in order to further implicate the already condemned leadership (27:54). It is in this light that the testimony of the guards (Gentiles), who witnessed Jesus' death, can be interpreted; they were convinced that Jesus had a divine connection—and yet Jerusalem remained unconvinced.[140]

---

137. Nolland, *Gospel of Matthew*, 1214. Harrington, *Matthew*, 403. France, *Matthew*, 1082.

138. There is also another connection to be made here: "The reference in Mt. 27.52 to the 'holy ones' is likely to be indebted to Zech 14:5, which may be echoed again in Mt. 27:53 ('entered into the holy city')" (Nolland, "The King as Shepherd," 133).

139. Not everyone accepts the "Holy City" to be Jerusalem. Kenneth Waters believes it could be an "apocalyptic, eschatological, heavenly complex" (Waters, "Matthew 27:52–53," 496).

140. Throughout Matthew's narrative, Gentiles have provided a foil against which to measure Israel's unwillingness to believe. From the Magi to Sodom, which would still exist had it witnessed the events attached to Jesus' ministry, Matthew had used non-Jews as models of reason and fair judgment. Israel, on the other hand, was presented as unconvincible and unwinnable.

The testimony of the Gentile witnesses is also critical to this climactic moment (27:54). Having witnessed the event of Jesus' death, they declared that Jesus had to be the Son of God. This, in Matthew's narrative, could only mean that Jesus was truly God's representative on earth.[141] The great question of the Gospel was now conclusively answered, and even the Gentiles could acknowledge it; Jesus truly was the man that represented heaven on earth, and, therefore, Jerusalem was wrong.

Before leaving Matthew's account of the death of Jesus and its relationship to God's covenant with Israel, it is noteworthy that Matthew did not include the prayer of Jesus for forgiveness for the perpetrators, which is peculiar to Luke (Luke 23:34). Matthew, like Mark, did not suggest ignorance on the part of the persecutors, or seek their absolution. This should further contribute to the proposition that Matthew intended the death of Jesus to be seen as Israel's apocalyptic moment, without denying its salvific implications for those who would be found in Jesus' house.

## The Attempt to Conceal the Evidence

Following the burial of Jesus, Matthew embarked on a unique direction in his narrative—he seemed intent to redress the false story that had been put out by Jerusalem, that the disciples had stolen the body. This was, however, not simply an apology for the resurrection, but a last and significant assessment of Jerusalem, who "will not be convinced even if someone rises from the dead" (Luke 16:31).[142] Jerusalem received the sign of Jonah, just as had been promised (12:39–40); yet it did not repent.

Matthew's indictment narrative is both obvious and subtle. Here the reader witnesses the chief priests and Pharisees going to meet with Pilate on the day after the day of preparation—the Sabbath (27:62).[143] This was a serious breach of their own purity conventions and further evidence of their lawlessness/hypocrisy. This may have been inserted to prepare the readers to understand what followed: the actions of the leaders were impure. Here they referred to Jesus as a deceiver, yet no charge of deceit had been laid against him, and they requested a guard to supervise the gravesite.

---

141. Kingsbury, "Composition and Christology," 583.

142. Matthew does not present Jerusalem as unbelieving, for there is nothing in the discourse where they question the validity of Jesus' miracles or his resurrection. It seems that they know that Jesus is God's Messiah, but like Satan, they refuse to acknowledge him.

143. Wenham, "The Resurrection Narratives," 49.

Matthew's concluding chapter commences with the women's arrival "after the Sabbath."[144] There they, along with the guard, were confronted with an earthquake and an angel of the Lord who proceeded to roll back the stone in the presence of the petrified guard. There the angel declared that Jesus was not present, having already risen. In this way, Matthew was able to demonstrate that the first witnesses to the extraordinary, though not completely unexpected events, included the Gentile guard who breached Sabbath for Caiaphas.[145]

This pericope was completed with the guards' report,[146] the Jerusalem deception and the bribe. Presumably, under Caiaphas, Jerusalem had put out its own dishonest version of events. It did not question the veracity of the resurrection report, according to Matthew, but simply entrenched itself further in its obstinate stand.[147]

## New Covenant, New Leaders, New People

Matthew's narrative is lengthy at times, but not at this critical conclusion. The fulfillment of the narrative, in this concluding declaration, is the declaration of both heavenly and earthly dominion (28:18). Jesus declared himself to be, in Matthew's narrative, the Son of Man of Daniel's vision.[148] His authority was therefore permanent and comprehensive; he had been given authority to judge the nations, including Israel.[149] As Jesus had been given this absolute authority, the reader is left to conclude that all other authority, particularly Jerusalem's, had now been revoked.

---

144. This must have been intended to contrast the righteous with the unrighteous according to Sabbath regulation.

145. This was followed by Jesus' appearing and the second instruction that the disciples meet him in Galilee (28:10). Jesus, according to Matthew, did not return to Jerusalem after the resurrection but left it.

146. Like the risen "holy ones" the guards "went into the city" where they reported the resurrection. Matthew was determined to establish the notion that Jerusalem was reliably informed of these events. Heil, "The Narrative Structure," 433.

147. It is reminiscent of the prophecy, "the rulers gather together against the LORD and against his Anointed One" (Ps 2:2). Unlike Judas, Jerusalem was incapable of showing remorse, even after it was revealed that they had betrayed innocent blood.

148. Matthew 28:18–20 conforms "to the pattern of a ritual of ancient enthronement" (Meier, "Two Disputed Questions," 417).

149. The final pericope of Matthew has been heavily disputed, particularly the trinitarian formula found within it. Kingsbury, however, asserts that the vocabulary and style of the passage is consistent with the rest of the Gospel. Kingsbury, "Composition and Christology," 379.

Having this authority, Matthew's Jesus commanded the new order. This included the commissioning of the disciples to teach the "Torah" of Jesus with the divine accompaniment to the ends of the earth.[150] The disciples' commissioning as the new shepherds, appointed by YHWH, could only support the proposition that Aaron/Levi's tenure as stewards of God's project was hitherto concluded (Ezek 34).[151] The disciples' message was the new covenant declared in advance through Jeremiah 31, which would be characterized by permanence, acceptance and forgiveness. Their field was the world; they would not be made unclean by association with Gentiles, for they had the assurance of Jesus' accompaniment. YHWH would no longer be found exclusively in Jerusalem, for the *missio Dei* would be both universal and international.

It was appropriate, then, for Matthew to complete the picture of judgment against the "old order" by establishing the parameters of the new in his narrative; just as the removal of Saul could not be complete without David's ascension to the throne, so the Jerusalem priestly tenure could not be fully terminated without the appointment of the new shepherds, and the disclosure of their perpetual commission.

---

150. The disciples were commissioned on the mountain where they were told to meet Jesus. Moses was also told to meet YHWH at the mountain Horeb (Exod 3:12). The mountain is significant for inauguration of covenant and the commissioning of the Twelve. Hanson, "Transformed on the Mountain."

151. An alternate possibility was that Matthew followed the Moses/Joshua paradigm; on the mountain Joshua was commissioned to go and slay the nations in Canaan. Jesus' disciples, by contrast, were sent to conquer the Gentiles in the whole world. Sparks, "Gospel as Conquest."

# 9

# Conclusion

THE INTENTION OF THIS book was to read Matthew's gospel through a particular lens, in order to ascertain whether there is sufficient evidence to propose that Matthew sought to advance and complete the Hebrew narrative by recording the Jesus data against the backdrop of the Law and the Prophets. It was proposed that Matthew perceived the importance of the prophetic anticipation of YHWH's arrival to his temple as the "Day of the Lord," and may have recognized the need to weave together many of the loose threads of the metanarrative, particularly those that pertained to the judgment of the Levitical community, which would involve the removal of its representative entitlement and the destruction of the temple which it administered. This, it has been argued, would need to be documented as a legal necessity, to complete and terminate a covenant that was both written and binding. Fulfillment of the Scripture would also need to be recorded in the form of Scripture, and for this reason, it is proposed that Matthew intentionally wrote what he believed to be Scripture. If this were Matthew's intention, he would need to have produced a polemical document that would demonstrate "just cause" for the termination of the Levitical constitution and its house/temple. That is what Matthew believed and that was the story he wrote. Otherwise, what purpose would a Jewish man have in compiling a document that suggested that the inviolable and permanent provisions of Torah, which insisted that Jerusalem would be God's earthly sanctuary (1 Kgs 9:3), and Aaron's offspring would always be its stewards (Exod 29:9), was now terminated? For Matthew, Jesus was YHWH, and he came to adversely judge the temple and its stewards, while, at the same time, choosing his treasured possession (Mal 3:16–18).

This reading has sought to examine the plotline of Matthew in order to ascertain whether Matthew had intended to write a document that was covenantal in its intention; that is, a document which intended to demonstrate

Israel's unwillingness to accept the peace treaty that YHWH sought to broker as the last expression of mercy within that covenant, leaving no alternative but to have the Mosaic administration terminated, with the necessity of imposing the penalties for failure on the temple, its stewards and the nation. These penalties were foreshadowed within the terms of the covenant (Deut 28:15–68). It is in this context that Jesus came to fulfill the Law and the Prophets (5:17).

Throughout this reading, it has been possible to observe the sustained conflict narrative, which is the center of Matthew's plotline. Matthew commenced by establishing Jesus' credibility by use of the genealogy, divine declaration, prophetic identification, connection with Israel's significant historical events, and personal determination to be YHWH's holy representative by refusing to capitulate to Satan. It is apparent from the beginning to the end of the narrative that Jesus was in danger from the leadership of Jerusalem (2:3; 26:4). And yet, it is also clear from the beginning to the end of Matthew that Jerusalem was in danger from Jesus, for he came to bring judgment to its community and temple (3:10; 23:38). Matthew did not have Jesus appear in Jerusalem until the end of the narrative, unlike other Gospels. By doing so it becomes evident within the narrative that Jerusalem could only mean death for Jesus (23:37). This pattern of conflict with Jerusalem was highlighted throughout the story by Jesus' own severe condemnatory words delivered as a consequence of the regular skirmishes with the priestly representatives wherever he ministered. This conflict intensified as Jesus made his way to the "holy City" where he would complete his divine task (16:21).

Jesus' gracious and miraculous actions contributed to the plotline to vindicate YHWH/Jesus, who was portrayed as doing everything possible to show mercy and win the allegiance of a recalcitrant nation. This, however, did not result in repentance from Jesus' opponents, but further intransigence and enmity. The portrayal of these institutional opponents, in their variegated yet monolithic hostility under the stewardship of Caiaphas, was consistent throughout Matthew, and there could be no doubt on the readers' part that this would end in a final eschatological conflict. It was through Jesus' death, then, as portrayed by Matthew, that YHWH terminated the Mosaic covenant, as symbolized by the tearing of the temple veil, and Caiaphas and Jerusalem had become tainted by the shedding of the ultimate "innocent blood" that would certainly result in the violent retribution of God (AD 70).

The parables within Matthew contribute to the hypothesis presented in this reading. The advancement of Isaiah's indictment as the rationale for Jesus' public teaching after the rejection of his mission proves to be a key turning point in the narrative. Other parables were clearly direct rebukes of Jerusalem's stewards, and, therefore, they were parables of indictment. Still other parables, which were mostly directed to the disciples, were intended to function as preparation for the task of the new community in the face of impending judgment. These parables certainly indicted the Jerusalem stewards also; however, they primarily functioned as warnings to the disciples who had to walk a different path to the stewards who were being deposed.

A key feature of this reading was to consider how Matthew used the Jesus tradition to inform his readers of his indictment intentions. We were able to observe that Matthew consistently drew the attention of his readers to the thoughts and actions of his opponents (2:3; 3:7; 9:3, 11, 34; 12:2; 10, 24, 33–39, 45; 15:1–9; 16:1–6, 21; etc.). This is particularly apparent in the post-resurrection narrative, where Matthew uniquely demonstrates the inconceivable recalcitrance of the Jerusalem leadership in its relationship to YHWH, even after it had been given reliable information about the resurrection of Jesus. They were aware that Jesus had prophesied the event (27:63), but nonetheless, they could not bring themselves to honor him. By doing this, Matthew had informed his readers that Jerusalem was intentionally opposed to YHWH's agenda, and not simply acting out of ignorance. Matthew was also prepared to label Jesus' opponents as evil, something that the other Synoptic writers were reluctant to do. Lastly, Matthew was prepared to unambiguously implicate Caiaphas by demonstrating his direct animosity to Jesus. This, along with the particular catalogue of Mosaic breaches by Caiaphas and his administration in Matthew's account, is a particularly provocative aspect to the Gospel. Caiaphas was the ruler of the kingdom that Jesus came to overthrow. In this way Matthew signaled the final encounter between the offspring of the woman and the offspring of the serpent. The opening of graves would provide evidence that Adam's death sentence had now been repealed for Jesus' new house.

A compelling argument can be made that Matthew is a type of prophetic indictment even from what appears, to the casual reader, to be the benign or "encouraging" texts within the narrative. If one accepts that New Testament writers did not simply "proof text" but intended their readers to import the context of the passage or verses cited, as many have now argued, these texts take on a different character. "Immanuel" (God with us), the fields that are "white for harvest," the offer of "rest" to the heavy laden, and the Isaiah verses used to confirm or clarify John's view of Messiah, when considered within their prophetic contexts, all conveyed an austere threat of accompanying punishment and even devastation. Reading these Matthean texts as signals which point to their contexts has been an integral part of this project, particularly as it applies to advancing the Day of YHWH narrative.

The ministry of Jesus has also been reassessed, to see whether his messianic role could be better understood as priestly, and so demonstrate the theology articulated by the writer of the Epistle to the Hebrews. Others have made compelling cases for the presentation of Jesus as Messiah priest in Mark and John,[1] so it is likely that in this most Hebrew of the Gospels, this theme/subtext would be apparent also. It does appear that the Messiah priest, anticipated by the Qumran community, reads easily within Matthew's narrative, and brings explanatory power to some significant Matthean conundrums. When Matthew's Jesus is considered to be a priest, Jesus' conflict narrative and his rivalry with Jerusalem becomes easier to comprehend. From this it is also possible to observe Matthew's use of building metaphors to identify the existence of the two competing communities. This allowed Matthew's gospel to be read as the story of two houses: one of these houses would survive the cataclysmic events of AD 70, while the other would become desolate. It is proposed that this two-house hypothesis has explanatory power within the Gospel, particularly as it relates to the Sermon on the Mount.

On the basis of this reading, Matthew was written to be a prophetic indictment designed to complement and advance the existing Hebrew narrative. It does seem plausible that Matthew may have intended his "historic" retelling of the Jesus story to be prophetic and authoritative in nature—an advancing of the Hebrew narrative to fit seamlessly with the existing story by projecting what the Prophets and the Law anticipated would take place when the theocracy of Israel would draw to a close. All the elements of a Hebrew theodicy are present, and more: the innocent "victim," the evil antagonists, the assembly of witnesses to testify, the courtroom scene, a corrupt judge, the execution, and the divine vindication, all point to a genre that Matthew's readers are familiar with from the Torah.[2] It is therefore proposed that there is indeed sufficient evidence to conclude that Matthew can be plausibly read as presenting a final prophetic judgment against Jerusalem and its priests, which, in turn, resulted in the termination of the Mosaic covenant. Matthew reads like a theodicy and may just be the conclusion to the great theodicy of the Hebrew nation and the human race.[3]

---

1. Fletcher-Louis, "Jesus as the High Priestly Messiah: Part 1." Fletcher-Louis, "Jesus as the High Priestly Messiah: Part 2." Heil, "Jesus as the Unique High Priest."

2. Examples of Hebrew theodicy where God is vindicated by the deliverance of his people include the stories of Joseph, Esther, Job and Daniel.

3. "And I will put enmity between you and the woman, and between your offspring and hers; he will crush your head, and you will strike his heel" (Gen 3:15).

# Bibliography

Abel, Ernest L. "Who Wrote Matthew?" *New Testament Studies* 17/2 (1971) 138–52.
Adler, William. "Exodus 6:23 and the High Priest from the Tribe of Judah." *Journal of Theological Studies* 48/1 (1997) 24–47.
Alexander, Joseph A. *Commentary on Isaiah*. Grand Rapids: Kregel, 1992.
Allen, Leslie C. *Ezekiel 20–48*. Word Bible Commentary 29. Dallas: Word, 2002.
Allison, Dale C., Jr. "The Structure of the Sermon on the Mount." *Journal of Biblical Literature* 106/3 (1987) 423–45.
———. *Studies in Matthew: Interpretation Past and Present*. Grand Rapids: Baker, 2005.
Anderson, A. A. *2 Samuel*. Word Biblical Commentary 11. Dallas: Word, 2002.
Anderson, Janice Capel. "Double and Triple Stories, the Implied Reader, and Redundancy in Matthew." *Semeia* 31 (1985) 71–89.
———. *Matthew's Narrative Web: Over, and Over, and Over Again*. Sheffield, UK: JSOT, 1994.
Argyle, A. W. "Evidence for the View that St. Luke Used St. Matthew's Gospel." *Journal of Biblical Literature* 83/4 (1964) 390–96.
Aune, David E. *The New Testament in Its Literary Environment*. Edited by Wayne A. Meeks. Library of Early Christianity. Philadelphia: Westminster, 1987.
Avni, Gideon, and Zvi Greenhut. "Akeldama: Resting Place of the Rich and Famous." *Biblical Archaeology Review* 20/6 (1994) 36–46.
Balabanski, Vicky. *Eschatology in the Making: Mark, Matthew and the Didache*. Edited by Richard Bauckham. Series for New Testament Studies (Monograph Series) 97. Cambridge: Cambridge University Press, 1997.
Bauckham, Richard. *The Gospel for all Christians: Rethinking the Gospel Audiences*. Edinburgh: T. & T. Clark, 1998.
———. *Jesus and the Eyewitnesses: The Gospels as Eyewitness Testimony*. Grand Rapids: Eerdmans, 2006.
———. "The Parable of the Royal Wedding Feast (Matthew 22:1–14) and the Parable of the Lame Man and the Blind Man (Apocryphon of Ezekiel)." *Journal of Biblical Literature* 115/3 (1996) 471–88.
Bauer, David R. "The Kingship of Jesus in the Matthean Infancy Narrative: A Literary Analysis." *Catholic Biblical Quarterly* 57/2 (1995) 306.

———. "The Major Characters of Matthew's Story: Their Function and Significance." *Interpretation* 46 (1992) 357–67.
Bautch, Richard J. "An Appraisal of Abraham's Role in Postexilic Covenants." *Catholic Biblical Quarterly* 71 (2009) 42–63.
Beasley-Murray, G. R. *Jesus and the Kingdom of God*. Grand Rapids: Eerdmans, 1986.
———. *John*. Word Bible Commentary 36. Dallas: Word, 2002.
Bird, Michael F. *Are You the One Who is to Come? The Historical Jesus and the Messianic Question*. Grand Rapids: Baker Academic, 2009.
———. "The Case of the Proselytizing Pharisees?—Matthew 23:15." *Journal for the Study of the Historical Jesus* 2/2 (2004) 117–37.
———. *Crossing Over Sea and Land: Jewish Missionary Activity in the Second Temple Period*. Peabody, MA: Hendrickson, 2010.
———. "The Crucifixion of Jesus as the Fulfillment of Mark 9:1." *Trinity Journal* 24/1 (2003) 23–36.
———. *Jesus and the Origins of the Gentile Mission*. Edited by Mark Goodacre. Library of New Testament Studies 331. London: T. & T. Clark, 2006.
———. "Jesus as Law-Breaker." In *Who Do My Opponents Say I Am?*, edited by Scot McKnight and Joseph B. Modica, 3–28. New York: T. & T. Clark, 2008.
———. "Who Comes from the East and the West? The Historical Jesus and Luke 13.28–29/Matt. 8.11–12." *New Testament Studies* 52/4 (2006) 441–57.
Black, Matthew. "The Use of Rhetorical Terminology in Papias on Mark and Matthew." *Journal for the Study of the New Testament* 37 (1989) 31–41.
Block, Daniel I. *The Book of Ezekiel: Chapters 25–48*. Edited by Robert L. Hubbard Jr. New International Commentary of the Old Testament. Grand Rapids: Eerdmans, 1998.
Bolt, Peter. *The Cross from a Distance: Atonement in Mark's Gospel*. Edited by D. A. Carson. New Studies in Biblical Theology. Downers Grove, IL: InterVarsity, 2004.
———. "Feeling the Cross: Mark's Message of Atonement." *Reformed Theological Review* 60/1 (2001) 1–17.
———. "Mark 13: An Apocalyptic Precursor to the Passion Narrative." *Reformed Theological Review* 54 (1995) 10–32.
Bond, Helen K. *Caiaphas: Friend of Rome and Judge of Jesus?* London: Westminster John Knox, 2004.
———. "Caiaphas: Reflections on a High Priest." *Expository Times* 113/6 (2002) 183–87.
———. *Pontius Pilate in History and Interpretation*. Society for New Testament Studies (Monograph Series) 100. Cambridge: Cambridge University Press, 1998.
Borgen, Peder. "In Accordance with the Scriptures." In *Early Christian Thought in Its Jewish Context*, edited by J. Barclay and J. Sweet, 193–206. Cambridge: Cambridge University Press, 1996.
Braun, Roddy L. *1 Chronicles*. Word Bible Commentary. Dallas: Word, 2002.
Brown, Schuyler. "The Matthean Apocalypse." *Journal for the Study of the New Testament* 4 (1979) 2–27.
Bruce, F. F. *Jesus and Christian Origins Outside the New Testament*. Grand Rapids: Eerdmans, 1974.
Brueggemann, Walter. *Isaiah 1–39*. Louisville: Westminster John Knox, 1998.
Byrne, Brendan. *A Costly Freedom: A Theological Reading of Mark's Gospel*. Collegeville, MN: Liturgical, 2008.

Callahan, Tim. "Who Really Killed Jesus?" *Skeptic* 11/1 (2004) 87–90.
Cargal, Timothy B. "'His blood be upon us and upon our children': A Matthean Double Entendre?" *New Testament Studies* 37 (1991) 101–12.
Carlston, Charles E. "Interpreting the Gospel of Matthew." *Interpretation* 29/1 (1975) 3–12.
Carson, D. A. "Christological Ambiguities in the Gospel of Matthew." In *Christ the Lord: Studies in Christology Presented to Donald Guthrie*, edited by Harold H. Rowden, 97–114. Leicester: InterVarsity, 1982.
———. "The Jewish Leaders in Matthew's Gospel: A Reappraisal." *Journal of the Evangelical Theological Society* 25/2 (1982) 161–74.
———. *When Jesus Confronts the World: An Exposition of Matthew 8–10*. Grand Rapids: Baker, 1987.
Carter, Warren. "The Crowds in Matthew's Gospel." *Catholic Biblical Quarterly* 55/1 (1993) 54.
———. "Evoking Isaiah: Matthean Soteriology and an Intertextual Reading of Isaiah 7–9 and Matthew 1:23 and 4:15–16." *Journal of Biblical Literature* 119/3 (2000) 503–20.
———. "Jesus' 'I have come' Statements in Matthew's Gospel." *Catholic Biblical Quarterly* 60/1 (1998) 44.
———. "Kernels and Narrative Blocks: The Structure of Matthew's Gospel." *Catholic Biblical Quarterly* 54/3 (1992) 463–81.
———. "Matthew's Gospel: An Anti-Imperial/Imperial Reading." *Currents in Theology and Mission* 34/6 (2007) 424–33.
———. "Some Contemporary Scholarship on the Sermon on the Mount." *Currents in Research: Biblical Studies* 4 (1996) 183.
Casey, Maurice. "Aramaic Idiom and the Son of Man Problem: A Response to Owen and Shepherd." *Journal for the Study of the New Testament* 25 (2002) 3–32.
———. "The Jackals and the Son of Man (Matt 8:20—Luke 9:58)." *Journal for the Study of the New Testament* 23 (1985) 3–22.
Catchpole, David R. "The Answer of Jesus to Caiaphas (Matt. xxvi.64)." *New Testament Studies* 17 (1971) 213–26.
Chae, Young S. *Jesus as the eschatological Davidic shepherd: studies in the Old Testament, Second Temple Judaism, and in the Gospel of Matthew*. Tübingen: Mohr Siebeck, 2006.
Chance, J. Bradley. "The Cursing of the Temple and the Tearing of the Veil in the Gospel of Mark." *Biblical Interpretation* 15/3 (2007) 268–91.
Chenoweth, Ben. "Identifying the Talents: Contextual clues for the interpretation of the parable of the talents (Matthew 25:14–30)." *Tyndale Bulletin* 56, no. 1 (2005) 61–72.
Childs, Brevard S. *Isaiah*. Edited by J. L. Mays et al. The Old Testament Library. Louisville: Westminster John Knox, 2001.
Chilton, Bruce D. *A Galilean Rabbi and His Bible: Jesus' Use of the Interpreted Scripture of His Time*. Wilmington, DE: Glazier, 1984.
Coleran, James E. "The Sons of God in Genesis 6:2." *Theological Studies* 2/4 (1941) 487–509.
Collins, Adela Yarbro. "The Charge of Blasphemy in Mark 14:64." *Journal for the Study of the New Testament* 26/4 (2004) 379–401.

Collins, John J. "Mowinckel's *He That Cometh* Revisited." *Studia Theologica* 61/1 (2007) 3–20.
Combrink, H. J. B. "The Structure of the Gospel of Matthew as Narrative." *Tyndale Bulletin* 34 (1983) 61–90.
Conard, Audrey. "The Fate of Judas: Matthew 27:3–10." *Toronto Journal of Theology* 7/2 (1991) 158–68.
Cotter, Wendy J. "The Parable of the Children in the Market-Place, Q (Lk) 7:31–35: An Examination of the Parable's Image and Significance." *Novum Testamentum* 29/4 (1987) 289–304.
Cousland, J. R. C. *The Crowds in the Gospel of Matthew*. Boston: Brill, 2002.
———. "The Feeding of the Four Thousand Gentiles in Matthew?" *Novum Testamentum* 41/1 (1999) 1.
Crossan, John Dominic. "Seed Parables of Jesus." *Journal of Biblical Literature* 92/2 (1973) 244–66.
Dahlberg, Bruce T. "The Typological Use of Jeremiah 1:4–19 in Matthew 16:13–23." *Journal of Biblical Literature* 94 (1975) 73–80.
Davies, W. D., and Dale C. Allison, Jr. *A Critical and Exegetical Commentary on the Gospel According to Saint Matthew*. Vol. 1, *Introduction and Commentary on Matthew I–VII*. International Critical Commentary. London: T. & T. Clark, 1988.
———. *A Critical and Exegetical Commentary on the Gospel According to Saint Matthew*. Vol. 2., *Commentary on Matthew VIII–XVIII*. International Critical Commentary. London: T. & T. Clark 1991.
———. *Matthew: A Shorter Commentary*. London: T. & T. Clark, 2004.
Davison, James E. "Anomia and the Question of an Antinomian Polemic in Matthew." *Journal of Biblical Literature* 104/4 (1985) 617–35.
de Jonge, M. "Matthew 27:51 in Early Christian Exegesis." *The Harvard Theological Review* 79/1–3 (1986) 67–79.
De Moor, Johannes C. "The Targumic Background of Mark 12:1–12: The Parable of the Wicked Tenants." *Journal for the Study of Judaism: In the Persian Hellenistic and Roman Period* 29 (1998) 63–80.
den Dulk, Matthijs. "Measuring the Temple of God: Revelation 11:1–2 and the Destruction of Jerusalem." *New Testament Studies* 54/3 (2008) 436–49.
Derrett, J. Duncan M. "Binding and Loosing (Matt 16:19, Matt 18:18, John 20:23)." *Journal of Biblical Literature* 102/1 (1983) 112–17.
Dillon, Richard J. "Ravens, Lilies, and the Kingdom of God (Matthew 6:25–33/Luke 12:22–31)." *Catholic Biblical Quarterly* 53/4 (1991) 605–27.
Dodd, C. H. *According to the Scriptures: The Sub-Structure of New Testament Theology*. London: Nisbet, 1952.
Draper, Jonathan A. "The Genesis and Narrative Thrust of the Paraenesis in the Sermon on the Mount." *Journal for the Study of the New Testament* 75 (1999) 25–48.
Drum, Walter. "Magi." In *The Catholic Encyclopedia*, vol. 9. New York: Robert Appleton, 1910. http://www.newadvent.org/cathen/09527a.htm.
Duling, Dennis C. "'Egalitarian Ideology, Leadership, and Factional Conflict within the Matthean Group." *Biblical Theology Bulletin* 27 (1997) 124–37.
Durham, John I. *Exodus*. Vol. 3 Word Biblical Commentary. Dallas: Word, 2002.
Ellingworth, Paul. *Commentary on Hebrews*. New International Greek Testament Commentary. Grand Rapids: Eerdmans, 1993.
Elliott, J. K. "The Anointing of Jesus." *The Expository Times* 85 (1973–74) 105–7.

Esler, Philip F. "The Incident of the Withered Fig Tree in Mark 11: A New Source and Redactional Explanation." *Journal for the Study of the New Testament* 28/1 (2005) 41–67.

Eusebius, and Christian Frederic Crusé. *Eusebius' Ecclesiastical History: Complete and Unabridged*. Peabody, MA: Hendrickson, 2006.

Evans, Craig A. "'The Book of Genesis of Jesus Christ': The Purpose of Matthew in Light of the Incipit." In *Biblical Interpretations in Early Christian Gospels*, edited by Thomas R. Hatina, 2:61–72. London: T. & T. Clark, 2008.

———. "Jesus' Action in the Temple: Cleansing or Portent of Destruction?" *Catholic Biblical Quarterly* 51/2 (1989) 237–70.

———. "Luke's Use of the Elijah/Elisha Narratives and the Ethic of Election." *Journal of Biblical Literature* 106/1 (1987) 75–83.

———. "'The two sons of oil': Early Evidence of Messianic Interpretation of Zechariah 4:14 in 4Q254 4 2." In *Provo International Conference on the Dead Sea Scrolls*, edited by Donald W. Parry and Eugene Ulrich, 566–75. Ithaca, NY: Snow Lion, 1999.

Faierstein, Morris M. "Why Do the Scribes Say that Elijah Must Come First?" *Journal of Biblical Literature* 100/1 (1981) 75–86.

Farnell, F. David. "The Synoptic Gospels in the Ancient Church: The Testimony to the Priority of Matthew's Gospel." *The Master's Seminary Journal* 10/1 (1999) 53–86.

Fee, Gordon D. "A Text-Critical Look at the Synoptic Problem." *Novum Testamentum* 22/1 (1980) 12–28.

Fitzmyer, Joseph A. *The Gospel According to Luke (I–IX)*. Edited by W. F. Albright and D. N. Freedman. The Anchor Bible 28. Garden City, NY: Doubleday, 1981.

Fleming, Daniel E. "The Biblical Tradition of Anointing Priests." *Journal of Biblical Literature* 117/3 (1998) 401–14.

Fletcher-Louis, Crispin H. T. "The High Priest as Divine Mediator in the Hebrew Bible: Dan 7:13 as a Test Case." *Society of Biblical Literature Seminar Papers* 36 (1997) 161–93.

———. "Jesus as the High Priestly Messiah: Part 1." *Journal for the Study of the Historical Jesus* 4/2 (2006) 155–75.

———. "Jesus as the High Priestly Messiah: Part 2." *Journal for the Study of the Historical Jesus* 5/1 (2007) 57–79.

Fockner, Sven. "Reopening the Discussion: Another Contextual Look at the Sons of God." *Journal for the Study of the Old Testament* 32/4 (2008) 435–56.

Forbes, Greg. "Darkness Over All the Land: Theological Imagery in the Crucifixion Scene." *Reformed Theological Review* 66/2 (2007) 83–96.

Foster, Paul. *Community, Law, and Mission in Matthew's Gospel*. Tübingen: Mohr Siebeck, 2004.

———. "Why did Matthew Get the Shema Wrong? A Study of Matthew 22:37." *Journal of Biblical Literature* 122/2 (2003) 309–33.

Foster, Robert. "Why on Earth Use 'Kingdom of Heaven'? Matthew's Terminology Revisited." *New Testament Studies* 48/4 (2002) 487–99.

France, R. T. *The Gospel of Matthew*. New International Commentary on the New Testament. Grand Rapids: Eerdmans, 2007.

———. "Matthew and Jerusalem." In *Built Upon the Rock*, edited by Daniel M. Gurtner and John Nolland, 108–27. Grand Rapids: Eerdmans, 2008.

———. "On Being Ready (Matthew 25:1–46)." In *The Challenge of Jesus' Parables*, edited by Richard N. Longenecker, 177–95. Grand Rapids: Eerdmans, 2000.

France, R. T., and John Nolland. "Reflections on the Writing of a Commentary on the Gospel of Matthew." In *Built Upon the Rock*, edited by Daniel M. Gurtner and John Nolland, 270–89. Grand Rapids: Eerdmans, 2008.

Friedrichsen, Timothy A. "A Note on και διχοτομησει αυτον . . . (Luke 12:46 and the Parallel in Matthew 24:51)." *Catholic Biblical Quarterly* 63/2 (2001) 258.

Gale, Aaron M. *Redefining Ancient Borders: The Jewish Scribal Framework of Matthew's Gospel*. New York: T. & T. Clark, 2005.

Garber, Zev. "The Jewish Jesus: A Partisan's Imagination." *Shofar: An Interdisciplinary Journal of Jewish Studies* 23/3 (2005) 137–43.

Gartner, Bertil. *The Temple and Community in Qumran and the New Testament*. Edited by Matthew Black. Society for New Testament Studies, Monograph Series 1. London: Cambridge University Press, 1965.

Gibbs, Jeffrey A. "Israel Standing with Israel: The Baptism of Jesus in Matthew's Gospel (Matt. 3:13–17)." *Catholic Biblical Quarterly* 64/3 (2002) 511–26.

Goldingay, John E. *Daniel*. Word Bible Commentary 30. Dallas: Word, 2002.

Good, Deirdre Joy. "The Verb Anachōreō in Matthew's Gospel." *Novum Testamentum* 32, no. 1 (1990) 1–12.

Goodacre, Mark. "Mark, Elijah, the Baptist and Matthew: The Success of the First Intertextual Reading of Mark." In *Biblical Interpretations in Early Gospels*, edited by Thomas R. Hatina, 2:73–84. London: T. & T. Clark, 2008.

Goulder, Michael. "Sections and Lections in Matthew." *Journal for the Study of the New Testament* 36 (1999) 77–94.

———. "Two Significant Minor Agreements (Mat. 4:13 Par.; Mat. 26:67–68 Par.)." *Novum Testamentum* 45/4 (2003) 365–73.

Grams, Rollin Gene. "Not 'Leaders' but 'Little Ones' in the Father's Kingdom: The Character of Discipleship in Matthew's Gospel." *Transformation* 21/2 (2004) 114–25.

Grassi, Joseph A. "Five Loaves of the High Priest: (Mt 12:1–8; Mk 2:23–28; Lk 6:1–5; 1 Sam 21:1–6)." *Novum Testamentum* 7/2 (1964) 119–22.

———. "Matthew as a Second Testament Deuteronomy." *Biblical Theology Bulletin* 19 (1989) 23–29.

Gurtner, Daniel M. "Lus' Syntax and the Identity of the NT Veil." *Novum Testamentum* 47/4 (2005) 344–53.

———. "Matthew's Theology of the Temple and the 'Parting of the Ways.'" In *Built Upon the Rock*, edited by Daniel M. Gurtner and John Nolland, 128–53. Grand Rapids: Eerdmans, 2008.

———. *The Torn Veil: Matthew's Exposition of the Death of Jesus*. Edited by John Court. Society for New Testament Studies Monograph Series 139. New York: Cambridge University Press, 2007.

Hagner, Donald A. *Matthew 1–13*. Edited by Bruce M. Metzger. Word Biblical Commentary 33A. Dallas: Word, 1993.

———. *Matthew 14–28*. Word Biblical Commentary 33B. Dallas: Word, 1995.

Ham, Clay Alan. *The Coming King and the Rejected Shepherd: Matthew's Reading of Zechariah's Messianic Hope*. Sheffield, UK: Sheffield Phoenix, 2005.

———. "Reading Zechariah and Matthew's Olivet Discourse." In *Biblical Interpretation in Early Gospels*, edited by Thomas R. Hatina, 2:85–97. London: T. & T. Clark, 2008.

Hamilton, Catherine Sider. "'His blood be upon us': Innocent Blood and the Death of Jesus in Matthew." *Catholic Biblical Quarterly* 70/1 (2008) 82–100.

Hannan, Margaret. *The Measure and Demands of the Sovereign Rule of God in the Gospel of Matthew*. Edited by Mark Goodacre. Library of Biblical Studies. New York: T. & T. Clark, 2006.

Hanson, Kenneth C. "Transformed on the Mountain: Ritual Analysis and the Gospel of Matthew." *Semeia* 67 (1994) 147–70.

Hare, Douglas R. A. "How Jewish is the Gospel of Matthew?" *Catholic Biblical Quarterly* 62 (2000) 264–77.

Harrington, Daniel J. "Problems and Opportunities in Matthew's Gospel." *Currents in Theology and Mission* 34/6 (2007) 417–23.

Harrington, Hannah K. *The Impurity Systems of Qumran and the Rabbis*. Edited by Pheme Perkins. SBL Dissertation 143. Atlanta: Scholars, 1993.

———. *The Purity Texts*. Companion to the Dead Sea Scrolls. London: T. & T. Clark, 2004.

Harrington, Daniel J. *The Gospel of Matthew*. Sacra Pagina. Collegeville, MN. Liturgical, 1991.

———. "Matthew and Paul." In *Matthew and His Christian Contemporaries*, edited by David C. Sim and Boris Repschinski, 11–28. London: T. & T. Clark, 2008.

Hartley, John E. *Leviticus*. Word Commentary 4. Dallas: Word, 2002.

Hasitschka, Martin. "Matthew and Hebrews." In *Matthew and His Christian Contemporaries*, edited by David C. Sim and Boris Repschinski, 87–103. London: T. & T. Clark, 2008.

Hauerwas, Stanley. *Matthew*. Brazos Theological Commentary on the Bible. Grand Rapids: Brazos, 2006.

Hays, Richard B. *The Conversion of the Imagination: Paul as Interpreter of Israel's Scriptures*. Grand Rapids: Eerdmans 2005.

Heil, John Paul. "Christ, the Termination of the Law." *Catholic Biblical Quarterly* 63 (2001) 484–98.

———. "Ezekiel 34 and the Narrative Strategy of the Shepherd and Sheep Metaphor in Matthew." *Catholic Biblical Quarterly* 55/4 (1993) 698.

———. "Jesus as the Unique High Priest in the Gospel of John." *Catholic Biblical Quarterly* 57/4 (1995) 729–45.

———. "The Narrative Structure of Matthew 27:55—28:20." *Journal of Biblical Literature* 110/3 (1991) 419–38

Hendriksen, William. *Matthew*. New Testament Commentary. Edinburgh: Banner of Truth, 1973.

Herzog, William R., II. *Parables as Subversive Speech*. Louisville: Westminster John Knox, 1994.

Hiers, Richard H. "'Binding' and 'Loosing': The Matthean Authorizations." *Journal of Biblical Literature* 104/2 (1985) 233–50.

Hill, David. "On the Use and Meaning of Hosea 6:6 in Matthew's Gospel." *New Testament Studies* 24/1 (1977) 107–19.

Himmelfarb, Martha. "Impurity and Sin in 4QD, IQS, and 4Q512." *Dead Sea Discoveries* 8/1 (2001) 9–37.

Holst, Robert. "The One Anointing of Jesus: Another Application of the Form Critical Method." *Journal of Biblical Literature* 95/3 (1976) 435–46.

Hood, Jason B. "The Coming King and the Rejected Shepherd: Matthew's Reading of Zechariah's Messianic Hope." *European Journal of Theology* 16/1 (2007) 58–59.

Hooker, Morna. *The Son of Man in Mark*. London: SPCK, 1967.

Horne, Edward H. "The Parable of the Tenants as Indictment." *Journal for the Study of the New Testament* 71 (1998) 111.

Howard, George. *The Gospel of Matthew according to a Primitive Hebrew Text*. Macon, GA: Mercer University Press, 1987.

———. "Stylistic Inversion and the Synoptic Tradition." *Journal of Biblical Literature* 97/3 (1978) 375–89.

———. "The Textual Nature of Shem-Tob's Hebrew Matthew." *Journal of Biblical Literature* 108/2 (1989) 239–57.

Hultgren, Arland J. *The Parables of Jesus: A Commentary*. Grand Rapids: Eerdmans, 2000.

Janzen, David. "The Meaning of Porneia in Matthew 5.32 and 19.9: An Approach from the Study of Ancient Near Eastern Culture." *Journal for the Study of the New Testament* 80 (2000) 66.

Jauhiainen, Marko. "Turban and Crown Lost and Regained: Ezekiel 21:29–32 and Zechariah's Zemah." *Journal of Biblical Literature* 127 (2008) 501–12.

Jerome and Gennadius. *Lives of Illustrious Men: Matthew, Surnamed Levi*. In Nicene and Ante-Nicene Fathers, ser. 2, vol. 3. http://st-takla.org/books/en/ecf/203/2030386.html.

Jewett, Robert. "Agitators and the Galatian Congregation." *New Testament Studies* 17/2 (1971) 198–212.

Jones, John Mark. "Subverting the Textuality of Davidic Messianism: Matthew's Presentation of the Genealogy and the Davidic Title." *Catholic Biblical Quarterly* 56/2 (1994) 256–72.

Kazen, Thomas. *Jesus and Purity Halakah*. Coniectanea Biblica: New Testament 38. Stockholm: Almqvist & Wiskell, 2002.

Kee, Min Suc. "The Heavenly Council and Its Type-Scene." *Journal for the Study of the Old Testament* 31/3 (2007) 259–73.

Keegan, Terence J. "Introductory Formulae for Matthean Discourses." *Catholic Biblical Quarterly* 44/3 (1982) 415–30.

Keener, Craig S. "'Brood of vipers' (Matthew 3.7; 12.34; 23.33)." *Journal for the Study of the New Testament* 28/1 (2005) 3–11.

———. *A Commentary on the Gospel of Matthew*. Grand Rapids: Eerdmans, 1999.

Keil, C. F., and F. Delitzsch. *The Pentateuch*. Vol. 1. Commentary on the Old Testament. Grand Rapids: Eerdmans, 1985.

Kelly, Balmer H. "Exposition of Matthew 4:1–11." *Interpretation* 29/1 (1975) 57–62.

Kingsbury, Jack Dean. "Composition and Christology of Matt 28:16–20." *Journal of Biblical Literature* 93/4 (1974) 573–84.

———. "The Developing Conflict between Jesus and the Jewish Leaders in Matthew's Gospel: A Literary-Critical Study." *Catholic Biblical Quarterly* 49/1 (1987) 57–73.

———. "Form and Message of Matthew." *Interpretation* 29 (1975) 13–23.

———. *Matthew as Story*. 2nd ed. Philadelphia: Fortress, 1988.

———. "The Plot of Matthew's Story." *Interpretation* 46 (1994) 347–56.

———. "Reflections on 'the Reader' of Matthew's Gospel." *New Testament Studies* 34/3 (1988) 442–60.

———. "The Rhetoric of Comprehension in the Gospel of Matthew." *New Testament Studies* 41/3 (1995) 358–77.

———. "Structure of Matthew's Gospel and His Concept of Salvation-History." *Catholic Biblical Quarterly* 35/4 (1973) 451–74.

———. "Title 'Kyrios' in Matthew's Gospel." *Journal of Biblical Literature* 94/2 (1975) 246–55.

———. "Title 'Son of David' in Matthew's Gospel." *Journal of Biblical Literature* 95/4 (1976) 591–602.

———. "Verb *akolouthein* ('to Follow') as an Index of Matthew's View of His Community." *Journal of Biblical Literature* 97/1 (1978) 56–73.

Kirk, J. R. Daniel. "Conceptualising Fulfilment in Matthew." *Tyndale Bulletin* 59/1 (2008) 77–98.

Klawans, Jonathan. *Impurity and Sin in Ancient Israel*. Oxford: Oxford University, 2000.

———. "Methodology and Ideology in the Study of Priestly Ritual." In *Perspectives on Purity and Purification in the Bible*, edited by B. J. Schwartz et al., 84–95. London: T. & T. Clark, 2008.

Klein, Ralph W. *1 Samuel*. Word Bible Commentary 10. Dallas: Word, 2002.

Kline, Meredith G. "Divine Kingship and Gen. 6:1–4." *Westminster Theological Journal* 24 (1962) 187–204.

———. *Glory in Our Midst: A Biblical-Theological Reading of Zechariah's Night Visions*. Overland Park, KS: Two Age, 2001.

Kloppenborg, John S. "Isa 5:1–7 LXX and Mark 12:1, 9, Again." *Novum Testamentum* 46 (2004) 12–19.

Kobelski, Paul J. *Melchizedek and Melchireša*. Catholic Biblical Quarterly Monograph Series 10. Washington, DC: Catholic Bible Association, 1981.

Kuhn, Karl A. "The 'One like a Son of Man' becomes the 'Son of God.'" *Catholic Biblical Quarterly* 69/1 (2007) 22–42.

Ladd, George Eldon. *A Theology of the New Testament*. Rev. ed. Edited by Donald A. Hagner. Grand Rapids: Eerdmans, 1993.

Langley, Wendell E. "The Parable of the Two Sons (Matthew 21:28–32) Against Its Semitic and Rabbinic Backdrop." *Catholic Biblical Quarterly* 58/2 (1996) 228.

Lawrence, Louise Joy. "'For truly, I tell you, they have received their reward' (Matt 6:2) Investigating Honor Precedence and Honor Virtue." *Catholic Biblical Quarterly* 64/4 (2002) 687.

Leuchter, Mark. "'The Levite in your gates': The Deuteronomic Redefinition of Levitical Authority." *Journal of Biblical Literature* 126/3 (2007) 417–36.

Levenson, Jon D. "The Last Four Verses in Kings." *Journal of Biblical Literature* 103/3 (1984) 353–61.

Levin, Yigal. "Understanding Biblical Genealogies." *Currents in Research: Biblical Studies* 9 (2001) 11.

Lindars, Barnabas. *Jesus Son of Man*. Grand Rapids: Eerdmans 1983.

Linton, Olof. "Parable of the Children's Game." *New Testament Studies* 22/2 (1976) 159–79.

Loader, William R. G. "Son of David, Blindness, Possession, and Duality in Matthew." *Catholic Biblical Quarterly* 44/4 (1982) 570–85.

Longenecker, Bruce W. "Evil at Odds with Itself (Matthew 12:22–29): Demonising Rhetoric and Deconstructive Potential in the Matthean Narrative." *Biblical Interpretation* 11/3–4 (2003) 503–14.

Longenecker, Richard N., ed. *The Challenge of Jesus' Parables*. Grand Rapids: Eerdmans, 2000.

———. *Galatians*. Word Bible Commentary 41. Dallas: Word, 2002.

Lowe, Malcolm F. "The Demise of Arguments from Order for Markan Priority." *Novum Testamentum* 24/1 (1982) 27–36.

Lowe, Malcolm F., and David Flusser. "Evidence Corroborating a Modified Proto-Matthean Synoptic Theory." *New Testament Studies* 29/1 (1983) 25–47.

Luz, Ulrich. *Matthew 1–7: A Commentary*. Translated by Wilhelm C. Linss. Edinburgh: T. & T. Clark, 1989.

———. *Matthew 8–20*. Edited by Helmut Koester. Hermeneia. Minneapolis: Augsburg Fortress, 2001.

———. *Matthew 21–28*. Edited by Helmut Koester. Hermeneia. Minneapolis: Augsburg Fortress, 2005.

———. *The Theology of the Gospel of Matthew*. New Testament Theology. Cambridge: Cambridge University Press, 1995.

Malbon, Elizabeth Struthers. "Narrative Criticism." In *Searching for Meaning: An Introduction to Interpreting the New Testament*, edited by Paul Gooder, 80–87. London: SPCK, 2008.

Marshall, John W. "Matthew's Christian-Jewish community." *Jewish Quarterly Review* 88/1–2 (1997) 85–88.

Martens, Allan W. "'Produce Fruit Worthy of Repentance': Parables of Judgment against the Jewish Religious Leaders and the Nation." In *The Challenge of Jesus' Parables*, edited by Richard N. Longenecker, 151–76. Grand Rapids: Eerdmans, 2000.

Martin, Brice L. "Matthew on Christ and the Law." *Theological Studies* 44/1 (1983) 53–70.

Mason, S. N. "Priesthood in Josephus and the Pharisaic Revolution." *Journal of Biblical Literature* 107/4 (1988) 657–61.

Matera, Frank J. "The Plot of Matthew's Gospel." *Catholic Biblical Quarterly* 49/2 (1987) 233–53.

Mathewson, David. "A Note on the Foundation Stones in Revelation 21.14, 19–20." *Journal for the Study of the New Testament* 25/4 (2003) 487–99.

McComiskey, Douglas S. "Exile and the Purpose of Jesus' Parables (Mark 4:10–12; Matt 13:10–17; Luke 8:9–10)." *Journal of the Evangelical Theological Society* 51/1 (2008) 59–85.

McEleney, Neil J. "The Unity and Theme of Matthew 7:1–12." *Catholic Biblical Quarterly* 56/3 (1994) 490.

McIver, Robert K. "The Parable of the Weeds among the Wheat (Matt 13:24–30, 36–43) and the Relationship between the Kingdom and the Church as Portrayed in the Gospel of Matthew." *Journal of Biblical Literature* 114/4 (1995) 643–60.

Meier, John P. "John the Baptist in Matthew's Gospel." *Journal of Biblical Literature* 99/3 (1980) 383–405.

———. "Two Disputed Questions in Matt 28:16–20." *Journal of Biblical Literature* 96/3 (1977) 407–24.

———. *The Vision of Matthew: Christ, Church, and Morality in the First Gospel*. Theological Inquiries. New York: Paulist, 1979.

Menken, Martinus J. J. "The Sources of the Old Testament Quotation in Matthew 2:23." *Journal of Biblical Literature* 120/3 (2001) 451–68.
Menninger, Richard E. *Israel and the Church in the Gospel of Matthew*. American University Studies, series 7, Theology and Religion. New York: Lang, 1994.
Merritt, Robert L. "Jesus, Barabbas and the Paschal Pardon." *Journal of Biblical Literature* 104/1 (1985) 57–68.
Milikowsky, Chaim. "Which Gehenna: Retribution and Eschatology in the Synoptic Gospels and in Early Jewish Texts." *New Testament Studies* 34/2 (1988) 238–49.
Miller, Fred. *Q—The Great Isaiah Scroll Page*. 2006. http://www.ao.net/~fmoeller/qumdir.htm.
Miller, Susan. "The Woman Who Anoints Jesus (Mk 14.3–9): A Prophetic Sign of the New Creation." *Feminist Theology* 14/2 (2006) 221–36.
Moffitt, David M. "Righteous Bloodshed, Matthew's Passion Narrative, and the Temple's Destruction: Lamentations as a Matthean Intertext." *Journal of Biblical Literature* 125/2 (2006) 299–320.
Morris, Leon. *The Gospel According to Matthew*. Grand Rapids: Eerdmans, 1992.
Moss, Charlene McAfee. *The Zechariah Tradition and the Gospel of Matthew*. Berlin: Walter de Gruyter, 2008.
Mullen, E. Theodore, Jr. "The Divine Witness and the Davidic Royal Grant: Ps 89:37–38." *Journal of Biblical Literature* 102/2 (1983) 207–18.
Neville, David J. "Toward a Teleology of Peace: Contesting Matthew's Violent Eschatology." *Journal for the Study of the New Testament* 30/2 (2007) 131–61.
Nolland, John. *The Gospel of Matthew*. Edited by I. Howard Marshall and Donald A. Hagner. The New International Greek Testament Commentary. Grand Rapids: Eerdmans, 2005.
———. "The King as Shepherd: The Role of Deutero-Zechariah in Matthew." In *Biblical Interpretation in Early Christian Gospels*, edited by Thomas R. Hatina, 2:133–46. London: T. & T. Clark, 2008.
———. *Luke 1:1–9:20*. Word Biblical Commentary 35A. Dallas: Word, 2002.
———. *Luke 18:35–24:53*. Word Biblical Commentary 35C. Dallas: Word, 2002.
Nowell, Irene. "Jesus' Great-Grandmothers: Matthew's Four and More." *Catholic Biblical Quarterly* 70/1 (2008) 1–15.
O'Brien, Julia M. *Priest and Levite in Malachi*. Edited by David L. Peterson and Pheme Perkins. Society of Biblical Literature Dissertations 121. Atlanta: Society of Biblical Literature, 1990.
Olson, Daniel C. "Matthew 22:1–14 as Midrash." *Catholic Biblical Quarterly* 67 (2005) 435–53.
O'Neill, John Cochrane. "The Unforgivable Sin." *Journal for the Study of the New Testament* 19 (1983) 37–42.
O'Toole, Robert F. "Acts 2:30 and the Davidic Covenant of Pentecost." *Journal of Biblical Literature* 102/2 (1983) 245–58.
Owen, Paul, and David Shepherd. "Speaking up for the Qumran, Dalman and the Son of Man: Was Bar Enasha a Common Term for 'Man' in the Time of Jesus?" *Journal for the Study of the New Testament* 81 (2001).
Pamment, Margaret. "The Kingdom of Heaven according to the First Gospel." *New Testament Studies* 27/2 (1981) 211–32.
Pennington, Jonathan T. *Heaven and Earth in the Gospel of Matthew*. Grand Rapids: Baker Academic, 2007.

Perkins, Pheme. "If Jerusalem Stood: The Destruction of Jerusalem and Christian Anti-Judaism." *Biblical Interpretation* 8/1–2 (2000) 194–204.

Petersen, David L. "Zechariah's Visions: A Theological Perspective." *Vetus Testamentum* 2 (1984) 195–206.

Phillips, Peter. "Casting Out the Treasure: A New Reading of Matthew 13:52." *Journal for the Study of the New Testament* 31/1 (2008) 3–24.

Plummer, Robert L. "Something Awry in the Temple? The Rending of the Temple Veil and Early Jewish Sources that Report Unusual Phenomena in the Temple around AD 30." *Journal of the Evangelical Theological Society* 48/2 (2005) 301–16.

Poirier, John C. "Purity Beyond the Temple in the Second Temple Era." *Journal of Biblical Literature* 122/2 (2003) 247–65.

Polkinghorne, Donald E. *Narrative Knowing and the Human Sciences*. Albany: State University of New York, 1988.

Powell, Mark Allan. "Do and Keep What Moses Says (Matthew 23:2–7)." *Journal of Biblical Literature* 114/3 (1995) 419–35.

———. "The Plot and Subplots of Matthew's Gospel." *New Testament Studies* 38/2 (1992) 187–204.

Przybylski, Benno. *Righteousness in Matthew and His World of Thought*. Society for New Testament Studies, Monograph Series 41. Cambridge: Cambridge University Press, 1980.

Reid, Barbara E. "Violent Endings in Matthew's Parables and Christian Nonviolence." *Catholic Biblical Quarterly* 66/2 (2004) 237–55.

Repschinki, Boris. "'For he will save his people from their sins' (Matthew 1:21): A Christology for Christian Jews." *Catholic Biblical Quarterly* 68/2 (2006) 248–67.

Richardson, Peter, and Stephen Westerholm. *Law in Religious Communities in the Roman Period: The Debate over Torah and Nomos in Post-Biblical Judaism and Early Christianity*. Edited by Peter Richardson. Studies in Christianity and Judaism 4. Waterloo, ON: Wilfrid Laurier University, 1991.

Ritmeyer, Leen, and Kathleen Ritmeyer. "Akeldama: Potter's Field or High Priest's Tomb?" *Biblical Archaeology Review* 20/6 (1994) 22.

Robertson, O. Palmer. *The Christ of the Covenants*. Grand Rapids: Baker, 1980.

Saldarini, Anthony J. "Delegitimisation of Leaders in Matthew 23." *Catholic Biblical Quarterly* 54 (1992) 659–80.

———. *Matthew's Christian-Jewish Community*. Chicago: University of Chicago Press, 1994.

Sanders, E. P. *Judaism: Practice and Belief 63 BCE—66 CE*. London: SCM, 1992.

———. *Paul and Palestinian Judaism*. Philadelphia: Fortress, 1977.

Sandt, Huub van de. "'Do not give what is holy to the dogs' (Did 9:5d and Matt 7:6a): The Eucharistic Food of the Didache in Its Jewish Purity Setting." *Vigiliae Christianae* 56/3 (2002) 223.

Scharen, Hans. "Gehenna in the Synoptics." *Bibliotheca Sacra* 149, no. 596 (1992) 454–70.

Schellenberg, Ryan S. "Kingdom as Contaminant? The Role of Repertoire in the Parables of the Mustard Seed and the Leaven." *Catholic Biblical Quarterly* 71 (2009) 527–43.

Schnackenburg, Rudolf. *The Gospel of Matthew*. Grand Rapids: Eerdmans, 2002.

Schnittjer, Gary E. "The Narrative Multiverse within the Universe of the Bible: The Question of 'Borderlines' and 'Intertextuality.'" *Westminster Theological Journal* 64/2 (2002) 231–52.

Schwartz, B. J., et al., eds. *Perspectives on Purity and Purification in the Bible.* London: T. & T. Clark, 2008.
Scott, Bernard Brandon. "The King's Accounting: Matthew 18:23-34." *Journal of Biblical Literature* 104/3 (1985) 429-42.
Scott, James W. "Matthew's Intention to Write History." *Westminster Theological Journal* 47/1 (1985) 68-82.
Segal, Michael. "The Responsibilities and Rewards of Joshua the High Priest according to Zechariah 3:7." *Journal of Biblical Literature* 126/4 (2007) 717-34.
Senior, Donald. "Between Two Worlds: Gentiles and Jewish Christians in Matthew's Gospel." *Catholic Biblical Quarterly* 61/1 (1999) 1-23.
———. *Matthew.* Edited by Victor Paul Furnish. Abingdon New Testament Commentaries. Nashville: Abingdon, 1998.
Shedinger, Robert F. "A Further Consideration of the Textual Nature of Shem-Tob's Hebrew Matthew." *Catholic Biblical Quarterly* 61/4 (1999) 686.
———. "Must the Greek Text Always be Preferred? Versional and Patristic Witnesses to the Text of Matthew 4:16." *Journal of Biblical Literature* 123/3 (2004) 449-66.
Sim, David C. *Apocalyptic Eschatology in the Gospel of Matthew.* Edited by Margaret E. Thrall. Society for New Testament Studies Monographs 88. New York: Cambridge University Press, 1996.
———. "The Gospels for All Christians? A Response to Richard Bauckham." *Journal for the Study of the New Testament* 84 (2001) 3-27.
———. *The Gospel of Matthew and Christian Judaism.* Edited by John Barclay et al. Studies of the New Testament and Its World. Edinburgh: T. & T. Clark, 1998.
———. "Matthew 7.21-23: Further Evidence of Its Anti-Pauline perspective." *New Testament Studies* 53/3 (2007) 325-43.
———. "Matthew and the Pauline Corpus: A Preliminary Intertextual Study." *Journal for the Study of the New Testament* 31/4 (2009) 401-22.
Sklar, Jay. "Sin and Impurity: Atoned or Purified? Yes!" In *Perspectives on Purity and Purification in the Bible,* edited by B. J. Schwartz et al., 18-31. London: T. & T. Clark, 2008.
Sloyan, Gerard S. *Jesus on Trial: A Study of the Gospels.* 2nd ed. Minneapolis: Fortress, 2006.
Smith, Christopher R. "Literary Evidences of a Fivefold Structure in the Gospel of Matthew." *New Testament Studies* 43/4 (1997) 540-51.
Smith, D. Moody. "When Did the Gospels Become Scripture?" *Journal of Biblical Literature* 119/1 (2000) 3-20.
Smith, Ralph L. *Micah–Malachi.* Word Biblical Commentary 32. Dallas: Word, 2002.
Snodgrass, Klyne R. *Stories with Intent: A Comprehensive Guide to the Parables of Jesus.* Grand Rapids: Eerdmans, 2008.
Spadaro, Martin. "An Examination of the Relationship between the Priesthood and the Law in Hebrews 7." ThM diss., Regent College, 2006.
Sparks, Kent. "Gospel as Conquest: Mosaic Typology in Matthew 28:16-20." *Catholic Biblical Quarterly* 68/4 (2006) 651-63.
Stanton, Graham N. *The Gospels and Jesus.* Edited by P. R. Ackroyd and Graham N. Stanton. Oxford Bible. New York: Oxford University Press, 1989.
———. *The Interpretation of Matthew.* Studies in New Testament Interpretation. Edinburgh: T. & T. Clark, 1995.

Stassen, Glen Harold. "The Fourteen Triads of the Sermon on the Mount (Matthew 5:21–7:12)." *Journal of Biblical Literature* 122/2 (2003) 267–308.

———. "Healing the Rift Between the Sermon on the Mount and Christian Ethics." *Studies in Christian Ethics* 18/3 (2005) 89–105.

Stegemann, Hartmut. *The Library of Qumran*. Grand Rapids: Eerdmans, 1998.

Stein, Robert H. "The Matthew–Luke Agreements Against Mark: Insight from John." *Catholic Biblical Quarterly* 54/3 (1992) 482.

Stevens, Marty E. *Temples, Tithes and Taxes: The Temple and the Economic Life of Ancient Israel*. Peabody, MA: Hendrickson, 2006.

Stuart, Douglas. *Hosea–Jonah*. Word Bible Commentary 31. Dallas: Word, 2002.

Sylva, Dennis D. "The Temple Curtain and Jesus' Death in the Gospel of Luke." *Journal of Biblical Literature* 105/2 (1986) 239–50.

Talbert, Charles H. *Reading the Sermon on the Mount: Character Formation and Ethical Decision Making in Matthew 5–7*. Grand Rapids: Baker Academic, 2004.

Thomas, John Christopher. "The Kingdom of God in the Gospel according to Matthew." *New Testament Studies* 39/1 (1993) 136–46.

Thompson, William G. "An Historical Perspective in the Gospel of Matthew." *Journal of Biblical Literature* 93/2 (1974) 243–62.

Throckmorton, Burton H., Jr., ed. *Gospel Parallels: A Synopsis of the First Three Gospels*. Nashville: Thomas Nelson, 1979.

Trevett, Christine. "Approaching Matthew from the Second Century: The Under-Used Ignatian Correspondence." *Journal for the Study of the New Testament* 20 (1984) 59–67.

Tuckett, Christopher M. "On the Relationship between Matthew and Luke." *New Testament Studies* 30/1 (1984) 130–42.

Turan, Sinai. "A Neglected Rabbinic Parallel to the Sermon on the Mount (Matthew 6:22–23; Luke 11:34–36)." *Journal of Biblical Literature* 127/1 (2008) 81–93.

Turner, David L. *Matthew*. Baker Exegetical Commentary on the New Testament. Grand Rapids: Baker Academic, 2008.

Van de Water, Rick. "The Punishment of the Wicked Priest and the Death of Judas." *Dead Sea Discoveries* 10/3 (2003) 395–419.

Vanderkam, James C. *From Joshua to Caiaphas*. Minneapolis: Fortress, 2004.

———. "Joshua the High Priest and the Interpretation of Zechariah 3." *Catholic Biblical Quarterly* 53/4 (1991) 553.

Vermes, Geza. *The Complete Dead Sea Scrolls in English*. New York: Penguin, 1997.

———. *The Dead Sea Scrolls in English*. 3rd ed. Sheffield, UK: JSOT, 1987.

———. *Jesus and the World of Judaism*. Philadelphia: Fortress, 1984.

———. *Jesus in his Jewish Context*. London: SCM, 2003.

Verseput, Donald. "Jesus' Pilgrimage to Jerusalem and Encounter in the Temple: A Geographical Motif in Matthew's Gospel." *Novum Testamentum* 36/2 (1994) 105–21.

———. "The Role and Meaning of the 'Son of God' Title in Matthew's Gospel." *New Testament Studies* 33/4 (1987) 532–56.

Viviano, Benedict. "The Least in the Kingdom: Matthew 11:11, its Parallel in Luke 7:28 (Q), and Daniel 4:14." *Catholic Biblical Quarterly* 62/1 (2000) 41–54.

Vos, Howard Frederic. *Nelson's New Illustrated Bible Manners and Customs: How the People of the Bible Really Lived*. Nashville: Thomas Nelson, 1999.

Waetjen, Herman C. "Genealogy as the Key to the Gospel according to Matthew." *Journal of Biblical Literature* 95/2 (1976) 205–30.
Waters, Kenneth L., Sr. "Matthew 27:52–53 as Apocalyptic Apostrophe: Temporal-Spatial Collapse in the Gospel of Matthew." *Journal of Biblical Literature* 122/3 (2003) 489–515.
Watts, R. E. *Isaiah's New Exodus and Mark*. Edited by M. Siebeck. Wissenschaftliche Untersuchungen zum Neuen Testament 2. Reihe 88. Tubingen: Mohr Siebeck, 1997.
———. "The Lord's House and David's Lord: The Psalms and Mark's Perspective on Jesus and the Temple." *Biblical Interpretations* 15/3 (2007) 307–22.
Weber, Kathleen. "The Image of Sheep and Goats in Matthew 25:31–46." *Catholic Biblical Quarterly* 59/4 (1997) 657.
Wenham, David. "A Note on Matthew 24:10–12." *Tyndale Bulletin* 31 (1980) 155–62.
———. "The Resurrection Narratives in Matthew's Gospel." *Tyndale Bulletin* 24 (1973) 21–54.
———. "The Rock on Which to Build: Some Mainly Pauline Observations about the Sermon on the Mount." In *Built Upon the Rock*, edited by Daniel M. Gurtner and John Nolland, 187–206. Grand Rapids: Eerdmans, 2008.
Wenham, Gordon J. *Genesis 16–50*. Word Biblical Commentary 2. Dallas: Word, 2002.
Weren, Wilhelmus Johannes Cornelis. "The Five Women in Matthew's Genealogy." *Catholic Biblical Quarterly* 59/2 (1997) 288–305.
Westerholm, Stephen. *Jesus and Scribal Authority*. Coniectanea Biblica: New Testament 10. Lund, Sweden: Gleerup, 1978.
———. *Understanding Matthew: The Early Christian Worldview of the First Gospel*. Grand Rapids: Baker Academic, 2006.
Westermann, C. *Genesis 1–11*. Darmstadt: Wissenschaftliche Buchgesellschaft, 1972.
Whitters, Mark F. "Jesus in the Footsteps of Jeremiah." *Catholic Biblical Quarterly* 68/2 (2006) 229–47.
Williamson, H. G. M. *Ezra-Nehemiah*. Word Biblical Commentary 16. Dallas: Word, 1985.
Woods, Edward J., ed. *The "Finger of God" and Pneumatology in Luke–Acts*. Edited by Stanley E. Porter. Journal for the Study of New Testament Supplement Series 205. Sheffield, UK: Sheffield Academic, 2001.
Wright, N. T. *Jesus and the Victory of God*. Minneapolis: Fortress, 1996.
———. "The Law in Romans 2." In *Paul and the Mosaic Law. The Third Durham Tübingen Research Symposium on Earliest Christianity and Judaism*, edited by J. D. G. Dunn, 131–50. Durham: Tübingen Mohr, 1994.
———. *The New Testament and the People of God*. Minneapolis: Fortress, 1992.

www.ingramcontent.com/pod-product-compliance
Lightning Source LLC
Chambersburg PA
CBHW071235230426
43668CB00011B/1445